MAIN STREET MOVIES

CINEMA AND THE AMERICAN EXPERIENCE
Kathryn H. Fuller Seeley, editor

Martin L. Johnson

MAIN STREET MOVIES

THE HISTORY OF LOCAL FILM
IN THE UNITED STATES

INDIANA UNIVERSITY PRESS

This book is a publication of

Indiana University Press
Office of Scholarly Publishing
Herman B Wells Library 350
1320 East 10th Street
Bloomington, Indiana 47405 USA

iupress.indiana.edu

© 2018 by Martin L. Johnson
All rights reserved

No part of this book may be reproduced or utilized in any form or by any means, electronic or mechanical, including photocopying and recording, or by any information storage and retrieval system, without permission in writing from the publisher.

The paper used in this publication meets the minimum requirements of the American National Standard for Information Sciences—Permanence of Paper for Printed Library Materials, ANSI Z39.48–1992.
Manufactured in the United States of America

Cataloging information is available from the Library of Congress.

ISBN 978-0-253-03252-2 (cloth)

ISBN 978-0-253-03253-9 (paperback)

ISBN 978-0-253-03254-6 (ebook)

1 2 3 4 5   23 22 21 20 19 18

For my parents,
whose support is unwavering

This afternoon the populace of the city paraded in procession before that wonderful instrument, the moving picture machine. A momentary glimpse of the town's life on the streets was caught and fixed in preservation. The images of the scene, moving in the sunlight of a day that will be gone tomorrow, living and breathing, on the instant, was snatched from the grasp of time and sealed beyond the power of change, a silent fadeless pageant of what we were.

Now the crowds have scattered, and the people have returned to their homes and from the canvas of memory the transitory scene has already begun to fade.

The same grouping will not again occur. The same people can never assemble again. They themselves have changed in the short time. The school children have passed a little further on to adult life. The boys and girls are older and the aged have stepped nearer the grave. Those moving pictures of civic life which daily fill our streets and the streets themselves are changing. New houses will be built and others torn down; new children will come and the grim reaper will bind the ripened grain, but the picture on the reel which was made today will never change. It will come back and march in silent pageant, the horses prancing, the throng gesticulating, laughing, talking, cheering silently like the ghost of time.

These will be the real ghosts of the coon hunt. There will be no ghosts caught at the camp grounds as marvelous as these ghosts of ourselves. We will sit in the picture show hereafter and see ourselves living in the past, the resurrection of the past, and live again this day. And soon there will be some on the picture screen whom we once knew but know no more. The panorama of the world is passing. All creation is a moving picture. Beings on the far off worlds toward which the light is traveling from this one will see in ages yet to come our pictures when we have passed away, and perhaps when our spirits have winged their way to those celestial homes, flying swifter by angel flight than sunbeams go, we may arrive in time to see the pictures of our whole past life unroll before us like this reel today. If so, make the pictures now the way you want to see them.

—"The Pictures of Today,"
Moberly (Mo.) *Weekly Monitor,* November 7, 1913

CONTENTS

	Accessing Moving Images	xi
	Acknowledgments	xiii
	Abbreviations	xvii
	Introduction: Defining the Local Film	1
one	The Silent Pageant: Municipal Booster Films	16
two	The Home Talent Film and the Origins of Itinerancy	56
three	"How Movies Are Made": Hollywood and the Local Film	95
four	Itinerants *Adopt a Baby*: The Local Hollywood Film and the Operational Aesthetic	114
five	Kidnapping the *Movie Queen*: Amateur Aesthetics as Cultural Critique	135
six	The Cameraman Has Visited Your Town: The Local Film and the Politics of Recognition	163
seven	Every Town Has Its Main Street: The Banal Localism of the Civic Film	201
eight	Reclaiming the Local Film: Artifacts, Archives, and Audiences	227
	Conclusion: See Your Town Disappear— The Historicity of the Local Film	255
	Filmography	261
	Bibliography	275
	Index	289

ACCESSING MOVING IMAGES

Audiovisual materials are available for this volume. In the enhanced ebook these materials are embedded and can be viewed or listened to by clicking the play button. For readers of the print book, the collected materials are available for viewing online at http://purl.dlib.indiana.edu/iudl/media/197x61fm50. Information and links for each individual entry follow.

Moving Image 1.1. Excerpt from *Present and Past in the Cradle of Dixie* (1914). Directed by O. W. Lamb. Courtesy of the Alabama Department of Archives and History, Montgomery
http://purl.dlib.indiana.edu/iudl/media/b98m40zz0f

Moving Image 4.1. Excerpt from *Wellston's Hero* (1932). Directed by Don Newland. Courtesy of the Wellston Historical Association, Wellston, Ohio
http://purl.dlib.indiana.edu/iudl/media/435g355k07

Moving Image 5.1. Excerpt from Lincoln, Maine, *Movie Queen* (1935). Directed by Margaret Cram. Courtesy of Northeast Historic Film, Bucksport, Maine
http://purl.dlib.indiana.edu/iudl/media/v33r86cb22

Moving Image 6.1. Excerpt from Henderson, North Carolina, *Movies of Local People* (1938). Directed by H. Lee Waters. Courtesy of the H. Lee Waters Film Collection, David M. Rubenstein Rare Book and Manuscript Library, Duke University, Durham, N.C.
http://purl.dlib.indiana.edu/iudl/media/v63f95km9t

Moving Image 7.1. Excerpt from Mooresville, North Carolina, *My Home Town* (1946). Directed by Don G. Parisher and George S. Gullett. Courtesy of the Mooresville Public Library
http://purl.dlib.indiana.edu/iudl/media/722h247s71

Moving Image 8.1. Excerpt from *Aliquippa in 1937* (1997). Produced by the Center for Industrial Heritage of Beaver County. Courtesy of Donald Inman

http://purl.dlib.indiana.edu/iudl/media/128n39z25v

ACKNOWLEDGMENTS

ACKNOWLEDGMENTS ARE GENEALOGICAL BY NATURE, interlocked intellectual and social histories of the author. Writing itself is a lonely endeavor, but one draws solace from the richness of scholarly engagement in classrooms and conferences, the warmth of family and friendship, and the joy of scaffolding new knowledge. While I have made every effort to thank people by name for their role in making this book possible, I also want to note that every person I have discussed local films with over the past decade has contributed to what you have in your hands today.

My undergraduate training in the Department of Modern Culture and Media at Brown University helped me realize the value of challenging dominant narratives of media history, and Wendy Chun, Michael Silverman, Elliot Colla, and Karl Schoonover helped me find my path as an academic and historian. This project germinated in 2003, when, in Robert C. Allen's graduate seminar on the history of moviegoing in the United States, I first encountered the movies of H. Lee Waters, an itinerant filmmaker from North Carolina whose work remains as engaging as the day I first saw it at Duke University's Special Collections. At the University of North Carolina, where I completed a master's thesis on Waters, I benefited from Allen's incisive commentary, as well as advice and mentorship from Robert Cantwell, Patricia Sawin, and, at Duke, Jane Gaines. At New York University, where I expanded my research into a dissertation, I added another roster of advisors and mentors, most notably Dan Streible, who, more than any scholar I know, has bridged divides between scholars and archivists, filmmakers and critics, bringing new vibrancy to film history, a field that for too long was stuck in the delta of Hollywood. Anna McCarthy, Jonathan Kahana, Dana Polan, the late Robert Sklar, and Moya Luckett also provided critical support for my project as it developed. My classmates, including Greg Zinman, Jinying Li, Dominic Gavin, Paul Grant, Jihoon Kim, Paul Fileri, Nate Brennan, Wyatt Phillips, Jennifer Zwarich, and David Parisi, were cheerful companions. Finally, I want to thank my colleagues in the Department of Media and Communication

Studies at the Catholic University of America. I appreciate the generosity and thoughtfulness of Steve McKenna, Alex Russo, Niki Akhavan, Maura Ugarte, Josh Shepperd, and Abby Moser, who were always there to give advice as needed.

As I presented my research at conferences, I developed colleagues and mentors at other universities. In particular, I wish to thank, in alphabetical order, Richard Abel, Michael Aronson, Stephen Bottomore, Joe Clark, Allyson Nadia Field, Caroline Frick, Oliver Gaycken, Marsha Gordon, Jennifer Horne, Sarah Keller, Jeffrey Klenotic, Paul S. Moore, Jennifer Peterson, Ryan Shand, and Gregory A. Waller. In addition, friends inside and outside of academia provided critical support, including Matt Cordell, Ben Healy, Alice Lovejoy, Kris Nesbitt, the late Johnetta Pressley, and Daniel Wilinsky.

Although I possess neither the training nor the manual dexterity to be a film archivist, I would like to think of myself as an honorary member of the archival community. Dwight Swanson, in particular, has been a generous friend, giving me his collection of VHS tapes and DVDs from his days as a pursuer of itinerant-produced films. Karan Sheldon, cofounder of Northeast Historic Film, and Margie Compton, of the University of Georgia, have been enthusiastic supporters of my research. I also wish to thank Kim Andersen, Snowden Becker, Skip Elsheimer, Karen Glynn, Siobhan Hagan, the late Cynthia Luckie, Meredith McDonough, the late Bill McFarrell, Julia Nicoll, Rick Prelinger, Amy Sloper, Albert Steg, Katie Trainor, Andy Uhrich, David Weiss, and Tim Wisniewski.

One never has enough time to spend at an archive, making the assistance of librarians and curators critical. For making my research trips more productive than they otherwise would have been, I would like to thank Maxine Ducey and Dorinda Hartmann of the Wisconsin Center for Theater and Film Research; David Kessler of the Bancroft Library at the University of California, Berkeley; Rosemary Hanes and Josie Walters-Johnston at the Library of Congress; Barbara Hall at the Margaret Herrick Library; Sandra Joy Lee Aguilar at the Warner Brothers Collection at the University of Southern California; Lydia Pappas of the Moving Image Research Collection at the University of South Carolina; and two archivists at Indiana University, Zach Downey of the Lilly Library and Brian Graney at the Black Film Center/Archive. This book has also benefited from the work of fellow researchers of itinerant filmmakers, and the descendants of the filmmakers themselves. Carl Ballenas, Hellen Newland Chaplain, John Dulaney, Anne Evans, Kathryn Gangel, Echo Heron, Hugh Jamieson, David Kuntz, Jeff Logan, Andy Poore, Joseph Tarabino, Nathan Wagoner,

Ken Walston, Tom Waters, Tom Whiteside, and James Winslow all shared their research materials with me, demonstrating the appeal of local films for the communities they depicted.

Indiana University Press has been great to work with, and I wish to thank my editors: Raina Polivka, who first showed interest in the book, and Janice Frisch, who has helped make it a reality. My outside readers, Kathryn Fuller-Seeley and Mark Lynn Anderson, helped me see the book through new eyes and provided useful advice as I made the final revisions. This book was completed with the assistance of a grant from the National Endowment for the Humanities, which gave me a full year to focus on completing the final chapters of the manuscript. Any views, findings, conclusions, or recommendations expressed in this book do not necessarily represent those of the National Endowment for the Humanities. While this book was written in home offices and coffee shops, in libraries and academic buildings, it was completed at the Writer's Room in Boston, where quiet and 24/7 access made it a welcome respite from home and work.

Finally, I want to thank my family. My parents, Bob and Pam Johnson, have been supportive of this work from the beginning, as have my brothers, Jeremiah and Spencer, and my grandmother Norma Johnson. Without the patience and love of my wife, Melissa Gilkey, this project would have been hard to complete, and her parents, John and Sally, and sister, Anna, have shown warmth and kindness throughout this process. Melissa and I have welcomed to the world two children, Soren and Laurel, who have given us great joy. I hope this book is a small return for the forgiveness and love they have shown me.

ABBREVIATIONS

ACFP	*Adams County* (Corning, Iowa) *Free Press*
ACUR	*Adams County* (Corning, Iowa) *Union Republican*
AMM	*Amateur Movie Makers* (New York)
DO	*Daily Oklahoman* (Tulsa)
EG	*Emporia* (Kans.) *Gazette*
HN	*Hutchinson* (Kans.) *News*
MA	*Montgomery* (Ala.) *Advertiser*
MAH	Marion Angeline Howlett Papers, Harvard Theatre Collection
MM	*Movie Makers* (New York)
MNC	*McAlester* (Okla.) *News-Capital*
MPW	*Moving Picture World* (New York)
MSC	Mack Sennett Collection
NBT	*New Brunswick* (N.J.) *Times*
PPIE	Panama Pacific International Exposition Records
RNC	Richard Norman Collection
SG	Shad Graham Papers
SNR	*Springfield* (Ill.) *News Record*
WEC	*Waterloo* (Iowa) *Evening Courier*
WECR	*Waterloo* (Iowa) *Evening Courier and Reporter*

MAIN STREET MOVIES

INTRODUCTION
Defining the Local Film

IN THE BEGINNING, ALL MOVING images were local. In Eadweard Muybridge's Animal Locomotion plates, taken at the University of Pennsylvania in the 1880s, we often see an old man with a long, white beard who was none other than Muybridge himself. In West Orange, New Jersey, Thomas Edison's technicians cast themselves in their early film experiments. Fred Ott saw his own sneeze.

And soon after Auguste and Louis Lumière first directed their cinematograph toward their employees leaving their factory in Lyon, they projected the results so their subjects could see themselves. The cinema was conceived as a solipsistic enterprise. To make a movie was also to see one, and those who saw movies often saw themselves in them.

But even after these early moving image experiments birthed a new industry, local films remained a central appeal of a movie show. Traveling exhibitors carried movie cameras with them as they went from fairground to amusement hall to tent show, confident that a local film made just hours before that night's show would be a surer draw than a reel purchased three years ago.

For the first fifteen years of the cinema, 1895 to 1910, local films were a regular feature of the picture show. In this period, the local film was a genre, often identified in newspapers, theater programs, and billboards as "local views," "topicals," or "actualities." Like other early cinema genres, the definition of local film was as much prescriptive as descriptive. Audiences and exhibitors alike recognized local views as motion pictures that were made near the site of their intended exhibition in order to give people the opportunity to see themselves on screen. One could "get in" a local film in much the same manner that one made the decision to go see a picture show—just by showing up. Even if many audiences saw local films in this early period, they were ephemeral experiences, much like the cinema itself.

This begins to change around 1910, when what André Gaudreault calls the "institutionalization" of the cinema commenced.[1] Distributors started to circulate film programs on a regular, and predictable, basis. Film production itself became more organized, and within a few years, the building blocks of the industry—genres and stars—were in place. In most cities and towns, the movies themselves went from an occasional spectacle to a permanent, settled fixture in local life. In many ways, the cinema's arrival as an institution occurred precisely at the moment that there was something called a "moving picture theater" in town.

These new purpose-built movie theaters were both appendages of the communities in which they were located and conduits for national, and occasionally global, content.[2] Unlike other manufactured goods, which became domesticated as they were integrated into the routines of everyday life, motion pictures themselves never stayed in town long enough to become familiar. Movies were a commodity—sold by the foot, produced by the reel, and exchanged between exhibitors and distributors. There appeared to be little room left for an artisanal moving image practice like making local films for the satisfaction of those who preferred to see their own images on screen. In fact, until recently film historians assumed that local movies lost favor toward the end of the first decade of the 1900s, one of many early cinema practices that did not survive the transition to classical narrative cinema.

And yet, local films continued to be made by traveling and, on occasion, local filmmakers. While a few exhibitor-filmmakers active in the early cinema period stuck to their old habits, new camera operators and directors adjusted their practices for the times. Instead of paying for production costs upfront, filmmakers asked business organizations and other local groups to sponsor their work. Rather than exhibiting their movies in a temporary location, they contracted with theater managers to show their films at the new movie house in town. Instead of leaving the subjects of their films to chance, filmmakers planned scenes of particular people and places, and, within a few years, began shooting narrative fiction pictures.

The consequences of this shift in the production of the local film were more substantial than has been previously understood. While some local movies were still received as images of the quotidian and contingent, an accidental record of both pastness and locality, many more local films were altered by the same stresses narrative and fictional conventions placed on film form in the early 1910s. Instead of deploying what Tom Gunning has called a "view aesthetic," in which the cinema apparatus produces the local out of an encounter between a camera operator and a future exhibition site, filmmakers captured a filmic local that had already been constituted in cooperation by theater owners and sponsors.[3]

We could choose to ignore this shift, reading the raw "footage" of local film as a remnant of forgotten people and distant places, a method that turns local films, like home movies, into an ahistorical film genre in a medium otherwise marked by change. Alternately, we could identify these films as the genres they mimicked—amateur comedies, newsreels, sponsored film—with their locality being a feature only of passing interest. In this book, I propose that we focus on how these films presented, and challenged, the local they claimed to represent.

This book attempts to answer two questions: did local film production continue in the United States after 1910, and, if so, how did local films change in response to the development of the motion picture industry that was, in many ways, the leading edge of a globalized, mass culture?[4] The answer to the first question is easy, even if it challenges longstanding assumptions about the narrowing path American film history is assumed to have taken starting in the mid-1910s. As I show, local films continued to be made, in large numbers, throughout the United States well into the 1950s, with the last itinerant producers making their rounds in the early 1970s. Seeing yourself in the movies was not an experience specific to early cinema, or something reserved for movie extras, but rather an ordinary part of going to the movies.

The answer to the second question is the occupation of this book. Following James M. Moran, I use the term "mode," rather than the more restrictive "genre," to describe the types of local films identified. As Moran notes, defining a moving image practice as a mode allows for "variations in social function, material resources, cultural competence, and phenomenology of spectatorship."[5] While locally produced and exhibited motion pictures shared modal traits, most notably the expectation that audience members would be able to recognize people and places in the film, difference began to emerge between modes of production in the early 1910s, and, over time, came to represent competing ideas about the form and function of the cinema.

I identify six significant modes of local film production—municipal booster films, home talent pictures, local Hollywood films, amateur fiction films, movies of mutual recognition, and civic films. Using case studies to analyze each mode, I consider the larger commercial, technological, and cultural shifts within and outside of the cinema that shaped the context in which these pictures were produced and exhibited. Rather than assuming the local film was a simple genre with an obvious and timeless appeal, I argue that the emergence of distinct modes of production and exhibition suggests that the definitions of the local and its filmic representation fluctuated over the course of the twentieth century. The local film, then, came to represent and document how the cinema, one of the leading propagators of mass culture, was experienced in the United States.

From Local Views to Local Films

The origin of the local film is coterminous with cinema itself. Traveling exhibitor-producers were shooting local views as early as 1896, and most, if not all, of the companies and cinematographers active in the early years of the cinema made them as a stock-in-trade. And yet, even early histories of the movies downplayed the importance of local views, preferring to focus on technical and aesthetic developments of film form and the rise of the motion picture industry. The first scholarly histories of the medium retained this industry focus, in part because the sources they used, particularly trade publications for movie producers, were consumed with achieving efficiencies of scale. For this reason, the absence of local film from canonical cinema histories is not due to the lack of evidence but rather a consequence of methodologies that favor national- and industry-focused narratives.

Even so, there is a rich scholarship on local films made in the early cinema period, and this work informs my own reading of such films made after 1910. Even the first histories of the cinema, mostly written by former industry employees, were aware of the local film's appeal. In *A Million and One Nights*, Terry Ramsaye noted that the Lumière brothers made "local scenes" for their programs but did not mention American exhibitors who did the same.[6] Other early histories of the American cinema also skip over local motion pictures, or mention them in passing.[7] In the 1980s, the first generation of academically trained cinema historians, including Gunning, Charles Musser, Robert C. Allen, and Miriam Hansen, began revisiting the myths of early cinema, many of which were spun by Ramsaye and other industry veterans.

In these revisionist histories, local films, which were often identified as "local views" or "actualities," were seen primarily as a phenomenon of the first decade and a half of the cinema.[8] Allen notes the popularity of local films throughout the early cinema period, particularly those produced by American Mutoscope and Biograph between 1897 and 1901.[9] Musser and Carol Nelson concur in their book on the traveling exhibitor Lyman Howe, noting that "by the turn of the century, local views were a well-tested method of boosting the popularity of a motion picture show."[10] Some of these researchers have suggested that the production of local motion pictures ceased by the end of the decade. Allen argues narrative fiction genres became dominant around 1905 because exhibitors found that such films were more profitable than local views.[11] Musser claims that the Film Service Association, a consortium formed in late 1907 to protect Edison patent interests by regulating distribution and exhibition practices, forced most producers and exhibitors to sharply curtail local films.[12] Even though Allen, in particular, emphasizes the continuing popularity of local scenes into the early 1910s, few scholars have engaged deeply with his claim for the popularity of local actualities. The absence of extant films has likely served to limit scholarly interest in locally produced motion pictures.[13]

A less historically nuanced but more provocative analysis of the possibility of local motion pictures occurs in Miriam Hansen's 1991 book *Babel and Babylon*. Citing Allen's research on the use of local actualities in vaudeville houses, Hansen attributes their appeal to the "primitive fascination" early cinema audiences had with the medium's capacity to capture everyday life. At the same time, Hansen argues, the promise of self-recognition in the local film was potentially political, as it suggested the possibility for a democratic screen in which anyone could appear. For her, local motion pictures were similar to other alternative and minority practices in early cinema that were shut out by classical film narrative. As she argues, "The viewer's investment in the screen as mirror differs from later, narratively mediated forms of identification—with characters, star images, and the look of the narrating camera—which effectively displaced interest in local and personal representation from the institution of cinema, relegating it to the private province of 'home' movies."[14] While this argument could be read as a restatement of her broader claims for the transformation of spectatorial practices between the early and classical cinema eras, Hansen's opposition between recognition and identification is particularly useful for a consideration of the local film.

Although the label "local film" was occasionally used in trade publications and newspapers starting in the early 1910s, the term does not appear in the scholarly discourse until the early 2000s, after a significant discovery of local views encouraged new research on the subject.[15] In 1994, three metal drums containing much of the output of the Mitchell and Kenyon Company (1899–1913) were found in the basement of an unoccupied building in Blackburn, England.[16] The discovery of 830 of the company's films, which consisted almost entirely of local views, changed cinema history in Britain by calling attention to the prevalence of such films in the first decade of the cinema. In 1997, several of the films were screened at the Pordenone Film Festival in Italy, and in 1998, the first article on the collection was published in *Film History*.[17] Vanessa Toulmin, the research director of the National Fairgrounds Archive in England, led the rediscovery of the Mitchell and Kenyon films, which were donated to the British Film Institute in 2000. In journal articles, books, and a BBC documentary, Toulmin demonstrates the potential of local films as artifacts of social and cultural history. Today, the Mitchell and Kenyon collection is the third largest from a single company in the early cinema period, after Lumière and Edison.[18]

The popularity of the Mitchell and Kenyon collection has had two consequences for scholarship on local motion pictures. First, archivists and scholars identified extant motion pictures as local films, often confusingly treating them as part of the same transnational genre. For example, when *Film History* published a special issue on the "local film" in 2005, collections from Sweden, Germany, Luxembourg, and the Netherlands, as well as the Mitchell and Kenyon films, were highlighted. Other collections, from H. Lee Waters's movies of the American South (1936–1942) to Rudall Hayward's "community comedies" produced in New Zealand in the late 1920s, were now identified as local films.[19] In a survey of what he called "amateur-commercial hybrid film[s]," Dan Streible describes a local version of an *Our Gang* comedy produced in Anderson, South Carolina, in 1926.[20] However, with a few exceptions—most notably, Gregory A. Waller's list of local films produced in Lexington, Kentucky, between 1907 and 1930, published in his 1995 exhibition history of the city—researchers have not had any way to measure the significance of any one title.[21] The absence of historical studies has encouraged scholars to speculate on potential ties between, for example, New Zealand's Hayward and Vermont's Margaret Showalter Cram, one of the itinerant directors of the *Movie Queen*, a local comedy filmed repeatedly throughout the United States in the 1930s.[22] While what could be called the "unified theory" of the local film may bring attention to little-known works, attempts to analyze discrete practices as part of a single phenomenon downplay historical exigencies.

The second consequence of the Mitchell and Kenyon collection was a reconsideration of the social and cultural significance of the local film. By the early 2000s, local films were well-known to scholars and archivists, and the latter group began making them a priority for preservation. In the United States, local films by H. Lee Waters and Melton Barker were named to the Library of Congress's National Film Registry, which recognizes motion pictures of great national and cultural significance, in 2004 and 2012, respectively. While these films were always of interest to local historical societies, it is only in recent years that they have been considered of national importance.

While the discovery of local films has encouraged archivists to look for other extant films and contextual material that describe their production and exhibition, many scholars continue to define the local film in relationship to theories of spectatorship. Tom Gunning characterizes the early cinema period as the "era of local cinema," with local and global views intermingled in an evening's show. As he notes, "The lure of virtual world tours and glimpses of distant, exotic places marked the global aspect of early cinema, while the gasp of recognition and the naming of familiar faces or places characterized its local identity."[23] For Gunning, the local film is not a genre, with formal traits embedded within the film itself, but rather dependent on audience recognition to accrue meaning.

While Toulmin demonstrates that one could recover much of the meaning of a film through contextual research, many scholars have argued that the film's principal pleasure, and meaning, comes when the audience performs what Gunning calls the "gasp of recognition."[24] He suggests such a response could be read out of the film themselves: "We can no longer hear the cries that welcomed these images at the turn of the century; one side of the dialogue has been silenced. But, as historians, we have a responsibility to recall and channel those departed voices, or at least to search for their echo in the images that, thankfully, have survived."[25]

Gunning's advice to recover an "echo" of the exhibition experience in the image itself leaves scholars to make connections between these idiosyncratic practices and the broader experience of cinema without sufficient supporting evidence. Such speculations are reminiscent of much of the scholarship on early cinema, in which the naming of the "first" motion picture of any genre or form turns into a debate on the properties and functions of the cinema itself.[26] By tasking themselves with the near impossible work of recreating the "lost world" in which local motion pictures were made and received, scholars risk burrowing into minutiae, what Carolyn Steedman has called the "dust" of history, and never accounting for the relationship of such films to the larger domain of the cinema, or to political, economic, and cultural life.[27] This book argues that local films are more than the sum of the individuals who recognized themselves in the movies, and thus seeks to position local film practices in the United States within broader contexts.

Notes on Methodology

This book provides a national perspective on local film production in the United States after 1910. Rather than limit my focus to a sampling of filmmakers or a geographic region, I used keyword searches of digitized materials, including newspapers, trade journals, and films, to identify and analyze distinct modes of local film production. Employing trade and local newspapers, extant films, and archival collections, I explicate these modes through case studies of filmmakers and film companies. This hybrid research method allows me to maintain the depth of a microhistory without losing the breadth of a survey of print discourse about the many variants of the local film. My methodological approach is strongly influenced by what Richard Maltby has termed the "new cinema history," which focuses on discrete events of cinema-going rather than audience experiences of the movies in a given period. Borrowing concepts from cultural geography, historians such as Jeffrey Klenotic, Deb Verhoeven, and Paul S. Moore suggest that we think of the cinema as an organic, ongoing process of place creation, with the moviegoing experience created anew with each screening, rather than one in which the early possibilities for moviegoing were abandoned in favor of a classical mode of spectatorship.[28] The cultural geographer Doreen B. Massey writes of what she calls the "event of place," the moment in which space and time intersect, involving "the coming together of previously unrelated, a constellation of processes rather than a thing."[29] The local film is the distillation of particular places, and for audiences, place recognition was as an important quality of the local film as self-recognition. By emphasizing the production of place, I analyze the potential meanings of the local film by considering the processes of production and exhibition as well as the film itself.

I began this project by looking closely at a source familiar to film historians, the pages of the *Moving Picture World*. In the late 1900s and early 1910s, the *World* was one of several new publications that emerged to serve the needs of the motion picture industry. Along with *The Nickelodeon*, *Motography*, *Motion Picture News*, and, later, *Exhibitors Herald*, these publications were particularly sensitive to the interests of small-town and rural exhibitors, who made up a substantial percentage of their readership. Several pages of each issue were devoted to exhibitor news, and their regional correspondents often noted the production of local films.

If national trade publications provide an overview of local motion pictures from the exhibitor perspective, articles and advertisements printed in small-town newspapers give insight into how these movies were presented to local audiences. In almost all cases, local newspapers covered the production of these films from start to finish, at times even signing on as sponsors. Itinerant filmmakers used newspapers to orchestrate elaborate publicity campaigns for their productions, placing articles and staging events with front-page headlines in mind. Using large, digitized newspaper collections, which together represent several thousand newspapers from towns and cities throughout the United States, I map the paths of the itinerants featured in my case studies and, through close analysis, examine how they adjusted their own publicity and business practices over time.[30]

In my research, I have located hundreds of extant local motion pictures held by film archives, historical societies, and public libraries throughout the United States. Rather than assessing these films as visual evidence of specific people and places, I pay close attention to their aesthetics and to the social and political circumstances of their production. My comparative analysis of Don Newland, for example, was only possible after acquiring access copies of five versions of the same film from libraries and historical societies in Wisconsin, Pennsylvania, and Ohio. Although I realize that this study just captures a sliver of the local films made in the United States in the twentieth century, by focusing on the modal qualities of extant films, I aim to provide a guide for how local films may be interpreted.

Finally, my research draws on archival collections that were donated by the filmmakers themselves, as well as brochures, pamphlets, photographs, and films that were found in other collections. Two of the filmmakers in the study donated their materials to archives, resulting in the H. Lee Waters Collection at Duke University and the Shad. E. Graham Collection at the University of Texas at Austin. A third director, Marion Angeline Howlett, one of several dozen directors for the Amateur Theatre Guild, donated materials to the Harvard Theatre Archive. I have also benefited from the use of digitized collections and research materials at the Alabama Department of Archives and History, Ball State University, Bancroft Library at the University of California, Black Film Center/Archive at Indiana University, Chicago History Museum, George Eastman House, Margaret Herrick Library at the Academy of Motion Picture Arts and Sciences, New York Public Library, Northeast Historic Film, Walter J. Brown Media Archives at the University of Georgia, and Wisconsin Center for Film and Theater Research.

CHAPTER SUMMARY

In this book, I argue that exhibitors and producers used local films to interrogate, negotiate, and assuage concerns about the spread of mass culture into everyday life. In eight chapters, arranged chronologically, I use case studies to show different aspects of local film practices. The first four chapters establish critical developments in local films in the transitional and classical period (1909–1932), including the use of local films in town advertising campaigns, the introduction of narrative techniques and fictional stories into local films, and the association of local films with stardom and Hollywood. The next three chapters explore how ideas of gender and amateurism, race and recognition, and nation and commerce inflect the construction of the local between 1936 and 1975. The final chapter focuses on the rediscovery and preservation of these films, which began in the 1980s and continues to this day.

In the first chapter, I consider the municipal advertising, or booster, motion picture. Sponsored by well-financed business clubs and chambers of commerce and produced by companies who specialized in industrial motion pictures, booster films were intended to promote a city to its own residents, as well as to nonresidents who might see the film at an exposition or even at a theater in their own city. While early producers distinguished their films from local views by shooting longer and more elaborately staged motion pictures, by 1913 producers began to integrate fictional and narrative sequences into what had previously been a nonfiction form. In a case study of the Paragon Feature Film Company, which claimed to have produced one hundred motion pictures between 1914 and 1917, I argue that the imperative for making a film that resembled the melodramas audiences were used to seeing overtook the sponsor's interest in portraying their city as a distinct and desirable place to live or invest. While early Paragon motion pictures used historical reenactments and narratives set in local factories, by their last film the company was using a melodramatic plot in which a spurned lover commits suicide at the end of the two-reel picture. By 1917, booster film production declined, most likely because the United States' entry into World War I disrupted the domestically oriented booster movement. Even though the municipal booster motion picture phenomenon was short lived, sizeable production budgets and experiments with narrative and fiction scenes make booster films important indicators of alternate uses for the cinema in the transitional era.

In the second chapter, I discuss the production of local fictional narratives featuring local actors, which I call "home talent" films, in the 1910s. Although the term "home talent" was in common usage in the late nineteenth and early twentieth centuries, by the time a reduced-width film gauge was introduced in 1923, the term "amateur" was more widely used to describe nonprofessionals. By reclaiming the term "home talent" for the amateur motion pictures of the 1910s, I reassert the importance of the geography of cultural production and dissemination. I focus on one exceptionally prolific filmmaker, Charles Tinsley of Corning, Iowa, who produced at least twenty photoplays in his hometown of two thousand people between 1914 and 1916, using box office receipts to help fund his practice. Initially, Tinsley wrote a new scenario for each picture, often tying them to local events, such as house fires, reunions, and, most prominently, the activation of Corning's National Guard unit to the US-Mexico border. In 1915, Tinsley began working as an itinerant filmmaker, using the same scenario for each home talent picture he produced. By 1918, Tinsley had abandoned his local work and instead joined the growing ranks of independents who traveled throughout the country shooting the same story again and again. Although these films were still labeled home talent pictures, they rarely featured original scenarios particular to a local community.

In chapter 3, I turn to the impact of the vertically integrated studio system on the local film. While the late 1910s is often thought of as a period in which producers, distributors, and theater chains began standardizing the experience of cinema, exhibitors used their community ties to demand more studio and distributor support in localizing motion pictures for particular audiences. By 1918, several studios had established publicity or exploitation departments, with dozens of regional managers tasked with helping exhibitors promote individual motion pictures. One technique used was the production of a local film, often a screen test, to attract audience attention. For the 1922 Mack Sennett feature *The Crossroads of New York*, an exploitation manager in Louisville, Kentucky, decided to make a more ambitious local picture, a two-reel comedy that would "mimic Sennett." After the success of the Louisville film, exhibitors across the country tried their own local *Crossroads* movies, with varying results. In some cities, inexperienced theater managers proved unable to pull off the local comedy, resulting in negative press coverage and, likely, disappointed moviegoers. The mixed results of the *Crossroads* experiment, accompanied by broader concerns about movie fans flocking to Hollywood after a local screen test, likely tempered studio enthusiasm for local pictures.

However, around 1923, itinerant filmmakers began claiming experience in the motion picture industry. In chapter 4, I consider their so-called Hollywood local motion pictures, in which they replicated the experience of Hollywood filmmaking at all levels, from the casting process to the public filming of special effects, like car crashes and rescues from burning buildings. I focus here on the career of Don Newland, who made difficult-to-verify claims of working with movie pioneers such as Mary Pickford, Flora Finch, and John Bunny, in order to secure work. Regardless of his actual experience, he was one of the most prolific itinerants of the 1920s, making dozens of pictures throughout the United States. Newland's filmmaking and business acumen was such that he even made the transition to sound filmmaking in the early 1930s, long before other itinerants.

In chapter 5, I consider the role small-gauge film technology played in democratizing the production of local films in the 1930s. Despite the introduction of the 16mm amateur film gauge in 1923, local films continued to be shot and exhibited using 35mm equipment for the remainder of the decade. But with the introduction of brighter 16mm film projectors in the early 1930s, filmmakers began to produce local movies with the smaller gauge equipment, transporting not just the camera but also the projector, a phonograph for sound accompaniment, and publicity material from location to location. Hollywood culture also changed the stakes for the people who appeared in local films. Seeing themselves in the movies was not enough. They expected to see themselves as potential stars, and their towns as movie sets. While early Hollywood-themed itinerant films, such as those discussed in chapter 4, were presented with a showman's sincerity, by the 1930s, appearing in a local film was often treated as a lark, often one with implicit gender assumptions. For example, working under the auspices of the Amateur Theatre Guild, young college-age women made a lighthearted comedy film series titled *Movie Queen*, which parodied Hollywood film culture, particularly its fascination with ingenues, vamps, and virgins. In contrast to earlier films, the *Movie Queen* films, which were preceded by a three-act play with the same title and a fashion show, satirized Hollywood and its small-town fans. The local film, then, served in the 1930s and later as a way for rural residents to participate in and mock Hollywood culture.

Other 16mm itinerants rediscovered the local view, producing nonnarrative and nonfiction pictures with titles such as *See Yourself and Your Town in the Movies*. In chapter 6, I consider the films of H. Lee Waters, a studio photographer from North Carolina who visited 118 small towns and cities in the mid-Atlantic South between 1936 and 1942, shooting 252 films. In this chapter, I consider the role "mutual recognition," or, in the terms of many itinerants, "seeing yourself as others see you," played in documenting and reproducing social difference. Waters, for example, filmed segregated communities, in some cases producing films specifically for white or African American audiences, and in others reproducing the segregation of the town in his films. In this chapter, I build on the philosopher Paul Ricouer's work on recognition to develop a theoretical underpinning for the pleasures and politics of recognition in local films.

Even after the long decline of the single-screen movie theater commenced in the late 1940s, local films continued to be made in many communities. In some cases, filmmakers who began their careers in the 1920s and 1930s continued to work, revisiting old territory and finding smaller towns where a local film could still draw interest. In chapter 7, I focus on a mode of production that became more significant in the postwar period, the civic film. Unlike the booster films of the 1910s, civic films were not advertising vehicles. Instead, these films, in most cases sponsored by local merchants, were intended to celebrate, and often commemorate, the small town, its institutions, and the business interests that sustained them. For example, in the 1940s, a number of filmmakers, including the Texas-based Shad E. Graham, begin making a series titled *Our Home Town*. Directors used a prerecorded soundtrack narrated by national radio announcers to assure local business communities their town was just like any other. In this chapter, I consider the "banal localism" of the postwar hometown movies and suggest that this shift in the function of local films was due to the increasing difficulty small towns had in establishing themselves as distinct, culturally and economically significant places.

If local films were made as frequently as this book documents, why were they missing, not just from film histories but also from social and local histories? In chapter 8 I consider narratives of discovery, preservation, and exhibition of local films in the past three decades. Beginning in the late 1980s, historians and archivists began finding local films in barns, basements, and attics. As archival moving images became an increasingly popular way of memorializing the past, communities used their own movies as a way to understand their history, as local films documented certain places and people while eliding others. In this chapter, I consider the recovery, reclamation, and reuse of local films as processes that change how we assess these moving images. Although much of this work takes place in the communities where the films were made, I also consider how these films are transformed when they circulate online, in scholarly and archival settings, and, in some cases, as raw material transformed by artists.

Mapping the Local Film

While previous studies of the local film have emphasized the basic appeal of "seeing yourself in the movies," I focus on the other pleasures a local film might offer. For many audiences, seeing oneself in the movies was not a timeless pleasure, as the "movies" were constantly changing. One year, audiences and sponsors may have wanted to see an advertisement for their town, while the next they instead preferred to see their home as the setting for a fictional drama. These types of seeing could still be called recognition, but the recognition was not just about seeing oneself reproduced in the cinema but also about seeing oneself embedded in larger national processes. Local films inculcated in movie audiences a sense of *mutual* recognition, which, as I explain in chapter 6, requires not only seeing yourself but seeing yourself with the awareness that others are watching. The enduring popularity of the local film can only partially be attributed to a fascination with the medium of cinema itself. Local films reflect and refract experiences of people as they saw themselves in booster films, home talent movies, local Hollywood films, movie industry parodies, civic pictures, and, now, archival footage. In order to fully understand this practice, it is necessary to place the local film in its social and cultural contexts.

Notes

1. Gaudreault, *Film and Attraction*, 69.
2. As Ross Melnick has shown in his recent study of the pioneer exhibitor Samuel "Roxy" Rothafel, theater managers elevated the status of the cinema in the teens by encouraging business groups, service clubs, and other organizations to see their local theater as a public space. See Melnick, *American Showman*, 80.
3. Gunning, "Before Documentary."
4. While I focus on local film production in the United States, where a shared and vibrant film culture created the conditions for the diversity of film practices I describe, local filmmaking was a global phenomenon.
5. Moran, *There's No Place Like Home Video*, 73.
6. Ramsaye, *A Million and One Nights*, 238.
7. In addition to Ramsaye's work, histories by Robert Grau, Benjamin Hampton, Lewis Jacobs, Garth Jowett, Kenneth MacGowan, and Robert Sklar downplay the importance of local views in early cinema. For example, MacGowan noted that Lumière cinematographers made local pictures wherever they went. As he wrote, "When the local pictures flashed on the screen, even the most cynical peasant was convinced that here was no trickery." MacGowan, *Behind the Screen*, 92.
8. The term "local topical" was mostly used in Britain. See Gomes, "Working People, Topical Films, and Home Movies."
9. Allen, *Vaudeville and Film*, 128–131.
10. Musser and Nelson, *High-Class Moving Pictures*, 109.
11. Allen, *Vaudeville and Film*, 142–143.
12. Musser reiterates this claim in a more recent encyclopedia entry on itinerant exhibitors, suggesting that "Edison's patent claims made filmmaking far riskier, and there was less small-time production" than in the United Kingdom. See Musser, "Itinerant Exhibitors," 341.
13. Allen, *Vaudeville and Film*, 216–219.
14. Hansen, *Babel and Babylon*, 31.
15. For example of the uses of the term "local film" in the 1910s, see an advertisement suggesting exhibitors "Make Your Own Local Films" that appeared in *MPW*, December 14, 1912, 1110, and the article "Expect Many to See Local Films," *La Crosse* (Wis.) *Tribune*, July 11, 1914, 6. The first scholarly use of the term appears to be in Toulmin, "'Local Films for Local People.'"

16. Vanessa Toulmin, Patrick Russell, and Simon Popple, "Introduction to the Mitchell and Kenyon Collection," in Toulmin et al., eds., *The Lost World of Mitchell and Kenyon*, 3–5.

17. Whalley and Worden, "Forgotten Firm," 51.

18. Toulmin, *Electric Edwardians*, 3.

19. See Hoorn and Smith. "Rudall Hayward's Democratic Cinema."

20. Streible, "Itinerant Filmmakers and Amateur Casts," 177.

21. Waller, *Main Street Amusements*. Other accounts of local film production after 1909 have appeared in Michael Aronson's study of moviegoing in Pittsburgh, Pennsylvania; Paul S. Moore's account of film exhibition in Toronto; and George Potamianos's dissertation on exhibition in Sacramento and Placerville, California. See Aronson, *Nickelodeon City*, 208–247; Moore, *Now Playing*, 207; and Potamianos, "Hollywood in the Hinterlands," 168.

22. Hoorn and Smith, "Rudall Hayward's Democratic Cinema," 79.

23. Tom Gunning, "Pictures of Crowd Splendour: The Mitchell and Kenyon Factory Gate Film," in Toulmin et al., eds., *The Lost World of Mitchell and Kenyon*, 52.

24. Stephen Bottomore, for example, defines the local film as a motion picture in which there is "significant overlap" between the people in the audience and the people in the film. See Bottomore, "From the Factory Gate to the 'Home Talent' Drama," 33.

25. Gunning, "Pictures of Crowd Splendour," 53.

26. For more on the historical and theoretical difficulties of establishing cinematic firsts, see Gaines "First Fictions." As Jane Gaines argues, in cinema history "'firstness' and its concomitant, 'origin,' are almost automatically challenged by the very possibilities of mechanical reproduction where reproducing is indistinguishable from producing" (1314).

27. Steedman, *Dust*.

28. Richard Maltby, "New Cinema Histories," in Maltby et al., eds., *Exploration in New Cinema History*, 3–40. In the same volume, see Klenotic's "Putting Cinema History on the Map." Deb Verhoeven has written on these issues in the essay "New Cinema History and the Computational Turn," in *Beyond Art, Beyond Humanities, Beyond Technology: A New Creativity, World Congress of Communication and the Arts Conference Proceedings*, COPEC–Science and Education Research Council, Guimarães, Portugal, http://hdl.handle.net/10536/DRO/DU:30044939.

29. Massey, *For Space*, 141.

30. These databases include ProQuest Historical Newspapers, America's Historical Newspapers, Old Fulton NY Post Cards, Newspaper Archive, Newspapers.com, and Genealogy Bank. The first two databases are academic, while the latter four are private and/or commercial. In some cases, this research was supplemented by looking through microfilm of newspapers that have not yet been digitized.

1

THE SILENT PAGEANT
Municipal Booster Films

> Quite recently a moving picture company sent its photographers to Springfield, Illinois, and produced a story with our city for a background, using our social set for actors. Backed by the local commercial association for whose benefit the thing was made, the resources of the place were at the command of routine producers. Springfield dressed its best, and acted with fair skill. The heroine was a charming débutante, the hero the son of Governor Dunne. *The Mine Owner's Daughter* was at best a mediocre photoplay. But this type of social-artistic event, that happened once, may be attempted a hundred times, each time slowly improving. Which brings us to something that is in the end very far from *The Mine Owner's Daughter*. By what scenario method the following film or series of films is to be produced I will not venture to say. No doubt the way will come if once the dream has a sufficient hold.
>
> —Vachel Lindsay, *The Art of the Moving Picture* (1915)

> Anyone can have a film made to his order. Several films have been made in this city, for some of them, not very big ones either, as much as $500 has been paid. But what good are they. They were shown at the local theatre. That was all. Now they are tucked away in a trunk perhaps. So it would be with county fair scenes. Distributors will not distribute such films free of charge, nor exhibitors exhibit them. They are regarded by them as advertising and charged as such.
>
> —"Educational Movies," *Oxnard* (Calif.) *Daily Courier*, August 26, 1922

WHEN VACHEL LINDSAY, THE SELF-MADE—and self-appointed—poet and cultural critic of the Midwest, turned his attentions to the cinema in 1915, he saw in the new medium an opportunity for what Garth Jowett later called a "democratic art."[1] In *The Art of the Moving Picture*, Lindsay presented a theory of film form and genre that locates the cinema in a specifically American context.[2] In one chapter, Lindsay described a film first exhibited in his hometown of Springfield, Illinois, in the summer of 1915, just a few months before the book's publication. In this passage, Lindsay

16

observed that the motion picture titled *The Mine Owner's Daughter*, which was made at the behest of local businesses, was a "mediocre photoplay" but brought about a "social-artistic event" in his hometown. Although he neglected to name the production company or describe the film's plot, Lindsay speculated that such local films would be made again and again, until one day they reached the level of capital-A "Art," using the cinema to produce local spectacles. Lindsay then summarized his own scenario for a local film in Springfield, one that would feature the goddess of the city emerging from the hills and telling the city fathers how to prepare for the future.[3]

Lindsay's hopes for the local film were quickly dashed, as structural changes in the film industry make it difficult for independent producers to distribute their work, a state of affairs that turned many would-be local film sponsors into skeptics. However, Lindsay failed to realize that *The Mine Owner's Daughter*, a film he almost certainly saw in July 1915 in his hometown, was not made for Springfield audiences alone. Instead, the Commercial Association that sponsored the film expected it "to be placed on show in 182 different cities throughout the United States."[4] By the time the Paragon Feature Film Company of Omaha, Nebraska, arrived in Springfield to produce *The Mine Owner's Daughter*, the company had made dozens of similar films in cities such as Oklahoma City, New Orleans, and Montgomery, Alabama. While Lindsay thought *The Mine Owner's Daughter* was on the leading edge of the cinema to come, its production company had in fact started several years earlier, and would make its last film in 1916.

Between 1910 and 1916, when the American cinema was itself undergoing what historians have identified, in retrospect, as the transition to the classical Hollywood era, there was a wave of production and theatrical exhibition of movies like *The Mine Owner's Daughter*. Called booster or town advertising films, these pictures were sponsored by business organizations interested in promoting the attractions of their town to potential residents and manufacturers, and exhibited both in the town or city where they were made and, if their producers are to be believed, other towns and cities throughout the United States. While early booster films were merely collections of local views, by 1914 motion picture companies began producing narrative, semi-fictional films. These industrial romances blended the tropes of historical pageantry and transitional cinema melodrama. Most often, they used a wedding plot to build a story that advertised local manufacturing plants and resources. Over time, booster films began to incorporate elements of common narrative film plots, including daring rescues of damsels in distress, explosions, and automobile crashes.

What I call the "municipal booster film" is a local film that was sponsored by a business organization, such as a board of trade, chamber of commerce, or commercial club, of a city or town for the express intent of advertising that municipality's virtues to its own residents as well as potential settlers and investors. The municipal booster film was not a genre but rather a mode of production that incorporated generic cues from industrial romances and melodramas. These films were distinct from the local views of early cinema in three ways. First, unlike the local view, the municipal view was not defined exclusively by the pleasure of self-recognition, that is, audiences seeing themselves on film. Instead, the films were often noted for their presentation of local places, first as attractions for businesses or people wishing to relocate and later as locations for fictionalized movie scenes. Second, in contrast to local views, which tended to be very short (one-hundred-foot reels were common) and rapidly processed and exhibited, municipal boosting films were both longer (at least a thousand feet) and more likely to be produced over a series of days or weeks. With the luxury of time to produce their film, sponsors were able to exercise much greater control over who and what appeared, and did not appear, in their production. Third, sponsors believed their motion pictures would be seen elsewhere, in neighboring cities, throughout the state, and even nationally and internationally. Although the historical evidence suggests that very few municipal booster films were exhibited so widely, sponsors were led to expect national distribution of their films, which in turn affected their production decisions.

The municipal booster film can therefore be located within ongoing debates about the possibilities for a moviegoing audience to constitute itself as a public. Miriam Hansen has argued that the classical Hollywood cinema that emerged in the late 1910s eliminated the "conditions around which local, ethnic, class, and gender-related experience might crystallize," thus ending the potential for the cinema to serve as an alternative public sphere.[5] While Hansen is interested in an urban, multiethnic, working-class, and gendered milieu, the phenomenon of the municipal booster film suggests that local experiences of spectatorship in more homogenous communities also thrived during the transition. As Robert C. Allen has argued, rural encounters with the cinema during the transitional era were of a markedly different character than its urban counterparts.[6] Rather than viewing films in class-segregated and neighborhood-based nickelodeons, rural and small-town inhabitants viewed movies downtown, in theaters that were once dedicated exclusively to live entertainment. Even after the construction of purpose-built movie theaters commenced in the early 1910s, the picture show remained a venue for live performances and civic functions, serving as a cultural center in many small towns. While histories of the movies and traveling mass amusements, such as circuses and vaudeville acts, are usually told in a national framework, Gregory A. Waller argues that by ignoring the "local configuration of sites, sponsors, and occasions" necessary for these amusements to occur, we miss much of what made them significant in the first place.[7]

The shift in emphasis from national to local histories of the cinema is not made out of a desire to fully represent the kaleidoscope of movie experiences in the early twentieth century, nor to suggest that, for the sake of historical accuracy, we need to substitute studies of bejeweled metropolises like New York and Chicago for more ordinary places like Lexington, Kentucky, and Wilmington, North Carolina. Instead, work by Allen, Waller, Kathryn H. Fuller-Seeley, Paul S. Moore, and many others suggest that differences between and among locales of moviegoing augurs for a reconsideration of how and why the cinema developed as a mass amusement.[8] Instead of a center-periphery model, in which all that is noteworthy about motion pictures passed through New York and, later, Los Angeles, these studies reveal multinodal networks of cinema cultures, with pathways extending in all directions. Rather than serving as *prima facie* evidence of the rise of national, mass culture in the early decades of the twentieth century, the cinema becomes a site where we can investigate these claims. Local studies open up new horizons of inquest, enabling a reexamination of old assumptions and revealing new fields of research.

For example, scholars have long argued for the historical significance of the cinema because of its close association with the advent of urban industrial modernity, which allowed working-class moviegoers to influence the direction the cinema would take.[9] Operating under the assumption that films such as *What Happened on Twenty-Third Street, New York City* (Edwin S. Porter, 1901) was emblematic of both the kinds of movies audiences saw and their everyday experiences, scholars conflated the production and reception of such films. The longstanding debate between Tom Gunning and Charles Musser over whether early cinema is best understood as a medium that delivered "attractions" that shocked audiences, or one in which audiences "contemplated" the complex operations of the cinema, assumes that modernity was essentially an urban phenomena.[10] Although Joe Kember supports the so-called modernity thesis in its broadest strokes, he suggests that scholars have missed the most salient quality of modernity for early cinema audiences: the fact that "individuals had become adept at objectifying others and detaching themselves from the responsibilities of genuine intimacy and empathy." Kember argues that early film institutions, such as fairgrounds and theaters, "not only reproduced some of the most widely disseminated perspectives on modernity... but also allowed them to be registered, deliberated, and worked through." Applying Anthony Giddens's theorization of modernity to the cinema, Kember argues that exhibition reveals in the cinema what Giddens calls the "duality of structure," in which the "screening of a film participates in the creation of the spectator at the same time as the conventions for film exhibition and styles of filmmaking are reassessed and reproduced by the spectator." In this way, Kember suggests, "institutions successfully connect local contexts of action with distant imperatives, often across large spans of time and space."[11] Urban sophisticates and country rubes were equally encouraged to see the cinema not just as a reflection of modern life but also as an opportunity to see in the cinema a capacity for empathy and intimacy that was elsewhere under threat.

By shifting emphasis away from experiences of shock and alienation, and toward a focus on immediacy and connection, Kember suggests that we take seriously those who made claims for the medium's educational and socially uplifting aspects. Audiences everywhere, even in small towns, were primed to see the cinema as an expression of modernity, and yet they were also continually reminded of its association with the lecturers, showmen, and theater managers who brought them in contact with distant people and places. As he notes, exhibitors produced and sponsored local views in the early cinema period in order to "foster varied bonds of recognition and empathy with their audiences, and to generate relationships that were characterized by intimacy as well as exhibitionism."[12] And while the local views of the early cinema period were never intended to be screened to other communities, these feelings of intimacy and exhibitionism continued to resonate in the early 1910s. The local view did not lose popularity in the transitional era, as some have suggested, but was rather transformed into new modes of local picture production that responded to the changing form and industry structure of the cinema.

In the transition, movie audiences began to think of themselves as a public, participating in the regulation and production of the cinema. One could shape the cinema by joining a censor board, by sending one's scenario off to a production company, or by appearing in a local film. Michael Warner argues that the salient quality of a public is the "reflexive circulation of discourse," which in a cinema context would mean the capacity for audiences to critically participate in film culture.[13] In contrast to Hansen's more grounded, tangible alternative public sphere, one in which audiences felt their "collective presence" in the movie theater, Warner's notion of a public relies on a social imaginary to serve as the audiences' interlocutor.[14] In this way, the public that was constituted and reproduced in print discourse, particularly newspapers, became visible through the production, exhibition, and, *imagined* distribution of local films.[15] Municipal booster films were produced in large numbers for a time because their sponsors believed their films could be circulated to other towns, thus constituting themselves as member of a moviemaking public that consisted of individuals from all factions of society.

The decline of the municipal booster film in the late 1910s was not due to a lack of interest in local filmmaking. Rather, it was, as an Oxnard, California, newspaper observed in 1922, a decline in interest in making local films to be exhibited elsewhere. While there is scant evidence that booster films were exhibited theatrically, there is substantially more evidence of their nontheatrical exhibition in sites such as regional conventions, trade tours, and, more prominently, at the 1915 Panama-Pacific Exposition in San Francisco. Many of the films produced by Paragon and other municipal film companies were exhibited at the Panama-Pacific Expo, supplementing the more elaborate displays states and cities usually sent to expositions. Reviews of the exposition note that motion pictures were shown at all the state halls, but very few visitors were interested in watching films like *Fifty Thousand Feet of Kansas* (1915), produced by Paragon and featuring no less than 50,000 feet of film, taken in 200 towns, of a state with a population of just 1.5 million.

By promising that their films would be circulated, booster film producers encouraged sponsors to invest more time and money in these pictures than they might have done otherwise. As a result, the municipal films of the 1910s were far more ambitious than any other mode of local film production of this or any other decade. At the same time, the transformation of the municipal booster film from a longer, carefully selected series of local views into a semi-fictional narrative film that turned a city's attractions into key plot elements was essential, as it allowed the local film to become a mode that was primarily concerned about the production and reproduction of place. In effect, the emergence of the municipal booster film, and its subsequent decline after 1916, reveals the potential, and the limits, of local film production and exhibition in the United States.

Municipal Advertising and Motion Pictures

In December 1909, the magazine *Town Development* published its first issue on topics it identified to be "in the interest of manufacturers as well as commercial clubs, business men's associations and like organizations."¹⁶ While the magazine often covered the more mundane issues of municipal development, like the building of sewer systems and the platting of industrial sites, many of its articles, editorials, and advertisements were dedicated to the cause of "town promotion." On the cover of the first issue, a prose poem printed on top of a map of the United States appears with the headline, "Our Town and the Map." An excerpt of the poem reads,

> Where is *our town* on this map?
> Ah, yes, there it is, right at the point of my pencil—see?
> Wonder who *else* sees
> Who *knows* our town is on this map?
> Who *cares*—other than our home folks?
> What does *our town* mean, *industrially*, to America?
> Anything?
> What is its *rank* in the American town development game?
> What's the *score*?
> Are we really *in* the game?
> Boys, it is almighty important, the position *our town* takes in this race for municipal supremacy,
> And the old town cannot fight her battles without *you* and *me* to *boost*. We can *boost*, at least, if we do not *build*.

The sentiments in this prose poem—the excitement that comes with someone's town being located on the map, the apprehension about whether anyone else knows or cares about the town, and the militaristic commitment to boosting, if not building, the town's identity—are often repeated in the pages of *Town Development, American City,* and other business and urban planning publications. Read by small-town mayors and council members, business owners and itinerant entrepreneurs, lawyers and other members of the professional classes, these publications documented and encouraged the transformation of urban life in the early twentieth century. One of the municipal services often covered in the pages of these magazines—the town advertising, or booster, campaign—helped transform the function of the local film from a mode of self-reflection to a mode of self-presentation. Town promoters used the cinema as another advertising medium, one that was more portable than the convention booth or the booster train and more enticing than the brochure or booklet. By producing its own motion picture, a local municipal organization could put its town on the map, or at least in local movie theaters, with the possibility of exhibition in other cities in the United States and throughout the world.[17] While the advantages of using film as a promotional tool were obvious to town promoters, motion picture producers were deterred by the difficult logistics of shooting and exhibiting pictures in all corners of the country. In fact, town promoters, not film producers, may have devised the concept of the "municipal film," establishing modes of production, financing, and distribution that fit, not always easily, with the cinema's fast-evolving institutional practices. The early history of the municipal film, then, is not found in the histories of film production or exhibition but, rather, in the history of municipal advertising.[18]

Municipal advertising, or booster, campaigns were not the most significant or longest lasting legacies of the town development movement, which transformed systems of government and brought forth major investments in infrastructure. But these campaigns were important because they allowed municipalities to create and manage their identities in a rapidly growing and centralizing nation. Given the great economic insecurities of the 1910s—when a factory relocation or a new highway or rail line could make the difference between a town's success or failure—booster campaigns gave town residents a sense of control over their own destinies, a fact that was repeated again and again in municipal and business magazines. As one editorial writer put it in the winter of 1912: "It does not require the application of much force to send a boulder tumbling down a mountain side, but once the boulder is started everything must give way before it. That's it! Perhaps your individual push will start the town on its way to greater prosperity."[19]

The municipal advertising campaign allowed a town to demonstrate its capacity for self-confidence, and booster magazines often praised successful efforts as ends in themselves. Although the booster is perhaps now best recognized as the subject of parody, deftly captured in Sinclair Lewis's 1922 novel *Babbitt*, in the 1910s boosterism was a major denomination of the American civic religion.[20] The booster movement was particularly strong in the Midwest, the South, and the West, regions with cities whose future prospects both seemed more promising and more fragile than those of well-established cities in the Mid-Atlantic and New England. The budgets for these advertising campaigns were substantial, with municipalities committing thousands of dollars annually to booster activities.

Although western expansion and speculative land development had fueled regional, state, and municipality promotion for decades, around the turn of the century a new phase in self-promotion was already underway.[21] The pamphlet, long the standard form of publicity, was being replaced by a multitude of advertising materials, from mass-produced booklets to full-page advertisements in general interest magazines. Advertising agencies began to handle accounts for city and town governments and business organizations, and took on the responsibility for full-scale campaigns that included the production of elaborate displays for installation at national expositions and regional trade shows. In addition, such firms helped communities produce advertising stunts in the hopes of being mentioned in urban newspapers and mass-circulation magazines. By the time *Town Development* began publishing in 1909, scores of people within its pages identified themselves as town promotion "experts," many of whom had backgrounds in advertising. By convincing civic and business leaders that a town could be advertised just like any other product, these promoters helped ignite a flourishing of commercial advertising campaigns in many towns and cities.[22]

Cities large and small, new and old, northern and southern, eastern and western, all promoted themselves through advertising campaigns, but southern cities still rebuilding after the Civil War and new, small western cities tended to launch the most ambitious campaigns. For example, the Tulsa Commercial Club, a group of businessmen organized in March 1901, saw their newly established Oklahoma town grow from a population of 1,391 in 1900 to a small city of 72,075 by 1920. In 1903, 1905, and 1907 the commercial club sponsored "booster trains" that were loaded up with displays and brochures about Tulsa (with titles like "Facts about Tulsa: A Coming Metropolis") and sent to cities on the East Coast and Upper Midwest in hopes of attracting new Tulsans. According to one history of Tulsa, in the early 1910s, "any visiting dignitary received red-carpet treatment, which usually consisted of beef barbecued over an open gas well, a Chautauqua-style lecture, and a medley of patriotic songs, which the club band performed."[23] Whether or not the boosters succeeded in attracting new industries and residents to their city, they did help foster a culture of town promotion that linked the production of an idealized image of the town with its material prosperity. By creating and then identifying with the ideal version of their town, boosters attempted to convince others, and themselves, that their town could achieve its full potential.

The municipal film, like any number of other promotional techniques, did not emerge as the idea of a single individual, company, or even industry, but rather appeared as a response to a number of factors. In a period of economic turbulence, towns and cities were eager to try new methods of advertising, and professional "boosters" were ready to offer their services. Motion picture companies who were trying to navigate the rapidly changing film industry found that the production of municipal films was a lucrative business, and certainly more stable than the search for which stories and stars would prove profitable in the marketplace. And, of course, some of the residents of small towns and cities who appeared in municipal films became entranced with the idea that appearing in a film was the first step in their quest for greater recognition or even national fame.

The confluence of these factors helped transform the local film from a mode of production associated with self-recognition to one that was primarily associated with self-promotion. In the early 1910s, sponsors of municipal advertising films boasted that the motion picture had unparalleled potential to reach audiences. Seemingly unburdened by the challenges of production and distribution that troubled many companies of the period, municipal film producers could rely on both substantial budgets and receptive local audiences. While some of these appeared to be no more than another set of local views, audiences saw them as something different precisely because they could imagine audiences elsewhere appreciating images of their town. As the Kansas City Chamber of Commerce, believing it had commissioned the first-ever municipal motion pictures, noted in its May 1913 newsletter, "The projection on a screen in the place of meeting before the entire assemblage of the beauties and advantages of Kansas City will be, beyond question, more forceful and convincing than all the 'wire-pulling' and distribution of expensive souvenirs possible."[24]

This shift in expectations for the cinema both recalled the cinema's earliest moments—when itinerant exhibitors inserted a local view into a program of views from elsewhere—and signified the increasing importance of distributors in determining which pictures could be seen where. The producers of municipal films offered products that were both local and had promise for distribution, which enabled them to convince sponsors to invest in their production. Moreover, a local film that audiences expected to be seen elsewhere proved to be a greater draw than the local views of the itinerant exhibition era. Once municipalities realized that they could make back some of their production budgets through local screenings, they were eager to produce such films.

The sponsors of municipal advertising films called attention to their novelty, making it difficult to identify just how widespread the practice was in the early 1910s. One indication of the popularity of the town boosting film, however, was a November 1912 article by Leo L. Redding, the editor of *Town Development*. In "Town Boosting with the 'Movies,'" Redding gave a thorough accounting of the use of the motion picture in booster campaigns. One of the first municipal campaigns to incorporate motion pictures, Redding wrote, took place in Wisconsin in the fall of 1910. J. F. Carter, the ambitious secretary of the Mobile Progressive Association in Alabama, sent out postcards to Wisconsin farmers inviting them to a film screening of life in the South. *Town Development* described what the farmers saw at one of five moving picture theaters in southern Wisconsin towns: "They saw actual pictures of actual things—the parade and crowds in the streets of Mobile at the bi-centennial celebration of the ancient city; the fertile pine stump land of the nearby country and the blasters at work blowing up the stumps with dynamite, and burning them. Striking pictures, these, with plenty of action in them."[25]

The film also included a view of the city from a ten-story building, shots of its port and railroad lines, and "some more farming pictures designed to emphasize such points as the plentifulness of cheap labor and the fact that the crop season is a long one in the sunny Southland." Farmers who attended the screening soon received publicity literature from real-estate promoters in Alabama. Redding wrote that as long as town advertising motion pictures appealed to "a miscellaneous public there is no surer way of arousing favorable comment, provided means can be found for getting the films widely distributed." Surprisingly, but perhaps reflecting the inchoate state of the film industry at the time, Redding claimed that distributing a town advertising film was "not particularly difficult," as long as the film was unique, had "plenty of action," and did not look too much like an advertisement. The article closed by listing a dozen other cities where films had been made in the past two and a half years, and noted, "It is a pretty slow town, in these days, that hasn't had its picture taken."[26] In two years, the municipal film went from being a novel form of advertising to a routine activity for ambitious towns.

Optimistic Twins: Industrial Films and Boosterism

While the origins of the local view lay in exhibition practices, the form and function of the municipal booster film was indebted to early industrial films. Frank Kessler and Eef Masson have argued that industrial films were often complex, multi-generic products that resisted classification and definition. In order to push against an impulse to over-categorize industrials, they argue for the films' evaluation in "historically specific, pragmatic contexts."[27] In the United States, industrial films produced in the early 1910s were intended to be advertisements for their sponsors. In 1911, Watterson Rounds Rothacker—who claimed that his Industrial Moving Picture Company, founded a year earlier, was the first company to specialize in advertising film—argued that the industrial motion picture was a natural evolution of both the medium and the advertising industry. Motion pictures could become "advertising educators" that had limitless possibility, potentially transforming the cinema into a site of industry-sponsored visual education.[28] By combining what were thought to be discrete fields—advertising, industry, education—Rothacker signaled the capacity for industrials to define, and be defined by, their circumstances of production and exhibition. By producing motion pictures that could be educational and entertaining, Rothacker could assure advertisers that their sponsored product would be able to compete in the film marketplace. For several years, advertising films appeared to be tolerated by exhibitors, a rare period of comity that abruptly ended in June 1913, when Epes Winthrop Sargent penned a strongly worded article against the advertising film in *Moving Picture World*. He pleaded to exhibitors, "Run a theater, not a bill board, and you'll be treated like a manager instead of a bill poster."[29]

Although the Industrial Moving Picture Company produced more traditional industrial pictures in the early 1910s—an early film, the Du Pont–sponsored *Farming with Dynamite* (1910), was particularly popular in rural areas—some of the company's most publicized clients were municipalities.[30] While Rothacker mentioned other uses for the industrial film in the articles he published in the first few years of his company's existence, he vociferously supported town advertisements. In a 1911 article that appeared in a compendium of advertising techniques, Rothacker wrote, "For advertising a community or a territory Moving Pictures are the medium par excellence. At Land Shows or at any exhibition they convey to an audience a graphic idea of the beauties and opportunities which the smoothest of tongues can at best but faintly conjure to the mind's eye. Moving Pictures are manifestly reliable exponents. Those who view them have not to make allowance for exaggeration."[31] While the company's activities were reported in *Moving Picture World* and local newspapers, in many cases the articles focused on the company's failures. In July 1911, the *World* reported that the chamber of commerce in Chattanooga, Tennessee, had rejected a film produced by the Industrial Moving Picture Company, calling it "inaccurate, badly shaded and lacking in vivid motion."[32] The following week, the *World* defended the film company, asking, "How is it possible to take a moving picture of a comatose town?"[33] A few months later, *The State*, in Columbia, South Carolina, reported that a camera operator from the Industrial Moving Picture Company had failed to arrive as promised, leaving the secretary of the city's chamber of commerce to explain the photographer's absence to an angry crowd. According to the newspaper, the group that had gathered on a Sunday in early October to have their pictures "tuk" was so angry that the secretary fled the scene "in terror of his life and limb." Within a few hours the film's sponsor sent a telegram to Rothacker demanding that the camera operator arrive in the next few days or he would cancel the contract for the state's films.[34]

Nevertheless, other companies soon joined the municipal film field. In February 1911, the Advance Motion Picture Company was founded in Chicago, and within three years was successful enough to increase its capital stock from $2,000 to $150,000.[35] In March 1911, Horatio F. Stoll, a California correspondent for *Moving Picture World*, noted an advertising scheme in the West where chambers of commerce sponsored the production of advertising films for exhibition in the state's theaters.[36] By October, the production of city booster films was so commonplace that the *World* reported, "this idea of picturing cities the motion picture way is becoming quite popular throughout the West, and the Advance Motion Picture Company" had landed many contracts to do so.[37]

In the examples cited so far, municipal films were produced at the behest of booster organizations, which sought out production companies to realize their campaigns. By 1911, however, motion picture companies were approaching municipalities to fund their own advertising films. In many cases, production companies advertised in local newspapers, even going so far as to send their query letters to newspaper editors in hopes that the prospect of a plan would itself be news. For example, on January 23, 1912, the Industrial Film Syndicate sent a letter to the mayor of New Brunswick, New Jersey, and to the editor of the *New Brunswick Times*, laying out its plans for the film it would make in their city:

> Immediately after we take your city, it is our intention to show the picture at your local theatre and then further exhibit it throughout the state and country where necessary, among a series of films, now so interesting to the public, under the title of "Civic America"; the system is our profit in this enterprise, there being no expense to your city further than such support as your merchants and industries might give us for personal additional representation and the assistance we require to have interesting events carried out in the streets while we are taking the city, such as parades, fire runs, and such activities as would tend to give your city a metropolitan air.[38]

Similar letters were sent to cities in New York, including Mount Vernon and Schenectady, though the films shot in those cities were not exhibited in New Brunswick.[39] The company's sales tactics were in keeping with those of other booster film producers. By first dangling the possibility of screening New Brunswick's film in other cities, the Industrial Film Syndicate was able to interest the mayor and, more importantly, the Board of

Trade in the film. Once they convinced sponsors to fund the film's production, the company asked the city to stage an event in order for them to have something of interest to film. After filming a local spectacle, the company found it easier to attract people to the theater, and the sponsor could make back its investment from local box office receipts alone. By asking the city to pretend to be "metropolitan," the company called attention to the booster agenda.

In fact, after reprinting the Industrial Film Syndicate's letter, the editor went on to speculate what might happen in New Brunswick were the city to take the company up on its proposition:

> If we wanted to, or if everybody wanted to, we could have a parade of the Rutgers faculty, duplicating, shall we say, the parade at the installation of the president or at commencement.
>
> Company H could turn out in full marching order, and show that New Brunswick is not lacking in patriotic fervor or in the means wherewith to sustain it.
>
> The firemen and the policemen might parade, the Rutgers sophomores might haze a few freshmen, the big factories might send forth floats and the banks might have a line of depositors marching to the receiving window.[40]

As in the earlier examples, the municipal film was imagined to be an amalgam of local views of city institutions and municipal leaders, displays of patriotism and advertisements for local businesses, who were expected to pay for the production under the auspices of the booster organization. The writer of this article turned the company's request for New Brunswick to put together activities worthy of being filmed into a challenge to the community. Because the letter from the Industrial Film Syndicate alludes to the "twenty million" people attending movies daily, the paper readily imagines an audience much larger than New Brunswick: "If the people of New Brunswick were to take the moving picture proposition seriously they could make a showing that would make theatre goers in other parts of the country sit up and take notice."[41] With just the promise of a motion picture, companies could excite the booster spirit, turning what could have been an ordinary "local view" into an event to be produced by the municipality.

Two months after the Industrial Film Syndicate's letter was printed in the *New Brunswick Times*, another article appeared on the front page, this time announcing that the board of directors of the Board of Trade had approved the motion picture proposal. With the contract signed, the New Brunswick Board of Trade prepared for the production of the city's motion picture. As the pithy editorial writer put it in the next day's newspaper,

"Everybody in the city is requested to get in motion before the film man comes to take the pictures."[42] The connection between a moving picture and a town "on the move" became a running joke in the newspaper for several months, underlining both the novelty of the film's production and the assumptions the community made about what a local motion picture should look like.

After winning local approval, Edwin S. Carman, the film's producer, visited the city's manufacturers, fire companies, and Rutgers College to arrange when and where to shoot the pictures and, presumably, to sell advertising space in the film. Two days later, the newspaper announced that New Brunswick would hold a "Boost New Brunswick" week in May, and that the moving pictures would be a feature attraction. New Brunswick's population was booming, and its boosters had no trouble raising $1,700—$50 dollars a piece from 34 Board of Trade members—as a down payment for the event.[43] One week later, the first moving pictures were shot in New Brunswick, with thousands of people showing up on Livingston Avenue, the central thoroughfare in town, to watch the city's firefighters on the run, just as if, the newspaper reported, "they were responding to an alarm of fire." The shot itself was staged, with the camera operator positioned at one street corner and the fire companies at another so they could all be filmed in passing. In addition, the paper reported that the day's footage would be edited with images shot at a later date in order to tell a narrative: "Tomorrow the camera man will visit all of the fire houses and photograph the companies as they are leaving houses. Then the pictures will be patched together, so that when the film is completed it will show just how the New Brunswick firemen respond in an alarm; will show the hitching of the horses. There was some talk of having an imaginary fire, with the placing of ladders up a house and the firemen at work with hose, but this was abandoned."[44]

Fires and firefighters were common themes in early American cinema, and "imaginary" fires, along with fake traffic accidents, were tropes of local films in the early 1910s, particularly once fictional elements began to be incorporated into municipal advertising films.[45] Over the next two weeks, the company shot many scenes in New Brunswick, including a Rutgers basketball game, interiors of the Johnson & Johnson manufacturing plant, and activity on business and residential streets. One of the more unusual scenes was made at the Rutgers campus, with cadets engaging in a "sham battle" on the university's football field, "using up a lot of cartridges and making much smoke."[46] Although filming ended in late April, the completed picture was not exhibited until late May, so it would coincide with New Brunswick's booster week.

On May 25, the *New Brunswick Times* announced plans for the exhibition of what the paper was now calling the "industrial films."[47] The films now ran 4,500 feet, far longer than the typical "feature" film of the period, and would debut in the Airdome, a seasonal open-air theater that opened in July 1910 in nearby Highland Park.[48] Three days later, the film was reviewed for the first of several times, with the paper observing that the mayor's smile for the camera was the most surprising scene in the four-reel film. Even though the untitled film was first exhibited at the Airdome, the camera operator chose to film crowds leaving the Opera House, the largest theater in New Brunswick, capturing people who did not expect to be filmed.[49]

After the New Brunswick films concluded their run at the Airdome, they moved to the Opera House, replacing a long running residency by a theater company. The picture had grown to a remarkable six thousand feet.[50] The films were shown with "several other reels of foreign make," implying that the company might not have been carrying out its proposed plan for a *Civic America* series featuring films made in many cities.[51]

By the end of 1912, dozens of companies specialized in the production of local films, and many of them advertised in national publications, including *Moving Picture World*, *Motion Picture News*, *Town Development*, and *American City*. Gunby Brothers, based in New York, placed an advertisement in the *World* in August 1912 offering to make "any local picture to order" for just ten cents a foot, half the cost charged by the Industrial Film Syndicate.[52] Another New York outfit, the Special Event Film Manufacturing Company, began advertising in the *World* in April 1912. After initially offering to make local films for theater managers, the company switched its marketing strategy in 1913, advertising "Moving Picture Cameras for sale cheap. Local Pictures Made. We rent cameras and cameramen."[53] The Commercial Motion Picture Company started in New York in 1913, and in August placed an advertisement in *Moving Picture World* announcing that they specialized in making "motion pictures of local events."[54] Even though the company promised a 25 percent commission to anyone who secured a film contract, its stint in the municipal film business was short-lived, a fate shared by many of its competitors. By October, the company was instead advertising its films of the World Series.[55]

As the municipal advertising film became more commonplace, theater managers and other entrepreneurs tried their hand in the business, but without access to film exchanges, these individuals and companies did not try to distribute their films to larger audiences. While local films were still being used for civic purposes, theater managers and metropolitan or regional companies had a more expansive definition of the municipal advertising film than the companies that had national aspirations. In Philadelphia, city businessmen started the H. B. B. Motion Picture Company in February 1914 for the "special purpose of featuring Philadelphia, her industries and developing the activities of Philadelphians."[56] The same month, the Magnet Film Manufacturing Company started in Evansville, Indiana, advertising that they made "Motion Pictures of Home-Comings, Carnivals, Conventions, Celebrations and Athletic Events," in addition to educational, industrial, scenic, historical, and scientific films.[57] Despite this ambitious menu of production possibilities, the company did most of its work in nearby towns.[58] In Manhattan, Kansas, O. W. Holt started an eponymous film company, producing a film in June 1914 of the dedication of the Grand Army of the Republic Memorial Hall in nearby Topeka. Instead of sending the film around the country, the local chapter of the GAR, a fraternity of Union veterans of the Civil War, decided to bury (literally) the film for fifty years so future generations could view their dedication ceremony.[59]

In her study of the standardization of everyday life in the early decades of the twentieth century, Marina Moskowitz argues that the widespread adoption of zoning codes helped manage the growth of cities and small towns. City planners, like the professional boosters discussed earlier, traveled from town to town giving speeches about their latest ideas and published articles in national magazines about the importance of their work. Moskowitz suggests that in the promotional literature and speeches by municipal boosters and planners, "zoning provided both a process, arranged daily life in a city, and a product, an image of urban life."[60] A municipal booster film had many of the same advantages as a zoning code, if not the same degree of permanence, because cities both had to change themselves to look suitable for the motion pictures and, once recorded, could use the film as a representation of their ideal selves. But by 1914, the local view was no longer a sufficient representational form. In order to make local films that would have nonlocal appeal, filmmakers needed to match the industry in its use of genre, narrative form, and special effects.

Paragon Feature Film Company

Many varieties of the municipal booster film were produced in the early 1910s, from parade and convention films to real-estate advertisements to memorial films. Producers told sponsors that their films would be screened elsewhere as distinct works, or that excerpts from their films would be included in newsreels or travelogues.[61] Made aware of the wider audience for their movies, sponsors and producers began rethinking the form of the local view as film style itself changed. Instead of shooting thousands of feet of film, companies began shooting one- or two-reel films that could more easily fit into an evening program. One of the most significant tendencies, however, was the incorporation of fictional and semi-fictional scenes into booster films. Filmmakers adopted narrative techniques from the theatrical motion picture. Several production houses made such movies, but the best examples come from the semi-fictional narrative versions of municipal booster films produced by the Paragon Feature Film Company, three of which are extant. Paragon's work is indicative of how producers responded to changing distribution and exhibition patterns.[62] In order to convince audiences that his films could be exhibited theatrically, Oliver William Lamb, the director of Paragon, defined his films as "motion pictures 'with a plot.'"[63] Lamb made as many as one hundred booster films between 1912 and 1916, but there is scant evidence of their exhibition in theaters in towns other than their sites of production.

In May 1912, Lamb, a thirty-four-year-old who had previously been employed as a secretary-treasurer for a manufacturer of streetcar equipment and, more recently the secretary-treasurer for a company that produced a treatment for hog cholera, entered the motion picture business.[64] Living in Topeka, Kansas, Lamb joined other local businessmen to form the short-lived Victor Film Advertising Company, which produced booster films in Topeka and Lawrence, Kansas, before selling the business in July of that year.[65] A few months later, Lamb rejoined the movie field, traveling to McAlester, Oklahoma, to make a picture. Now representing the Special Event Film Company of New York, Lamb told the *McAlester News-Capital* that the films had been sent to his address in Illinois from New York.[66] The Special Event Film Company was incorporated on January 12, 1912, and advertised in *Moving Picture World* throughout that year. In April it first offered "motion pictures taken to order."[67] Lamb may have encountered the company through the magazine *Popular Mechanics* in July 1912, in which its classified ad stated, "Have a local motion picture taken. It will pay you. We make 'em. Write for terms. State how many feet you want. We do the rest. Moving picture cameras and printers, bought, sold and exchanged. We rent Moving Picture Cameras."[68]

Lamb's exact role with the company was unclear. On October 15, 1912, the Commercial Club of McAlester signed a contract to produce a picture of their city and the coalfields nearby. A camera operator and stage manager were expected to come to McAlester to take the pictures, and once the film was made, the paper reported that the reel would be sent "on the road in charge of a competent operator [presumably Lamb] throughout

Illinois, Indiana, Ohio and Pennsylvania."⁶⁹ That very evening, company director Fred Beck left New York for McAlester with a camera operator and stage manager, a trip of 1,400 miles.

Like the Industrial Film Syndicate, the Special Event Company asked its sponsor to stage a parade for the benefit of the cameras. But the *News-Capital* also reported that "the pictures will be staged just as the pictures in a regular company," in order to make the film attractive to other audiences. The paper summarized the film's plot as follows: "Six young ladies will be picked out who are to act as escort for the picture people. They will be taken aboard the Katy flyer, probably from the south, and the train will be shown coming into town. This gives an excuse for showing the union station, also."⁷⁰

The plot summary notes that the women will be shown visiting the Busby Hotel, five of the best houses in McAlester, coal mines, cotton gins, and the agricultural exhibits at the county fair. The set-up for the film was common. Edwin S. Porter made a similar picture, *Boarding School Girls*, in Coney Island in 1905. Charles Musser has argued that the Porter film's use of young women to provide a "seamless mimetic consistency" between scenes anticipated classical cinema.⁷¹ While the MacAlester film was made to advertise the surface rights to nearby coalfields, the newspaper points out that the picture will also "show to the east that this wild western country is as highly civilized as the most effete portions of 'back east.'"⁷²

Renting the Forum Theater, the commercial club ran the film, titled *Seeing McAlester*, November 13–17, 1912.⁷³ While community members funded the film's production, the film's exhibition was intended to raise enough money for it to be distributed, for free, to the eastern states. The newspaper reviews were critical of the film, which was highly unusual as publishers were often aligned with booster organizations. In one scene, a local bank president appears with a hoe handle, which the newspaper describes as "the poor man's golf stick," and pretends to labor at a cottonseed oil mill, which some viewers perceived as a parody of either the bank president or common laborers.⁷⁴ After the first day of exhibition, the newspaper defended what appears to have been strong criticism of the film by those who saw it: "It should be remembered that the folks are not trained motion picture actors. The admonition to 'not look at the camera' had little effect. It was impossible to keep some folks from looking square at the camera and to that degree the pictures were impaired."⁷⁵

Others complained that the people were too self-conscious before the camera and that some appeared repetitively, while others were left out entirely. The newspaper also admitted that the "story is necessarily not very thrilling." The two-reeler was exhibited every hour during its run at the Forum, with comedy pictures added to fill out the program.[76]

One month later, in December 1912, Lamb visited Wichita Falls, Texas, this time as a representative of the Special Scenic Film Company of Denver. Having adopted Special Events' business model whole-cloth, Lamb proposed to the directors of the local chamber of commerce that he would shoot a thousand-foot film showing the scenes of Wichita Falls.[77] As part of his presentation, Lamb screened *Seeing McAlaster* at the Gem Theater. For $750, Lamb promised he would make the film and distribute it for a year, with the chamber picking the theaters where the film would be seen. While the Wichita Falls picture was not made, likely due to the expense of the production, Lamb proposed making similar films for dozens of towns.[78] On April 28, 1913, Lamb incorporated the Special Scenic Film Company in Colorado, with his wife and the owner of the hotel where they were staying serving as witnesses.[79] Soon after Special Scenic incorporated, Lamb either left it to start another company or, more likely, unofficially changed the name of his firm to the Paragon Feature Film Company.[80] By exchanging "Special Scenic" for "Paragon Feature," Lamb signaled his awareness of what audiences were now expecting from the movies. Scenic films, a popular genre in the early cinema era, were receiving less play as narrative fiction films began to dominate movie theaters. Likewise, Paragon Feature suggested both the high expectations audiences had for films in the early 1910s and the growing popularity of the feature film, which in this period was as likely to connote the film's distinction within the regular program as it was to indicate the length of the film.[81] For the remainder of 1913, Lamb continued to make his sightseeing films, producing motion pictures in Oklahoma City, Tulsa, Wichita, Little Rock, Kansas City, Houston, and several small towns in Texas, Oklahoma, and Missouri.

Even though Lamb continued to produce sightseeing films throughout 1913, he experimented with the addition of fictional and narrative elements into a genre that had hitherto been strictly nonfiction and, for the most part, non-narrative. Lamb might have been influenced by the work of other industrial film companies, who began adding more fictional elements to local films in order to make them more attractive for audiences in other cities. For example, in June 1913, the Industrial Moving Picture Company turned an assignment to shoot a track meet in Springfield, Illinois, into an opportunity to write a scenario based on "one of the popular boys' stories," in which a track star is kidnapped by his rivals in order to keep him from competing but is rescued just in time for him to win the race. The *World* noted nationwide attention because "a scenario was written around what

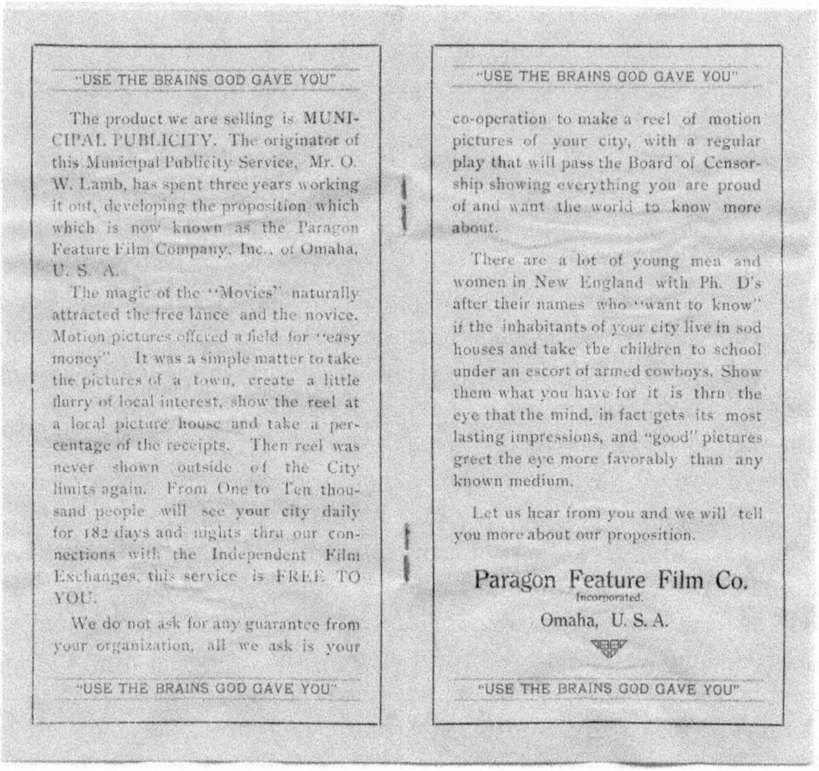

"USE THE BRAINS GOD GAVE YOU"

The product we are selling is MUNICIPAL PUBLICITY. The originator of this Municipal Publicity Service, Mr. O. W. Lamb, has spent three years working it out, developing the proposition which which is now known as the Paragon Feature Film Company, Inc., of Omaha, U. S. A.

The magic of the "Movies" naturally attracted the free lance and the novice. Motion pictures offered a field for "easy money". It was a simple matter to take the pictures of a town, create a little flurry of local interest, show the reel at a local picture house and take a percentage of the receipts. Then reel was never shown outside of the City limits again. From One to Ten thousand people will see your city daily for 182 days and nights thru our connections with the Independent Film Exchanges, this service is FREE TO YOU.

We do not ask for any guarantee from your organization, all we ask is your

"USE THE BRAINS GOD GAVE YOU"

"USE THE BRAINS GOD GAVE YOU"

co-operation to make a reel of motion pictures of your city, with a regular play that will pass the Board of Censorship showing everything you are proud of and want the world to know more about.

There are a lot of young men and women in New England with Ph. D's after their names who "want to know" if the inhabitants of your city live in sod houses and take the children to school under an escort of armed cowboys. Show them what you have for it is thru the eye that the mind, in fact gets its most lasting impressions, and "good" pictures greet the eye more favorably than any known medium.

Let us hear from you and we will tell you more about our proposition.

Paragon Feature Film Co.
Incorporated.
Omaha, U. S. A.

"USE THE BRAINS GOD GAVE YOU"

Figure 1.1. Brochure (c. 1913) from the Paragon Feature Film Company, Panama-Pacific International Exposition Records, 1893–1929. *Courtesy of the Bancroft Library University of California, Berkeley*

is generally a common place event."[82] By incorporating fictional scenes into the municipal film, Lamb was able to both distinguish his films from competitors offering similar services and assuage any fears that the films would be unsatisfactory to local audiences and unappealing to audiences elsewhere.

In July, Lamb approached the Oklahoma City Chamber of Commerce with a plan to make a film about the rapidly growing city. Again, Lamb proposed to make a two-reeler (1,300 feet in this case), which had become Paragon's standard. His business model had also changed slightly. Instead of requiring the booster organization to pay up front, Lamb said he would make the film at no charge but would use the receipts from its local exhibition to pay for production and distribution costs, thereby reducing risk for the sponsoring organization. Lamb also detailed his distribution plans. According to the newspaper, the Oklahoma City film would first be screened throughout the state, and then in theaters across the nation. As he told the chamber, the company would "furnish weekly reports showing the number of persons who see the film daily when it is exhibited." While Lamb's sales pitch was not new, the more interesting moment came when he described the film he planned: "My idea of taking Oklahoma City for the 'movies' would be to first show Oklahoma City as it was in 1889, a small town with a boxcar for a railroad station and cowboys and Indians about. It is somewhat like many persons suppose Oklahoma is today. Then we would show Oklahoma City in 1913."[83]

From there, Lamb went on to describe his formula to find six attractive young women and record them touring local sights. But his proposal that the city recreate a fictional version of Oklahoma City's recent past is revealing, in part because Lamb once again supposed that the imagined audience for this film—namely, the large moviegoing public in the East—would be drawn to a narrative that depicted the city's past, not its present. Lamb added more details to his distribution plans, suggesting the Oklahoma City film would be seen by three thousand people daily, just a small portion of the 20 million who regularly went to the movies.[84] Local businesses took him seriously. Speaking before the chamber of commerce in a special Saturday meeting, Lamb argued that "the clamor now is not for rough comedy, but for educational reels, as may be seen from the popularity of the animated weeklies," using a synonym for newsreels.[85] Lamb proposed that the films could be shown at the Oklahoma building at the Panama-Pacific Exposition in San Francisco, then being organized. Lamb also screened films of Sherman, Texas, and Lincoln, Nebraska, before the chamber at the Overholser Theater, the largest in the city. Speaking to the local newspaper, Lamb speculated that the Oklahoma City reels would be superior to any his company had produced thus far.

The contract was signed on July 14, and the title—*Seeing Oklahoma City in the Days of '89*—was announced in the next day's paper, along with the estimate that 2 million people would view the film in a year's time. For the first, historical reel, Lamb proposed recreating the scene of the 1889 land rush.[86] As Lamb described the scene in the shot-by-shot list reprinted in the newspaper, the event would feature "firing of gun, staking off claims, a gun fight or two, something that will cause the audience to raise up in its seats and reach for the ceiling."[87] After a two-week delay, the scene was filmed at Northeast Lake on Sunday, July 27, with two thousand spectators. More than one hundred people participated in the scene itself, all of them dressed in regalia appropriate to 1889. The newspaper noted that automobiles, telephone poles, and other signs of modernity were left out of the scene. Lamb's commitment to historical accuracy was evident in an encounter with a participant in the film, which was recorded by the newspaper:

> In staging the scene, one man insisted on climbing to the top of a small oak tree and watching the scene. Director Lamb spied him and yelled:
> "Say, you in the tree; climb on out—it wasn't stylish to do that in '89 I'm told."
> "Oh, yes it was," the old timer replied. "That was just where I was when the run was made."[88]

As this interaction shows, Lamb used reenactment of locally important, nationally known events to appeal to larger audiences, as well as to give "old-timers" an opportunity to participate in a movie reproduction of the recent past. Soon after shooting the scene, Lamb called the picture the "greatest thing we have ever attempted" and noted a similar film shot with professional actors would cost three thousand dollars and take two weeks.[89] William Lou Gullett, the camera operator and scenario writer for Paragon, went even further in this self-praise, claiming, "It is probable that the Gaumont company will build a story about this feature of the Oklahoma City reel and advertise it throughout the United States."[90]

Before shooting in Oklahoma City was even finished, Lamb had already started soliciting towns for other Paragon films. For the rest of the year, Lamb produced films in Muskogee, Oklahoma; Wichita, Kansas; Billings, Montana; Cheyenne, Wyoming; Tulsa, Kansas City, Little Rock, and several more cities in Missouri and Texas.

From Pilgrim Films to Industrial Romances

In January 1914, Lamb made what was probably his first industrial romance, *A Council Bluffs Courtship*, in Council Bluffs, Iowa, located just across the Nebraska border from Omaha, where Paragon had relocated a month earlier.[91] The term "industrial romance" was often used to describe narrative industrial films, and such films used the word "romance" in their titles, including the International Harvester Company's *The Romance of the Reaper* (1911).[92] Although Lamb's new narrative centered on romantic love, his films also reflected the literary tradition of the romance, in which the ideals of the city are personified in its native youth. Produced in an era in which civic promoters were considered the vanguard of business culture, municipal booster films were well suited for romantic themes.

Industrial romances inserted the views emblematic of the local film into the mise-en-scène of narrative fiction films. For Paragon's industrial romances Lamb, or the sponsor, cast a young man and woman, in most cases the sons and daughters of prominent society members, to play the leads. The particularities of the films differed. Some included historical reenactments, while others explored contemporary political tensions over class, labor, and gender equality. However, they all incorporated the narrative of a courtship, often set against a backdrop of views of local industries, culminating in a wedding. In each, a couple meets, the man proposes, the woman accepts, and they marry. While this plot was not unusual, Lamb may have been the first itinerant filmmaker to make narrative "wedding" films, a trope that was used by many of his successors.[93]

Soon after producing the Council Bluffs picture, Lamb traveled to San Antonio, Texas. While Lamb had already made his pilgrim films in Dallas, Fort Worth, and Houston, as well as a number of smaller Texas towns, he had more ambitious plans for San Antonio. On January 12, 1914, Lamb signed a contract with the chamber of commerce to produce a "dramatic scenario" of the city that Lamb estimated would be seen by 500,000 people by the end of the film's twenty-six-week run. Instead of shooting a reenactment of the Alamo, which had been staged for cameras in San Antonio in 1911, Lamb chose a contemporary story, which he titled *An American Citizen*.

According to the scenario printed in the newspaper, the film opens with a shot of a small house in the Chicago suburbs.[94] John Mason, a municipal engineer, is walking home when he sees his wife in tears, and her physician, Dr. Tadmas, leaving their house. The doctor informs him that his wife must be taken to a higher, warmer climate in order to get better. The couple's daughter joins her parents on their porch, and Mason pulls out a publicity brochure for San Antonio. In the next scene, the family arrives to San Antonio, visits the Alamo immediately upon arrival, and then settles into their new home. In the first few scenes, the film establishes both San Antonio's historical importance and its sunny weather, considered to be a key advantage over northern cities. While most of Lamb's films did not portray life in other places, sponsors and audiences alike assumed that one of the purposes of their films was to entice people from larger cities to smaller, growing ones, and from the East to the West. By making this dynamic explicit in *An American Citizen*, Lamb represented in fictional form the possibility for cities to win new residents by producing attractive brochures or sponsoring interesting films.

After this optimistic beginning, the narrative turns darker, as we learn that, six months later, Mason has still not been able to find work. At that moment, Mason's wife hands him a newspaper with the headline "Citizens Will Vote for Bonds." The next day, Mason picks up the newspaper and learns that the city approved $20 million of bonds for municipal improvements to be made in the city over the next five years. Buoyed by this good news, the couple takes a sightseeing tour of San Antonio. While on tour, the Masons meet the Warrens, old friends from Chicago who also relocated to San Antonio. Frank Warren, the couple's son, and Louise Mason, the Masons' daughter, reconnect, and within a few minutes of screen time, Frank kisses Louise. As the scenario put it, "the flames of an old love are fanned afresh." The elder Warren offers John Mason a job on the project that will widen Commerce Street. A few scenes later, Frank decides to visit Louise at her home. When he arrives, he discovers that the house is in flames. Although the fire department has already arrived, it is up to Frank to rescue Louise. With the Mason house destroyed, Frank and Louise go back to the Warren home, where the couple's parents both bless the marriage. A wedding follows, and the film closes with a shot of the couple at the railroad station, about to embark on a honeymoon. The final scenes in *An American Citizen*—a courtship, a fire, a rescue, and a wedding—are repeated in almost every Paragon film made between 1914 and 1916.

For most of 1914 and 1915, Lamb produced moving pictures in the Midwest and Upper Midwest, working in Michigan, Wisconsin, Illinois, and Kansas. Three shot in this period have been preserved and are among the few extant municipal booster movies. All three films—*The Lumberjack* (1914, Wausau, Wisconsin), *Present and Past in Cradle of Dixie* (1914, Montgomery, Alabama), and *The Blissveldt Romance* (1915, Grand Rapids, Michigan)—are mostly intact and indicate the vibrancy and skill of Lamb and his crew. While these films represent a small percentage of the work the company produced in its brief yet prolific history, the films show the changing status of local scenes in Lamb's mostly pre-scripted narratives.

In February 1914, just after he finished *An American Citizen*, Lamb returned to the historical reenactment film, shooting *Present and Past in Cradle of Dixie* in Montgomery. Six months earlier, Lamb had treated the Oklahoma land rush as a historical event spatially and temporally disconnected from the rest of the film. But for the Montgomery film, Lamb used this historical event as the backdrop for a story that addressed the tension between the South's agricultural past and its industrial present. In addition to resonating with other movies commemorating the Civil War, with 1915's *The Birth of a Nation* being the most prominent, *Present and Past* was also in keeping with the newly popular historical pageants, elaborate outdoor stage dramas used to celebrate local history.[95]

In Montgomery, Lamb had William Gullett, his "scenario expert," write a plot that featured a reenactment of Jefferson Davis's 1861 inauguration as the president of the Confederacy. In this fictional film a group of businessmen from the North come to Montgomery to witness this reenactment. After touring local sights and industries, one of the visitors, Bertram C. Lawton, falls in love with southern belle Elinore Harrison, who is described in a plot summary printed in the *Montgomery Advertiser* as the "beauteous link of the chivalrous past and the dreaming present."[96] But the past is not really past, as Elinore's grandfather, a Confederate colonel in the Civil War, refuses to allow his granddaughter to marry a northerner. The couple agrees to break off their wedding plans, but soon after a fire breaks out in the colonel's home. Lawton races to the house and saves the life of Elinore's grandfather, who then blesses the wedding.

Lamb's decision to make another historical reenactment film was in part driven by market considerations and, likely, his sense that white southerners would be interested in participating in yet another commemoration of the Civil War. In an interview with the *Montgomery Advertiser*, Lamb said that "one of the most attractive features of all moving picture productions is the reproduction of the scenes of the past through a series of shadow or memory pictures," and that viewers of *Present and Past* would witness a "glimpse, dramatic and vivid, of the epic past, through incidents of the day."[97] The film, including the "memory pictures," was sponsored by the Business Men's League.

In one early scene, Elinore brings Lawton and the other visitors to the capitol, where they all take out binoculars to observe the city. Although the party is shown to be on the steps of the Greek Revival capitol building, only some of the subsequent point-of-view shots were taken from the capitol. Others were taken from the higher vantage point of high-rise office buildings. Matte framing is used to simulate the binocular point of view, underlining the importance of seeing these scenes as a tourist would.

After the sightseeing shots, *Present and Past in Cradle of Dixie* transitions to the historical reenactment of the early days of the Confederacy. The first intertitle announces that the event is the fiftieth anniversary of the inauguration of Jefferson Davis at the Alabama State Capitol, even though the actual anniversary took place three years earlier. The next intertitle reads "Crowd cheers as Governor appears," although it is not immediately clear whether the governor being cheered is the 1914 governor or the 1861 governor. The two intertitles are followed by a pan of the crowd, with many feather-hatted women and top-hatted men waving to the camera, making this shot one of the few in the film where local audiences would see themselves on screen. As the *Montgomery Advertiser* reported, members of historical and patriotic societies were invited to participate in the scenes, and

Figures 1.2 and 1.3. Still frames from *Present and Past in Cradle of Dixie* (1914). *Courtesy of the Alabama Department of Archives and History, Montgomery*

men were asked to "wear the big old fashioned black bow ties, Prince Albert coats, and high hats."⁹⁸ While the paper assured its readers that those not in costume would still be able to appear on camera, it is significant that one of the few crowd scenes in the film asked participants to be reenactors. The next intertitle introduces Alabama's governor, Emmet O'Neal, himself the son of a former governor and Confederate general, informing the viewer that his speech "paints thrilling word pictures of the stirring days of the early sixties." The next shot shows the governor giving a speech, followed by a shot of several men in a conference room.

Unlike the Oklahoma City film, which featured a reenactment of the dramatic land rush, *Present and Past* depicts the early days of the Civil War as a series of heated discussions, all taking place within the confines of the capitol. Even the reenactment of the Davis inauguration is shot more like a newsreel than a fictional narrative. Lamb told the Montgomery newspapers that the scenes would be used in Pathe's Weekly, the Mutual Weekly, and the Animated Weekly newsreels.⁹⁹ Audiences could thus read these reenactment scenes in two ways. First, they could be seen as fictional scenes within a narrative that was filmed in Montgomery. Alternatively, they could be read as documentation of the people of Montgomery reenacting an historical event. In the first case, the picture would only be legible if it was seen in its entirety. In the second, the reenactment scenes could be cut out of the film and inserted into a newsreel. Based on Lamb's statements to the local press, he intended for the film to be used in either way.

With the historical section of the film complete, Lamb returned to the wedding narrative, which starts with a ball at Morning View, an antebellum mansion used as the location for the remaining scenes. Bertram proposes to Elinore at a fountain, a prop that appears in several of Lamb's films. The lovers visit Colonel Harrison, who signals his disapproval. Bertram returns to the dance and a crowd gathers round to hear his troubles. An intertitle informs the viewer that Bertram has decided to steal Elinore away, which in effect realizes grandfather's fears and, by extension, the fears of many white southerners wary of northern investors. In the next sequence, a horse-drawn fire engine races to the house where Elinore lives. Three women, shown earlier to be on the second floor of the house, jump out the window, and in the next shot we see firemen rush into the building. The film ends with a quick intertitle—"A Happy Reconciliation"—followed by a shot of Bertram and Elinore with a minister. (See Moving Image 1.1.)

This tidy ending connects Montgomery's past with its present and suggests that the future of the city lies in greater economic and cultural ties

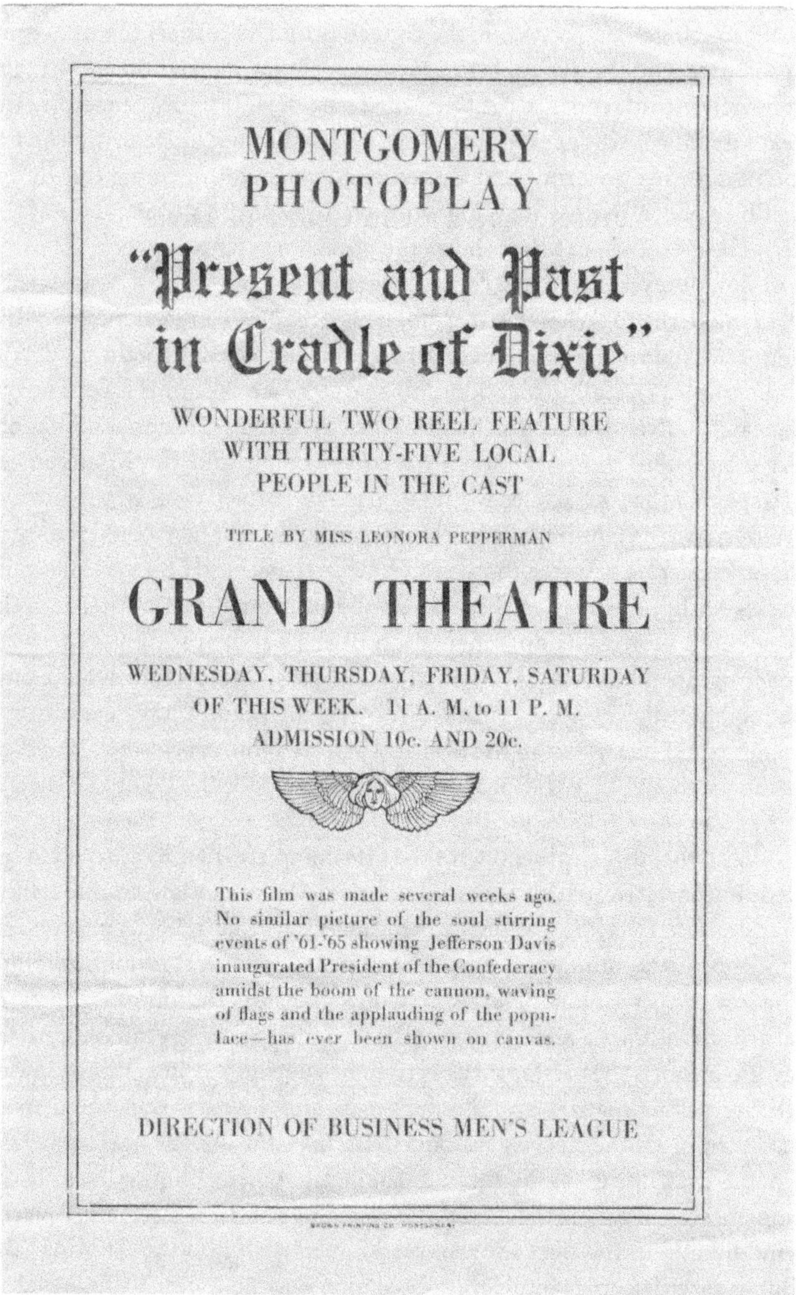

MONTGOMERY
PHOTOPLAY

"Present and Past in Cradle of Dixie"

WONDERFUL TWO REEL FEATURE
WITH THIRTY-FIVE LOCAL
PEOPLE IN THE CAST

TITLE BY MISS LEONORA PEPPERMAN

GRAND THEATRE

WEDNESDAY, THURSDAY, FRIDAY, SATURDAY
OF THIS WEEK. 11 A. M. to 11 P. M.
ADMISSION 10c. AND 20c.

This film was made several weeks ago. No similar picture of the soul stirring events of '61-'65 showing Jefferson Davis inaugurated President of the Confederacy amidst the boom of the cannon, waving of flags and the applauding of the populace—has ever been shown on canvas.

DIRECTION OF BUSINESS MEN'S LEAGUE

BROWN PRINTING CO. MONTGOMERY

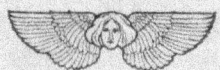

Figure 1.4. Program from *Present and Past in Cradle of Dixie* (1914). *Courtesy of the Alabama Department of Archives and History, Montgomery*

between New England and points south and west. In a Paragon Feature Film brochure, likely produced in 1913, Lamb claimed that the purpose of his films was to counteract regional prejudices. For example, he told potential clients that "there are a lot of young men and women in New England with PhDs after their names who 'want to know' if the inhabitants of your city live in sod houses and take the children to school under an escort of armed cowboys."[100] In a few cases, like the Montgomery picture, Lamb incorporated reenactments of widely known historical events from a town's history into the narrative, but he was careful to include scenes of modern life as well. While sponsors saw scenes of coalfields as suitable attractions for Lamb's early film of McAlester, Oklahoma, by 1914 sponsors were enticed by films that integrated local attractions—factories, local landmarks, and prominent citizens—into a film narrative. In Muscatine, Iowa, Lamb highlighted the city's pearl button industry by incorporating the process of their manufacture into the plot.[101] For his romance of Jackson, Michigan, Lamb staged a race between two automobiles made in the city.[102] Unlike the pilgrim films, where the various sights of the city were treated equally, with a shot of a local church just as important as a shot of farm land or an industrial plant, the industrial romance films centered their narratives around particular industries.

For *The Lumberjack*, filmed in Wausau, Wisconsin, in July 1914, Lamb used the industrial romance storyline, with the town's lumber mill serving as the principal attraction. A married couple, Hans and Helen Hagge, played the leading roles. Hans Hagge had moved to Wausau several years earlier to head a new mutual insurance company, while his wife, Helen, was the daughter of a lumber pioneer.[103] In the fictional story, Helen and Hans spend their courtship visiting the town's industries, including a lumber mill and granite quarry. One scene, which takes place at the park where the couple plans to marry, features shots of log rolling, a local folk practice that Lamb filmed in many Wisconsin cities in the summer of 1914. At one point, Helen takes out glasses to survey the city. As with other Paragon works, her point-of-view shot is framed by a matte. The following shots, all pans, demonstrate the size of the city and its principal attractions, including the river and lumberyards. These industrial scenes are followed by views of the country club, including shots of golfers. One obvious, if not directly stated, difference between the municipal booster film and the local view is the former's emphasis on the upper class, or "society," instead of the latter's emphasis on democracy before the eye of the camera.[104]

For the rest of 1914 and early 1915, Paragon produced more films in Wisconsin and Kansas, and received contracts to produce films for the

Panama-Pacific International Exposition in San Francisco. In April 1915, Paragon returned to the South, shooting *From Wedding Bells to Cotton Bolls* in Memphis, Tennessee, and *The Spirit of Columbus, 1865–1915* in Columbus, Georgia. In Memphis, Lamb staged the burning and sinking of a steamboat on the Mississippi River, an event that was spectacular enough to win the film limited distribution in Ohio.[105] For the Columbus film, Lamb appears to have reused the reenactment footage originally shot in Montgomery and filmed a new reenactment of the "last battle" between the North and South, with local people playing soldiers on both sides.[106] Even though the stunts in Lamb's Midwestern films were not as spectacular as those used in the South and Southwest, he made up for the lack of special effects with increasingly complex narratives.

Although Lamb had been flirting with melodramatic plots for more than year, by September 1915 he had fully committed to the mode. Film theorist Linda Williams argues that melodrama was the dominant form of popular cinematic narrative in the silent era, one particularly suited to address questions of morality. In Paragon's late films, the moral question appears to have been, what is the human price of progress? The factories that boosters once fought to get were now depicted as hazardous workplaces. Urbanization meant an abandonment of rural life. Access to national markets brought with it threats to family unity. As Williams argues, melodrama promises that we can always reverse time, return to a "space of innocence." She continues, "Melodrama offers the hope, then, that it may not be too late, that there may still be an original locus of virtue, and that this virtue and truth can be achieved in private individuals and individual heroic acts."[107] The wedding scenes in the Paragon films signal the close of a progressive narrative. The couple overcomes physical danger and protestations by family members in order to ensure the community's continued development and growth. At the same time, these scenes are an attempt to wish away the tensions between modernity and tradition, nationalism and localism, the uncertain present and the unviable past. Entering its last year of production, Paragon began making pictures that overflowed with melodramatic scenes, threatening their very function as town boosters.

In the early autumn of 1915, Lamb traveled to Grand Rapids, Michigan, to make *The Blissveldt Romance*, a melodrama contrasting rural and city life. The film opens in Jennison, Michigan, a small town a few miles from Grand Rapids. John Graham has just accepted a job offer from a bank in Grand Rapids, leaving behind his girlfriend Lizzie Johnson, who works at the Blissveldt dairy farm. When John arrives at the train station in downtown Grand Rapids, he is so overwhelmed by city life that he is struck by a car when he tries to cross the street. The driver of the car, the urbane and wealthy Amelia Brown, takes him to her palatial estate and nurses him back to health. Within a few days, John asks Amelia's father if he can marry his daughter, but he is turned down. However, the mansion soon catches fire, as mansions tend to do in Paragon films, and John rescues Amelia, convincing her father to approve the marriage.

At this point, *The Blissveldt Romance* takes an unexpected turn. Back in Jennison, Lizzie reads of John's nuptials in the Grand Rapids newspaper. She gets on a horse, not in a car, and heads to town to find John. In the next scene, she stops the horse and takes out a telescope, which she uses to find John in the crowd. The matte shots we see do not show John, however, but instead the crowd scenes for which local films are best known. The people waving to the camera are not waving to Lizzie but instead to audiences in Grand Rapids and other cities where the film might be shown. Once Lizzie locates the wedding party at an elite rowing club, she makes the brash and unexpected decision to commit suicide by jumping off a pier. This melodramatic scene is unusually dark for a town promotional film, and Lamb only managed to pull off a happy ending by showing a scene of Amelia and John with their young daughter a few years later.

When Lamb used the same ending for *The Maid of the Mississippi*, produced in Rock Island, Illinois, in October 1916, he ran into censorship troubles. Described in the *Moving Picture World* as a "home talent photoplay," the film stood out because it lacked the "traditional happy ending" for which such pictures were known.[108] While the mayor of Rock Island eventually relented and approved the sponsored film's local exhibition, the fact that such a confrontation happened at all suggests the perils of making local films that were thrilling enough for the national marketplace. In an effort to match the standards of popular narrative movie productions, Lamb ended up producing pictures that aimed to succeed as entertainment rather than as town advertisements.

Although its pace of production slowed sharply after 1915, Paragon continued to make films in the Midwest for another year or two. In May 1916, Paragon shot *A Cedar Valley Romance* in Waterloo, Iowa. While Lamb still told the film's sponsor that he planned to exhibit the film for 182 days and nights, he no longer emphasized the appeal of local monuments and buildings as attractions in themselves. Instead, Lamb set narrative pieces in locations within the city. "He will make use of St. Francis hospital for an injured patient," the Waterloo paper reported, "Grace Methodist church for a wedding, the rear of an observation car on the Cedar Valley line for a honeymoon scene, the Cedar river for a boat regatta, and the Fourth street bridge for a parade."[109]

The paper also reported that similar films had been made in eighty-six cities, of which fifty titles have been identified. While the film's production and initial reception was not unusual, its distribution was covered in more detail than the typical Paragon film. In December 1916, six months after the film was first exhibited in Waterloo, the newspaper reported that Westinghouse Electric & Manufacturing Company wrote the town's commercial club, asking if they could exhibit its sponsored film in cities where they had branch factories.[110] In April 1917, a Waterloo resident reportedly saw herself on screen in a movie theater in Clarksville, Kentucky, which exhibited her hometown's moving picture.[111] The same month, John S. Conger, then president of Paragon, wrote the commercial club that its film had been seen in dozens of cities in Indiana and Kentucky.[112] In June, the club was informed by Paragon, now based in Des Moines, that the film print would be returned to them after its exhibition in Minneapolis and St. Paul.[113] A year after its return to Waterloo, *A Cedar Valley Romance* was shown at Electric Park, an amusement center.[114]

One bright spot in the waning years of the booster film was the Panama-Pacific Exposition in San Francisco. As early as September 1913, Lamb encouraged the Oklahoma City Chamber of Commerce to turn over *Seeing Oklahoma City* to the state's Panama-Pacific Exposition Commission, which took the films on a tour to raise funds for the Oklahoma State Building.[115] At the end of 1914, Lamb signed a contract with the Panama-Pacific Commission of Kansas to take fifty thousand feet of film in two hundred towns in Kansas.[116] In January 1915, the city commissioners of Emporia, Kansas, agreed to pay seventy-five dollars for a thousand-foot film of their town, which would be screened at both the Panama-Pacific Exposition and the later Panama-California Exposition in San Diego.[117] The films were to be accompanied by a lecture from Major W. L. "Iron Jaw" Brown, then the speaker of the Kansas House of Representatives.[118] For *50,000 Feet of Kansas*, Lamb returned to shooting local views, including ample footage of schoolchildren, prominent buildings, fire engines, and automobiles.[119] In addition to being screened at the two expos, the films would be shown, Lamb said, in the eastern United States by the National Association of Real Estate Dealers.[120]

Paragon was not the only film company making films for states interested in novel methods of fundraising. For example, the Kentucky commission contracted with the National Film Products Company of

Cincinnati to produce a state film for two dollars a foot, with some of the proceeds being used to erect a state building.[121] Similar schemes were used in Michigan, Colorado, and Tennessee.[122] By the time the exposition opened in February, many state buildings featured motion picture rooms, where expo-goers could see films of the state. One observer counted seventy-seven motion picture projectors at the state and country halls.[123] Many of the films produced by Paragon and other municipal film companies were exhibited at the expo, supplementing the more elaborate displays states and cities usually sent. In some cases these served as fundraisers to erect buildings. The sheer amount of footage shot in preparation for the exposition may have exhausted business groups' enthusiasm—and budgets—for such productions.

Around 1917, the Paragon Feature Film Company dissolved.[124] In September 1918, O. W. Lamb registered for the draft, identifying himself as a shoe salesman for a company in Akron, Ohio.[125] A few years later, he moved to Detroit, where he died on July 19, 1931. While Lamb appears to have been a particularly successful itinerant filmmaker, his relatively brief stint was typical of the trade. Of the dozens of companies that specialized in the production of municipal boosting films, few lasted more than three years. The Industrial Moving Picture Company, renamed the Rothacker Film Manufacturing Company in February 1916, is the only significant producer of booster films that survived the wave of industry consolidation and centralization in the late 1910s, but it too limited production of booster films by the end of the decade.[126]

There is little evidence that booster films received national distribution, and the trade press suggests that many producers misled sponsors about the potential reach of their films. As early as March 1914, an editorial in the *Moving Picture World* warned that municipal film producers exaggerated the circulation of their films.[127] The sponsors for municipal booster films quickly lost their aspirations for national audiences. By 1922, trade paper suspicions of booster films had filtered down to the local press. That year, following yet another story announcing a plan for motion pictures to be made of the county fair, an Oxnard, California, newspaper complained that as easy as it was to make a motion picture, distributing it was all but impossible.[128]

By 1915, municipal advertising film producers were already curtailing their ambitions. The national consolidation and centralization of motion picture distribution operations made it difficult for companies like Paragon to promise towns that their films would be screened in other cities. While booster pictures were occasionally produced after 1915, such films tended to either be limited to the local market or one-off projects with uneven results.[129] Furthermore, the booster movement itself shifted directions soon after the entry of United States into the Great War in 1917, as national unity became paramount. Local film producers once again had to be content to make films that created, as Lamb put it in one of his company's brochures, "a flurry of local interest" and were then "never shown outside of the City limits again."[130]

The producers of municipal advertising films expanded the category of local motion pictures by making films that boosters saw as equal to those produced by the national companies, even if they failed to received distribution. While local movies of all modes continued to be made after the transitional era, by 1917 producers rarely promised that their films would be screened elsewhere. Instead, the municipal advertising film retained one function: showing local people themselves and the attributes of the place where they lived in hopes that they would stay put. The production and exhibition of municipal advertising films in the early 1910s established both the possibilities and limits for the local film in the transitional era.

Notes

1. Jowett, *Film*.
2. In fact, the work could also be said to put cinema in a local contest. Lindsay's hometown newspaper noted that the book, originally entitled *A Higher Criticism of the Movies*, was "based entirely on personal observation of the movies in this city." See "Criticizes 'Movies,'" *SNR*, July 17, 1915, 7.
3. Lindsay, *The Art of the Moving Picture*, 146–150.
4. "Society to Show in Elopement of Beautiful Heiress, Filmed in Novel City 'Booster' Drama," *SNR*, June 16, 1915, 1.
5. Hansen, *Babel and Babylon*, 44.
6. See Robert C. Allen, "Decentering Historical Audience Studies: A Modest Proposal," in Fuller-Seeley, ed., *Hollywood in the Neighborhood*, 20–36.
7. Waller, *Main Street Amusements*, 64.
8. Although this project focuses on the United States, moviegoing research is increasingly an international field, with recent contributions only confirming how narrow, and atypical, New York was as an early site of cinema culture.
9. This argument is presented most succinctly in Vanessa Schwartz and Leo Charney's edited volume *Cinema and the Invention of Modern Life*.
10. For an overview of this debate, see Wanda Strauven's edited volume *Cinema of Attractions Reloaded*.
11. Kember, *Marketing Modernity*, 26, 22, 32, 27.
12. Ibid., 142.
13. Warner, *Publics and Counterpublics*, 90.
14. Hansen, *Babel and Babylon*, 43.
15. On the central role newspapers played in shaping movie publics, see Abel, *Menus for Movieland*.
16. *Town Development*, December 1909, 1.

17. In 1914, a thousand-foot municipal film of St. Louis produced by the St. Louis Motion Picture Company and sponsored by the Business Men's League was sent to South America. See *MPW*, April 18, 1914, 381. A similar film of Cincinnati also toured cities in South America that year. See *MPW*, June 13, 1914, 557.

18. For a very broad overview of municipal advertising, see Ward, *Selling Places*.

19. E. L. McColgin, "Putting Your Town upon a Map: A Few Intensely Practical Suggestions from a Town Developer Who Takes His Own Advice and Delivers the Good Thereby," *Town Development*, December 1912, 175.

20. See Daniel J. Boorstin's chapter on boosters in *The Americans*, 113–161.

21. See Wrobel, *Promised Lands*. See also Teaford, *Cities of the Heartland*.

22. This movement to standardization took place across a number of areas of civic life. See Novak, *The People's Welfare*; Reps, *The Making of Urban America*; and Moskowitz, *Standard of Living*.

23. Vaughn-Roberson and Vaughn-Roberson, *City in the Osage Hills*, 69.

24. "The First Municipal Motion Pictures Ever Made," *Kansas Citian*, May 1913, 64.

25. Leo L. Redding, "Town Boosting with the 'Movies,'" *Town Development*, November 1912, 129–131, 129 (quotation). The piece was reprinted in the short-lived film advertising trade publication *Moving Picture Publicity* a year later. See *Moving Picture Publicity*, December 1913, 3–8.

26. Ibid., 131.

27. Kessler and Masson, "Layers of Cheese."

28. Watterson Rothacker, "Advertising by Moving Pictures," in Johnson, comp. and ed., *Library of Advertising*, 250.

29. Epes Winthrop Sargent, "Advertising for Exhibitors," *MPW*, June 21, 1913, 1244.

30. Watterson Rothacker, "Industrial Uses of the Motion Picture," *Scientific American*, June 15, 1912, 536. There are a handful of examples of industrial municipal advertising films made before 1910, including films of Chicago's factories, which were produced for the Alaska-Yukon-Pacific Exposition, held in Seattle in 1909. See "Chicago to Be Advertised," *Chicago Daily Tribune*, November 20, 1908, 13.

31. Rothacker, "Industrial Uses of the Motion Picture," 536.

32. *MPW*, July 29, 1911, 221.

33. *MPW*, August 5, 1911, 297.

34. "Crowd Was There, But No Pictures," *The State* (Columbia, S.C.), October 8, 1911, 9. The telegram was reprinted in the newspaper.

35. *MPW*, May 23, 1914, 1131.

36. Horatio F. Stoll, "Value of the Moving Pictures for Advertising," *MPW*, March 11, 1911, 521.

37. *MPW*, October 14, 1911, 133.

38. "Moving Pictures Will Show Busy New Brunswick to the Rest of the State and Country," *NBT*, January 26, 1912, 1. The company identified themselves as the Commercial Film Syndicate in this letter, but the company later returned to using the name Industrial Film Syndicate, which was also the name used to register their incorporation in the state of New York on May 31, 1912, New York State Division of Corporations, State Records. In Iowa, the company called itself the Independent Film Syndicate.

39. See "Moving Pictures Will Show Busy New Brunswick to the Rest of the State and Country," and "Moving Picture Films Will Advertise City's Attractiveness," *Municipal Journal*, February 29, 1912, 323.

40. "Moving Pictures Will Show Busy New Brunswick to the Rest of the State and Country."

41. Ibid.

42. *NBT*, April 6, 1912, 4.

43. "Starting to Get Town on the Move," *NBT*, April 9, 1912, 1; "Boost New Brunswick Is Helped Along by Donations of $1,700," *NBT*, April 11, 1912, 1. Between 1910 and 1920, the city's population grew by 40.2 percent, to 32,779. See *Fourteenth Census of the United States* (Washington, DC: Government Printing Office, 1921), 1:524.

44. "Firemen Snapped on the Run," *NBT*, April 20, 1912, 1.

45. For more on fire and early cinema, see Moore, *Now Playing*, 45–74.

46. "Take Pictures That Show City Is on the Move," *NBT*, April 23, 1912, 1; "Moving Pictures Taken of Times Plant," *NBT*, April 26, 1912, 1.

47. "Latest News Concerning Booster Week," *NBT*, May 25, 1912, 1.

48. "New Airdome Opens Tonight," *NBT*, July 7, 1910, 1. While the theater featured live performances, films were screened between acts. See advertisement, *NBT*, July 27, 1910, 5.

49. "Mayor's Wink at Camera Man Is Discovered," *NBT*, May 28, 1912, 3.

50. "Week of Moving Picture Views of Local Scenes," *NBT*, June 5, 1912, 3.

51. "Can See City All on the Jump at One Glimpse," *NBT*, June 6, 1912, 3.

52. *MPW*, August 24, 1912, 781.

53. *MPW*, April 12, 1913, 200.

54. *MPW*, August 2, 1913, 574.

55. *MPW*, October 18, 1913, 247.

56. *MPW*, February 14, 1914, 828. For more on local films in Philadelphia, see Frykholm, *Framing the Feature Film*, 131–132.

57. *MPW*, February 7, 1914, 708.

58. For example, in July 1914, Magnet made a film of the Elks state convention and silver jubilee and exhibited it throughout Indiana. See *MPW*, July 11, 1914, 324.

59. *MPW*, June 13, 1914, 1556.

60. Moskowitz, *Standard of Living*, 184, 216.

61. Raymond Fielding suggests that in the silent era, freelance cameramen provided a significant portion of the footage used in the national newsreels. See Fielding, *The American Newsreel*, 134. For more on travelogues, see Peterson, *Education in the School of Dreams*. While some municipal booster films could also be classified as travelogues, there is scant evidence that booster films were received as such.

62. For example, in 1914, the Scenic Film Company of Atlanta produced a film in connection with the business-led "Buy-a-Bale" campaign, which asked Georgians to purchase extra bales of cotton in order to keep up commodity prices. The film starred Atlanta mayor James G. Woodward and was written and directed by Mrs. J. Garnett Starr, who the paper claimed had acted in films by D. W. Griffith. See *Atlanta Constitution*, October 11, 1914, 11M.

63. PPIE, carton 58, folder 21.

64. "Factory Company Will Build Here," *Topeka* (Kans.) *Daily Capital*, February 18, 1908, 7.

65. The company used a variation of the "tourist" plot described below. See "A Kansas 'Rube' in Topeka's Film," *Topeka* (Kans.) *Daily Capital*, May 17, 1912, 14, and "Films Tuesday," *Jeffersonian-Gazette* (Lawrence, Kans.), May 29, 1912, 5. The company was bought by James Calvin and renamed the Best Film Manufacturing Company. See "Victor Film Company Has Changed Hands," *Topeka* (Kans.) *Daily Capital*, July 24, 1912, 10.

66. "Pictures Shown. McAlester 'Movies' Being Shown by Commercial Club at the Forum," *MNC*, November 13, 1912, 1.

67. A certificate of incorporation was filed with the state of New York. According to the same records, the company dissolved on November 23, 1915. In January 1913, the *Moving Picture News* reported that the company's president, Fred Beck, had covered ten thousand miles that month alone, taking pictures for his educational series and promoting his company's new camera. See *Moving Picture News*, January 25, 1913, 22.

68. *Popular Mechanics*, July 1912, 19.
69. "Picture of City," *MNC*, October 15, 1912, 1.
70. Ibid.
71. Musser, "The Travel Genre in 1903–1940," 125.
72. "Picture of City."
73. "Pictures Shown," *MNC*, November 13, 1912, 1.
74. Ibid.
75. "All 'Seeing McAlester,'" *MNC*, November 14, 1912, 1.
76. Ibid. See also the advertisement for the Forum in the same issue, 5.
77. *Wichita* (Kans.) *Daily Times*, December 3, 1912, 1.
78. *Wichita* (Kans.) *Daily Times*. December 11, 1912, 4.
79. Incorporation records, Secretary of State, Colorado, April 28, 1913, Colorado State Archives, Denver.
80. The secretary of state's incorporation office in Colorado does not have a record of a Paragon Feature Film Company. Personal correspondence with the author, August 20, 2010. The state of Nebraska also does not have a record of Paragon's incorporation. Personal correspondence with the author, June 1, 2010.
81. As Charlie Keil notes, 1913 also marks the advent of the feature film. See Keil, "1913."
82. *MPW*, June 14, 1913, 1149.
83. "'Movies' of Oklahoma City Made in 1889 and 1913, Proposal Made to Chamber of Commerce," *DO*, July 12, 1913, 10.
84. "Motion Picture Plan Considered," *DO*, July 13, 1913, 5. Russell Merritt estimates that by 1910, nickelodeons drew 26 million Americans every week. See Merritt, "The Nickelodeon Theater, 1905–1914: Building an Audience for the Movies," in *Exhibition: The Film Reader*, ed. Ina Rae Hark (New York: Routledge, 2002), 22.
85. "Motion Picture Plan Considered."
86. "Contract Signed to Show City in Motion Pictures," *DO*, July 15, 1913, 1.
87. *DO*, July 15, 1913, 2.
88. "Run of '89ers Was Picturesque Sight," *DO*, July 28, 1913, 8.
89. Ibid.
90. Ibid. In 1913, Gullett was listed as the manager of the Empress Theater in *Ballenger and Richards Forty-First Annual Denver Directory* (Denver: Ballenger and Richards, 1913).
91. *MPW*, January 24, 1914, 428.
92. See *MPW*, April 15, 1911, 822. As the *Educational Film Magazine* defined the term in 1919, an industrial romance is a "motion picture advertising feature in which business is combined with sentiment to form a basic theme." See "'Industrial Romance' in Theatre," *Educational Film Magazine*, March 1919, 32.
93. For example, Walter Steiner, of the Hudris Film Company, also made wedding films in the 1910s.
94. "Begin Taking Film Showing San Antonio," *San Antonio* (Tex.) *Light*, January 14, 1914, 11.
95. For more, see Glassberg, *American Historical Pageantry*.
96. *MA*, March 22, 1914, 23.
97. "Moving Pictures to Hold Sway in City for Two Days," *MA*, February 22, 1914, 12.
98. Ibid.
99. "Merchants to Be Shown on Screen," *MA*, February 20, 1914, 9.
100. Brochure, PPIE, carton 58, folder 21. Thanks to Paul Moore for suggesting that the flyer is from 1913. According to Moore, the list of distributors is identical to those used by the Universal Film Company.
101. *MPW*, June 6, 1914, 1426.

102. *MPW*, June 20, 1914, 1717.

103. See "Marathon County Historical Society: People of Marathon County," http://www.marathoncountyhistory.com/PeopleDetails.php?PeopleId=157.

104. In some cases, local views also privileged the upper classes, but given the large number of street scenes, it was possible for someone like an overeager child to appear in a local view multiple times even if he or she was not invited to do so.

105. See Advertisement, *Evening Tribune* (Marysville, Ohio), December 9, 1915, 2.

106. "Columbus Pictures to Be Shown Tomorrow," *Columbus* (Ga.) *Ledger*, April 11, 1915, 10. The battle referred to an actual "last battle," which took place on April 16, 1865, in Columbus. See Charles A. Misiulia, *Columbus, Georgia, 1865: The Last True Battle of the Civil War* (Tuscaloosa: University of Alabama Press, 2010).

107. Williams, *Playing the Race Card*, 28, 35.

108. "Censorship and Home Talent Films," *MPW*, October 28, 1916, 583.

109. "Waterloo Women to Act in Movies; Suffragists Will Play Their Part," *WEC*, May 19, 1916, 1.

110. "Waterloo Film Sought," *WECR*, December 18, 1916, 11.

111. "Sees Self in Movies in Kentucky Theatre," *WECR*, April 17, 1917, 3.

112. "Show the Waterloo Film in Minneapolis," *Waterloo* (Iowa) *Times-Tribune*, April 6, 1917, 6.

113. "Cedar Valley Romance Coming Home after Long Tour for Last Showing," *WECR*, June 9, 1917, 3. In July 1915, the company was identified in the *SNR* as being located in Des Moines, Iowa. See *SNR*, July 24, 1915, 3.

114. *WECR*, August 24, 1918, 7.

115. See *MPW*, September 20, 1913, 1294.

116. "Emporia in Panama Show," *EG*, December 28, 1914, 1.

117. "Pictures for Big Shows," *EG*, January 19, 1915, 1.

118. "Children in Movies," *HN*, January 9, 1915, 2.

119. In 1916, Lamb also shot fifty thousand feet of Texas towns for the picture titled *Texas as It Is Today*. See "Films to Show Industries in the Southwest," *Kerrville* (Tex.) *Mountain Sun*, January 29, 1916, 1.

120. "Getting in the Movies," *HN*, January 18, 1915, 3. Lamb may not have lived up to his promises to the people of Hutchinson, as visitors from that town to the exposition could not find the Kansas films on display. See "But Where Are the Films?" *HN*, December 16, 1915, 10.

121. Telegram from F. G. Hogue. November 18, 1914, PPIE, carton 58, folder 22.

122. Michigan used proceeds from film production to pay for its building. See Telegram to George Hough Perry, July 9, 1914, PPIE, carton 58, folder 28. In Colorado, boosters planned to raise fifty thousand dollars by charging towns to shoot ten thousand feet of film, which would then be exhibited in their state hall. See letter to Frank Burt, June 11, 1914, PPIE, box 12, folder 3. In Tennessee, state boosters reported receiving seven thousand dollars from the sales of film contracts to go toward construction of their hall. See Telegram from F. G. Hoge, November 23, 1914, PPIE, carton 59, folder 14.

123. Macober. *The Jewel City*, 149.

124. *City Directory of Greater Omaha* (Omaha: Omaha Directory Company, 1917), 1255.

125. Draft card, September 12, 1918, "U.S. World War I Draft Registration Cards, 1917–1918," Ancestry Library Edition, ancestry.com.

126. Rothacker's name change, which was accompanied by the company's expansion, was reported in the *Chicago Daily Tribune* ("Industrial Changes Its Name"), on February 19, 1916, 14. For an account of the company's post-1916 work, see A. S. Witmer, "Motion Picture and City Publicity," *American Municipalities* 38, no. 2 (November 1919): 198. The film described was produced in Louisville for the benefit of the shareholders of the

Louisville Industrial Foundation. While the film was exhibited theatrically, and the article discusses plans to distribute the film, neither was proposed by the Rothacker Film Manufacturing Company.

127. *MPW*, March 14, 1914, 1405.

128. "Educational Movies," *Oxnard* (Calif.) *Daily Courier*, August 26, 1922, 2.

129. For example, in 1923, the Rothacker Film Company produced the seven-reel booster film *The Spirit of St. Louis*. See Louis J. Manar Papers, 1915–1935, Missouri History Museum Archives, St. Louis. Personal correspondence with the author, June 5, 2010. While the film was intended to be distributed nationwide, its producers focused on nontheatrical exhibition.

130. Paragon brochure, PPIE, carton 58, folder 21.

2

THE HOME TALENT FILM AND THE ORIGINS OF ITINERANCY

IN THE EARLY 1910S, LOCAL actors, scenario writers, and directors began making their own narrative fiction local films, encouraging them to think of the cinema as a participatory medium. Following common usage of the time, I label these pictures as "home talent," a term that connotes the theatrical tradition of using local actors in traveling productions, as well as larger turn-of-the-century debates about the qualifications of native-born professionals in a country increasingly governed by national systems of training and assessment. In other words, "home talent" could be used as a positive term, when referring to the skill of a local actor, writer, or filmmaker, or as a pejorative, describing someone who did not have proper training. The home talent productions I discuss featured local actors and, in some cases, were also written and directed by a resident aspiring filmmaker.

Previously overlooked in histories of transitional-era cinema, the home talent film operated in a middle space, with neither the familiarity of the local view nor the national orientation of the municipal booster film. My focus here is on home talent pictures produced for exhibition in theaters in rural areas, which were particularly hospitable to artisanal modes of moviemaking or, at the very least, had residents who reported the local production of motion pictures in trade and hometown newspapers. In order to demonstrate the possibilities for home talent pictures in the mid-1910s, I have focused on a particularly prolific filmmaker from Corning, Iowa, a town of two thousand people. After producing more than a dozen original motion pictures in Corning between 1914 and 1916, Charles D. Tinsley turned to itinerant work, shooting the same scenario in towns throughout the Midwest for the next two decades. Several home talent directors became itinerant filmmakers by the end of this decade, which, ironically, dampened interest in locally written and directed films, as audiences proved to be content to see themselves act before the camera in standardized scripts. The home talent film, originally conceived as an alternative cinema practice that enabled the expression of local and regional identities, lost its uniqueness by the early 1920s and instead became a routine response to the mass entertainment culture that began to dominate small-town life.[1]

This chapter is divided into two sections. In the first, I consider the origin of the term "home talent," with a focus on its use in theatrical and rural contexts. In contrast to the term "amateur," which implied nonprofessionalism, home talent was distinguished instead by a contrast between local and nonlocal practitioners.[2] In the 1910s and early 1920s, "home talent" was often used to describe theatrical or motion picture performances by local actors and only later became replaced by the term "amateur," which filmmakers also claimed for their own in the late 1920s. In the second section, I document the emergence of home talent motion pictures in the transitional period of the American cinema. The consolidation and concentration of the film industry in Los Angeles ensured that motion picture production would primarily take place in an urban area far from where most rural Americans, who made up a majority of the population, lived.[3] Home talent productions represented an earnest, if ultimately short-lived, attempt by theater managers and filmmakers to produce local movies that were the equals of those made by national, well-capitalized companies.

Very few of the films discussed in this chapter are known to have survived and just fragments of Tinsley's films have been found, so my descriptions of them rely on titles, reviews, and plot summaries printed in trade and local newspapers. Unlike the booster films discussed in chapter 1, home talent pictures were not sponsored by business interests or, at least at first, produced by outsiders. But, like its more sophisticated and ambitious counterpart, the home talent movie was a short-lived phenomenon. While other forms of local culture, such as the folk drama or regional music, survived encounters with mass culture, home talent productions were quickly overwhelmed by commercial cinema. At the same time, they served as a transition between the local views of the early cinema period and later narrative fiction motion pictures that reflected popular national genres.

The Origins of Home Talent

In the late 1800s, the colloquial term "home talent" began to be used as a way to set apart local actors, teachers, engineers, and other untrained and poorly trained professionals from the nonlocal educated professionals who had infiltrated rural and small-town life. As Robert Wiebe has argued in his study of American society between 1877 and 1920, residents of towns and small cities enjoyed social, cultural, and political autonomy in the late 1800s, only to see their way of life threatened at every turn in the early twentieth century.[4] Corporations and social movements had perhaps the most significant impact on small-town life, as both sought to systematize laws and folkways in order to establish a unified nation. The same railroad lines that connected agricultural producers with urban markets enabled the development of regional and national networks of cultural production and dissemination.[5] Likewise, the rise of national fraternal and civic organizations, city planning departments, and various Progressive-era movements to reform social activity led to an informal, if no less consequential, nationalization of everyday life.[6] In these contexts, the term "home talent" was used to signify the exception to the general case that many local activities, from the performance of a play to the laying of a sewer line, were planned and conducted by outside professionals and experts.

In its broadest usage, "home talent" referred to local people who filled occupational roles that were increasingly held by trained professionals. For example, education journals of the late 1800s and early 1900s printed heated editorials defending the use of home talent teachers in opposition to reformers who believed that those teachers were inferior to their professionally trained counterparts.[7] An article in a telephony journal published in 1910 noted that independent telephone companies "are not able to employ the best engineering talent, so they are managed and operated by home talent, which has been trained by previous home talent."[8] In 1916, the magazine *The Western Architect* noted that an "old adage about home talent being unappreciated by the citizens of a community" was particularly true in St. Louis, the focus of a feature article on that city's architects.[9] While many rural residents welcomed new systems of governance, the debates over home talent suggest that pockets of resistance still existed.

This denigration of home talent was informed by a larger anxiety about the effects that both immigration and rural-urban migration had on the nation's small towns, which were, as Richard Lingeman argues, at their apotheosis at the turn of the century.[10] Despite the prosperity of the country's rural regions, which profited from the demand for agricultural products in the urban areas of the United States and Europe, the diversity of occupational opportunities in cities encouraged many people to leave family farms and small towns for fast-growing metropolitan centers.[11] In his history of small towns in the Midwest in this period, Lewis Atherton observed that by 1900, artists, writers, and members of the professional classes, like doctors and lawyers, were disproportionately likely to live in Chicago, while teachers and preachers were more likely to live in rural areas.[12] As the cultural historian Timothy Spears has argued, "Chicago dreaming" afflicted middle-class residents of small towns who, on moving to the city, shaped its culture.[13] Writers such as Hamlin Garland, who left the rural Midwest for Boston in the mid-1880s, spent their careers trying to recover their rustic childhoods in their literary work, which only accelerated the tendency for rural life to be associated with the past.[14]

The rise of national mass media, including general interest magazines, cinema, and the news from afar that began to fill the pages of local newspapers, connected small towns with cities while reminding them how distant they were, culturally and socially, from the metropolitan centers.[15] With regards to cinema, Richard Abel has written that female Midwestern movie fans, through reading the columns of Gertrude Prince from 1912 to 1914, inhabited female star roles as "projective sites of fantasy adventure" and, at the movies, vicariously took on "active, attractive worker or professional" occupations that were otherwise unavailable to them.[16] As Abel argues, the growth of movie fan culture in the early 1910s was in part attributed to the connection that middle- and working-class people, particularly women, made between the movies and their own aspirations. By expressing pride in their own "home talent," whether on film, on stage, or in the workplace, small-town residents could legitimate their own decisions to resist the charm, and greater opportunities, of the city.

While home talent was for many a colloquialism more than an ideological commitment, rural advocates in the Progressive movement became invested in the idea that local culture could be a salve to wounds caused by a rapacious capitalist economy. Even though Progressives promoted expert-driven scientific farming methods, in the cultural field they lent their support to rural promoters of home talent.[17] Reformers found sympathizers in the hinterlands, mostly farmers and educators with shared concerns about the ills of modernity. In 1908, President Theodore Roosevelt formed the federal Country Life Commission, which spent the next year assessing the social, economic, and cultural status of rural areas.[18] After the commission issued its report, many of its members formed the Country Life Movement, which sought to carry out the taskforce's recommendations. Although President William Taft set aside the commission's recommendations when he took office the next year, the movement received support from academics and preservationists who wanted to sustain agricultural folkways for future generations.[19] The movement's political platform is largely forgotten, but they achieved some success, such as the formation of the education-focused Extension Service of the US Department of Agriculture, which started in 1914.

That same year, Alfred Arvold, an English and oratory instructor at North Dakota Agricultural College, started the Little Country Theater, which produced regionally written and locally performed plays in rural areas. In making his case for the theater in *The Drama*, a quarterly magazine published by the Drama League of America, Arvold presented a view of small-town life that was familiar from popular novels and films about small towns, if not necessarily to the inhabitants themselves: "Social stagnancy is a characteristic trait of the small town and the country. Community spirit is at a low ebb. Because of the stupid monotony of the village and country existence, the tendency of the people, young and old, is to move to large cities."[20]

Arvold went on to argue that as long as rural areas lacked cultural opportunities, their residents would be no better off than those who lived in urban squalor. He suggested that the only way to stop rural-urban migration was to allow small town residents to "find their *true expression in the community*."[21] This argument was a familiar one in this period, echoing Chicagoan Jane Addams's attempts to help working-class immigrants adjust to factory work by celebrating the cultural aspects of the nonmechanized and domestic labor they performed in the old country.[22] What distinguished Arvold's project was that he assumed that rural areas, unlike urban ones, lacked any local amusements, and that the pastoral ideal would survive only if rural people were able to meet demand for entertainment without outside help.[23]

The Little Country Theater, which Arvold built on the campus of the agricultural college in Fargo, North Dakota, was based on the opera houses, schools, and churches already used as theaters in small towns. Although the model theater included a "place for a moving picture machine," Arvold's intent was to produce theatrical work that would "stimulate an interest for good clean drama and original entertainment among the people living in the open country and villages, in order to help them find themselves, and that they may become better satisfied with their surroundings."[24] By conceiving of the theater as a "sociological force" that would allow for people to come together and celebrate their own lives, Arvold refuted not just the cinema but also other forms of popular entertainment, such as local performances of Shakespeare, which relied on the works of outsiders to draw audiences.[25] Arvold argued that the "home talent play," where neighbors worked together to put on their own entertainment, "introduces a friendly feeling in a neighborhood."²⁶

In the process of producing these plays, which often dealt with experiences shared by audience members and performers, town residents could discover their own talents as actors, musicians, writers, or directors. Although the theater was just a year old when Arvold wrote of its accomplishments in *The Drama*, he could already point to several successful plays, including the literally titled *A Farm Home Scene in Iceland Thirty Years Ago*, which featured twenty North Dakotans from Iceland reenacting the native customs of their home country.²⁷ The *Moving Picture World* commented on Arvold's project, noting that the "photoplay could easily be fitted into this plan by the educators."²⁸ Arvold's success in producing "home talent plays" won him national fame, as other states started their own university theaters to foster the development of home talent. For example, in 1918, the University of North Carolina hired Frederick Koch, who had worked with Arvold in North Dakota, to start the Carolina Playmakers, which produced regional "folk drama" throughout the state. In cities, the Little Country Theater idea was mirrored by the Little Theatre movement, which started in 1912 to promote the performance of small-stage plays.²⁹

If the Progressive movement argued for the educational and social benefits of home talent productions, some critics noticed a crasser side as well. In 1922, the theater critic Walter Prichard Eaton observed in *Scribner's Magazine* that "a totally new and different theatrical system is springing up," one in which "the people themselves are producing drama, not professionally, not as commercialized entertainment, but as a means of community enjoyment and self-expression."³⁰ While Eaton, the author of several books about the professional theater, mourned the decline of touring Broadway productions that had long provided live theater outside of urban centers, he found much to like about their local replacements.

But Eaton also observed another variation of the home talent play, one in which local people acted in plays written by outsiders. While these plays fostered community spirit, their stated purpose was to raise money for charity or school activities. Eaton argued that these plays, often produced by high school students, were "not done with any education end in view, with any sense of social services, above all with any faintest realizations of what dramatic art means. It is done solely to raise money for some school purpose (such as uniforms for the basket-ball team), and the cheapest sort of farce-comedy is chosen. Under the auspices of our education, the drama is commercialized as no Broadway manager ever dared to commercialize it. It is that idea of 'home talent' production which the new movement has got to fight, and to fight through the schools and colleges first of all."³¹

These commercial home talent plays were produced with efficiency in mind, allowing local people to put on a theatrical production in a matter of weeks.³² The largest producer of home talent plays, the Universal Producing Company, was based in Fairfield, Iowa, and best known for *Aunt Lucia* (1925), a take on the English cross-dressing farce *Charlie's Aunt* (1892), which proved to be immensely popular with rural audiences.³³ By the early 1930s, Universal was booking hundreds of shows every summer all over the United States and southern Canada, with the highest density in the Midwest.³⁴ Sponsored by fraternal and civic organizations, schools, and churches, home talent plays were among the most popular amateur productions of the 1920s and 1930s, supplanting older standbys, such as the minstrel show.³⁵

If rural reformers hoped that one day every town would produce a play of its own creation, the home talent craze of the first few decades of the twentieth century instead resulted in hundreds of towns producing the same play again and again. Home talent was most valorized in towns and small cities where live theater had become difficult to see, due in part to the success of motion pictures. According to one estimate, more than 95 percent of the professional theaters that operated in the United States in 1890 had closed by 1939.³⁶ The producers of home talent plays made work that reflected local or regional cultures but also allowed participants to take part in cultural forms that were increasingly associated with mass entertainment.

While the home talent play itself survives, as the enduring popularity of high school musicals and community theater attests, the disappearance of the term, and the rise of the term "amateur" in its stead, suggests a shifting set of cultural values. While "home talent" implies a spatial and geographic definition, with the centers of entertainment connected to the hinterlands through overlapping circuits, "amateur" instead posits that local performers are decisively disconnected from their professional counterparts. While local films are often read, retrospectively, as comprising "amateur" performances, the term "home talent" offers a more nuanced, and critical, way to understand how producers and audiences alike understood their goals in making their own movies.

The Home Talent Film

Even though home talent had particular meanings for disputes over professional qualifications, rural-urban quarrels, and theatrical productions, in the early 1910s the term also began to be used to describe local films. While motion pictures and the theater have been studied as competing entertainments with distinct histories, audiences and producers alike often saw them as alternate paths to a creative end.[37] As Charles Musser has noted in an article on the relationship between early race films and the New Negro Theater movement, many playwrights and directors did not draw sharp distinctions between film and theatrical work, and as a result, he argues that such works should be seen as "complementary theatrical experiences."[38] While newsreels, scenics, advertising films, and industrials were also produced and exhibited in small towns in the early 1910s, the directors of home talent films emphasized the role scenario writers and actors played in creating narrative fiction shorts that resembled those released by the national producers of the period. Changes in the motion picture industry encouraged local producers to adapt their films to meet audience expectations, and home talent productions influenced other modes of local motion pictures.

In this section, I wish to consider the dual meaning of the home talent film, that is, films written and produced by locals, and motion pictures starring local actors. While other scholars have considered screenwriting and acting competitions in the mid-1910s, in which many aspired (and failed) to find their place in the cinema, these aspiring directors had the resources to experiment with local motion picture production.[39] I have chosen to focus on an individual filmmaker in a small town in Iowa because this example suggests the possibilities for motion picture exhibition and production that existed in the mid-1910s.[40] In contrast to the municipal booster films discussed in chapter 1, early home talent films did not seek to advertise a town to either the community or outsiders. Instead, local directors, screenwriters, and actors made work that could be appreciated by an audience composed of the people who contributed to the film's production as well as their neighbors. As a result, home talent films had a dual address. Some in the audience were there to see themselves on screen, fitting Stephen Bottomore's definition of a local film whereby there is a "significant overlap" between those on screen and those in audience.[41] Others in the audience who were not in the film, however, instead recognized their neighbors and their community. Furthermore, all were encouraged to evaluate local motion pictures as the coevals of nationally distributed product. While some cinema historians have argued that the mid-1910s was distinguished by the rise of the feature film, Ben Singer has countered that one- and two-reelers remained popular until the late 1910s.[42] Local directors, screenwriters, and actors made one- and two-reelers with the awareness that their movies would be compared with an industrialized cinema made for mass consumption.

Home Talent and Film Technology

Unlike well-capitalized industrial motion picture companies, producers of home talent films could not afford to make significant investments in camera equipment, particularly if they intended to shoot just a few reels of film. While camera operators could be hired to realize any project, and itinerant producers plied their trade in even small towns, many people desired to make their own films nonetheless. One of the earliest signs of new possibilities for local motion picture making came in 1911. Eberhard Schneider, who had been involved in the film industry since its inception, placed an advertisement in the *Moving Picture World* that spelled out the appeal of the local film: "Mr. Theater Manager and Exchange Man—why don't you yourself buy the greatest Christmas present your town, your customer, your patron and your heart desires. Buy a local Motion Picture Making outfit and photograph your town occurrences; photograph the one who has a grouch against you, show him on the sheet and he will smile and be your friend. This local picture outfit has been reduced from $800 down to $395, for real professional work, guaranteed; no toy."[43]

Schneider's entry into the semiprofessional camera market, made only after he was sued for copyright infringement by Thomas Edison and failed to get a motion picture license from the Motion Picture Patents Company, was a bit premature, as his camera kit was too expensive for the typical theater owner.[44] A second attempt at selling cameras to exhibitors came almost a year later, in September 1912, when the Chicago-based company Lavezzi Machine Works began advertising their motion picture camera kit in trade publications.[45] In the *Moving Picture News*, Lavezzi offered a booklet for sale for $2.50 with "100 POINTERS on big money-making stunts, repairing, operating and care of the Moving Picture Camera."[46] Although Lavezzi's camera kit likely cost under a hundred dollars, only exhibitors and amateurs with considerable technical skill would be able to assemble a camera from a kit.[47] Before 1913, few exhibitors would have been able to afford a camera and instead relied on contracts with industrial film companies and newsreel camera operators.

But starting in early 1913, more camera manufacturers began advertising amateur and semiprofessional cameras in the *World*.[48] In January, the Photo Records Company began advertised its Quiverless Picture Producing "Precision" Camera, which it claimed was modeled after the "best French types."[49] In early February, the American Cinematograph Company advertised its new camera in the *World*, calling it "just the proper equipment for taking local, scenic and industrial views."⁵⁰ Later that month, the *World* published an article on the Sept motion picture camera, which was being imported from France by Arthur G. Whyte of the Whyte-Whitman Company in New York.⁵¹ As the article stated, "there was need for some sort of a camera that could be rated somewhere between the professional and the amateur instruction; amateur in point of size, but professional in efficiency." In the article, the Sept Camera was described as the first camera to meet this need, with the author noting that its ability to shoot local films made it uniquely suited for "providing many drawing cards for the theater that could not be otherwise obtained."⁵² The article went on to suggest that the camera be used to record "local scenes such as employees leaving a factory, an Elks' parade, the laying of a corner stone, a baby show, a fire, or comedy pictures using local characters."⁵³ Whyte-Whitman began regularly advertising in the *World*, joining Schneider, who was now advertising his "Junior Professional" camera, as well as American Cinematograph, Lavezzi, and, in April, the Motion Picture Camera Company.⁵⁴ Industrial film producers also began renting or selling cameras, including the Special Event Film Manufacturing Company, which offered a "small moving picture camera" for ninety dollars.⁵⁵ Other models soon followed, which helped drive camera prices down below one hundred dollars.⁵⁶ By the end of 1913, anyone with the means to purchase a camera could quickly make back the investment by exhibiting pictures at a local theater. This point was not lost on camera sellers. In an advertisement for its $150 Williamson camera, which ran in the *World* in October 1914, the Whyte-Whitman Company claimed that "any exhibitor can pay for this outfit in four weeks. Write us and we will prove it to you."⁵⁷

Exhibitors and the Home Talent Show

While inexpensive cameras bolstered the prospects for home talent pictures, producers also needed a paying audience and a place to exhibit their films. Small town theaters proved to be particularly welcoming sites for home talent pictures, perhaps because they already featured home talent on stage. Although the history of film exhibition has mostly been studied in isolation from the history of other popular entertainments, in small towns the cinema and live entertainments regularly shared the same theatrical space throughout the 1910s.⁵⁸ An earlier boom in traveling live entertainment encouraged many towns to construct a permanent venue for such acts, many of which were called "opera houses," in a nod to the cultural aspirations of the period, and became multipurpose spaces for performances and gatherings of all sorts. When motion pictures were exhibited at the opera house, they supplemented or even replaced live entertainment that appeared in those spaces. By the end of the decade, many theaters and opera houses were under joint ownership, with the opera house being used primarily for live theater and special film events due to their greater seating capacity.[59]

Even after opera houses and movie theaters began to be routinely used for film exhibition, live theater remained an integral part of an evening's entertainment. When expensive Broadway shows started to cut their traveling units in the face of declining returns due to film competition, smaller theater groups picked up much of their business. In addition, movie theater managers used local talent to supplement film screenings to both increase box-office receipts and to build relationships with the communities. In 1913, David S. Hulfish, in one of the first handbooks for motion picture theater owners, proposed that theaters in small towns host a weekly "Amateur Night" where local patrons could compete with each other to win prizes.[60] While many theaters remained locally owned, out-of-town owners and managers became increasingly common in this decade, as did theater chains and houses affiliated with major producer-distributors. This often placed the interests of the feature film industry at odds with those of the theater manager, who pursued strategies to differentiate his or her theater from the competition.

By 1913, trade publications began stepping up their efforts to promote the benefits of what they called "exhibitor cameras." While this chapter focuses on the production of fictional films, many camera owners also shot local news events, obviating the need to hire cinematographers to shoot local views and newsreels, with the result of making such local films so ordinary that they were rarely noted in the trade press. At its annual international exhibition for exhibitors in July 1913, the *Moving Picture World* commented on the trend: "Cameras for exhibitors are commanding unusual attention. It will not be long before many exhibitors will have their own camera and outfit and add the always interesting local attractions to the run of photoplays. A freight wreck just at the edge of town, with only a few box cars in the ditch and no one hurt, is a bigger money getter than a thousand feet of some smash-up with a loss of life sufficiently serious to command national attention."[61]

The *World* regularly reported on innovative uses of exhibitor cameras, both in the United States and elsewhere. For example, in September 1913, the *World* reported that "a new kind of local picture—not a topical—is coming into vogue" in Britain, and went on to describe a fictional film starring members of the Reading Thespian Society in which "a local dude persistently follows a charming local lady."[62] That same month, a semi-fictional film starring members of the local fire and police departments was produced in Youngstown, Illinois, with the proceeds going toward the Policeman's Pension Fund.⁶³ By October, the production of local films had grown to such an extent that Epes Winthrop Sargent, whose "Advertising for Exhibitors" column in the *World* kept a close eye on developments in the field, warned exhibitors to "be careful of locals," noting that "few local companies or camera men are yet competent to turn out really good work, and to book a feature of this sort for the sake of the local pull without having seen it in advance is to take a pretty long chance."⁶⁴ He advised exhibitors take a railroad trip, if necessary, to see the film in advance, which suggests that most filmmakers processed and edited their films in large cities. Sargent's warning is also a reminder that even local filmmakers relied on regional networks of distribution and production in order to show their work.

In 1913, regional reporters for the *Moving Picture World* expanded their coverage of local picture production. In addition to noting local views or booster films, reporters detailed the production of dozens of fictional and semi-fictional local motion pictures, ranging from a series of "home film society dramas" produced by Elite Production Company of Waukegan, Illinois, to a comedy in Princeton, Indiana, in which "a perfectly good flank roast was dragged through the streets attached to an automobile. The bloodhounds got the scent and followed it with drooling chops—all in focus."⁶⁵ By August 1915, the home talent phenomena had become so widespread that one Illinois reporter just listed the towns where home talent productions had been shown the previous week:

> Illinois managers are doing some "sharpshooting" at possible patrons to keep the houses comfortably filled in a gloomy season. . . . Playing local pictures is one method that helped bring out crowds as people like to see themselves as others see them. Home made films were found in the week's programs at the Criterion Skydome, in East St. Louis; the Apollo, at Peoria; the Empire, at Morris; the Washington Skydome, at Belleville; the Gaiety, at Springfield, which had "The Mine Owner's Daughter," a mediocre home-talent reel, and the Knights of Pythias opera house, at Pittsfield, which ran the films of its sister city, Barry.⁶⁶

Although these news items rarely ran for more than a few lines and were mixed in with more mundane reports of theater openings and changes in management, the fact that national trade papers noted the production of local films at all underlines just how visible this mode of production was in the mid-1910s.

Exhibitor manuals also supported featuring home talent in the cinema, both off-screen and on. In 1915, less than two years after warning about the possible pitfalls of exhibiting local films, Sargent published a manual for exhibitors in which he supported the production of local films, particularly those that featured home talent:

> With the spread of the topical film and the news weeklies, the locally owned motion picture camera is getting more common. Try making your own production. It has been done and with success. Offer ten dollars for the best script. Put the local players in and use as many as you can. Get a script with a couple of scenes showing a crowd. Advertise that at a certain house Saturday you will make these scenes in some convenient place. There will be a mob there. They cannot act, but all who get in the picture will come and bring their friends. In cutting the film let the mob run well down instead of flashing. Give the volunteer players plenty of time (say 30 feet) to look at themselves.[67]

By 1915, Sargent was familiar with a wide variety of home talent productions. In the previous year alone, the *World* had run items on dozens of local pictures. In Evanston, Illinois, local theater owners Alpha Bodkin and John Keane had produced *Love against Wealth*, one of many "home pictures" starring students at Northwestern University, in September 1914.[68] The previous month, a South Dakota filmmaker shot *It Happened in Joyland*, which the *World* reported was the first scenario ever written and produced in that state.[69] With exhibitor support, home talent productions blossomed in the mid-1910s, with the *Moving Picture World* reporting on several pictures a week made all over the country.

The First Step to Fame Begins in the "Local Field"

The third factor that contributed to the increased production of home talent pictures in the mid-1910s was the growth of the motion picture industry itself. What Ben Singer has called the two cinema "revolutions"— the nickelodeon boom and the advent of the feature film—created new opportunities for producers.[70] An industry that had been based in the New York and Chicago metropolitan areas faced new competition from companies in Jacksonville and Los Angeles.[71] Smaller cities like New Orleans, Denver, Omaha, and Kansas City were not left out of the boom in production either.[72] While many of these companies aspired to make one- and two-reelers for the national market, others announced their intentions to target local, state, and regional markets. These companies offered a range of motion picture services, from developing film to renting cameras, and also produced newsreels, industrials, and advertising films. They even offered to shoot what would later be known as home movies. Studio photographers similarly took up filmmaking in the 1910s to make extra income. When these filmmakers found it difficult to obtain regional or national distribution for their films, they turned to the production of local films to work on their technique. As Ernest A. Dench wrote in 1915, "The curse of the [motion picture] industry is over-production of commonplace material, so the photographer in a small way would be well advised to confine himself to the local field until he feels confident that his product can compete with that turned out by the standard producers."[73]

Of course, home talent producers benefited from the emerging movie fan culture. Producers and theater managers interested in securing regular patrons boosted local participation in the movies. In the early part of the decade, fledgling producers, eager to win fans for their films, engaged audiences as potential partners in the production of films. For example, the Balboa Amusement Producing Company launched a scenario contest, with cash prizes for the best scripts.[74] In the early 1910s, small ads requesting original scenarios ran in trade publications, which resulted in a flurry of submissions and the development of a cottage industry of scenario-writing manuals. Aspiring camera operators and directors were not as numerous, perhaps due to the fact that even the least expensive camera cost more than the pen and paper (or typewriter) one needed to write scenarios, but they too were encouraged to try out their talents by making local films. For example, in 1916, a writer for a photography publication in California advised aspiring filmmakers to engage local talent:

> The local photoplay idea is quite popular in most localities. By getting in touch with those who write scenarios, and almost everybody is a scenario writer now, one can find people desirous of producing photoplays using home talent, and thereby create a camera job for himself. To those who fear their own particular community is free from scenario fans and photoplay actors and actresses, I would suggest a want advertisement calling for scenarios and talent. Unless you have a private secretary, give only your telephone number, otherwise the one advertising will be kept mighty busy handling the result of a quite modest announcement.[75]

Mail-order camera storesv also encouraged the production of home talent films. The David Stern Company, a camera exchange based in Chicago, placed an advertisement in *Moving Picture World* in the summer of 1916 telling the paper's readers that "big money" could be made by taking moving pictures for "news, advertising and home talent."[76] While local news films were likely indistinguishable from earlier local views and advertising films, Stern's identification of home talent as the third important local film genre suggests its viability for even the casual filmmaker.⁷⁷

Many home talent film producers appealed to theater groups who were already interested in acting. In 1916, Chicago resident Richard E. Norman, who later moved to Florida and became a producer of race films, published a brochure provocatively titled, "Have You Talent? If So Give It the Acid Test of the Screen." In the brochure he reprinted a letter from one satisfied client, the Illini Photoplayers, who, with Norman's help, produced the home talent drama *Pro Patria* in August 1916. The club's business manager described Norman's camerawork as follows: "Sharp, clear, steady photography with judicious close ups, cut backs and fades combined with excellent directing in both the dramatic and comedy parts, contribute to make our first attempt a success."⁷⁸ Norman's proposal for local photoplayers clubs suggested one possible future for the local film:

> People everywhere are always anxious to see their friends or local people in moving pictures, especially if the picture has a real plot, is properly directed and photographed and each member of the cast playing a role best suited to him or her. Such pictures have never failed to play to capacity business when shown at the local theatre, and have created a demand for more good pictures. The reason this demand has never been satisfied is because there was no local organization to further the local picture and much good talent has not had a chance to express itself on the screen.⁷⁹

The rest of the booklet resembled the guidebooks on scenario-writing that were published in the same period. As Torey Liepa has argued, in the early 1910s, film studios responded to their need for new film scenarios by "engaging and stimulating the public interest in film writing through advertising, contests, screenwriting schools and other enticements."⁸⁰ While this experiment in motion picture democracy was short-lived, its codification of screenplay and filmmaking techniques influenced the producers of local motion pictures.

Scenario guidebooks, in particular, tended to express faith in formulas for movie scripts, with authors contributing original ideas, preferably based on their own experiences. As one guidebook stated, if "your characters are taken from every day life of the present and your story is familiar to the great majority of Americans, your success is almost certain," provided scenario writers follow the book's recommendations for the formatting and narrative structure of their photoplays.⁸¹ Even if actual opportunities for scenario writing were limited, guidebooks suggested otherwise. As William R. Kane wrote in a guide to the writer's markets in 1915, "Unless a motion picture manufacturer makes only local views or advertising pictures he offers some sort of opportunity to writers for the screen."[82]

In his "Have You Talent?" brochure, Norman played to the acting aspirations of movie fans. He assured audiences that "the market is not over-supplied with desirable photoplayers," and that it would be possible to determine if an actor had a "screen personality" without filming them. Several pages were devoted to *Pro Patria*, which suggests that the film may have been the only one Norman made in cooperation with a photoplayers club. All of the other testimonials appear to refer to the home talent pictures produced by the Superior Film Company, including *The Man at the Throttle* (1915), which I discuss later. Norman closed the brochure with instructions on how one could form his or her own club and asked his readers to consider the following: "Maybe you have a special scenario you wish produced, a big local idea filmed, a pageant or other big local occurrence that a story can be woven around. Let us hear from you."

The home talent phenomenon of the 1910s was not limited to film itself. In many spheres of cultural production—theater, music, art, photography, dance—individuals became aware of the transformative possibilities of mass culture and the potential for their own efforts to be rewarded with fortune and fame. While the boosters that backed industrial romances expected their films to reach millions, the participants in home talent production instead wanted to witness their own performances on screen. The popularity of the home talent film in the 1910s was driven by a belief, quickly proved to be a fantasy, that anyone had a shot at success.

The Career of C. D. Tinsley

To date, no home talent films from the 1910s that were directed, written, and acted in by locals are known to survive. In the absence of actual films, I instead consider the work of C. D. Tinsley, a portrait studio photographer and filmmaker unknown to cinema historians despite his long and prolific career. Tinsley produced almost two dozen movies in his hometown of Corning, Iowa, between 1914 and 1919; worked as an itinerant director of home talent productions from 1915 to 1933; and produced industrial and news films from the late 1910s to 1941, including work for the US government.[83] Although Tinsley was not the typical theater owner or studio photographer, his ambition as a filmmaker demonstrates the possibilities for home talent films in even small towns. To my knowledge, Tinsley's movies contained no advertising, and he did not intend for them to be seen by regional or national audiences. Neither did he claim to be affiliated with the larger picture industry nor did he make any attempts to enter the national industry. Instead, Tinsley, like a number of producers of local films, worked regionally and never lived outside his home state. Tinsley was a "home talent" filmmaker in more ways than one.

From Photography to Motion Pictures

Charlie David Tinsley was born in 1873 on a farm in eastern Iowa to a German mother and a native Iowan father who served on the Union side in the Civil War.[84] Later, one writer remembered Tinsley as being "always anxious and ambitious to learn all there was to know about everything in general."[85] Sometime in the 1890s, he entered the field of photography, first working in nearby Batavia, Iowa, a town of just three hundred people.[86] In 1898, he moved to Corning, in western Iowa, and started a photography studio.[87] Corning was a small town, which struggled to maintain a population of more than two thousand people, and Tinsley became intensely loyal to it, starting traditions like an annual Christmas brunch that he maintained even when his itinerant work kept him on the road for much of the year.[88] The town's two weekly newspapers were keenly interested in Tinsley's work, regularly reporting on his business trips, vacations, and the motion pictures he made.

In 1908, when he was still running his photography studio, Tinsley was described by one of the local papers as "one of our up-to-date photographers," someone who "never lets anything new pass him by," so it was not surprising that Tinsley was captivated by the movies.[89] In October 1912, he purchased an interest in the Lyric Theater, Corning's first purpose-built movie theater.[90] A few months later, the newspaper proudly printed a letter the Lyric had received from the Motion Picture Patents Company–controlled General Film Company's distribution office in Omaha, Nebraska, that praised the theater's "Anniversary Jubilee program," which included local entertainment.[91] In February 1913, Tinsley arranged for a "moving picture man" to come to Corning "for the purpose of taking everything and everybody in the city and all the people from the country that can be present when the machine is in operation."[92] Given the exuberant tone of the long article that announced its production, this picture was likely the first made in Corning. Although the film, which was expected to depict local businesses, schools, and civic clubs, was sponsored by the town's commercial club, the article was careful to emphasize that neither the newspaper nor the theater would profit from the picture's production. Instead, the article noted that the "filmmakers are striving for something good, something that will be a big advertisement for our town and that may be preserved as one of the special occasions in our history—something to be remembered for years."[93] While the movie that resulted was never reviewed in the paper, it had a weeklong engagement at the Lyric starting on March 3, 1913.[94]

Tinsley did not enter the moving picture business until May 1914. In late April of that year, his photography studio burned down, resulting in a loss of $1,200 worth of equipment.[95] One of the local newspapers reported that Tinsley had $650 in insurance on his possessions, so his decision to start his film career a few weeks after the fire suggests that he used part of the insurance money to purchase a motion picture camera.[96] His first film, a military drama called *Saved by the Stars and Stripes*, engaged the militias of Corning and nearby Villisca, with a cast of one hundred people.[97] When the film was exhibited almost two months after its mid-May filming, the newspaper praised the photoplay for the quality of the pictures and its setting, noting that "the play will be much appreciated and doubly interesting because of the local color added in having home people and home scenes."[98]

After the success of this initial film, Tinsley found himself in high demand. As one Corning newspaper reported, "since staging the local picture play *Saved by the Stars and Stripes*, Mr. Tinsley has had a number of calls from surrounding towns for the use of the film when completed and also offers to make other home talent plays at different places."[99] On July 29 of the same year, a few weeks after the debut of his first film, one of the local newspapers reported that Tinsley, who now identified himself as a representative of the Tinsley Film Company, "had his moving picture machine working overtime" for the past few weeks.[100] One paper noted that Tinsley took pictures of an automobile parade in Corning as well as automobile stunts at the fairgrounds on a Wednesday afternoon and exhibited them the very next evening at the Lyric Theater. As the same paper noted in August, "Mr. Tinsley takes pride in getting out his films on very short notice after the acting of the drama has been accomplished."[101] Tinsley worked at the breakneck pace typical of the period, producing at least eight films in the second half of 1914 and another half-dozen in 1915. His films quickly became part of the regular moviegoing experience in Corning, not the special events promised by itinerant filmmakers. Tinsley even hosted his own night of movies in November 1914, competing that week with Francis X. Bushman, John Bunny, the serial *Million Dollar Mystery*, and a Paramount program.[102]

Unlike itinerant filmmakers, who either filmed permanent structures, such as government buildings and schools, or asked sponsors to stage events for the benefit of their camera, Tinsley, who also worked as a local newsreel camera operator, incorporated news event footage into his home talent pictures.[103] In November 1914, the newspaper reported that Tinsley

Figure 2.1. Photograph of the Superior Film Manufacturing Company making a film in Cedar Rapids, Iowa, in 1913. *Courtesy of the Black Film Center/Archive, Indiana University, Bloomington*

turned footage of a major fire in Corning that was taken the past summer into the centerpiece for a new narrative, *Between Two Fires*.[104] The same article alluded to another picture made by Tinsley, *Last Drill of the Boys of '61*, taken at a reunion of Civil War veterans, and mentioned that his next project, *Chariton's Heroes*, would be made in the town of Chariton, eighty miles to the east. In February 1915, Clyde A. Glougie captured a wolf on his ranch outside of town for Tinsley's next film, *The Wolf Hunt*, which cast two hundred people and up to fifty dogs for a film that climaxed with a wolf slaughter.[105] The paper also printed the rather simple plot of the film: One of Glougie's sheep is killed, and Glougie responds by accusing his neighbor's dog of committing the crime. Just before Glougie is about to shoot the dog, he realizes that his daughter is missing and goes to find her. When he finds her, she tells him that she saw a wolf on the property, after which the wolf hunt begins. Calling Tinsley "the man who 'knows how,'" the newspaper expressed confidence in his abilities to turn out a motion picture. In late May 1915, Tinsley left Corning for Des Moines, where he went to work as a camera operator for the Superior Film Company, which, as the Corning newspaper noted, "puts on local home talent stories and stunts, similar to those Mr. Tinsley has given in this city and nearby communities."[106]

With the Superior Film Manufacturing Company

The newspaper's description of the Superior Film Manufacturing Company was not fully accurate, as the company specialized in newsreels and booster pictures and had moved into home talent productions only recently. In November 1913, a Des Moines newspaper reported that the company had won a contract to "present pictures of all interesting local and state events" at the Orpheum Theater.[107] A few months earlier, the company was paid $500 by the Iowa Department of Agriculture for a 1,530-foot film of the Iowa State Fair, which took place in late August.[108] In late 1913, the company expanded its sights, running a quarter-page advertisement in the December 6 issue of *Moving Picture World* announcing that the company would shoot "Local Pictures at half the cost."[109] The company's low costs made them competitive with more established firms. For example, railway officials and business owners in Gettysburg, Pennsylvania, selected the company to produce a four-thousand-foot film for seven hundred dollars after rejecting a higher offer from the Philadelphia-based H.B.B. Motion Picture Company.[110] In May 1914, the *World* reported that the company had made films in Trenton, Missouri, with the intention of showing them at the Missouri building of the Panama-Pacific International Exposition in San Francisco.[111] Newspaper accounts of the company suggest that they employed several camera operators, and the 1913 city directory in Des Moines lists four employees.[112] One employee, Richard E. Norman, produced home talent films, including *Sleepy Sam the Sleuth*, which he copyrighted in 1915, and filmed in a number of cities for several years before turning to the filming of race movies in the early 1920s.[113]

An undated brochure for the company, produced after 1914, boasted that it produced industrial, feature, advertising, and special films, and offered developing and printing services from its new studio in Des Moines. The company also provided cameramen for all occasions, including "Parades, Festivals, special events, celebrations, civic pictures, etc."[114] Sponsors were charged fifteen dollars a day, plus hotel and traveling expenses, for the camera operator and an additional five cents a foot for the developed film, with additional charges for titles. A typical thousand-foot film would cost a theater exhibitor at least eighty dollars, assuming that the camera operator was in town for two days. The exhibitor would have to sell eight hundred ten-cent tickets to break even.[115]

When Tinsley joined the Superior Film Company in May 1915, he discontinued his practice of writing original scripts and instead shot two scenarios, *The Man at the Throttle* and, later, *Two Troublesome Tramps*, again and again. The newspaper articles about Superior's films rarely mentioned the director, so it is difficult to know just how many films Tinsley made for the company and how many were made by other directors, like Norman, who similarly filmed *The Man at the Throttle* in 1915 and later the same film under a different title, *The Green-Eyed Monster*, which he also remade as a race film.[116] Although these films were called "home talent" productions, Norman's sales pitch to exhibitors emphasized just how little original film needed to be shot for each production. In an undated flyer for *Sleepy Sam*, now under his eponymous company name, Norman spelled out the appeal of his home talent films to skeptical exhibitors: "R. E. Norman of the Norman Film Manufacturing company was convinced that the Home Talent motion picture was a winner—not merely a novelty, but a steady winner, provided the heavy expense could be reduced to a minimum and the time consumed in making the Home Talent motion picture to not more than one day for each City."[117]

The flyer goes on to reveal the secret to Norman's success—he would film no more than two hundred of the thousand-foot motion picture in each town, splicing in footage that, Norman assured exhibitors, appeared to be also shot in the community. Like the producers of booster films, home talent directors were drawn to more efficient models of production, even if such tactics undermined the original lure of local footage.

Tinsley, whose relationship with Norman is unclear, may have made his first *Throttle* film in Oelwein, Iowa, in early June, soon after joining Superior. The local paper in Oelwein summarized the film's scenario: "Jack Manning and Joe Hilton are rivals for the hand of Helen Powers, daughter of the Superintendent of the Railroad. Bernard Powers, Superintendent, promises Jack Manning the hand of Helen Powers in marriage and a promotion to Assistant Superintendent if he wins the mail race between the railroad and a rival road. Joe Hilton throws a switch which wrecks two passenger trains and delays the mail train for three hours. In spite of the delay Jack Manning brings the mail train on time and wins the race. He wins the bride, the race and his promotion."[118]

Like the municipal booster films discussed in the previous chapter, a wedding serves as the film's dénouement, an easily staged event that resolves any narrative conflicts in the plot and allows for the crowd scenes that were an important element of local films. As Lynne Kirby has noted, the railroad romance was popular in the mid-1910s, although most of the

Thrilling Railroad Drama
"The Man at the Throttle"

A Local Photo-play

Acted by Home Talent

We are offering you the opportunity of gratifying your long cherished desire—that of seeing your home people in a photoplay acted in this city.

The story of "The Man at the Throttle" is based on a race to carry the fast mail. The jealous rage of the villain, because of his love for the heroine, prompts him to wreck the fast mail. The steel monsters crash together and a fearful catastrophe is revealed to your view (the scenes are of an actual wreck and at the time the pictures were taken, the fireman of one of the engines lies buried beneath it). The engines buried in the mud, the overturned steel cars and torn up tracks delay our hero in his race for the fast mail contract, but in spite of the heavy odds he is victorious.

Beautiful, sharp photography, by the SUPERIOR FILM MFG. CO., directed by *a master hand*.

Figure 2.2. Playbill for *The Man at the Throttle* (n.d.). *Courtesy of the Black Film Center/ Archive, Indiana University, Bloomington*

plots of nationally distributed serials centered on female characters.[119] While for Kirby the railroad film is a "medium of condensation" that finds its meaning by alternating different times and spaces, *The Man at the Throttle* appealed to local audiences who instead saw railroad operators as unaccountable and dangerous. Reporting on a train wreck near Corning in 1913, a local newspaper noted, "Might as well try to get Milwaukee water out of a Corning cistern as to get particulars of a railroad wreck from railroad people."[120] While the producers of early municipal booster films may have been reluctant to use a train wreck as the spectacle for a booster film, producers of home talent films could be assured that such scenes, even if they were not filmed locally, would be of interest to audiences.

The railroad plot was also appealing to communities because it offered a diversity of acting opportunities to the members of local society. Unlike municipal booster producers, home talent producers appealed to their sponsors' desire to be in a motion picture, rather than to advertise their towns in cinemas throughout the country. While Superior's business plan was not evident from the newspaper stories about their films, all imply that the local theater manager presented the film, which suggests that the company and the theater shared proceeds from the box office. The producers of home talents appeared to be satisfied with a single revenue stream and did not charge entry fees to vie for a spot in their films, sell advertising screen space to local businesses, or ask booster groups to sponsor the films, all practices that were widely used by other producers of local pictures.

At the same time, home talent pictures often shared with municipal booster productions a tendency to cast the town's elite in their productions. A 1916 film produced by Superior in Des Moines titled *Unto the Least of These* and sponsored by the women and children's hospital was described by the company as a "society film," a term that held true for most of the films made by Superior.[121] For example, in April 1915, the *Throttle* film in Cedar Rapids starred the superintendent of the Northwestern Railroad, the managing editor of the local paper, and the cashier of the Boone National Bank.[122] Tinsley used a similar casting strategy in his Corning films, but the number of films he made in town increased the likelihood that most residents would eventually have their turn on screen.

The directors associated with the Superior Film Company did not claim that their films were unique. As the paper in Waterloo, Iowa, put it, Superior was "a Des Moines concern which goes from town to town and films [*The Man at the Throttle*] with local characters."[123] Instead of emphasizing its unique product, Superior focused on the quality of the films themselves, even if it meant that such films contained nonlocal

WANTED

150 MEN AND BOYS

On horseback, with guns, blank cartridges and large straw hats, to volunteer to take part in a home talent moving picture play entitled

"THE MEXICAN RAID"

Company K will play an important part in the chase of the Mexican Raiders.

MEET AT LYRIC THEATRE, FRIDAY, MAY 12
AT 1:00 O'CLOCK P. M.

The picture will be staged at the Mose Straughan log cabin, 1 mile south of Corning

REMEMBER THE DATE, FRIDAY, MAY 12, 1916

Figure 2.3. Advertisement for *The Mexican Raid*. From the *Adams County* (Corning, Iowa) *Union-Republican*, May 10, 1916, 4

scenes. For example, one of the two collisions in *The Man at the Throttle*, the train wreck, was not filmed locally but instead near Creston, Iowa, in early 1915.[124] Although the *Moving Picture World* editorial quoted above assumed that audiences would be more interested in an ordinary, locally filmed accident than a spectacular one filmed far away, Tinsley and other Superior directors offered audiences local scenes alternated with spectacles. In Iowa City, the railroad wreck was described as a "scenic effect of thrilling type" but a head-on car collision, which Tinsley staged locally, attracted "hundreds of interested spectators" who wanted to see themselves in the film.¹²⁵ When the film was presented in Iowa City, its combination of the local and the spectacular proved to be the "delight of the pulse-stirred, heart-throbbing onlookers," an observation that may well have come from a Superior press release.¹²⁶ For Richard Norman, *Sleepy Sam*'s use of stock scenes proved to be an asset to convince skeptical theater owners to participate in the scheme. As one exhibitor noted in the brochure, "It took us about 15 minutes to get the cast of characters and all told about an hour to make the film," suggesting how limited Norman's ambitions were for local filmmaking.¹²⁷

The War at Home

While Tinsley worked as a representative of the Superior Film Company for the next several years, he continued to make motion pictures in Corning. However, he shifted his filmmaking practice from making fictional films that used local events as their central attraction to more politically salient works. Tinsley's *The Mexican Raid*, a home talent production made in Corning, Iowa, in the spring of 1916, is a particularly compelling example of this kind of local moving picture. Like other home talent productions, this picture relied on audience recognition of local people and places. But *The Mexican Raid* also depended on a politically sophisticated audience that could understand the implications of the depicted event—a recreation of Mexican revolutionary Francisco "Pancho" Villa's attack on the small border town of Columbus, New Mexico, on March 9, 1916—for the town's volunteer militia.

By the time Tinsley made *The Mexican Raid*, he was already well known in Corning for his motion pictures. The event depicted in the film precipitated President Woodrow Wilson's decision to send US troops into Mexico to capture Villa. In early May, two months after the raid, an article ran in the local paper describing the plot of Tinsley's film and his production plans:

> The title of the picture is *The Mexican Raid* and will be up-to-the-minute stuff, since it will picture Mexicans making a raid on Americans. The principal scenes of the film will be taken on the above date at the Mose Straughan farm, south of town. Co. K will take a leading part in the battle scene and the management of the picture wants the services of 150 men and boys on horse back to act as Mexicans and make the raid. The log cabin, a landmark on the Straughan farm, will be used in the picture and the cabin will be burned.¹²⁸

Tinsley's use of the Corning-based Company K of the Third Infantry of the Iowa National Guard to participate in the reenactment is interesting for three reasons. First, Wilson's commitment of troops to the conflict led

> **SEE THE HOME TALENT**
>
> # MOVING PICTURE
>
> Production staged and acted by local people of this city, featuring Miss Theressa Hight, Carlton Cummings, Orval Church, D. H. Meyerhoff, Mrs. E. F. Miner. The picture, staged and directed by C. D. Tinsley of this city, is entitled
>
> # "THE MEXICAN RAID"
> ### A DRAMA IN TWO PARTS
>
> Don't fail to see this great picture. See train No. 6 hit the Reese Chalmers Six and the hero and heroine buried in the wreck. See the heroine rescued by the rival of the hero. See the Mexicans raid and burn the log cabin. See Company K route the bandits and rescue the American women and children. Regular program in addition and change of program each day.
>
> # LYRIC THEATRE, FRIDAY AND SATURDAY, JUNE 9 AND 10, '16
>
> Saturday Matinee at 2:30. Continuous Performance Each Evening
>
> **Special:** Matinee Saturday at 2:30 p. m. for children under 12..5c
>
> **PRICES, 10c and 15c**

Figure 2.4. Advertisement for *The Mexican Raid*. From the *Adams County* (Corning, Iowa) *Free Press*, June 3, 1916, 4

many to suspect that the National Guard would be called into action for the first time since the Spanish-American War (1898), meaning that the actions of Company K soldiers in the film anticipated prospective real-life military service. Second, by casting other Corning residents as Mexicans, Tinsley was asking his audiences to imagine those not in the militia, which was made up of volunteers, as a potential enemy force, one marked as an

> **MEXICAN RAID, 1,000 FT. FILM ADDED**
>
> Directed and Produced by C. D. TINSLEY
>
> Since we made the story first, new developments have taken place, and we have made new scenes to cover the new history. While "The Mexican Raid," will appear nearly as before, the new scenes bring out the mobilization of the troops of the National Guard which makes the story complete. Some of the scenes in Part Two—Gov. Clarke signing call for National Guard, **pathetic scenes at station as Company K leaves for Mexican war.** Company K in service at Camp Dodge, aeroplane scouts dropping bombs, sharp shooters bringing down air craft. See yourself in the crowd at the station, Etc., Etc.
>
> LISTEN—Mary Pickford in "Rags," a great Paramount Feature also included in this program. This will be the biggest movie program you ever got for the money in Corning—home talent "Mexican Raid" and "Little Mary"---think of it.
>
> **OPERA HOUSE, ONE DAY ONLY, SAT., JULY 15**
>
> MATINEE 2:30 P. M.   ADMISSION, 5 AND 10c.

Figure 2.5. Advertisement for *The Mexican Raid*. From the *Adams County* (Corning, Iowa) *Union Republican*, July 12, 1916, 1

"ethnic" other. And third, by planning to burn a log cabin that the newspaper considered a "landmark" in the community, Tinsley was calling attention to the importance of the events depicted in the film by destroying something that was part of local history. In this way, *The Mexican Raid* asked audiences to recognize the place of the film—the Mose Straughan farm—as both a familiar site and a landscape that could stand in for the US-Mexico border. In *The Mexican Raid*, which was first shown in Corning on June 9 and 10, real soldiers reenacted a real military conflict on a real farm that had been reimagined by Tinsley as a battlefield.[129]

On June 18, Wilson called all members of the National Guard into service to protect the Mexican border, including 4,500 troops from Iowa, 78 of whom were from Corning.[130] Tinsley went to Camp Dodge, a training base twelve miles northwest of Des Moines, to film another thousand feet of film to add to *The Mexican Raid*. In an advertisement published on July 13, 1916, Tinsley listed the new scenes in the film: "Gov. Clarke signing call for National Guard, pathetic scenes at station as Company K leaves for Mexican war. Company K in service at Camp Dodge, aeroplane scouts dropping bombs, sharp shooters bringing down air craft." In Tinsley's description of this new reel, which appears to feature footage of training activities, he also added that the viewer might "see yourself in the crowd at the train station."[131] While the appeal of the first reel of *The Mexican Raid* was seeing a farm near Corning transformed into a battlefield, the second attracted audiences because it showed scenes featuring local people training for an actual battle. In the first reel, the soldiers in Company K were merely actors. In the second, the soldiers were the subjects of a newsreel assembled by Tinsley to show the real-world military response to the fictional scenes he had created a month earlier.

As Richard Abel has noted, World War I inspired the production of many "feature-length non-fiction films" on the war between 1914 and 1916, which were produced or distributed by small companies who saw a market opening for motion pictures about a war the United States had not yet officially entered but was nonetheless following very closely. Abel notes that the pictures often took an editorial stance on the war itself, making them more like propaganda for one side or another, in contrast to the neutral stance that newsreels claimed. Tinsley's early, semi-fictional pictures were different from the war pictures because they focused on an incident closer to home but likely played on audience interest in representations of war, which had before only been depicted in newsreels and short reenactments and actualities.[132] Tinsley made at least four more films about Corning's involvement in military conflicts of the 1910s, including *On the Mexican Border*, which was made in Brownsville, Texas, on behalf of the Iowa YMCA in early 1917, and several World War I films.

In October 1917, Tinsley turned the basement of his house into a film manufacturing plant and officially started the Tinsley Film Company. As the *Adams County Free Press* noted, Tinsley no longer had to travel to Des Moines, one hundred miles northeast of Corning, to process and edit his films. The newspaper also reported that it was printing intertitles for Tinsley, which helps explain its close coverage of Tinsley's films.[133] In December 1917, eight months after the United States entered World War I, Tinsley traveled to Washington, DC, to obtain permission to film soldiers from Corning in training at Camp Cody, located in Deming, New Mexico.[134] From Washington, Tinsley and his wife left for New Mexico, first stopping in several towns in Texas to make other films, likely home talent productions. The *Adams County Union-Republican* justified Tinsley's trip by noting that "a motion picture of Washington's army or Grant or Lee's Army would today be valuable and these pictures will be just as valuable in time to come."[135] In mid-February 1918, the Tinsleys returned from New Mexico to edit the film.[136] When the film was finished in mid-March, Tinsley sent it to the Committee on Public Information in Washington, DC, for approval. According to the Corning newspaper, "only two scenes in the entire six reels were ordered cut out by the authorities," and with the government's approval, Tinsley went back to New Mexico to show the film.[137] At the end of March, Tinsley returned to Corning for the film's local premiere and brought back "Woodrow," an eagle, as an added attraction.[138] A few months later, the paper reported the Tinsley had screened the film throughout Nebraska and South Dakota, carrying a different animal attraction from New Mexico—two horned toads—from town to town.¹³⁹ At the end of 1918, Tinsley produced another war film, *Over There*, a moving image illustrated song described as such: "Corporal Archie Ammon, and seven other boys from the Rainbow division, from overseas, put on a trench scene especially for this production. They went into the trenches at Camp Dodge and reproduced the scenes really produced in the great world war 'over there.'"¹⁴⁰

For the film's exhibition, a local Corning resident sang the popular World War I song from which it took its name, while Corrie Peregrine, the wife of Tinsley's former business partner, played the piano.¹⁴¹ In June 1919, Tinsley made his final war film, *Our Rainbow Boys*, so called because National Guard troops from three regiments in Iowa had joined National Guard troops in other states to form a "rainbow division." Tinsley traveled to New York in early 1919 to film the arrival of the *Leviathan*, a large military ship with Iowa's infantry regiments on board. Unlike Tinsley's previous war films, this one was commissioned by the Iowa Historical Society to "make a permanent record" of the event so that "the coming generations may see and be proud of the way we received our heroes of the World War." Unfortunately for those coming generations, the motion pictures are not known to survive.¹⁴²

Tinsley left Superior in either late 1917 or early 1918 but did not stop making films. Instead, he began an itinerant practice, producing one home talent film, *Two Troublesome Tramps*, throughout Iowa and nearby states for at least fifteen more years. Tinsley may have written the scenario himself. A newspaper article on a screening of Tinsley's films in Clearfield, Iowa, referenced a *Two Troublesome Tramps* produced in nearby Afton before Tinsley joined Superior.¹⁴³ The *Malvern* (Iowa) *Leader* summarized the film's comic narrative when the film was produced there in March 1916:

> The play is entitled, Two Troublesome Tramps, and they certainly prove troublesome to numerous Malvern people as they go their happy go lucky way, from the time they strike the town from a Wabash box car until they land behind the bars, placed there by the firm hand of the law as administered by Chief of Police Jones.
>
> They first apply for a "hand out" at the back door of the Baton Tenant home where Mrs. Tenant chases them off with a broom. This was done so vigorously that they tumbled over each other in their haste breaking Hixson's nose, which wasn't figured on in the original play. But it goes in the movies just the same, now. Next they appear at the back door of the D. R. Martin home but Mrs. Martin sets the dog on them to such effect that they beat a hasty retreat. Down at the livery barn they unexpectedly find some money and at once resolve to dress up and try another tack—Break into

society. They go to Kneeland's and purchase a complete new outfit and start out as dudes. They make a break at the lady in the case and get into a fight to liven things up a bit. They later overturn a couple of men busily reading the war news and afterward break up a party when they are nabbed by the eagle eyed minion of the law, J. W. Jones, who lands them safely behind the bars in the last scene.[144]

As with his previous home talent pictures, Tinsley incorporated scenes taken elsewhere into the *Tramp* movies, inserting a "snake scene" and a scene where a Ford automobile is driven off a bridge.[145] Although *Two Troublesome Tramps* had very few named roles, the "tramps," who were played by locals, interacted with their neighbors in various circumstances, allowing for a large cast of unnamed bit players to appear in the film. In Anita, Iowa, an advertisement placed in the newspaper noted the film depicted "more than 100 of our home people you all know" and called the film a "Feast of Fun!"[146]

Tinsley continued producing *Two Troublesome Tramps* throughout the Midwest and beyond, shooting films in Missouri, Kansas, Nebraska, North and South Dakota, Arkansas, and possibly Oklahoma and Texas in the 1920s and early 1930s. Although the picture's basic storyline and attractions remained unchanged, the descriptions of the films became more detailed, and Tinsley appears to have experimented with the mode. In Jefferson City, Missouri, Tinsley brought a blackface comedian from Chicago, Charles Weiss, to play the "mammy" role, which was not mentioned in the descriptions of the film in the 1910s but became an increasingly central character in the film in the 1920s and 1930s. Blackface was popular in small towns in the early part of the twentieth century, particularly in amateur theatrical productions, making Tinsley's use of the practice not unusual.[147] In 1933, Tinsley added another attraction to the film, "an attack by a monster reptile," an inserted scene possibly filmed in the Southwest, where Tinsley and his wife visited frequently.[148]

Tinsley turned sixty in April 1933. He produced only a handful of films after that date, though he lived another thirty-two years. In 1937, his house was foreclosed upon, and afterward he may have moved away from Corning.[149] In 1941, the Corning paper reported that Tinsley had returned to town to film *Watch Your Speed*, a traffic safety film sponsored by the National Safety Council, but there are no records of the picture's production.[150] By 1948, Tinsley had moved back to Corning and lived there until his death in 1965.[151] His obituary made just a brief mention of his movie career and did not comment on what happened to the many films he made in Corning and elsewhere.[152]

Itinerancy Begins at Home

The prevalence of home talent production in the mid- and late-1910s was but one example of the difficulties small-town residents had in accepting the movie industry's plans for their local theaters. Although traveling theater troupes, circuses, vaudeville acts, medicine shows, itinerant preachers, and live performers of all stripes refused to cede their careers in the face of the Hollywood behemoth, the industry had little interest in sharing their theaters with these two-bit acts. The seasonal rhythms of live performance were replaced by the daily onslaught of new films, with stars and genres designed for mass appeal. As Barbara Wilinsky has noted, in the 1910s movie producers, newspapers, and other large media outlets "selected and transformed different pieces of US subcultures not only to attract but also to construct and shape the mass audience."[153] Small-town audiences may have been a comparatively neglected group but were nevertheless swept up in this social and cultural transformation. From this perspective, the producers of home talent productions were attempting, and mostly failing, to gain a toehold on the screen of their local theater.

A few home talent filmmakers followed Tinsley's path and turned their success as directors of local films into a career. For example, Hugh V. Jamieson produced the home talent film *Won from the Flames* before starting his eponymous industrial film company in 1916, which remained in business for more than sixty years. Born in Kansas in 1889, Jamieson ran a movie theater in Baldwin City, Kansas, in the early 1910s while he was studying at Baker University. After graduating, Jamieson moved to Kansas City and around 1913 signed on as a traveling salesman for Edison's Home Projecting Kinetoscope.[154] Jamieson quickly sold twelve projectors, but a fire destroyed Edison's studio in December 1914, ending Edison's early foray into the amateur market.[155] Around that time, Jamieson purchased a Williamson Camera for seventy-five dollars and, according to a company history published in 1974, "started touring, making pictures, processing them in the hotel bathtub and showing them in the respective town where they had been shot."[156] With a script featuring a love story, a fire, and crowd scenes, Jamieson produced *Won from the Flames* in Kansas, Oklahoma, and Texas in 1915 and 1916.[157] In December 1915, Jamieson, looking to break ground in yet another aspect of production, contracted with a sign company to produce advertising trailers for use in Texas movie theaters, which would have been among the earliest film trailers. In 1916, Jamieson started the Jamieson Film Company, which became a leading regional producer of industrial films for decades.[158]

In other cases, home talent film producers had backgrounds in traveling entertainment and returned to those fields once they had exhausted their interest in filmmaking. For example, Basil McHenry, a circus promoter, worked as an itinerant film producer in the mid-1910s, producing a melodrama titled *The Man Haters* in Indiana, Ohio, West Virginia, Kentucky, Virginia, New York, and likely other states. The ten-minute version McHenry produced in Muncie, Indiana, in the fall of 1915 is extant.[159] McHenry did not direct the pictures himself but instead hired cinematographers to shoot the films. Like the Paragon films discussed in the first chapter, *The Man Haters* was a wedding picture, only in this case the lead actress had to first be persuaded to leave her club of "man haters," an allusion to feminist groups who rejected men.[160] The films were made with the cooperation, and likely sponsorship, of local newspapers, which held a "Who Will Be Ruth?" casting competition in the weeks leading up to the film's production. McHenry quit making films by the late 1910s and became a longtime traveling publicity agent for Hollywood films.[161]

It was far more common, however, for home talent filmmakers to announce their entry into the movie industry with great aplomb but never complete a production. The home talent field was marked with a series of false starts and unfulfilled promises. In trade newspapers like *Moving Picture News* and *Moving Picture World,* bold schemes for local picture productions would receive ample publicity, but the company or filmmaker discussed would never be mentioned again. For example, in early 1915, *Moving Picture World* printed a notice about a studio founded in Waterloo, Iowa, by Arthur L. Runyan for the production of advertising pictures: "Local talent will be engaged to enact the parts of the 'lover,' 'hero' and 'villain,' and a big studio will soon be in course of construction in Waterloo. As to outdoor scenery, the company will draw upon the natural resources of the immediate vicinity of Waterloo."[162]

There is no evidence that Runyan ever produced a film in Waterloo, which had a population of almost thirty thousand people in 1910, but the town still had its opportunity to appear in a number of home talent, industrial romance, and other local films made over the course of the next few decades.[163] Even if not every town had a filmmaker as ambitious as Tinsley, most towns saw a number of home talent productions made in the first decades of the cinema.

While producing home talent films could be a profitable enterprise, an overcrowded marketplace made it difficult for many producers to succeed. One bad experience could sour an exhibitor's openness to home talent productions, and poorly made pictures and scams were also reported in local papers and the trade press. In October 1915, a *Moving Picture World* correspondent in Illinois asked, "Do Local Films Pay?" offering several examples of films that were so bad that they hurt business for the three or four days they were booked at the theater.[164] While the producers of local views promised—and delivered—just the chance to see oneself on screen, the additional assurances made by home talent producers were often more difficult to fulfill.

Ironically, the difficulty any individual or company had staying in the business long term increased the variety and longevity of the practice. While a few producers were able to stay in business for a decade or more, it was far more typical for someone like Jamieson or Norman to shoot local films for a few years and then move on to make other types of motion pictures or quit the business altogether. If a town had a resident like Tinsley who owned a movie camera and used it to photograph local events or even produce home talents, it was difficult for an itinerant to come to town and do the same.

While Tinsley approached Alfred Arvold's goal for home talent productions to tell local stories, most directors found producing the same script again and again to be more economically viable. Many of the startup studios that opened in the far-flung corners of the United States had gone out of the business by the late 1910s or moved into the production of educational and industrial film. While itinerant filmmakers continued to produce narrative fiction films in the coming decades, these directors were no longer seen as autonomous agents within the world of motion pictures. Instead, they claimed to be representatives of the movie industry that everyone now called Hollywood.

Notes

1. For more on the infiltration of mass culture on rural life, see Barron, *Mixed Harvest*, 193–241. Barron argues that rural areas participated in cultural markets before they became part of mass culture around 1920.

2. See Zimmermann, *Reel Families*, 1–11. As Zimmermann argues of the contrast between amateurs and professionals, "Despite the propagation of an idea that amateurism protected equality through artistic, economic, or inventive opportunity, on a less-abstract level there remained a hierarchy of those who performed a task for a living and those who engaged in it for the self" (10). In contrast, home talent was often a remunerative activity, even if the work was temporary or if one could easily be replaced by a professional.

3. See US Bureau of the Census, *Fourteenth Census of the United States Taken in the Year 1920*, vol. 2, *Number and Distribution of Inhabitants* (Washington, DC: Government Printing Office, 1921), 50.

4. Wiebe, *The Search for Order*.

5. On the spread of consumer goods, the leading indicator of the general trend toward a national culture, see Strasser, *Satisfaction Guaranteed*, 124–161.

6. See Kaufman, *For the Common Good?* 56–82, and Reps, *The Making of Urban America,* 497–525.

7. See "Home Talent." School administration was a particularly contentious issue in rural communities, who resisted the consolidation of schools and the requirement that schools hire professional educators. For more on this issue, see Barron, *Mixed Harvest,* 43–77. For more on the new professional classes, see also Bledstein, *The Culture of Professionalism,* 80–128.

8. Cousins, "Combination for Better Engineering."

9. C. F. Johnson, "A Tribute to St. Louis," *The Western Architect,* June 1916, 62.

10. Lingeman. *Small Town America,* 258–320.

11. Danbom, *Born in the Country,* 163.

12. Atherton, *Main Street on the Middle Border,* 119–121.

13. Spears. *Chicago Dreaming.*

14. Ibid., 58–59. Spears notes that nostalgia for one's hometown was a common affliction for writers in this period (126–127).

15. See Abel, "Film Discourse in the Heartlands."

16. Ibid., 146.

17. Kett, *The Pursuit of Knowledge under Difficulties,* 293–330. As Kett notes, "The twin goals of Progressive-style popular education—the enhancement of the public's receptivity to scientific solutions and the intensification of feelings of community—frequently overlapped" (314).

18. Bowers, *The Country Life Movement in America,* 24–27. See *Report of the Country Life Commission.*

19. Bowers, *The Country Life Movement in America,* 94–95.

20. Arvold, "The Little Country Theatre," 88.

21. Ibid., 89.

22. Elshtain, *Jane Addams and the Dream of American Democracy,* 146. Liberty Hyde Bailey, chair of the Country Life Commission, himself echoed similar sentiments, instead proposing that rural people produce drama that depicts "the end of the planting, the harvest, the seasons, the leading crops, the dairy, the woods, the history and traditions of the neighborhood or the region." See Bailey, *The Country-Life Movement in the United States,* 213.

23. Of course, Arvold's assumptions depended on a narrowed, even elitist sense for what counted as culture, as evidenced by the popularity of rural music in the 1920s and 1930s.

24. Arvold, "The Little Country Theatre," 90.

25. See Levine, *Highbrow/Lowbrow.*

26. Arvold, "The Little Country Theatre," 91.

27. Ibid., 92–93.

28. *MPW,* April 4, 1914, 92.

29. See Chansky, *Composing Ourselves,* 64–66. The Little Cinema movement of the 1920s likely took its name from these earlier theatrical movements, but its supporters were not interested in using the cinema to establish local or regional identity. See Morey, "Early Art Cinema in the U.S."

30. Eaton, "The Real Revolt in Our Theatre," 598.

31. Ibid., 601–602.

32. See Glassberg, *American Historical Pageantry,* 345.

33. Senelick, *The Changing Room,* 328.

34. Eckey et al., *1,001 Broadways,* 32–33. Universal's most successful booker was Lauren Kenyon Woods, who went on to found the Boston Amateur Theatre Guild, a prominent producer of local motion pictures in the 1930s. See chapter 5.

35. The noted theater historian Brooks McNamara defines home talent plays merely as shows that were "sponsored by companies that provided directors—often young women with a college drama department background—... with a playscript suitable for amateurs." McNamara, "Popular Entertainment," 398. For a more complete history of the home talent play, see Eckey et al., *1,001 Broadways*.

36. In theater producer Norris Houghton's 1941 survey of American theater, *Advance from Broadway*, he noted that the number of professional theaters in the United States dropped from 5,000 in 1890 to 192 in 1939, 44 of which were in Times Square (14).

37. For more on the relationship between theater and film, see Jacobs and Brewster. *Theatre to Cinema*.

38. Musser, "Towards a History of Theatrical Culture," 12.

39. Liepa, "Figures of Silent Speech," 204–294; Luckett, *Cinema and Community*, 117–125.

40. As Robert C. Allen notes in the so-called Manhattan debates, which were published over a series of *Cinema Journal* issues in the mid-1990s, "if we were forced to choose only one locality to represent the way the movies became a part of most communities in America, we would have more reason to choose Anamosa, Iowa, than New York, New York." Allen, "Manhattan Myopia," 96.

41. Bottomore, "From the Factory Gate to the 'Home Talent' Drama," 33.

42. Singer, "Feature Films, Variety Programs, and the Crisis of the Small Exhibitor."

43. *MPW*, December 23, 1911, 1019.

44. *MPW*, September 16, 1911, 814. Schneider also ran an advertisement for his camera in *Popular Mechanics*, September 1912, 20. In order to make a return on his or her investment, an owner of Schneider's camera would have to sell more than four thousand ten-cent tickets for a single film.

45. *MPW*, September 14, 1912, 1130.

46. *Moving Picture News*. October 26, 1912, 33.

47. Lavezzi Machine Works, which was founded in Chicago in 1908, sold its camera kit for fifty dollars by 1913, although a company representative told the *World* in September 1913 that the camera was intended for home use. The lens and tripod were sold separately, for fifteen and ten dollars respectively. See *MPW*, September 13, 1913, 1162.

48. As Ben Singer has noted, in 1912 and 1913, a number of amateur motion picture cameras and projectors were released, some of which used 35mm film. See Singer, "Home Cinema and the Edison Home Projecting Kinetoscope."

49. *MPW*, January 18, 1913, 287. The quotes around "Precision" are in the advertisement.

50. *MPW*, February 8, 1913, 613.

51. "An Exhibitor's Camera: A Mechanically Perfect Instrument on a Small Scale Which Should Help Exhibitors to Fill Their Houses," *MPW*, February 22, 1913, 765. Before importing the Sept camera, Whyte-Whitman sold another import, the Williamson camera from Britain. See *Moving Picture News*, October 12, 1912, 5.

52. *MPW*, February 22, 1913, 765. Because these camera manufacturers targeted a semiprofessional market, the cameras they produced have not been studied as extensively as those produced for either the professional or amateur markets. For example, Alan Kattelle's *Home Movies*, an authoritative source on the history of amateur film equipment, only mentions the Sept 35mm semiprofessional camera in passing and suggests that it was not introduced into the United States until the 1920s (58). In James R. Cameron's history of amateur and semiprofessional cameras, published in 1927, he suggested that the Sept camera was the first "moderately priced camera" that used 35mm film, followed by the Victor Cine Camera, the De Vry Automatic Camera, and the Eyemo. See Cameron, *The Taking and Showing of Motion Pictures for the Amateur*, 14–15. Barry Salt suggests that

many of the cameras described here were modeled after the Williamson camera, first sold in 1904 and later copied by other companies. See Salt, *Film Style and Technology*, 70.

53. *MPW*, February 22, 1913, 765.

54. The Motion Picture Camera Company sold the Ideal Motion Picture Camera. *MPW*, April 26, 1913, 408.

55. *MPW*, April 12, 1913, 225. In December 1912, Special Event Film Manufacturing Company, discussed in chapter 1, sold its camera, lens, and tripod for one hundred dollars, with two hundred feet of film included as a bonus. See *Moving Picture News*, December 7, 1912, 31.

56. By January 1914, cameras were selling for seventy-five dollars in the *Motion Picture World*. See *MPW*, January 24, 1914, 462.

57. *MPW*, October 4, 1914, 81.

58. Notable exceptions include Allen, *Vaudeville and Film,* and Jacobs and Brewster, *Theatre to Cinema.*

59. A discussion of the relationship between movie theaters and opera houses in small towns can be found in William Faricy Condee's *Coal and Culture*. While Condee's argument is specific to opera houses in the southern Appalachian region, my research suggests that the pattern he identifies held true in towns throughout the United States.

60. Hulfish, *Motion-Picture Work*, 37.

61. *MPW*, July 26, 1913, 324.

62. *MPW*, September 13, 1913, 1164–1165. This example is also cited in Bottomore, "From the Factory Gate to the 'Home Talent' Drama," 40.

63. *MPW*, September 13, 1913, 1194. According to the *World*, the film "showed the rescue of a young woman from a burning building and the department was given an opportunity to display the workings of its apparatus."

64. *MPW*, October 4, 1913, 40–41.

65. *MPW*, September 5, 1914, 1394; February 21, 1914, 980.

66. *MPW*, August 21, 1915, 1341. *The Mine Owner's Daughter* was produced by Paragon, discussed in chapter 1.

67. Sargent, *Picture Theater Advertising*, 248.

68. *MPW*, September 26, 1914, 1796.

69. *MPW*, August 8, 1914, 850.

70. Singer, "Feature Films, Variety Programs, and the Crisis of the Small Exhibitor," 76.

71. For an account of Jacksonville's importance in the transitional era, see Bean, *The First Hollywood,* and Nelson, *Florida and the American Motion Picture Industry.*

72. With the exception of a few case studies, scholars have not written about small studios in far-flung cities in the transitional era. For a sampling of those studios that could be studied, see Karr, "Hooray for Providence."

73. Dench, "Openings for the Free Lance Cinematographer."

74. *MPW*, January 17, 1914, 305.

75. Hill, "Will the Moving Picture Camera Pay?"

76. *MPW*, June 10, 1916, 1949. In 1917, *Camera Craft* noted that David Stern was selling the Davsco Camera for use by directors of "news film and home talent pictures." See *Camera Craft*, January 1917, 39.

77. As Michael Aronson has noted, in the spring of 1916, *Motion Picture News* launched an advice column ("The Camera") for exhibitor-camera operators but encouraged them to stick to local newsreels. See Aronson, *Nickelodeon City*, 223–228. For more on local newsreels, see Abel, *Menus for Movieland*, 64–71.

78. "Have You Talent?" brochure, RNC, box 4, folder 75. In a herald for the film, Norman described it as a "lavish production" featuring "university notables" and "college studios" in a "story of University life with a plot of national interest." The "Have You

Talent?" brochure lists the scenes in the film, including "the blowing up of a house, a big ball room scene, showing a number of people dancing, registration, rushing and pledging scenes, a big fight scene in which a laboratory of chemical apparatus was broken up, also a scene showing the villain breaking a flask of chemical on the hero, disabling him and being blinded by an accidental explosion, finally falling downstairs, breaking his neck." According to the brochure, two of the actors in the film were cast in the Chicago-based film company Essanay's *The Prince of Graustark* (1916) as a result of their performances. Herald, RNC, box 4, folder 75. *Moving Picture World* also reported on *Pro Patria* in its September 2, 1915, issue, almost a month after its local exhibition (1577).

79. "Have You Talent?" brochure.
80. Liepa, "Entertaining the Public Option," 12.
81. Stoddard, *The Photo-Play,* [10–11].
82. Kane, *1,001 Places to Sell Manuscripts,* 230.
83. After contacting the state archives in Iowa for more information on Tinsley, I received a clipping file from Paula Mohr, an architectural historian who now works for the Iowa Historic Preservation Office in Des Moines. The file was assembled by Mary Jones, a historian in Iowa.
84. *ACFP,* February 18, 1965, 20. In the 1880 federal census, Tinsley was identified as living on a farm in Locust Grove, Iowa, where his father, David, was a merchant. Ancestry Library Edition, www.ancestry.com. More information about the family appears in the obituary for Tinsley's mother, Mary, in the Corning newspaper. See *ACFP,* July 9, 1931, 4.
85. *Anita* (Iowa) *Record,* October 25, 1917, 1.
86. *ACFP,* October 6, 1898, 6. Batavia's population is from the 1890 federal census. Ancestry Library Edition, www.ancestry.com.
87. *ACFP,* February 18, 1965, 20.
88. "Xmas Dinner," *ACFP,* December 28, 1933, 5. Tinsley regularly filmed these dinners and exhibited the results in the host's home in subsequent years.
89. "Of Local Interest," *ACFP,* March 25, 1908, 5.
90. "Business Change," *ACUR,* October 30, 1912, 12.
91. "Tribute to Enterprise," *ACUR,* January 1, 1913, 2.
92. "Corning to Be Taken," *ACUR,* February 14, 1913, 3.
93. Ibid.
94. "Additional Locals," *ACFP,* March 1, 1913, 4.
95. "Tinsley Studio Burned," *ACFP,* April 29, 1914, 1.
96. "Photo Play Is Staged," *ACUR,* May 20, 1914, 8.
97. Ibid.
98. "Pictures Are Fine," *ACUR,* July 1, 1914, 4.
99. *ACFP,* June 6, 1914, 7.
100. "Mighty Quick Word," *ACUR,* July 29, 1914, 1.
101. "Home Talent Films," *ACUR,* August 12, 1914, 4.
102. *ACFP,* November 7, 1914, 10.
103. In addition to the home talent films described here, Tinsley, like many local home talent filmmakers, also shot footage of important local events.
104. "Between Two Fires," *ACUR,* November 4, 1914, 2.
105. "The Wolf Hunt," *ACUR,* February 17, 1915, 2. Two weeks earlier, *Moving Picture World* published an account of a home talent film with the same plot that was shot in Tekamah, Nebraska, by the Hartman Brothers of Omaha, another producer of local motion pictures. It is not clear if Tinsley was inspired by this account or if he had connections with the company in Omaha, which is eighty miles west of Corning. See *MPW,* January 30, 1915, 701.
106. "Good Situation," *ACUR,* May 26, 1915, 7.
107. *National Democrat* (Des Moines), November 6, 1913, 3.

108. Iowa Department of Agriculture, *The Iowa Year Book of Agriculture*, 182.
109. *MPW*, December 6, 1913, 1226.
110. "Will Advertise Town With Film," *Adams County* (Gettysburg, Penn.) *News*, May 30, 1914, 1.
111. *MPW*, May 9, 1914, 840.
112. Des Moines City Directory, *Polk's Real Estate Register*. Richard E. Norman, Clarence Kramer, Morgan Howells, and Charles Vogman were also listed as working for the company.
113. See Bernstein and White. "'Scratching Around' in a 'Fit of Insanity'"; Lupack, *Richard E. Norman and Race Filmmaking*.
114. Superior brochure, RNC, box 4, folder 75. Because Norman quit working for the company by 1920, it seems likely that this brochure dates from the mid-1910s.
115. Ibid. In some cases, theater managers charged higher admission prices to see home talent films or ran them for up to a week. In almost all cases, these films were part of a two- or three-film program, which was changed two or three times a week.
116. See RNC, box 4, folder 72. Norman also appears to have produced the same film under another title, *The Wrecker*. See Lupack, *Richard E. Norman and Race Filmmaking*, 39–45, 324–325n38.
117. "Money Making Motion Picture Proposition" flyer, RNC, box LL-4, folder 75.
118. "The Man at the Throttle at the Gem," *Oelwein* (Iowa) *Daily Register*, June 2, 1915, 4. A herald for the same film is in RNC. The plot summary is the same, but the herald's writing is more vivid: "The steel monsters crash together and a fearful catastrophe is revealed to your view (the scenes are of an actual wreck and at the time the pictures were taken, the fireman of one of the engines lies buried beneath it)." Herald, RNC, box 4, folder 72.
119. Kirby, *Parallel Tracks*, 111.
120. *ACFP*, July 5, 1913, 5.
121. "Society Folk Take Part in Hospital Movie," *Des Moines News*, September 29, 1916, 2.
122. "Prominent Men to Be in Movie," *Cedar Rapids* (Iowa) *Daily Republican*, April 22, 1915, 5.
123. "At the Crystal," *WECR*, June 25, 1915, 3.
124. Ibid.
125. "Real Life Vs. Reel Life Now," *Iowa City* (Iowa) *Daily Press*, August 13, 1915, 1.
126. Ibid.
127. "Money Making Motion Picture Proposition" flyer.
128. *ACFP*, May 6, 1916, 5.
129. *ACFP*, June 3, 1916, 4. The attractions of the film are described in this ad as follows: "See train No. 6 hit the Reese Chalmers Six and the hero and heroine buried in the wreck. See the heroine rescued by the rival of the hero. See the Mexicans raid and burn the log cabin. See Company K route the bandits and rescue the American women and children."
130. Dick Dreyer, "Iowa Troops in Mexican Border Service: 1916–1917," Iowa National Guard Museum, http://www.iowanationalguard.com/museum/ia_history/1900%20Mexican%20Border.pdf.
131. *ACUR*, July 12, 1916, 1.
132. Abel, "Charge and Countercharge," 366–367, 370, 379.
133. *ACFP*, October 6, 1917, 4.
134. "Movies of the Soldiers," *ACUR*, December 12, 1917, 8.
135. *ACUR*, December 15, 1917, 8.
136. *ACFP*, February 16, 1918, 4.
137. *ACFP*, March 16, 1918, 9.
138. *ACFP*, March 30, 1918, 4. Just over a year later, the Corning paper reported that the eagle was donated to the Lincoln Park Zoo in Chicago. See "To Zoo," *ACFP*, April 16, 1919, 5.

139. *ACFP*, July 6, 1918, 8.
140. "Tinsley's Latest Production," *ACUR*, December 11, 1918, 7.
141. Ibid.
142. "Our Rainbow Boys," *ACFP*, June 7, 1919, 2.
143. "New Week, Friday, April 16," *Clearfield* (Iowa) *Enterprise*, April 8, 1915, 6.
144. "A Malvern Movie Play," *Malvern* (Iowa) *Leader*, March 9, 1916, 1.
145. "Griswold *American*," *ACFP*, November 3, 1917, 1.
146. *Anita* (Iowa) *Record*, October 18, 1917, 4.
147. None of the other itinerant filmmakers discussed in this book made blackface films, with the slight exception of Don O. Newland, whose 1927 film *Janesville's Hero* includes a scene in which a character lights a trick cigar, turning his face black. Two filmmakers discussed in this book, Richard E. Norman and Salvatore Cudia, produced race films in the 1920s and 1930s.
148. *Humboldt* (Iowa) *Independent*, January 3, 1933, 2.
149. "Foreclosure Notice," *ACFP*, April 29, 1937, 20.
150. "To Film Safety Picture Here," *ACFP*, November 13, 1941, 13. According to Alaina Kolosh at the National Safety Council Library, Itasca, Illinois, no records of this film exist. Personal correspondence with the author, January 17, 2011.
151. "Locals," *ACFP*, September 16, 1948, 3.
152. "Charlie D. Tinsley," *ACFP*, February 18, 1965, 20.
153. Wilinsky, "Flirting with Kathlyn," 52.
154. For more on the projectors, see Singer, "Home Cinema and the Edison Home Projecting Kinetoscope." Singer observes that Edison saw schools as an important secondary market for his projectors. By 1913, Edison had decided that the educational film market was the primary one for his projector and distributed a catalogue to sixteen thousand school superintendents (51–54, 61). Based on Singer's research, it seems likely that Jamieson did not start work as a traveling salesperson for Edison until 1912 or 1913. For more on Jamieson's experience with Edison, see Kuehn, "Jamieson Leaves the Scene," 913.
155. Singer, "Home Cinema and the Edison Home Projecting Kinetoscope," 61.
156. Kuehn, "Jamieson Leaves the Scene," 913.
157. "Hugh V. Jamieson Interview at KERA [TV—Dallas, Texas]," Texas Archive of the Moving Image, http://www.texasarchive.org/library/index.php?title=Hugh_V._Jamieson_Interview_at_KERA&gsearch=jamieson. According to Bruce Jamieson, Hugh's son, the family disposed of the films in 1958, when they decided that they were too dangerous to keep. Personal correspondence with the author, January 21, 2010. In the 1930s and 1940s, Jamieson processed many of the films shot by the itinerant filmmaker Melton Barker.
158. Kuehn, "Jamieson Leaves the Scene," 913.
159. See The Man Haters Film Collection, Ball State University, http://libx.bsu.edu/cdm4/collection.php?CISOROOT=%2Fmnhtrs.
160. The film's title may have been inspired by Clyde Fitch's 1908 play *Girls*, which features a club of "man haters" infiltrated by male suitors. In 1919, a film of the play, also entitled *Girls*, was produced by Paramount.
161. Turner, *Having Fun with It*, 14.
162. "New Moving Picture Company Formed," *MPW*, January 9, 1915, 200.
163. These films include the *Romance of Waterloo*, made in 1920, an industrial film made by the Tisdale Film Company in 1921, and *Things You Ought to Know about Waterloo*, produced in 1933 by Pacific Film Productions. *WEC*, October 1, 1920, 1; *WECR*, May 25, 1921, 4; *Waterloo Daily Courier*, November 1, 1933, 3.
164. Frank H. Madison, "Do Local Films Pay?" *MPW*, October 23, 1915, 485.

3

"HOW MOVIES ARE MADE"
Hollywood and the Local Film

IN 1922, *MOVING PICTURE WORLD* ran an item on a minor event in its local news section. A pair of "movie scouts" were wandering the streets of South Boston, persuading parents that their child could be the next Jackie Coogan if they only paid a small fee to have a picture taken for submission to movie executives.[1] But instead of seeing this as just another variation on the screen contests that were commonplace in the 1910s, the *World* alerted its readers that the police were pursuing these scouts as frauds, using promises of stardom to rob their victims of ten dollars or more. A year earlier, the Motion Picture Theater Owners of America issued a warning to exhibitors "entering into or lending their names to the production of home talent motion pictures made by traveling operators" after an Ohio theater was reportedly taken for $490.[2] The local film, like the head shot and the screen test, proved to be an easy way to con an unsuspecting public who increasingly associated all moving images with the national motion picture industry, or, as many came to call it, Hollywood.[3]

The rise of Hollywood *qua* Hollywood in the early 1920s is well known. Less well known are the processes that produced and disseminated Hollywood culture, particularly in the thousands of small-town movie theaters that served up to half of the moviegoing public. While discursive readings of early Hollywood culture have used fan magazines, trade journals, extant films, and, to a lesser extent, archival collections to reconstruct the experience of cinema, they neglect the role individuals affiliated with the industry played in creating this culture. In this chapter I focus on local film production that was coordinated by movie theater managers and industry representatives. Because these practices were iterative, close examination makes it possible to document the development of Hollywood culture on a much smaller scale. The local film itself was transformed by its encounter with Hollywood, changing audience expectations of what it meant to appear in a motion picture screened in their very own theater.

Hollywood Takes on the Local Film

While motion picture companies began to take an interest in movie fans in the early 1910s, it was not until they acquired theaters that they saw both the opportunity and the need to produce local pictures in which aspiring movie actors could appear. Through intermediaries—exhibitors, publicists, and independent camera operators—major producers made local shorts and exhibited them before their own products. Unlike the screen competitions of the mid-1910s, such as the national beauty contest Universal held in 1915 to promote the opening of their California studios, local films were not intended to promote the industry.[4] Instead, they were made to boost the box office returns of specific films and were seen as just one of many publicity stunts a studio could try in an effort to secure the loyalty of a skeptical exhibitor. Hollywood's interest in the local film was not as a vehicle for discovering new stars but, rather, proving that what one journalist called a "whiskered idea" still worked in the 1920s.[5]

In recounting this history, I rely heavily on the exhibitor trade press, which was particularly sensitive to the plight of small and independent exhibitors who made up a majority of their readership and ran most of the movie theaters in the small towns where local films were made. My focus on the exhibitor breaks from approaches to classical Hollywood centered on industry studies. For example, in her pioneering examination of the inner workings of the Hollywood studio system, Janet Staiger applies Alfred Chandler's analysis of the corporation to Tinseltown to argue that the industry was best understood as a top-down system in which producers determined industry operations, and lower-level employees were merely functionaries.[6] I instead concur with the business historian Olivier Zunz, who argues that the development of a management culture, which is transmitted from company headquarters to regional managers and local sales representatives, was equally important to the rise of the corporation as the dominant business form in the twentieth century. Zunz suggests that the new corporate culture destabilized local cultures, particularly in small towns and rural areas, and put in its place a "localized" culture that depended on national products and processes to thrive.[7] Small theater chain owners, promotional staff, and distributors were among the mid- and low-level managers who were familiar with the day-to-day operations of the theaters they oversaw, or, at the very least, tracked closely, and made decisions about how best to promote Hollywood products.[8]

In the late 1910s, the leading exhibitor trade publication, *Moving Picture World*, ran editorial after editorial about whether it was the "pictures" or the "presentation" that brought movies audiences back week after week.

Invariably, the *World*'s writers sided with exhibitors. For example, in a prose poem published in *Moving Picture World* in June 1917, Louis Reeves Harrison, one of the paper's more prolific writers and a frequent critic of motion picture quality, defended exhibitors against criticism by producers, noting that "No producer made our audiences / Those audiences have been recruited / From home life and from the family."[9] Eight months after publishing his ode to the exhibitor, Harrison took his praise a step further, suggesting that exhibitors were pioneers in the industry, "gradually evolving ideas and ideals which may compel a revolution in producing and distributing methods."[10]

In Harrison's account, which was echoed by many other *World* editorialists, exhibitors were the vanguard of the entertainment industry, embracing change and leaving the old ways of the live theater manager behind.[11] Instead of sticking with the old slogan "Give the People What They Want," Harrison suggested that exhibitors were shaping the public's taste for new and more adventurous films. In a period of immense economic pressure—with theater attendance down due to World War I, the war tax imposed on ticket sales to help pay for military operations, and, later in 1918, a flu epidemic that closed movie theaters nationwide for several months—exhibitors were portrayed in the trade press as both survivors and innovators. But they were not prepared for what came next—the formation of national theater chains and a vertically integrated industry that threatened to disrupt the intimate relationship exhibitors had with their patrons.[12]

Independents and Exploitation

Independent theater managers were, of course, no strangers to national film markets, and many were likely well versed in the expectations set for their houses by trade newspapers and guidebooks.[13] But several developments in the late 1910s alarmed exhibitors, particularly those in small towns who already felt besieged.[14] As Robert Sklar has noted, small-town theater managers changed their programs as often as three times a week so their regular customers would have something new to see, and their collective demand for new, high-quality films was such that it likely forced film companies to adopt a mass-production model.[15] In the spring of 1917, a group of theater chains, mostly based in large cities, formed the First National Exhibitors Circuit with plans to begin producing films. At the same time, both Famous Players-Lasky and Fox began experimenting with booking policies that allowed them to maximize returns on their own productions. In order to show the most popular films of the year, exhibitors had to agree to book a full slate of films, sight unseen, and were held to those contracts even if the films turned out to be duds. These developments threatened what independent exhibitors appeared to value most—the ability to select the films they felt would appeal to their customers.

But further changes were afoot, undermining even the area of expertise exhibitors believed was theirs and theirs alone—how best to sell the pictures to their customers. When Epes Winthrop Sargent started a column on film advertising in the *World* in September 1911, he saw it primarily as a venue for exhibitors to trade tips about how to design posters, programs, and publicity materials. After all, as writers in the *World* routinely argued, even if exhibitors could not control *which* films they screened, they could control *how* they were screened.[16] But in a special section devoted to motion picture publicity published in the *World* in July 1918, this conventional wisdom was upended. Newly appointed heads of publicity departments for major production companies criticized current exhibition practices, patiently explaining the purpose of the press books, halftone sheets, and advertising copy that they were now routinely supplying to exhibitors. Dwight S. Perrin, publicity director for Goldwyn Pictures Corporation, summarized producer views on exhibitors when he published this analysis in the *World* in 1918: "The average exhibitor of motion pictures feels contented with himself. He regards himself, without outside assistance, as being a good showman. He thinks that none of these men from New York or Chicago understand either him, his field or his particular house. He thinks that they know nothing of his public. He does not stop to measure his clientele on the yardstick of human nature. He does not admit that humanity measures up about the same regardless of geography."[17] Perrin's final claim—that all audiences were more or less alike, regardless of locality—quickly became a universal truth in the pages of the *World*. In September 1918, when the journal put out a call for "descriptions of 'stunts' or any showmanship ideas they may invent," the writers echoed Perrin's argument, noting that "an idea that will attract business in one town is likely to 'repeat' in another."[18]

The publicity stunt, or, as it was more commonly called in this period, "exploitation," was the key development in movie publicity in the late 1910s. Jane Gaines argues that the term evades definition, noting that its practice "can divert the attention of the onlooker, expand or contract to fit the occasion, and take the shape of the forms at hand."[19] Unlike the print methods of theater publicity—heralds, posters, newspaper advertisements—which were reproducible and thus easily adapted to the chain-store model of theater ownership, exploitation was rooted in performance and as such not easily described or disseminated. At the same time, its bombast gave it an outsized presence in *Moving Picture World*, particularly once national producer-distributors endorsed its use. As Gaines suggests, the shape-shifting capacities of exploitation "produces its own inflated reception simultaneously with its transmission."[20] As a result, exploitation became both a privileged form of publicity, one that theater managers might brag about and one whose reach and efficacy was difficult to prove.[21]

While Sargent's weekly column continued to circulate ideas about how exhibitors could best advertise pictures, "exploitation" experts affiliated with producer-owned exchanges began interjecting their own ideas about how a particular film was best advertised. In 1918, First National placed an advertisement in the October 19 issue of the *World* announcing a publicity contest for theater managers, who were asked to contribute their advertising ideas for *The Romance of Tarzan*, a sequel to the popular *Tarzan of the Apes*, made earlier that year. In the advertisement, the company revealed how little it knew about the theaters it was servicing:

> For the edification of the industry, as an illustration to other distributing agencies of the possibility for more intimate and practical cooperation with exhibitors by keeping all of them informed of what the comparative few are doing to attain consistent returns on their bookings, and for the particular benefit of those exhibitors who play features after they are ninety days old, and want a comprehensive illustration of how all earlier run accounts advertise and sell to the public, the First National Exhibitors' Circuit announces this contest, to be conducted with one specific release as a means of more accurately gauging the retail sales capacity of theatre variations in method according to house location, class of patronage, competition, and conditions generally affecting the box-office.[22]

In this advertisement, the company codified what had already been implied in trade publications for many years, that the purpose of such columns as Sargent's "Advertising for Exhibitors" was not to spotlight the creativity of exhibitors but to allow less resourceful exhibitors to borrow publicity ideas already in circulation. Even as First National executives sought to apply management theory to their newly acquired theaters—breaking them down into categories ("classes") and determining which publicity techniques were most successful in specific types of theaters—they also created a structure whereby individual exhibitors could experiment with publicity techniques, often in cooperation with regional publicity managers, and let others know about their successes.

The results of the First National contest were reported in March 1919. Sargent, characteristically, chose to spotlight the winning entry for "fourth class" theaters, those with fewer than 750 seats: L. L. Willey, manager of the Colonial Theatre in Rochester, New Hampshire. After noting Willey's print publicity campaign for *The Romance of Tarzan*, which included a half-page advertisement on the weekly newspaper's front page, Sargent described Willey's "Stunt Publicity" entry: "He wrote a prologue with a full scenic setting, for which he composed an original score. This used a man for Tarzan, some sailors, savages and a lion, tiger and ape, obtaining the costumes from a theatrical costumer. These players were paraded through the town with a band in addition to appearing in the prologue. The prologue even offered a rain effect with real water and calcium lights."[23] By showing that even a small theater could produce an exceptional advertising campaign, Sargent proposed that the local theater manager take on a new role. Instead of assembling picture programs and advertising campaigns for provincial tastes, the manager was instead responsible for promoting movies with the materials given to them by film producers. As a junior partner to the regional "exploitation manager," who in turn answered to the major film exchanges, the theater exhibitor was now fully part of a national system, rather than an independent owner or manager.

First National continued its efforts to redefine the exhibitor's role as the purveyor of both a standardized product and localized, but not local, advertising campaigns for that product. Just as exhibitors used screen contests to determine the type and intensity of movie fans, First National used advertising contests to find exhibitors who were particularly talented at promoting their films. In effect, company executives wanted to prove their conviction that the failure or success of a film was not due to its intrinsic quality, as exhibitors implied, but its publicity campaign. While holding to their belief that audiences everywhere were generally alike, advertising executives acknowledged that there were differences between small theaters and large theaters, first-run houses and those that operated on the margins. As C. L. Yearsley, the publicity director for First National, told *Moving Picture World* in April 1919: "There is little use in trying to create advertising that will appeal to everybody, everywhere, in the thought that all classes of showgoers can be attracted to every film that is screened. We aim here to have pictures of sufficient variety to appeal to all types of theatergoers and fit each picture with publicity helps and advertising copy that will appeal directly to the class of people whom we believe will be most interested."[24] Here Yearsley presented the central tension in First National's publicity campaigns: nationally coordinated campaigns were more efficient, but localized campaigns were more effective. As exhibitor Edward L. Hyman put it in 1920, a poorly managed theater would soon go bankrupt, but "when you turn the job of managing your house into a cut and dried proposition and lock out individuality and personality you are going to hit the down grade so fast that efficiency can't avert the smash-up."[25] For exhibitors in the early 1920s, the production of outstanding, original, and local publicity campaigns was the ticket to a successful theater.

Localizing the Movies

Two factors shaped the localization of the film experience in the late 1910s: trade paper advice to exhibitors and distributors' industry-wide creation of exploitation and publicity departments. First, the trade papers continued to be valuable sources of information about publicity techniques. Sargent's "Advertising for Exhibitors" column began including more ideas for publicity stunts in 1919, and as a result the column grew from its two- to three-page average throughout the 1910s to up to ten pages a week in 1920.[26] In March 1920, Sargent even changed the name of his column to "Advertising and Exploitation." Previously, exhibitors had referred to exploitation as "ballyhoo," extravagant publicity campaigns such as street parades and crowd-gathering performances, that were intended to draw people into the show. Because ballyhoo was associated with the circus and other "lower" forms of entertainment, some exhibitors preferred to use the term "exploitation" to raise the status of an effective, if expensive advertising technique.[27] In August of the same year, Sargent defended his decision to focus on exploitation, arguing, "Some few films are sold through interest in the star. The rest must be sold through locally created interest, intelligently aroused. The better the exploitation, the larger the receipts."[28] By investing so heavily in local publicity efforts, Sargent helped exhibitors, particularly independent and small-town theater managers, find a foothold in a rapidly changing industry in which each development seemed to strip away more of their autonomy.[29]

The second mechanism for the localization of the film experience did not occur through the trade papers but, rather, through the distribution arms of theater and motion picture conglomerates, which initially meant First National, Famous Players-Lasky, and Loew's. Studios invested in exploitation departments because standardizing publicity practices allowed them and their affiliated or wholly owned theaters to determine cost-effective ways to increase box office returns. Furthermore, by organizing exploitation departments that attended to the needs of local exhibitors, producer-distributors could secure their own revenue sources by persuading reluctant independent and small-town exhibitors that they would deliver the box office returns necessary for their long-term contracts to pay off. By establishing these departments in the late 1910s and early 1920s, studios also created a direct link to individual exhibitors. These departments had relatively small staffs. In August 1920, for example, Famous

Players-Lasky's exploitation department had just thirty field managers for twenty-eight exchanges, serving up to twenty thousand theaters.[30] However, these managers traveled constantly, so even small-town managers had the opportunity to make direct contact with a representative from the studio.[31]

While localization usually meant an advertising campaign tailored for particular audiences, in some cases exhibitors were also able to present the film itself as local. In January 1920, the Garden Theatre in downtown Baltimore promoted the Universal feature *Paid in Advance* by noting the hometown roots of the film's star, Dorothy Phillips. As *Moving Picture World* noted, "There is a certain amount of local pride which can be appealed to for a bigger clean-up than the play angle although the Garden by no means neglected to advertise the play as well; making it secondary to the star. This works so well that it even pays in a small place to boom a supporting player above the star; provided that the I-knew-him-when Club does not have too much material for reminiscence."[32] The next week, the *World* observed another way a film could be localized, this time by noting its location shooting. In New Orleans, the Trianon Theatre promoted the William S. Hart picture *John Petticoats* by printing a map of where key scenes were filmed. In the same article, which was printed in a special section titled "Proven Profitable Publicity Plans," a history of local motion pictures was published. Written with a breezy familiarity that marked much of the movie history printed in the trade press, the anonymous author observed, "Twenty-three years ago the Lumiere machines were thrown out of American theatres because they could only supply a limited number of local subjects while the Edison and Biograph companies offered nothing else. At no time in the interval has the charm of seeing your own neighborhood failed to draw, and the local angle is still the most powerful selling stunt. Because of the centralization of production not many cities can use the locally produced pictures."[33] This brief history, which suggests that the "local angle" was an enduring selling point for an exhibitor, signals what was to become a regular, if not commonplace, tactic of the studio-affiliated exploitation manager: the local film produced in association with a studio product. While the local film was not seen as novel, its proven success meant that exhibitors could be convinced that making hometown movies was worth the effort. By tying the local production to the promotion of a specific, nationally distributed motion picture, exhibitors once again used the "local" as a way to orient themselves, and their audiences, amid the dominance of the centralized film industry.

For the next several years, *Moving Picture World* printed numerous accounts of exhibitors teaming with exploitation departments to produce local films. In June 1920, Mildred Harris Chaplin, then in the middle of a high-profile divorce from Charlie Chaplin, traveled to San Francisco to witness a screen contest held at the Sun Theater on Market Street. As the *World* reported, "several hundred girls are competing for the honor of being selected to enter the company of Mildred Harris Chaplin at Los Angeles." Jack Laver, identified as a director for Chaplin, and Pliny Goodfriend, a cinematographer, ran the contest. The screen tests were shown in conjunction with Chaplin's latest film, *The Inferior Sex*.[34] The Australian actress Louise Lovely also produced local pictures in the early 1920s, first in the United States and Canada, and later back home in Australia.[35] In 1921, the *World* reported that a theater manager in Madison, Wisconsin, hired a local camera operator to take five hundred feet of film of local babies to publicize *Scrambled Wives*, which was distributed by First National.[36] Sargent advised, "Scout around and see if you can locate a news camera in your own or a nearby town. They are numerous these days, and there are several hundred titles the stunt will fit besides this First National."[37] In Sargent's view, the local film was most valuable because of its versatility, as any motion picture could be associated with audience desire to appear on screen. In fact, press accounts suggest that many of the local motion pictures made were advertised as "screen tests," which played into Hollywood studio and fan magazine discourses of the time.[38]

The Crossroads of New York

While most of the local films produced in association with Hollywood in the early 1920s were variations on the screen test or the local view, the exploitation campaign for Mack Sennett's *The Crossroads of New York* was considerably more ambitious—and likely contributed to the film's success in certain markets. A follow-up to Sennett's hit 1921 film *A Small Town Idol*, which stars Ben Turpin as a young man who goes to Hollywood to escape false charges of being a thief, *Crossroads* was originally intended to be a melodrama about a rural youth who travels to New York in search of a job with his rich uncle.[39] After early screenings were poorly received, Sennett reworked the film as a comedy, but his efforts were for naught as the film was still widely panned.[40]

Despite, or perhaps because of, unfavorable reviews, First National's exploitation staff put considerable effort into promoting the film, which premiered in New York on May 21, 1922, at the Capitol Theater, one of the city's flagship venues. According to the *World*, the summer of 1922 was a poor season for motion pictures, and, as Sargent noted in mid-July, exploitation was seen as the answer to exhibitors' woes.[41] First National itself was also in trouble due to the poor performance of its pictures and lost 20 percent of its sub-franchise holders between the fall of 1921 and the spring of 1923.⁴² In an effort to stem these losses, First National had started its own exploitation division just weeks before the *Crossroads* premiere, making the film an ideal test case for novel forms of publicity.

In June 1922, Joseph Goldberg, advertising manager of the Mary Anderson Theater in Louisville, Kentucky, devised a unique promotion for *The Crossroads of New York*—a local version of the First National release, including recreations of several key scenes that appeared in the film. As Goldberg told *Moving Picture World* in late July, "As soon as I saw the advance literature of 'The Crossroads of New York' it struck me that a 'Crossroads of Louisville' picture, to be run in conjunction with the Mack Sennett feature, would prove a good thing."⁴³ Goldberg enlisted Al Sobler, one of First National's exploitation representatives, and the local newspaper, the Louisville *Courier-Journal*, to participate in the production of a home talent film. Sobler was a former journalist and publicity man whose crowning achievement was the establishment of a Mark Twain anniversary celebration in order to promote the Fox film *A Connecticut Yankee in King Arthur's Court* (1921). Based in Louisville, he was one of twenty-nine First National representatives in the United States.⁴⁴ According to an article published in the *World* just before the *Crossroads* premiere, these representatives were "subject to the call of any exhibitors in putting over a First National attraction anywhere."⁴⁵ Ned Holmes, a former journalist who had experience as a publicity manager for a variety of entertainers—including Buffalo Bill and Jack Dempsey—led the organization, and most of his employees had similar backgrounds.⁴⁶

According to *Film Daily*, which glowingly reviewed Sobler's publicity stunt in August, Louisville had actually banned all forms of ballyhoo, so it was illegal for Sobler to use traditional forms of live publicity, such as a parade.⁴⁷ Eager to make a name for himself, Sobler realized that he could skirt the city's regulations by producing a film instead. He ordered eight hundred feet of film stock and convinced the International News Service camera operator to shoot the film in exchange for the newspaper publicity he would attract. Sobler wrote the film's script, which integrated local views into a narrative film. In a follow-up article, the *World*, this time crediting the idea to George A. Sine, the manager of the Mary Anderson Theater in Louisville, described the film's production in greater detail:

> Three men were picked for comedy leads, with others in the support, and for three days the scenes were shot in the busiest streets of the town while the ballyhoo-hating cops industriously pushed back the populace.

Figure 3.1. "Film Stunt Stirs All Louisville," *Exhibitors Trade Review*, July 29, 1922, 650

Then the paper came out with the announcement that, unknown to them, the crowds had been worked into some of the scenes, and there was a stampede for the M.A. [Mary Anderson Theater] to see who was in the picture. As a result an investment of $160 brought in so much money they had to raise the salary of the receiving teller in the bank where Sine makes his deposits.[48]

Sobler's success in both pulling off the stunt and circumventing laws against ballyhoo drew him considerable praise in the trade press. But the *World* downplayed the significance of the film itself, calling it a "revival of a whiskered idea" while noting that "if it still works there is no need to worry about its antiquity."[49]

Antiquated or not, the success of *The Crossroads of Louisville* prompted many imitators. Seven days after the Louisville film premiered, casting began in Kentucky for *The Crossroads of Lexington*.[50] As the *Lexington Herald* noted on June 30, 1922, "In addition to getting an unusual opportunity to break in the movie game via the Mack Sennett Company, those participating in the picture are having the time of their lives acting before the camera."[51] In August, First National ran a two-page advertisement in *Moving Picture World* on the success of the "exploitation stunt" for *Crossroads*, which included several photographs of the filming of *The Crossroads of Louisville* and *The Crossroads of Lexington*. While the ad did not explicitly mention that the stunt was a local film, it exhorted exhibitors to "Read How to Put It Over in Your Theatre and Clean Up" and noted that "Exhibitors Are Doing It All Over the Country." On the first page, the headlines from eleven newspaper articles were arranged in a collage, as if to suggest the quantity of publicity that resulted from the stunt, while the second page featured three photographs from the Kentucky films and a write-up in *Film Daily* praising the stunt.[52] First National's decision to place an advertisement on a local publicity campaign, rather than *The Crossroads of New York* itself, shows the importance of such campaigns to maintaining exhibitor interest in a motion picture long after it was first reviewed in the trade press, particularly if the film was perceived to be a flop. First National encouraged exhibitors to screen *Crossroads* not for its own merits but, instead, to see for themselves whether they could repeat the stunt in their own towns.

Several exhibitors saw the publicity around the Louisville film as an opportunity to make their own local motion pictures. For example, *The Crossroads of Cincinnati*, produced in July 1922, was intended to be a booster film for the city. According to *Reel Facts*, a Cincinnati-based exhibitor trade publication, the film "depicted the experiences of a man and his wife who had grown tired of the city and decided to look for a better place to live. When they reached the crossroads they were halted by the traffic cop, 'C. Vie Pryde,' who referred them to 'Cincinnatus,' the spirit of civic loyalty and the latter took them over the scenic detour, proving to them that there was much opportunity for pleasure and happiness in the old home town. In the end the couple decides to remain in the home town."[53] While *The Crossroads of New York* focused on the small-town resident who went to the city, *The Crossroads of Cincinnati* instead attempted to convince audiences never to leave their hometown. Like previous *Crossroads* movies, Cincinnati's version was to star several prominent people, including representatives from the chamber of commerce and the Underwriters' Salvage Corporation.[54]

Unlike itinerant filmmakers, who were accustomed to location shooting and tight production schedules, the greenhorn producers of *The Crossroads of Cincinnati* were unprepared to meet the challenges of shooting local pictures.[55] As the headline reads in a *Cincinnati Times-Star* article on the film's production problems, "We Learned about Movies from It":

> More terrible things—tragic things—happened than ever happened before to 1,000 feet of film. First the "soot" that, at a crucial moment, rained upon

the hero and heroine—photographed white! Undaunted, the scenario writer wrote a line showing WHY soot is white in Cincinnati. Next the most comical bit of comedy performed by the chief comedians—failed to record itself in the celluloid.

"We ran out of film at that point," explained the cameraman.

But worse than this was to come. Either as a result of the weather—or something else—came a day when the result of much "shooting" of scenes was nothing at all. The film melted.[56]

Although the film was eventually produced, the difficulties of production suggest that many theater managers may have chosen not to make local films because of the possibility of failure. While a poorly filmed scene in a local view or a screen-test reel could easily be excised from the finished product, the demands for continuity in narrative films meant that the exhibitor would have to reshoot scenes that were under- or overexposed. Tying a local film to a nationally distributed one meant that exhibitors had to finish their local pictures on a deadline determined by booking schedules, adding to their challenges. While the Cincinnati film fulfilled its ambition to "mimic Sennett," the trouble it gave its producers made it unlikely they would be hired to repeat their efforts.

After initial success in Louisville and Lexington, the news quickly turned for the worse for the *Crossroads* films. In July, a newspaper in Syracuse, New York, reported that their city "lacks comedy characters suitable for places in the movies from indications so far in the response to the call for amateur actors to be filmed for the 'The Crossroads of Syracuse.'"[57] In Watertown, New York, the paper called its *Crossroads* film, produced in August 1922, "disappointing," a view shared by former state senator George H. Cobb, who was then serving as the chairman of the New York State Motion Picture Commission. While Cobb did not object to the film's content, he told the local people that "the pictures are poorly represented," and that the "camera man did not make the best of his opportunities and many features that he should have presented were omitted and some of them were worthless."[58] Curiously, the scrapbook kept by Mack Sennett does not mention any additional local *Crossroads* pictures, but other versions continued to be produced. In Fort Wayne, Indiana, a local *Crossroads* picture was exhibited in September 1922.[59] In Iowa, *The Crossroads of Dubuque* was produced in March 1923.[60]

Trying out the Local Film

While the local films made for *Crossroads* exploitation received considerable attention in the trade press, it was not the only feature to be promoted with a local film in the early 1920s. In December 1922, the Regent Theatre in Paterson, New Jersey, held a "winking" contest in connection with the First National melodrama *East Is West*, which starred Constance Talmadge.[61] The *World* described the contest, which likely only featured women winkers, as follows: "Seventy-three pretty winkers, ranging in age from three to forty, winked twice before the Paterson News' special photographers, one a still photographer and the other a motion picture cameraman.... The special 'Winkers' reel was exposed Saturday, delivered Sunday afternoon, assembled Sunday night and shown for the first time at Monday's matinee. Opening with a shot of the city, it went through a scholastic exercise of winks from 73 people with a slow motion picture camera finishing the reel to show what the wink did to Paterson."[62] By playing off an element in the feature itself—Talmadge's winks—this exploitation competition tied the longstanding attraction of seeing oneself on screen to a specific publicity campaign. In January 1923, Jacob Fabian, the manager of the Regent Theater, published an essay in the *World* on the benefit of "welding exploitation into the program" and used his campaign for *East Is West* as an example. As Fabian, who pointed to his previous experience as the manager of a department store in order to demonstrate his familiarity with advertising practices, wrote, "Our own locally made wink reel, 1,000 feet long, got more laughs than the two-reel comedy. Nothing we have ever done attracted so many people to our theatre." According to Fabian, 22,000 votes were cast in the contest, which also attracted extensive newspaper publicity. Fabian revealed that he placed a "portable moving picture studio" on a truck, which allowed his exploitation staff to film local scenes as well as travel to various parts of Paterson to seek out the "cutest, the wisest, and the most effective winks."[63]

A month after Fabian reported on his success in Paterson, an exhibitor in Memphis, Tennessee, set up a studio in the foyer of the Loew's Palace Theater and filmed "winkers" after they paid admission to see *East Is West*. As the *World* noted, this variation was particularly clever due to the possibilities for multiple ticket sales:

> The urge to see oneself on the screen was just as potent as would be the winning of a prize, so nothing is lost and much is gained.
> And a lot of the posers came first to see Connie wink and absorb her technique so they could do it better—and that made a third admission.[64]

In contrast to earlier screen contests, the unnamed Memphis exhibitor did not feel the need to tie the screen test to the promise of a trip to Hollywood. Seeing oneself on screen proved to be a sufficient draw.

With the success of the *East Is West* campaigns duly noted in the trade press, other exhibitors continued to experiment with new modes of incorporating the local into national film publicity campaigns. In Atlanta, exhibitor Howard Price Kingsmore produced his own "home made trailer." Casting a local woman as the "Paramount Girl," Kingsmore filmed her presenting a card to Atlanta's mayor at city hall. After this shot, the viewer saw a close-up of the card itself, which announced the film, *A Gentleman of Leisure*.[65] According to the *World*, Kingsmore planned to create a series of trailers using the same concept. Other exhibitors used local films to promote the Goldwyn film *Souls for Sale*, including exhibitors in White Plains, New York; Butler, Pennsylvania; and Madison, Wisconsin.[66] In Indianapolis, Ace Berry used a local screen test to promote *Ashes of Vengeance*, starring Norma Talmadge, with the winner "put into the 'original' costume worn by Miss Talmadge and permitted to do some of the scenes in which the star appears alone."[67]

While the exploitation staff of First National appears to have been particularly fond of the local film as a publicity tool for their films, other studios also encouraged exhibitors to use the same technique. As mentioned above, Paramount and Goldywn supported the use of local pictures in publicity campaigns. Famous Players-Lasky suggested in the pressbook for the 1924 picture *Merton of the Movies* that it "might even be possible to take a picture of audiences as they enter your theater a couple of days before 'Merton' opens. Then 'See yourself on the screen here. . . . See how 'Merton' must have felt when he first saw himself in pictures.'"[68] The dozens of ideas listed in the typical pressbook indicated that local films were often suggested as a stunt. At the same time, the local film appeared to have been more viable in the mid-1920s, when a spike of interest in Hollywood stardom and a cycle of films about Hollywood encouraged their production.[69] While the screen-test competition continued to be used as a promotional technique in the late 1920s and 1930s, exploitation crews produced fewer films after the mid-1920s.[70] Jane Gaines suggests that by 1927 exploitation had fallen out of favor, as producers began to prefer national advertising campaigns.[71]

THE TROUBLE WITH MAKING LOCAL FILMS

While Hollywood studios could have used screen tests and other modes of local films more effectively in this period, several widely publicized scandals probably convinced studio executives that they should keep film fans far from Hollywoodland.[72] Unable to play their strongest card, exhibitors did their best to associate local films with Hollywood but could never deliver what at least some of their patrons really wanted—a chance to show off their acting skills in the movies. Hollywood's arms-length relationship with local film production reveals an uneasiness about the use of the means of production, so to speak, in the hometowns of their fans. When stunt publicity moved from the margins to the center of accepted promotional practices in the late 1910s, the tried-and-true trick of the "see yourself" movie was brought out as a cure for box office woes. And yet, the local film was never used systematically by any of the publicity and exploitation departments. As the case of the *Crossroads* local movies shows, even in the rare instance in which the publicity stunt was successful enough to get studio backing, exhibitors still had difficulty making it work in their towns. In many ways, the local film was like any other elaborate, hard-to-pull-off exploitation: spectacularly successful when it worked but an expensive, potentially damaging failure when it did not.

In the early 1920s, theater managers, often under the influence of the exploitation divisions of major film producers, saw the local film as one of many tactics that could help them publicize national releases. Ironically, their focus on tying local films to specific releases prevented them from embracing the most obvious appeal of being in a motion picture—the opportunity to see for oneself how movies were made and what it took to be a star. The people who gave motion picture audiences an inside view of the industry were not exhibitors, exploitation agents, or producers of films about the industry. Rather, it was itinerant filmmakers who claimed industry experience and demonstrated their ability to make a "Hollywood" film regardless of the resources at hand that brought Klieg lights and special effects to the masses.

Notes

1. "Boston Police on Trail of Self-Style 'Movie Scouts,'" *MPW*, October 6, 1922, 464.
2. "M.P.T.O.A. Tells Exhibitors to Beware Traveling Operators," *Exhibitors Herald*, September 17, 1921, 43.
3. Accounts of the bad effects of local films were not uncommon in this period. For one cautionary tale of a woman who ran away from home with an itinerant filmmaker, see Reeves and Trott, "Itinerant Filmmaking in Knoxville in the 1920s." In 1926, an individual came to Rushville, Indiana, to make a film, and absconded with $150 before production began. See "Decamps with $150 He Collected in Advance," *Daily Republican* (Rushville, Ind.), December 18, 1926, 1.
4. "Universal to Start Beauty Contest," *MPW*, April 10, 1915, 215.
5. "Home Talent Picture Gained Record Houses," *MPW*, August 5, 1922, 438.
6. See Janet Staiger, "The Hollywood Mode of Production to 1930," in Bordwell et al., eds., *The Classical Hollywood Cinema*, 94.
7. See Zunz, *Making America Corporate*, 8.

8. As Olivier Zunz writes of turn-of-the-century US business culture, "The silent corporate revolution that was taking place led the new generation of town elites to participate in the development of new knowledge, new professions, and new associations." Zunz, *Making America Corporate*, 33. Although he does not address the motion picture industry specifically, *Moving Picture World* and other trade publications, exhibitor conventions, and similar groups all fostered a sense of community among exhibitors that supplemented civic bonds. On the importance of fraternal and civic organizations in this period, see Kaufman, *For the Common Good?*

9. Louis Reeves Harrison, "Taken on Trust," *MPW*, June 16, 1917, 1758.

10. Louis Reeves Harrison, "Exhibitors in the Lead," *MPW*, February 9, 1918, 790.

11. On the subject of the cinema and live theater, see Pearson, "The Menace of the Movies."

12. As Ross Melnick and Andreas Fuchs note, the so-called picture palace era of the 1920s was also a period in which many independent exhibitors "feared for their very survival" against the competition from well-financed studio-owned theaters. See Melnick and Fuchs, *Cinema Treasures*, 46. For more on the small-town exhibitor, see Kathryn H. Fuller, "'You Can Have the Strand in Your Own Town': The Struggle between Urban and Small-Town Exhibition in the Picture Palace Era," in Waller, ed., *Moviegoing in America*, 88–99.

13. Hulfish, *Motion-Picture Work*; Sargent, *Picture Theatre Advertising*.

14. One overarching issue was the declining economic value of the independent theater to major producers, as the studio system that evolved in this period allowed film producers to draw most of their profits from big-city theaters that they owned or controlled. Douglas Gomery estimates that by 1926, half of all moviegoers in the United States attended 2,000 key theaters located in just 79 cities with populations over 100,000. The other half of moviegoers, attending one of an estimated 18,000 smaller theaters in suburban and rural areas, were often neglected as a result. See Gomery, *Shared Pleasures*, 57–66, and "The Picture Palace," 26.

15. Robert Sklar, Introduction, in Putnam, *Silent Screens*, 7–8. By the 1920s, Sklar notes, the average small-town theater demanded 150 films per year, while the urban picture palace could make do with just 25.

16. Harold B. Franklin, whose *Motion Picture Theatre Management* is often cited as a guide to exhibitor norms of the classical era, argued that exhibitors should distinguish themselves by their personality. In 1918, he wrote in the *World*, "A theater sells two things—entertainment and service. Give them choice entertainment and generous service. Make your theater wear a smile." See Franklin, "The Personality of a Theater as an Advertising Factor," *MPW*, July 20, 1918, 354.

17. Dwight S. Perrin, "What Can Advertising Accomplish?" *MPW*, July 20, 1918, 335.

18. *MPW*, September 7, 1918, 1401.

19. Gaines, "From Elephants to Lux Soap," 31.

20. Ibid. In his history of exploitation films, which focuses on sexually or otherwise salacious motion pictures, Eric Schaefer notes that "exploitation" as Gaines defines it was rarely used but the equivalent term "ballyhoo" was common. See Schaefer, *"Bold! Daring! Shocking! True!"* 117–135.

21. For more on exploitation departments, albeit from a different era in studio history, see Miller, "Promoting Movies in the Late 1930s."

22. *MPW*, October 19, 1918, 320.

23. *MPW*, March 1, 1919, 1179.

24. "Make an Audience for Every Picture," *MPW*, April 5, 1919, 79.

25. Edward L. Hyman, "Must Inject Personality into Your Theatre to Be Really Successful," *MPW*, February 14, 1920, 1102.

26. In the early 1910s, Sargent's column focused on print advertising and theater displays, which the theater manager had to prepare or assemble. Once producer-distributors began supplying predesigned newspaper display advertisements, Sargent turned to discussing other forms of advertising and publicity.

27. Fabrice Lybcza has argued that "ballyhoo" continued to be a viable term in the 1920s, but the practices he describes are very familiar to those discussed here. See Lybcza, "Fictions incarnées."

28. Epes Winthrop Sargent, "Why Exploitation Is a Necessity in Promotion Motion Pictures Properly," *MPW*, August 14, 1920, 907.

29. In late 1923, the *World* started another column, "With the Advertising Brains," written by Ben H. Grimm, which aspired to keep exhibitors "in intimate touch with 'the men at headquarters.'" *MPW*, September 22, 1923, 340.

30. Most estimates published in the 1920s assumed that there were twenty thousand theaters in the United States. See Halsey, Stuart & Co., "The Motion Picture Industry as a Basis for Bond Financing" (1927), reprinted in Balio, ed., *The American Film Industry*, 196.

31. "Meet Claud Saunders: He's Worth Knowing," *MPW*, August 14, 1920, 909.

32. *MPW*, January 3, 1920, 92.

33. *MPW*, January 10, 1920, 270.

34. *MPW*, June 19, 1920, 1614.

35. For more on Lovely, see Jeannette Delamoir's dissertation, "Louise Lovely."

36. *MPW*, July 23, 1921, 401.

37. Ibid.

38. See Orgeron, "'You Are Invited to Participate.'"

39. For a plot description of *Crossroads*, see *American Film Institute Catalog*, 156.

40. A fragment of *The Crossroads of New York* was found in 2010 at the Deutsche Kinemathek, which posted stills from the film as part of their "Lost Fragments" project. See https://www.lost-films.eu/identify/show/id/4402. *Variety* reported on the changes made to the film on May 26, 1922. See "Scrapbook: Crossroads of New York," MSC. For a full production history, see Sherk, *The Films of Mack Sennett*, 39. Many trade papers noted the film failed to match up against *A Small Town Idol*, which *MPW* called a "reviewers' paradise." June 3, 1922, 500. Fan magazines also criticized the film, with *Motion Picture Magazine* calling *Crossroad*'s plot "unadulterated nonsense." September 1922, 116.

41. *MPW*, July 15, 1922, 219.

42. Lewis, *The Motion Picture Industry*, 18–19.

43. "Ran Local Film to Exploit 'Crossroads of New York,'" *MPW*, July 29, 1922, 349. This article ran not in "Selling the Pictures to the Public," Sargent's exhibitor-focused column, but in the front news section, perhaps because the First National exploitation staff was involved in the film's production.

44. "Promotion Division Formed," *MPW*, May 20, 1922, 314.

45. "First National Exploitation Division Formed to Serve Exhibitors Everywhere," *MPW*, May 20, 1922, 313.

46. Ibid.

47. Advertisement, *MPW*, August 5, 1922, 403.

48. "Home Talent Picture Gained Record Houses," *MPW*, August 5, 1922, 438.

49. Ibid.

50. Gregory A. Waller also documents the production of *The Crossroads of Lexington*. See Waller, *Main Street Amusements*, 267–268.

51. "Work in 'Crossroads of Lexington' May Win Places with Mack Sennett's Company for Lexington Actor," *Lexington* (Ky.) *Herald*, June 30, 1922, MSC.

52. Advertisement, *MPW*, August 5, 1922, 402–403.

53. "The Crossroads of Cincinnati," *Reel Facts* (Cincinnati), July 19, 1922, MSC.

54. Ibid.

55. The article does not name the producers of the local picture, but they may have been representatives from First National rather than newsreel camera operators.

56. "We Learned about Movies from it," *Cincinnati Times-Star,* July 12, 1922, MSC.

57. "Movie Company Seek Comedy Players in Film," *Syracuse* (N.Y.) *Herald,* July 13, 1922, MSC.

58. "Crossroads of Watertown Disappointing," *Watertown* (N.Y.) *Standard,* August 16, 1922, MSC.

59. Advertisement, *News-Sentinel* (Fort Wayne, Ind.), September 2, 1922, 9.

60. "Crossroads of New York at Grand," *Dubuque* (Iowa) *Telegraph-Herald,* March 7, 1923, 5.

61. A print of *East Is West* was recently restored by Nederlands Filmmuseum. Elif Rongen-Kaynakçi, personal correspondence with the author, February 3, 2009.

62. "Unique Exploitation on 'East Is West,'" *MPW,* December 2, 1922, 428.

63. Jacob Fabian, "Wants Others to Profit by Plan That He Found Helpful," *MPW,* January 20, 1923, 224.

64. "Took Wink Contest Inside the Theatre," *MPW,* February 24, 1923, 784.

65. "Home Made Trailer Sells the Howard," *MPW,* September 8, 1923, 151.

66. In Madison, the film was publicized using a local screen test, which was particularly fitting given the film's star, Eleanor Boardman, had herself recently been "discovered" in a similar competition. In a full-page advertisement, which included ads from several department stores and a tire store, the theater noted that the theater would be visited by "Walter D. Nealand, director for the Goldwyn Pictures [who] is seeking 'new faces' and 'talent' for the movies." See *Wisconsin State Journal* (Madison), May 10, 1923, 7. In White Plains, manager C. A. Schauple produced a local film in association with *Souls for Sale* and, according to the *World,* made plans to start a local newsreel. See *MPW,* June 9, 1923, 470. In Butler, manager John C. Graham placed a camera on a truck and filmed in between heats of races at the county fair. See *MPW,* November 3, 1923, 135.

67. "Resemblance Contest Used Motion Picture," *MPW,* November 23, 1923, 395.

68. *Merton of the Movies* pressbook, September 9, 1924, Famous Players-Lasky, L 20550, Library of Congress, Washington, DC.

69. Between 1922 and 1924, film studios produced at least six feature films about Hollywood, including *Night Life in Hollywood* (1922), *Hollywood* (1923), *Souls for Sale* (1923), *The Extra Girl* (1923), *Mary of the Movies* (1923), and *Merton of the Movies* (1924).

70. For example, in 1932, Paramount launched a screen-test competition to find an actress to play the role of the "Panther Woman" in *The Island of the Lost Souls*. See "Film Company Seeks Movie Star in Southeastern Ohio," *Times Recorder* (Zanesville, Ohio), July 11, 1932, 1. See also Dan Streible's discussion of local *Our Gang* films in the late 1920s, in "Itinerant Filmmakers and Amateur Casts."

71. Gaines, "From Elephants to Lux Soap," 40.

72. See Stamp, "'It's a Long Way to Filmland.'" For more on the impact of the star scandals of the early 1920s on the industry and its fans, see Anderson, *Twilight of the Idols.*

4

ITINERANTS *ADOPT A BABY*
The Local Hollywood Film and the Operational Aesthetic

IN THE EARLY 1920S, JUST as the term "Hollywood" began to be used as a synecdoche for the movie industry as a whole, many itinerant filmmakers began associating themselves with the film industry in Los Angeles and then Hollywood itself.[1] While the motion picture industry was referred to by spatial metaphors throughout the 1910s—"Movieland" and "Filmland" were among the most popular terms—itinerant filmmakers were usually identified by the putative home of their production company, which in most cases was New York or Chicago, and was not of significant interest to their sponsors.[2] Instead, itinerant directors were often evaluated by their success in other cities, and many carried recommendation letters with them as confirmation.[3] Although itinerant filmmakers made fleeting references to actors and newsreel companies, sponsors focused on the local reception of the moving pictures they commissioned and the possibility, which grew dimmer with each passing year, that their film might receive national distribution.

When itinerants began to identify themselves as Hollywood directors, the effect was more than semantic. Itinerants emphasized their professional qualifications in press releases and interviews, suggesting ties, however tenuous or false, to well-known actors, directors, and production companies. Assistant directors to D. W. Griffith, employees of Selig Polyscope, and cameramen for Erich von Stroheim were among the many individuals who, if these itinerants are to be believed, decided to leave the movie colony for an uncertain life on the road. For skeptics of the inflated biographies of their crews, itinerant directors traveled with heavy, large, and presumably expensive equipment—cameras, lights, and, in the early 1930s, sound-recording technology that were of the same quality as those used in Hollywood. Furthermore, these directors recreated the social, cultural, and aesthetic forms of classical cinema. They held screen contests, staged special effects in the central business districts of the towns they visited, and sold themselves as educators who were in town to show people "how movies are made."

Considered in isolation, each of these developments would not be of much significance. As I have argued throughout this book, however, the local film is more a mode than a genre, a constellation of different technologies and networks that expressed themselves in unique and historically specific ways. The local film modes that were profitable, and produced most often, were ones that were easy to repeat, attractive to sponsors, and engaging to participatory audiences. The emergence of the Hollywood mode of the local film in the early 1920s was more than just a variation on the home talent productions, screen contests, and booster films of the previous decade. Instead, it helped bring about a new "horizon of expectations," to use Hans Robert Jauss's term, which transformed how audiences saw local movies and what they expected from them.[4]

Hollywood films were distinct from other modes of local film production, such as the home talent film and the municipal booster film, because their audience appeal rested in part on textual and extra-textual references to the motion picture industry. As a result, when audiences for Hollywood films saw themselves and places they recognized, they were encouraged to see these sights as if a professional director had filmed them. By performing as Hollywood directors, itinerant producers robbed the industry of some of its mystique, turning the screen test into just another film shoot and the special effect into easily explained camera tricks. At the same time, itinerants—almost always identified as *former* Hollywood directors—felt justified in critiquing the industry for trite storylines and poor acting. As a result, the Hollywood film, like the local films that were "tied in" with national releases as discussed in the previous chapter, absorbed some of the interest people had in entering the film industry, with the result of distancing local audiences from the national center of film production.[5]

Interstate *Adopts a Baby*

While there were scores of directors who worked in the Hollywood mode, including Melton Barker, Salvatore Cudia, and Louise Lovely, each of whom had varying degrees of actual industry experience, the directors associated with Interstate Film Producers were among the most active during the period in which the mode emerged. Between 1914, when the Chicago company made its first film in northern Indiana, and 1934, when the company ceased operations after its last working director, Don

Figure 4.1. Don Newland, right, with camera and audio recording equipment (n.d.).
Courtesy of Hellen Newland

O. Newland, retired from the road, Interstate made at least eighty films, almost all of which were slight variations of a single plot. But even though the company kept its plot, its directors readapted almost everything else about the production twice, first during the emergence of Hollywood in the early 1920s, and then for the sound era in the early 1930s. At least seven of the company's films, produced between 1926 and 1932, are extant.

Like many small film companies of the period, Interstate Film Producers' origins are murky. The earliest known reference to the company appears in July 1914, when a representative of the company traveled to Mishawaka, a small town in northern Indiana, to produce *Mishawaka Adopts a Baby*, the film title Interstate used almost exclusively for its films until 1923.[6] Although it is not certain whether Interstate was based in Chicago in the 1910s—city directories of the period list no company by that name, and there are no state incorporation records—its film production in the 1910s centered in the upper Midwest, mostly towns within 150 miles of Chicago.

While a number of individuals were associated with the company in the 1910s, including, intriguingly, two directors—Charles N. David and Ralph Phillips—who went on to work for the Chicago-based race film producer Ebony Films, it is unclear how the company was structured or who was in charge.[7] Based on local newspaper accounts of the company's productions in this period, it appears that Interstate's representatives tended to work in teams, with a director and cinematographer traveling together to produce the film. Most likely, the company was structured in a manner similar to the Superior Film Company in Des Moines, in which independent camera operators borrowed the company's materials, including professionally produced footage, such as a car chase scene or train wreck, that could easily be spliced into the film's narrative. Regardless, the absence of company records, extant films, and, with rare exception, newspaper accounts of Interstate's early years makes it difficult to locate clues about why its directors were able to manage the transition from producing home talent pictures to movies that could have been made in Hollywood.

Don Newland and the Hollywood Turn

While Don Newland was not the only director affiliated with Interstate to work in the 1920s, he quickly made it his company, producing at least fifty films over the next dozen years, and possibly many more. A Michigan native who had previously worked for the Magnet Feature Film Exchange in Chicago, Newland was first identified as a director with the company in early 1922, when he went to Kokomo, an industrial town in north-central Indiana, to make *Kokomo Adopts a Baby*, using the same film title as that used by Interstate's directors in the 1910s.[8] Like his predecessors, Newland produced the same narrative fiction comedy, but, unlike them, he expanded his geographic range to include the mid-Atlantic and South, and later added sound to his productions. More importantly, however, he broke from his predecessors by emphasizing that his films should be compared to those made in Hollywood, as he himself had experience in the movie industry.

While exploitation agents and theater managers struggled to produce local films that captured the Hollywood mystique, Newland proved to be a remarkably efficient and effective director of local films that matched the industry's bombast. He accomplished this by turning the very process of making a motion picture into a spectacle. Newspaper articles focused on every step of the production, from selecting the cast to staging shoots to developing and editing the finished product. Newland simultaneously directed motion pictures and performed as a director of motion pictures.

Here I focus on this latter aspect of Newland's practice, both as an entry point to the films themselves and as a way to emphasize the performative aspects of the local film. My analysis is informed by recent work on film exhibition by Robert C. Allen, Richard Maltby, and Paul S. Moore, which emphasizes the relationship between the eventfulness of an individual film's exhibition and the ordinary rhythms of everyday moviegoing.[9] Local films, like exploitation stunts, were intended to disrupt the routine of the movie experience. My inquiry focuses on the tactics Newland used to position himself as an emissary from Hollywood and to position his filmmaking practice as identical to those used in the movies audiences usually saw. My reading of Newland's performance is based primarily on newspaper articles written about his practice, which were numerous, as newspapers sponsored the production of his films, and repetitive, as he supplied much of the copy that was written about his films. Then, I turn to the relationship between Newland's performance as a director and the films he actually screened before audiences. Like some home talent pictures, Newland's films were hybrid productions, with title cards and some sequences reused in every film, while other scenes were shot anew for each town. But unlike the filmmakers behind previous productions, Newland made slight changes to his films over the twelve years he was an active filmmaker, adding, deleting, and altering scenes. Newland, it seems, grasped that the Hollywood genre formula of difference and repetition would work for local films, and he refined his filmmaking process to ensure that he could adapt to changes in the industry without losing the efficiencies he developed after years of practice.

A "Battery of Klieg Lights": The Operational Aesthetic at Work in the Hollywood Film

While there were aesthetic differences between the home talent films of the 1910s and Newland's Hollywood films, the primary distinction between the two was a bonus feature that Newland and similar directors added to their production—a demonstration of motion picture technology, most often described as an exhibition of "How Movies Are Made." For example, when Newland went to Elyria, Ohio, in late 1922 to film *Elyria Adopts a Baby*, he described his plans in this manner: "The film company will use the stage of the American theatre for making the 'interior' scenes. They convert the stage into a real movie studio. A powerful studio lighting system, special scenery, costumes, professional cameramen, director and all that goes to make up the fascinating process of 'big picture' making will be employed. The 'exterior' scenes for the comedy will be shot on the streets of Elyria. The public will be able to witness the making of both interior and exterior scenes thereby giving an idea 'How "Movies" are Made.'"[10]

In this passage, Newland took care to distinguish his work from those made by other itinerant filmmakers, particularly those home talent productions that were now being denigrated as amateurish.[11] In fact, Newland's promotional tactics borrowed from an earlier performance tradition, that of the "confidence man," whose hoaxes and frauds were a source of endless fascination and fear in the United States from the mid-nineteenth century forward. Karen Halttunen argues that the "confidence man," who connived naive young men into engaging in sinful behavior, was a contradictory figure, as his adoption of upper-class codes of behavior and dress made him indistinguishable from laudatory individuals, such as the characters in Horatio Alger's rags-to-riches novels.[12]

Likewise, itinerant producers of Hollywood films exaggerated, or lied about, their film background, even as they delivered what they promised. In his study of the preeminent confidence man of the nineteenth century, the showman P. T. Barnum, Neil Harris argues that Barnum's success as a promoter was due in part to his ability to generate controversy around the authenticity of his marvels without turning off those who become convinced that they were fakes. As Harris wrote, "Experiencing a complex hoax was pleasurable because of the competition between victim and hoaxer, each seeking to outmaneuver the other, to catch him off-balance and detect the critical weakness. . . . The opportunity to debate the *issue* of falsity, to discover how deception had been practiced, was even more exciting than the discovering of fraud itself."[13]

While Harris was most interested in understanding Barnum's success as a promoter, even when he took on an act that had failed for others, the term he developed to explain Barnum's appeal, the "operational aesthetic," has broader applications. By equating "beauty with information and technique," the operational aesthetic transfers some of the appeal of a medium,

Figure 4.2. Photograph of the production of *Durham's Hero* (1925), Alvin Talmage Parnell Photographs, David M. Rubenstein Rare Books and Manuscript Library, Duke University, Durham, N.C.

such as the motion picture, from its immediate experience, either being filmed or watching oneself on screen, to the circumstances of its production, distribution, and reception.[14] While one could read Newland's entire filmmaking practice as embodying an operational aesthetic or, to put it less kindly, a con game, four elements of his practice stand out: "special effects" to entice people to participate in his films; on-location and interior shooting to contrast between different modes of Hollywood filmmaking; exaggerated, and likely falsified, claims of professional experience; and a "star contest" to obscure, rather than democratize, casting decisions.

As we saw in the earlier discussion of home talent productions, audiences were particularly fascinated with "special effects" in the cinema, and filmmakers often announced the local production of such effects in advance so the scene's production could be witnessed by anyone who was interested in seeing how movies were made. One of the most discussed scenes Newland filmed was a car crash in the town's central business district, which served to amplify public interest in his film. The special effect was accomplished entirely in-camera, with Newland's cinematographer slow-cranking the camera, which was held upside down, as he moved the two cars in reverse. After a blast of smoke, the new cars are moved away and replaced with automobiles from the junkyard, giving the illusion that the earlier cars were destroyed. Despite the simplicity of this trick, Newland convinced newspapers, like one in Belvidere, Illinois, to boast of its novelty: "Spectators will have an opportunity to see how real comedy wrecks are staged as they do it in Hollywood. Trick photography can do some wonderful things and those in the crowd can see how the trick is done, how in the pictures they are made to see great accidents and yet nobody hurt. The trick is staged right there before their eyes."[15] Unlike the magician who performs a trick and then asks the audience to marvel at how it was done, itinerant filmmakers announced themselves by showing how professionals filmed a stock special effect scene well-known to film fans—a car crash, a rescue from a burning building, or a high-speed chase—and only later exhibited the filmed illusion to an audience who already knew how the trick was performed. For Newland, the special effect allowed him to establish his own credibility as a Hollywood director and simultaneously make the special effects themselves appear ordinary and easy to produce.

The operational aesthetic was also at play in Newland's discussion of film locations. The location shoot was, of course, intrinsic to the production of the local film, yet itinerant directors used it in very different ways. For the producers of booster films, locations were chosen to depict the town in its best light, while home talent filmmakers wanted locations that would be instantly recognizable to audiences. While Newland shot some of his scenes in well-known locations around town, he was most enthusiastic about his ability to shoot interior scenes, which were filmed on the stage of the movie theater before an audience, using equipment and props that Newland supplied. In each town, Newland told the newspaper that the "most interesting part of the picture making is the shooting of 'interior' studio scenes."[16] Newland's preference for interiors reveals an important shift in the function of the local film. By shooting in the movie theater, Newland associated his films with the glamor and universal appeal of the motion picture industry, not the places communities could recognize as their own.

By 1923, which coincided with a cycle of industry films that took Hollywood as their subject, itinerant directors also began identifying themselves with this semi-fictionalized film industry. In the early 1920s, Newland associated himself with the Interstate Film Producers of Los Angeles, even though it did not appear to have an office in that city and he continued to develop and edit his films in Chicago and New York.[17] By 1926,

Newland regularly gave newspapers a complete biography, including this one to the newspaper in Belvidere, Illinois: "Director Newland is a pioneer in the moving picture industry, having worked in the olden days with such stars as Mary Pickford, James Kirkwood, Flora Finch, Johnny Bunny and others when they were making one-reelers in a New York office building. Having worked as property man, electrician, studio manager and finally as director and recently having been connected with the famous Sennett, he has acquired considerable knowledge of beauty and screen types from his close connection with the beautiful Sennett bathing beauties."[18]

If Newland's autobiography is factual, the Vitagraph Company would have employed him by April 1915 (the date of Bunny's death), when Newland was eighteen. While Newland could have been working at Vitagraph in the mid-1910s, it seems highly unlikely.[19] Likewise, Newland's "connection" with Mack Sennett cannot be confirmed. Newland also made a habit of claiming that his cinematographers had previously been assistants to Erich von Stroheim.[20] But even if Newland and similar itinerant filmmakers were not the out-of-work Hollywood directors they claimed to be, their practice nonetheless depended on their affiliation with the industry. In interviews, Newland offered critiques of the movie industry, advice for aspiring actors, and praise for the beauty of the place where he was filming, which, he told the local paper, would make an excellent place for moviemaking if only they had as much as sunlight as they do in Los Angeles.

Newland also turned his claims of Hollywood expertise to his favor in another aspect of his film practice, the screen contest. While the screen contest was, as discussed earlier, by now a well-developed ploy to entice movie fans to participate in the cinema, itinerants like Newland began instead casting local people to play well-known character types or even specific stars. For example, when Newland produced a motion picture in Sandusky, Ohio, in early 1923, the local newspaper announced Newland's selection of the lead actor in this way: "Miss Beryl V. Starr, daughter of Mrs. Frances M. Starr, 1012 Fulton-st, stenographer in the office, of The Erie Food Products Co., E. Water-st, looks more like Miss Constance Talmadge, famous film actress, than any one of the other Sandusky girls bearing marked resemblance to the delightful 'Connie' and will take the part of 'Ethel,' the principal character in 'Sandusky's Hero,' the Sandusky movie, Director Newland of the Interstate Film Co., is here to make."[21]

Like previous star contests, the newspaper printed the full names and detailed information about the winner, which revealed the disconnect between the star the winner aspired to be and his or her current occupation. But unlike earlier screen competitions, which used a multiweek election conducted by the sponsoring newspaper to select the contestants, Newland chose his own cast. Soon after arriving in a town he placed a "Movie Application" in the local newspaper, which asked "girls" interested in appearing in the picture to submit their name, address, phone number, age, height, weight, complexion, and a "photograph if you have one" to Newland for his review.[22] While the star contests of the 1910s were conducted with a democratic spirit, with the winner being the entrant who received the most votes from moviegoers, Newland operated his contest according to the same mystifying logic of the Hollywood screen competitions of the period.

Like many confidence men, Newland's own story is difficult to tease out. He was not the first director for Interstate, and it is highly unlikely that he developed the publicity materials that made the company's Hollywood turn so successful. And yet, if one measures an itinerant's success by output, Newland is perhaps the most significant producer of local films in the 1920s, shooting dozens of pictures from New York to Florida, Wisconsin to North Carolina. In 1924, Newland employed Charles C. Fetty to be his cinematographer. Fetty, the cinematographer for the 1920 Alice Howell comedy *Lunatics in Politics*, is the only Newland employee whose experience in the film industry can be independently verified. Fetty worked with Newland in 1924 and 1925, leaving to start his own venture producing local films using the same script and production formula, titling his series *A Day in Hollywood*.[23] Newland ceased producing the *Adopts a Baby* series in the mid-1920s and turned to another series, *Hero*, which he made until the mid-1930s.[24]

Henpecked Husbands and Baby Ethels: The Aesthetics of the *Hero* Films

If Newland tried, with varying success, to update his performance as an out-of-work Hollywood director, the film he remade again and again remained surprisingly staid, holding over the same plot and stock characters from the *Adopts a Baby* films produced in the 1910s for his *Hero* series, which began in the early 1920s. Newland did change how he discussed the film over time. For example, while Interstate's directors in the 1910s described the film's plot as a "Mr. and Mrs. Bowser" story, a reference to the fictional bickering couple created by the humorist Charles Bertrand Lewis in the late nineteenth century, Newland instead told sponsors that he was making a "Mr. and Mrs. Sidney Drew" picture, after the series of films by the mid-1910s Vitagraph stars.[25] One of the earliest plot summaries appeared in 1916, when the *Alexandria Times-Tribune* in Indiana recounted the story of what appears to be a one-off, *Alexandria Adopts Twins, or Mr. and Mrs. Bowser*. The film opens with a scene at the household of Mr. and Mrs. Bowser, soon changed to Henpeck, a bickering older married couple. A letter arrives in the mail notifying the couple that they will soon by visited by twins—in other versions, just a single "baby"—who they are expected to adopt or, in later versions, care for while their parents are on vacation. The newspaper reprints the film's first gag as follows: "Bowser has the baby carriage all ready to meet them, thinking, of course, that they are babies and will be in care of the conductor. (Mrs. Bowser had thought so too). Such a chase as Lady Bowser is to have. For these are two good-looking young ladies that meet their uncle and as he is showing them the sights . . . Mrs. Bowser is informed of the perfidy of her husband and—immediately the chase is on."[26]

The "chase" of the film is emphasized in the description of *Alexandria Adopts Twins* and most of its successor films. Here, the chase is described as "Helen Holmes 'stuff,'" and its thrills are so moving that the writer claims that he or she is unable to describe them in words.[27] Although this early summary does not reveal the rest of the plot, the resolution of the chase runs as expected in the extant films. Mrs. Bowser realizes that the babies—later, just a single "Baby Ethel"—are in fact young women, and she forgives Mr. Bowser. From this skeleton of a plot, Newland added additional storylines and new characters in the early 1920s. In addition to Mr. and Mrs. Henpeck and Baby Ethel, Newland added two young men—Billy Brown, who serves first as Mr. Henpeck's accomplice and later wins Ethel's affections, and a "troublesome neighbor" who informs Mrs. Henpeck of her husband's imagined infidelity.[28] In later versions, Newland adds another young woman visitor, Katrinka, a "country cousin" who plays a comic role, and changes the troublesome neighbor character to "The Rival," a newspaper reporter who also pursues Ethel. In addition to giving Newland more roles to cast—a challenge for all producers of home talent pictures—the addition of a reporter signaled that Newland was turning to the local newspaper, not the movie theater, for sponsorship assistance. In fact, Newland added a second act to his *Hero* films, which he began making in 1923, in which the car crash climax sets the stage for the production of a newspaper article about the events that led up to the event. Only after the car crash is turned into a newspaper article can the film's third act begin, in which Billy Brown proposes to Baby Ethel and The Rival plays one last trick on Mr. Henpeck.

In order to underscore the interplay between the *Hero* films and Newland's use of the operational aesthetic to generate interest in them, it is helpful to look at two extant films and the press coverage they received. Both *Belvidere's Hero*, produced in Illinois in late March 1926, and *Janesville's Hero*, made in Wisconsin in early January 1927, were typical Newland productions of the period. Newland's publicity materials were placed effectively, with news of the film's production receiving multiple front-page articles. Newland also produced these films rather quickly, spending five days shooting the Belvidere film and just four in Janesville. For both films, he went back to a studio in Chicago to process and edit the movies, which took a full day, before returning to town to show the finished product for a three- or four-day run. Unlike his Hollywood counterparts, who found the home talent film a difficult stunt to pull off, Newland brought industry efficiency to his operations, taking just thirteen days to make the Belvidere film and fifteen to make the Janesville film, which may have been delayed because he did not work during the New Year's holiday.

While *Belvidere's Hero* and *Janesville's Hero* both received praise from their respective local newspapers and sponsors for giving audiences an opportunity to witness the production of a Hollywood motion picture, the surviving films offer a somewhat different lesson. For example, *Belvidere's Hero* opens not with an allusion to Hollywood but rather a paean to the newspaper, with the scrolling text noting that it is the "one institution in which ALL are interested, regardless of creed or condition."[29] While the newspaper articles about the film emphasize its affinity with Hollywood, this opening text suggests that the true purpose of the picture was to show how "one of the countless events that make up your daily newspaper" is put into print. Even though this opening credit does not appear in *Janesville's Hero*, a later sequence, which depicts the production of a newspaper, appears in both films, suggesting that Newland sold the film to newspapers as an opportunity for self-promotion.

For both versions, Newland began shooting at the local movie theater—the 845-seat Apollo Theater in Belvidere and the 500-seat Beverly Theater in Janesville—soon after he arrived in town, cementing the connection among the motion picture, Hollywood, and the theater where it would eventually be seen. Newland shot scenes in the movie theater for three consecutive nights, blocking off two hours each night. Newspaper advertisements noted that "Everybody Wants to See How Movies Are Made," and that an "Expert Director and Cameraman from Hollywood" would be on hand to show them how.[30] As suggested above, these interior scenes were critical to the film's success, as they allowed Newland to demonstrate his proficiency as a director and give audiences an opportunity to compare the picture's production to the finished project. While it is unclear from the newspaper articles when Newland shot particular scenes, there is some evidence suggesting that Newland largely shot in sequence, possibly to maintain audience interest in the picture as it was being made.

Following conventions of the period, each of the *Hero* films introduces its characters with title cards. While the title cards in *Belvidere's Hero* are just typed text, *Janesville Hero* uses highly stylized title cards with language to match. According to these title cards in the Janesville film, Mrs. Henpeck is "a loud-speaking mama with plenty of static and no interference," while Mr. Henpeck's "batteries are run down . . . and can't even listen in." The early interior scenes are overexposed and poorly framed, likely due to the difficulty of filming in a movie theater.³¹ The first significant plot event to take place is the arrival of a letter from a "college chum" now living in Cambridge, Massachusetts, who informs the Henpecks of Baby Ethel's impending arrival. In the letter, Mr. Henpeck's friend reminds him of Mr. Henpeck's earlier infatuation with Mrs. Henpeck. A medium shot of Mr. Henpeck scratching his head dissolves to one of him surrounded by young children, suggesting earlier, and now abandoned, plans for procreation.

The next scene opens with another title card, this time for The Rival, "a reporter with a nose for news and an eye for the girls." The shot that follows, of a young man sleeping in an office, was also filmed indoors, but in the newspaper's offices, not on the stage of the Beverly. On his editor's orders, The Rival leaves the office in search of a story. The next scene returns to the Henpeck narrative, with Mr. Henpeck pushing a carriage to meet Baby Ethel at the train station. While walking down one of the town's main thoroughfares, Mr. Henpeck meets Billy Brown. In the Belvidere film, the title card describes him as "the village cut-up and lady-killer," while the Janesville film instead notes that "what it takes to get shebas, he has *nothing else but*," using period slang for sexually attractive women, a reference to the Egyptomania of the period.

While Mr. Henpeck and Billy Brown are talking, an African American man also pushing a carriage enters the frame from the left. A close-up of an African American baby girl follows—intriguingly, the same shot is used in both films, as well as in *Wellston's Hero* (1932), a later film—and then a cut back to a shot of Mr. Henpeck and Brown that shows the baby's caretaker, possibly her father, leaving the carriage for Mr. Henpeck to accidentally take. Unaware of the baby in the carriage, Mr. Henpeck continues to the train station, where he meets The Rival, who is in search of news.

An iris shot shows the train arriving to the station. After a medium-shot of a woman in a fur coat stepping off the train car, a cut to a title card introduces Baby Ethel, "the cause of it all." Ethel hands Mr. Henpeck a letter of introduction confirming her identity, and the two leave The Rival and Billy Brown behind. They hear a sound and realize that there's a baby inside the carriage, who is once again shown in close-up. The Rival leaves Billy Brown to take care of the child, who is never again seen in the picture. This odd storyline is not mentioned in its press coverage, suggesting that Newland intended for it to surprise audiences who assumed they had witnessed the production of the entire film. Jacqueline Stewart argues that such "baby-switching" plots in transitional-era cinema challenged "traditional racial and gender roles" and, in effect, threatened "the stability of the white family and, by extension, the social order."[32] If marriage served a civic function in the municipal booster films of the 1910s, the *Hero* pictures suggest that marriage is merely palliative, unable to resolve sexual tensions and issues related to social reproduction. In fact, one could see the *Hero* films as being obsessed with the wrong kinds of babies—too many, in the case of a pair of sight gags that enclose the film; of the "wrong" race, as in this scene; and, in the case of "Baby" Ethel, not a baby at all.

The next scene takes place back in the Henpeck home, with a title card introducing yet another character, Katrinka, "a country flapper [who] visits auntie for the first time." The first shot of Katrinka, in a threadbare coat and checkered scarf, reveals the contrast between her and the sophisticated Ethel. Newland uses parallel editing to show Katrinka settling into the Henpeck home, while Mr. Henpeck takes Baby Ethel on a tour of town. Billy Brown sees the couple again and vows to win over Baby Ethel. He races to the Henpeck home, where he tells Mrs. Henpeck and Katrinka that Mr. Henpeck is "promenading around town with a strange woman." When Mrs. Henpeck and Billy Brown spot Mr. Henpeck and Baby Ethel, a chase commences, with Katrinka, who is wearing roller skates, serving as comic relief. Both odd couples get into automobiles to commence their chase in the countryside. For the Janesville version, Newland includes a curious sequence in which another character, Ezra Fetlock, described as "the inventor of skid chains and blow-out patches for balloon trousers," is introduced, followed by a close-up of him spitting tobacco at a dog. In the film credits, Newland identifies Fetlock as "Guess Who?" although the repetition of this sequence in other films suggests that this was another Newland gag, as audiences proved unable to guess the identity of a character who was played by a nonlocal.[33] For the car chase scene, Newland had his camera operator turn the crank slower, in order to produce the illusion of a high-speed chase. The chase circles back into town, at which point the most extravagant special effect in the film, a head-on collision between the cars driven by Mr. Henpeck and Billy Brown, is shown. The puff of smoke that appears was likely caused by some kind of explosive, but the wreck itself is rather anticlimactic. (See Moving Image 4.1.)

Mr. Henpeck leaves his automobile, and he and Baby Ethel attempt to escape on foot, but Mrs. Henpeck, Billy Brown, and Katrinka, still on roller skates, quickly catch up with the wayward couple. Once Mrs. Henpeck realizes that the "strange woman" is in fact Baby Ethel, she reconciles with Mr. Henpeck. The Henpecks presumably return home with their two houseguests, and the narrative focus shifts to the aftermath of the car wreck.

A scene at the car wreck reveals that an older man was hurt during the collision, and he is escorted away from the scene by two police officers. With a front-page story to write, The Rival heads back to the newspaper office. At this point, the film becomes an industrial, as it shows the mechanics of publishing a newspaper using linotype. Although Newland recycles the intertitles, the scenes of the newspaper production appear to be different for each film, an odd decision as only newspaper staff would likely be able to identify their machinery. While most of these shots are overexposed and ordinary, the scene in the Janesville film closes with a particularly compelling crowd scene. Instead of workers leaving a factory, Newland shows a dozen or more newsboys exiting the underground printing press via a flight of stairs onto a previously empty street, filling the space from below.

With the special edition of the newspaper out, the focus returns to the Henpecks. Billy Brown and The Rival are outside the Henpeck home, saying goodbye to Baby Ethel, when Mr. and Mrs. Henpeck and Katrinka come home. Mr. Henpeck picks up the just-delivered newspaper, which announces that the car wreck was a "scandal." Each town produced its own mockup newspaper, and the headlines are different in all extant films, suggesting that this was one place where Newland gave his sponsors creative input. Mr. Henpeck pledges revenge on the author of the damaging article. Several days pass. In the next shot, Billy Brown gives The Rival a trick cigar. Night falls, and The Rival visits the Henpeck home in hopes of seeing Baby Ethel. The Rival gives Mr. Henpeck the cigar and proceeds to court Baby Ethel. With parallel editing, Newland contrasts The Rival's romancing of Baby Ethel with the Henpeck's more tiresome life. Just after The Rival proposes to Baby Ethel, the trick cigar goes off, turning Mr. Henpeck's face black, a possible allusion to the earlier scene at the train station. Mr. Henpeck picks The Rival up by the shoulders and takes him outside, where Billy Brown is waiting for Baby Ethel. Mr. Henpack throws The Rival onto the street, and Billy Brown comes into the Henpeck home to propose to Baby Ethel, who accepts.

THE COMING OF SOUND AND *HUNTINGDON'S HERO*

Like many itinerant filmmakers, success was double-edged for Newland. Working at a frenetic pace for many years, he quickly ran out of the easiest and closest marks, and repeat visits to the same town were not received with the enthusiasm necessary to make his pictures a success. In 1923, just as Newland began producing his own films, another director of the *Adopts a Baby*, series had to assure residents of Huntington, Indiana, concerned they were being asked to remake a film produced in their community only four years earlier, that despite "having a few scenes somewhat similar, changes in scenes will be made and an entirely different plot is promised theater goers."[34] In addition, the *Hero* films sparked a slew of imitators, some of which were of markedly lower quality and cast disrepute on Newland's line of work. More obviously, Newland's own claims as a Hollywood director were undermined by his continual presence in small towns in the upper Midwest. For example, in 1928, Newland was described in an article in the *Wellsboro* (Penn.) *Agitator* as a "director from Hollywood," but went on to disclose that he was there as part of an area tour where he had or was planning to make local films in a half-dozen nearby towns.[35]

But Newland, like many other itinerants, did not give up when he seemingly exhausted the goodwill of his sponsors. Instead, he made the transition to sound, going back to the same city in Pennsylvania to produce a sound version of the same script. Although Newland's return to Wellsboro in late 1933 was not considered important enough to merit a front-page article, he promised audiences a new experience: "In this picture will be talking, singing and music, all produced by people that you know. Most of the interior or studio scenes will be made on the stage of the Arcadia theatre on the three days mentioned above. This will give the people of Tioga County an opportunity to see just how a talking picture is made. A motion picture sound studio will be set up on the stage with the director, cameraman, sound man and all the necessary equipment, including camera, microphones, recording apparatus involving a cost of $15,000, in actual operation."[36]

Newland's description of the film's production suggests an upgrade of his previous practice, rather than a rethinking of what might be possible in the sound era. Because he had already become accustomed to shooting interior shots, the sound transition was easier for him than it was for most itinerants. For the Wellsboro film, Newland added a scene with the 140 piece Wellsboro Boys' Band and employed a local orchestra for the film's musical selections, which itself was a way to bring local sounds back in the movie theater.[37] This time, Newland upgraded his resume, suggesting that he had spent the past five years working for Warner Brothers and Universal Pictures, and told the newspaper that *Wellsboro's Queen* would be "on a par with the average two-reel comedy that is shown on the screen of any theatre today."[38]

Huntingdon's Hero, filmed five months later, reveals the challenges Newland faced with sound.[39] Like *Janesville's Hero*, the first scene is inside the Henpeck household, only this time Mr. Henpeck, who is played by the mayor of Huntingdon, is sleeping and can be heard snoring. Although these scenes are not overexposed, the camera movement is unsteady, and there are frequent jump-cuts to mask flubbed lines. Two new characters are introduced in this scene, Mr. Henpeck's nieces, who happen to be musicians. Like many early sound films, musical numbers run throughout the film, perhaps to both call attention to the technology and mask any problems with synchronization.

Although the plot of *Huntingdon's Hero* is very similar to Newland's silent version, sound allows him to eliminate some shots, like the close-up of the letter Mr. Henpeck receives from Baby Ethel's parents. In addition, Newland abandons some of the visual gags of the earlier *Hero*, such as the dissolve showing the Henpecks surrounded by children. The sound is synchronous and was recorded on location, so street noises, birdsongs, and other aural debris fill up the film's soundtrack. At the same time, Newland declines to shoot what might be the loudest scenes, such as the arrival of the train carrying Baby Ethel. While the train is not heard or seen at the station, the whistle is heard when Billy Brown informs Mrs. Henpeck that her husband has been seen around town with a strange woman, suggesting either fortuitous timing or Newland's attempt to aurally match the train's arrival with Mr. Henpeck's trip around town with Baby Ethel. *Huntingdon's Hero* also contains more medium shots and longer takes than the silent version, allowing for patches of silence between the scripted and poorly delivered dialogue.

The central tension between the technological limits of sound film and the silent-era plot of the *Hero* films is realized in the chase scene. When Mr. Henpeck and Baby Ethel search for a getaway car, they have to talk to a car salesman first, who gives a twenty-second sales pitch before allowing the wayward couple to make their escape. The chase scene itself, including the car wreck at the end, is almost a shot-by-shot remake of the silent version, turning what was previously the picture's special effect into a relic. Instead of expressing marvel at the effect, the crowd gathered to witness the filming of the wreck can be heard laughing.

The next scenes proceed in much the same order as the *Janesville* film, but some jokes, like Henpeck's trick cigar, do not work in the same way, given the absence of the subplot of the abandoned African American baby. In the cleverest scene in the film, Billy Brown goes to turn on the radio just when the station is broadcasting a song dedication to Baby Ethel. The camera pans from the couch to the radio and then sweeps across the stage to a shot of the announcer's face, connecting these two separate spaces through the radio sound. The camera then swish pans back to Billy Brown, who sings to Baby Ethel. In this way, the Henpeck home becomes one with the radio studio, both of which are in fact the movie theater where *Huntingdon's Hero* is being filmed. In this long take, the camera pans from the couple to the orchestra and back again, in a move that seemingly mimics those used in Busby Berkeley musicals of the period.

While *Janesville's Hero* closes with the engagement of Billy and Ethel, *Belvidere's Hero* and *Huntingdon's Hero* continue for several more scenes, which, as a title card notes, occur several years later.[40] Billy and Ethel are walking down a street at night, followed by a little girl. Like the visual gag in the silent *Hero*, more and more children appear in the Huntingdon film, with the camera eventually revealing the sign for an orphanage. In the background one can hear someone, perhaps Newland himself, encouraging the children to "wrap it up" and exhorting them to move "faster" so the scene can conclude. By adding sound Newland also leaves subtle traces of its production in the picture itself, turning the "gasp of recognition" Tom Gunning wished to recover from local pictures into a quite audible plea to keep the film under budget.[41]

Huntingdon's Hero closes with a local view, only this time the audience is filmed from the stage of the movie theater itself, so they will, as Newland tells them in the film, "be able to see yourself sitting down there, up here, and down there." By producing a local view in a movie theater, Newland unwittingly strips the local film of much of its value. The seated audience could not approach the camera, and the unmarked space of the theater did not have any distinguishing characteristics that created much of the interest in local motion pictures. By filming the audience in the movie theater, the same place where much of *Huntingdon's Hero* was shot, Newland suggested that the "local" was only interesting in as much as it was connected with the presence of Hollywood culture in small towns.

Everyone Can Be a Star

While Newland was one of the most prominent itinerants in the 1920s, he had many rivals, all working in much the same manner but developing their own distinctive characteristics. For example, Salvatore Cudia, a Sicilian immigrant who worked in the New York film industry, announced his arrival to town by setting a fire in an abandoned building, for which actual firemen were called, and proceeded to shoot a rescue scene, which formed the centerpiece of the film.⁴² Cudia produced many films in the mid-Atlantic, including a sound film shot of the African American community in Baltimore in 1934.⁴³

Melton Barker, who began producing his series *The Kidnapper's Foils* in the early 1930s, claimed to have discovered the child star George "Spanky" McFarland of Hal Roach's *Our Gang* series.⁴⁴ Unlike Newland, Barker used his casting process as a revenue stream, with families paying a few dollars in order for their children to audition for the film. In the film, local thugs kidnap a young girl, Betty Davis, after her birthday party. Several child-only search parties form to try to find Davis. After a few days, the search parties join together, and finally Davis's call for help is heard. Once she is rescued, the children celebrate, and song and dance performances were often included in the film.⁴⁵ Barker produced local *Kidnapper's Foils* productions for more than four decades, from the early 1930s to the late 1970s, and film historian and archivist Caroline Frick has located documentation of 280 productions to date.⁴⁶

While Hollywood had limited success making local movies, the local Hollywood film, on the other hand, was much hardier. Unlike exploitation managers, itinerant filmmakers were particularly good at addressing the difficulties of shooting on location. Refining the formulas used by their predecessors, they were able to replicate the special effects, narrative conventions, and acting styles associated with classical cinema. Itinerants began claiming Hollywood origins precisely at the time that the major studios had won control of almost all of American cinema. Working at the margins of both production and exhibition, itinerant filmmakers gave those interested in seeing themselves in the movies their chance on the silver screen.

Notes

1. For an extensive history of Hollywood—the city, the real-estate development, the sign, and its cultural symbolism—see Braudy, *The Hollywood Sign*.
2. See Bean, "The Imagination of Early Hollywood."
3. For example, Paragon's O. W. Lamb, discussed in chapter 1, reprinted excerpts of such letters in his company's brochure. See PPIE, carton 58, folder 21.
4. Jauss, "Literary History as a Challenge to Literary Theory."
5. For more on the relationship between movie fans and Hollywood, see Morey, *Hollywood Outsiders*. While Anne Morey is also interested in how "film cultures were shaped by forces outside Hollywood" (3), her approach emphasizes national, if still marginal, enterprises, such as the Palmer Photoplay Corporation, which offered screenwriting courses to movie hopefuls.
6. "Film Man Here to Make 'Movie' of Mishakawa," *South Bend* (Ind.) *News-Times*, July 14, 1914, 10.

7. David listed his association with the company in the 1916, 1917, and 1918 editions of the *Motion Picture Studio Directory and Trade Annual*, published by *Motion Picture News*. In the 1920 and 1921 editions of the same publication, he claimed to have founded the company. See *Motion Picture Studio Directory and Trade Annual* (New York: Motion Picture News, 1920), 297.

8. Newland's previous employer was listed on his World War I draft card, which he filled out on June 5, 1918. Newland's name appears in a newspaper advertisement in the *Kokomo* (Ind.) *Daily Tribune*, January 14, 1922, 10.

9. For an excellent introduction to this shift in cinema historiography, see Richard Maltby, "New Cinema Histories," in Maltby et al., eds., *Explorations in New Cinema History*, 3–40.

10. "Elyria People to Take Part in Movie Here This Week," *Chronicle-Telegram* (Elyria, Ohio), December 4, 1922, 8.

11. See "'Cumberland Hero' to Be Filmed in This City Next Week," *Cumberland* (Md.) *Evening Times*, August 9, 1923, 9. The article leads by noting that Cumberland is "taking another fling at the home-talent movies," after a motion picture made earlier in the year failed to meet audience expectations.

12. See Halttunen, *Confidence Men and Painted Women*.

13. Harris, *Humbug*, 77.

14. See ibid., 57, for Harris's definition of the "operational aesthetic." Several film historians have used this term to describe cinema attractions. Charles Musser sees an operational aesthetic at work in the performance of a variety of technologies in the nineteenth century, including the cinema, while Tom Gunning has argued that silent film comedy of the 1920s relied on gags about the operation of machinery. My use of the term is somewhat different, as audience fascination was not with the operation of the camera itself but rather the operation of the multiple technologies—lighting equipment, scenery, and, later, sound-recording equipment—necessary to reproduce both the experience of witnessing the production of a Hollywood film and, later, the film itself. See Musser and Nelson, *The Emergence of Cinema*, 135, and Gunning, "Crazy Machines in the Garden of Forking Paths."

15. "Full Cast Is Made-Up; Will Start on Film This Afternoon," *Belvidere* (Ill.) *Daily Republican*, March 25, 1926, 8.

16. *Steubenville* (Ohio) *Herald-Star*, February 16, 1923, 1.

17. The company does not appear in the 1923 Los Angeles City Directory, for example. See *Los Angeles City Directory* (Los Angeles: Los Angeles Directory Company, 1923).

18. "To Name Girl Who Will Star in 'Belvidere's Hero' Picture," *Belvidere* (Ill.) *Daily Republican*, March 24, 1926, 8.

19. For example, Newland's name is not listed in Paolo Cherchi Usai's filmography *Vitagraph Co. of America*.

20. "Who'll Be Lucky Girl to Star in Janesville Movie?" *Janesville* (Wis.) *Daily Gazette*, December 28, 1926, 5.

21. "Miss Starr Is Chosen for Leading Rose in 'Sandusky Hero' Movie," *Sandusky* (Ohio) *Register*, March 1, 1923, 1.

22. *The Toledo News-Bee*, November 2, 1925, 2. In other towns, Newland did not specify the gender of applicants. See "Movie Stars Wanted," *Chronicle-Telegram* (Elyria, Ohio), December 4, 1922, 8.

23. Another company, Globe Films of New York, also copied Interstate's model in 1925, producing an *Adopts a Baby* film in New Castle, Pennsylvania. See "'New Castle Adopts a Baby,' The Capitol's Made in New Castle Photoplay Completed and Will Be Shown at the Capitol All Next Week," *New Castle* (Penn.) *News*, August 21, 1925, 16.

24. Newland also made a film titled *Wellsboro's Queen*, discussed below, and *Mamma's Choice* in 1928. See "Local Movie Is Great Success," *Morning Herald* (Gloversville, N.Y.),

March 27, 1928, 1. But the *Hero* film was produced far more often than these titles. In the late 1920s, Newland had changed the name of his company from Interstate Film Producers to Consolidated Film Producers.

25. "'Cumberland Hero' to Be Filmed in This City Next Week."

26. "Picture to Show Some Home Folks," *Alexandria* (Ind.) *Times-Tribune*, July 15, 1916, 1.

27. To wit, "It's screen stuff and even paper goes right through it, can't be described except as you SEE it." Ibid.

28. For a reference to a "troublesome neighbor," see "Miss Starr Is Chosen for Leading Role in 'Sandusky Hero' Movie."

29. The same sequence appears in *Wellston's Hero* (1932), one of the last silent films made by Newland.

30. Advertisement, *Janesville* (Wis.) *Gazette*, January 3, 1927, 4.

31. Alternately, the poor framing of select scenes in the film could have been introduced when it was reduced to 16mm.

32. See Stewart, *Migrating to the Movies*, 84.

33. "Alton's Hero to Close Run at Grand Tonight," *Alton* (Ill.) *Evening Telegraph*, July 21, 1926, 3.

34. "Will Start Work on Movie Today," *Huntington* (Ind.) *Press*, February 1, 1923, 3.

35. "Mr. Newland Interviewed," *Wellsboro* (Penn.) *Agitator*, February 1, 1928, 1.

36. "Make Movie in Wellsboro," *Wellsboro* (Penn.) *Agitator*, December 13, 1933, 6.

37. While Donald Crafton has argued that sound production was standardized by 1931, Gregory A. Waller has more recently shown that as many as a third of movie theaters had not upgraded to sound by 1933. See Crafton, *The Talkies*, 4, and Waller, "Robert Southard and the History of Traveling Film Exhibition," 8.

38. "Make Movie in Wellsboro."

39. Nathan Wagoner, a film instructor at Juniata College in Huntingdon, rediscovered *Huntingdon's Hero* in 2000. See Wagoner, "The *Huntingdon's Hero* Story."

40. Of course, it is possible that this closing scene in the Janesville film was lost.

41. Gunning, "Pictures of Crowd Splendour," 53.

42. See "To Shoot Big Fire Scene," *Washington* (N.J.) *Star*, November 26, 1925, 1.

43. "Aspirants for Movie Career to Get Chance," *Afro-American* (Baltimore), July 7, 1934, 3.

44. Frick, "Jackrabbit Genius," 9. While Caroline Frick has not been able to confirm that Barker "discovered" McFarland, he did know the child star, and there is substantial photographic and newspaper documentation of their association.

45. Texas Archive of the Moving Image, "About 'The Kidnappers Foil,'" http://www.meltonbarker.com/kidnappersfoil.html.

46. Frick, "Jackrabbit Genius," 13. Barker started his career with Hugh V. Jamieson, discussed in chapter 2, and even revived Jamieson's *Won from the Flames* series in the early 1920s.

5

KIDNAPPING THE *MOVIE QUEEN*
Amateur Aesthetics as Cultural Critique

IN THE SUMMER OF 1927, Marion Gleason, a member of the Rochester, New York, Community Players, spent several weeks directing a troupe of "Part Time Pickfords and Vacation Valentinos" in an amateur production.[1] The motion picture that resulted, *Fly Low Jack and the Game*, had the backing of Rochester's leading company, Kodak, who saw it as an opportunity to prove that its new 16mm amateur-gauge movie camera, the Cine-Kodak Model B, was as easy to use as its still cameras.[2] Produced with the assistance of Kodak employees and screened initially in a private home, the picture was a great success. Soon after its completion, Kodak arranged for it to be shown at the University of Rochester's Little Theater and, according to company publicity, more than 150 cities throughout the United States.[3] One of the cinematographers, Harry Tuttle, produced a local newsreel at many of the stops, giving audiences a first look at the potential of a camera that would make it almost as easy to shoot movies as it was to watch them.[4]

While one would expect that the birthplace of the amateur movie industry would also be an early production center, Kodak's decision to roadshow *Fly Low Jack*, a parody of Hollywood adventure films, was at odds with the company's strategy of encouraging consumers to use its 16mm equipment to make home movies. In addition, the local films Kodak made as part of this campaign suggested a commercial and theatrical application for a technology that the company might have foreseen but did not emphasize in the 1920s. While Kodak promoted many possibilities for its amateur-gauge cameras and projectors—from personal moving image libraries in every home to the production of community dramas and family portraits—creating local films for public exhibition was not on their list.[5]

In this chapter, I consider the impact 16mm, and the amateur and nontheatrical industry it enabled, had on the production and theatrical exhibition of local movies between 1923, when the gauge was standardized, and

1941, when the United States entered the Second World War and amateur film production was curtailed. Even though Kodak successfully branded 16mm as an "amateur" gauge, one that was unsuitable for theatrical exhibition, a new generation of filmmakers began using 16mm to produce and show local pictures independent of the movie industry that serviced Hollywood. Some were home movie enthusiasts in search of larger audiences for their work. Others were small-town theater owners who seized the opportunity to produce local newsreels. And, still others were traveling moviemakers who reinvigorated the field of local film production. The itinerant field became more inclusive in the 1930s, with greater participation from racial minority groups, women, and members of the working class, and local films became more widespread, with mill villages, hamlets, and rural outposts joining small towns and cities as sites suitable for production. This growth and dispersal of local film practices occurred as home movies remained the province of the upper middle class until after World War II, in part due to the expense of camera equipment.[6] But for the generous budgets of itinerant filmmakers, 16mm stock was more affordable than 35mm, allowing them to shoot more footage than their predecessors. While what I call small-gauge itinerants did not attempt to record synchronous sound for their productions, the introduction of Kodachrome in 1935 gave them the opportunity to shoot movies in color when it was still a novelty for Hollywood features.[7]

Despite the promise of 16mm, its popularity among itinerants in the 1930s had very little impact on the dominant modes of production described in the previous chapters. In fact, the rush of new entrants to moviemaking meant that many rediscovered the local view, non-narrative, and nonfiction pictures that had more in common with early cinema than Hollywood. What did change, however, was how filmmakers related to their subjects, and what expectations both had for their participation in a motion picture shot using technology that, in other contexts, would be treated as a home movie or amateur production. Working in a smaller gauge allowed itinerants to be more nimble than those who stuck with larger cameras and higher budgets. They could reasonably claim to shoot everyone in town and worked in a looser, more improvisational style than was the case for their more rigid 35mm counterparts, who stuck to scripted narratives to keep costs under control.

But these small-gauge itinerants also carried the burden of associating themselves with professional, not amateur, moviemaking. Cameras were designed for ease of use, not replicating the look of classical Hollywood, effectively closing certain aesthetic choices off to all but the most determined filmmakers. Rather than running their films through the projector in the booth, small gauge itinerants had to supply their own, and often ran it in the theater itself in order to ensure the image was bright enough to be seen. Before the introduction of the semiprofessional Cine-Kodak Special in 1933, even the cameras were small and simple, making it hard for filmmakers to mimic Hollywood when they were in town. At the same time, the arrival of 16mm also enabled companies to develop new, often exploitative business models, as the ease of making a film meant that professional camera operators were no longer required. Although improved transportation networks made it easier than ever to travel from one place to the next, and loosened social and cultural restraints made it possible for many more people, including women, to consider a life on the road, making local films continued to be a difficult enterprise, particularly for those directors who desired to match Hollywood's bravado.

While most of these *nouveau* itinerants accepted their lot by shooting scenes of everyday life, the women directors of the Amateur Theatre Guild saw in amateur culture and technology the opportunity to explore professional identities. Unlike other directors, these women were more than filmmakers. Trained as producers of commercial "home talent" plays, they were expected to assemble their productions from scratch, doing everything from fundraising to casting actors to acquiring costumes, props, and scenery to directing a three-act play, a fashion show, and a multireel film, all in the space of three weeks. As Angeline Howlett, one of many guild directors under contract in the 1930s, noted of her role in the process, "She Is the Show," the instigator of the entire event.[8]

Even though 16mm expanded, rather than redefined, the local film, the versatility of small-gauge cameras allowed new entrants to the field to explore how moving images could depict and challenge social and cultural structures. For the directors of the Amateur Theatre Guild's best-known production, a Hollywood farce titled *Movie Queen*, the play and film together served as a site where they could negotiate their own complicated relationships with the movie industry. The play's narrative of a naive young woman who gets swept up in the sinister machinations of a male-dominated industry mirrored the experiences of many *Movie Queen* directors, who were misled into thinking that their positions would give them more autonomy than they were actually granted. At the same time, the third act of *Movie Queen* voiced a feminist critique of Hollywood in which a movie queen ("Marlena Slarbo") and a hometown heroine ("Mary Brown") outwit male agents and studio executives and make off with fame and fortune. But it was in the movies themselves, which served as a fourth act to complete the story, that we can find evidence of the guild's directors using amateur equipment to make their sharpest critiques of Hollywood style and culture. While the local film performed many functions in the 1930s, from ethnography to documentary to publicity, it also took on the role of giving people who had grown weary of Hollywood an opportunity to mock the movies.

Hollywood Comes to Hohokus: Amateur Film and the Rejection of Professionalism

One of the key reasons the local film retained its appeal well into the twentieth century was that most people did not have the opportunity to see moving images of themselves on a regular basis. Early experiments with manufacturing and selling amateur film production equipment to the masses were unsuccessful, particularly in the United States.[9] While audiences quickly acclimated to a moving image culture, for the first fifty years of cinema, seeing images of oneself was such an uncommon event that even avid moviegoers could conceivably go years without watching themselves on screen. In the late 1910s, fan magazines wrote of the magical properties of the movie camera, which could reveal a "screen personality" invisible to the naked eye with just a few turns of the crank.[10] Itinerant filmmakers took advantage of this desire for being on camera, but the logistics and economic structure of their business meant that they could not meet the demand for local movies. But in 1923, the same year when Hollywood solidified its hold on the popular imagination as the center of the movie industry, Eastman Kodak released its first 16mm camera, designed to give anyone, of means, a chance to make or star in their own movies.

Hollywood and what came to be called "home movies," however, grew further apart in the 1920s and 1930s. Even after an amateur film market developed in the United States in the mid-1920s, its chief promoters sought to keep it far from the movie colony. Kodak set the tone by defining its cameras and projectors as parallel technologies to those used in its profitable still photography business, which privileged ease of use and depictions of domestic life. As early as March 1924, one of the company's publications alerted potential customers that for its home movies, "you press the button, we do the rest," reusing the slogan that originated with its first Kodak camera in 1888 and effectively created the field of amateur photography.[11] Home movies were intended to be shot and shown in domestic environments, and for the next decade Kodak did little to pursue professional users. Early projector bulbs were too dim to shed sufficient light in even a small theater, and early cameras were fairly unsophisticated.[12] When the Amateur Cinema League (ACL), an association of moviemaking enthusiasts, was founded in 1926, its members made a full-throated defense of amateurism, recalling its Latin cognate, *amator,* or lover, as the very opposite of the crass, profit-driven commercialism that dominated the professional studios in Los Angeles and elsewhere.

Ironically, the ACL itself supplied some of the individuals who were the exceptions to the general rule that most 16mm films were made for home use in the 1920s and 1930s. Charles Tepperman argues that so-called practical amateurs, those who sought to make money from their movie equipment, were initially supported by the ACL, who "defined and encouraged the production of four different subcategories of the genre: educational, industrial, social problem, and religious."[13] The ACL's monthly magazine, *Amateur Movie Makers,* later shortened to *Movie Makers,* was an important resource for these practical amateurs, advising them about how they might make their hobby profitable or, for a lucky few, a new career.

In the very first issue of *Amateur Movie Makers,* published in December 1926, J. H. McNabb, then the president of Bell & Howell, one of the leading manufacturers of amateur film equipment, wrote an article titled "The Amateur Turns a Penny," which anticipated a variety of applications of 16mm technology. After speculating on industrial, scientific, educational, civic, athletic, and home uses for the camera, McNabb closed by contending that "the element of pleasure and entertainment are secondary to the actual value in the more serious things which no other form of communication can possibly produce."[14] McNabb implicitly suggested that the movie camera was profitable because it saved the user money—for example, a coach might be able to more quickly train an athlete if he or she was shown their flaws on film—not because it provided new avenues of work for the nonprofessional. A few months later, in March 1927, a staff editorial promised articles on the "relation of amateur motion pictures to medicine and surgery, architecture, charitable fund raising, law and public safety, community advertising, and a score of other practical problems of our complex modern life."[15] Amateur filmmakers were encouraged to justify their hobby by exploring its many "practical uses" rather than focus solely on its commercial potential. When money-making opportunities were mentioned in *Amateur Movie Makers,* it was often in the context of producing income for cinema clubs, groups of filmmakers that joined together to produce longer and more elaborate amateur films. The magazine reported in late 1927 that the Little Screen Players of Boston raised money by charging fifteen dollars for screen tests of young men and women interested in "getting an opening in the professional movie world." As the article noted, "Five tests a week means a fifty-dollar profit and with fifty dollars—well, just take another glance from the advertising pages."¹⁶

Despite publishing the occasional article about the commercial potential of 16mm production, the magazine dismissed filmmakers who sought to generate revenue from their hobby. In 1928, an editorial went so far as to define an amateur filmmaker as a "person who makes movies but who does not devote the major part of his time to making them for profit."¹⁷ In an article in *Movie Makers* (the "Amateur" had been dropped) in late 1928, Epes Winthrop Sargent, author of the long-running "Advertising for Exhibitors" column for *Moving Picture World*, admitted that "the sincerest form of appreciation" a filmmaker could receive was a paying audience, but rather than advising the magazine's readers to go professional, he suggested that they make movies for charity events.¹⁸ While Sargent laid out a business model for the production and exhibition of local films—which he had discussed more than a decade earlier in a guidebook for exhibitors—he did not encourage amateurs to follow in their footsteps. Instead, he argued that a successful director should not grow his or her own business but instead "spread interest in amateur movies and lead others to share in this delightful pastime."¹⁹

Left out of many of the discussions about whether amateur filmmakers should profit from their hobby was the largest sector of the motion picture industry—Hollywood. As Patricia Zimmermann has argued, many amateur filmmakers did not achieve mastery of continuity editing and instead looked to other film forms, particularly the avant-garde, for inspiration.²⁰ Many scholars, including Jan-Christopher Horak and David James, have explored the connections between amateur filmmakers and avant-garde films in the 1920s and 1930s.²¹ But Hollywood is not absent from the pages of *Movie Makers*. Instead, it was initially presented as an aesthetic, one that amateurs could mimic in order to produce films that would please their audiences, before the magazine turned decisively against the mainstream in the 1930s. In February 1927, *Amateur Movie Makers* published one of its first scenarios for its readers to replicate in their own towns. Jerome Beatty described his scenario, titled "The Great Yonkers Jewel Robbery," by noting that the "story goes back to the sure-fire 'chase' idea, which was basis of early motion pictures, and has combined it with the 'U.S. Cavalry to the rescue' motif which also is not original with this writer."²² Although Hollywood was not mentioned by name in the script, the published scenario employed many of the formal techniques associated with commercial films of the period, including extensive use of close-up shots. A 1935 editorial in *Movie Makers* openly dismissed "trite or 'sure fire' scenes" that mimicked those found in Hollywood.²³ In their view, amateurs were free of the constraints placed on Hollywood production precisely because they did not expect to make a profit. Hollywood was used pejoratively in *Movie Makers* as shorthand for any profitable use of amateur equipment, which allowed the ACL to dismiss the production of film for profit as a whole.

Hollywood did have a place, however, in amateur film production as the object of farce and satire. In a 1932 article in *Movie Makers* on the advantages of Hollywood burlesque as an amateur film motif, Theodore Huff argued that "while it is difficult to compete with Hollywood producers on their own ground in a straight story since amateur actors are apt to suffer by comparison, in a burlesque, errors and crudities only add to the fun."²⁴ Huff went on to write that filmmakers should cast children, given their natural ability to mimic others, and that Hollywood's failure to convincingly mock itself meant that satire was one area where the amateur "can outdo the professional."²⁵ An article in the November 1935 issue of *Movie Makers* reveals how amateur filmmakers might have seen itinerant filmmakers who claimed to be associated with Hollywood in order to make a profit on their activities: "News items in the daily press on the activities of local movie makers are fairly common by this time, and sometimes pretty silly. 'Hollywood Comes to Hohokus!'—you know the kind of thing we mean. In the articles which follow such headings, the editors suggest their amazed belief that a unit of Paramount or M-G-M has just hit town, simply because a group of movie makers was seen on Main Street with a camera and a couple of reflecting boards."²⁶

The article went on to downplay the significance of such events because it assumed that there were so many amateur filmmakers in the country that every town had at least one or two producing films for fun. But, as the directors of *Movie Queen* and many other itinerants who hit the road with amateur-gauge equipment in 1930s learned, there were many people left in Hohokus who were eager to see themselves in the movies.

SHE IS THE SHOW: MOCKING HOLLYWOOD FOR PROFIT

While it is unclear when the first itinerant filmmaker picked up a 16mm camera and hit the road, by the mid-1930s there were dozens of them traipsing through the countryside, asking townspeople to "Watch for the Cameraman [or -woman]" who was there to take their picture. In most cases, these itinerants were lone operators, hiring extra crew only when absolutely necessary. Taking advantage of the economies of scale set up for amateur filmmakers, itinerants shot several hundred feet of film, mailed the exposed footage to Eastman Kodak or Agfa-Ansco, and waited a few days to get back the results. Reels could be quickly spliced together to make for longer movies, and itinerants routinely projected up to an hour of footage, the same length as the "B" movies of the period. Because most theaters were not equipped with a 16mm projector, filmmakers supplied their own, along with any sound equipment they thought necessary for the show.[27] In fact, it might have been developments in projectors, not cameras, that allowed the itinerant business to boom in the mid-1930s. As *American Cinematographer* noted in April 1934, projector lamps introduced between 1933 and 1934 were "300 per cent" brighter than those in use earlier in the decade, and the corresponding push by theatrical exhibitors to project more dimly to save money meant that 16mm projection could be the equal, in terms of the size and brightness of the image, of 35mm.[28] Compared to the elaborate and costly productions discussed in previous chapters, these 16mm productions were of drastically smaller scale, so much so that it is surprising that the filmmakers were able to maintain the bravado of their "big picture" predecessors. There is not any evidence of 35mm itinerants switching to a smaller gauge, or the reverse occurring once an itinerant became a professional.

Local views were the stock in trade of many 16mm camera operators. Directors from Amateur Service Productions, one of the most active producers in the 1930s, made such movies throughout the country. The company appeared to pick up on a business model established years earlier by companies such as Special Event Film Manufacturing Company of New York and Superior Film Company of Des Moines. They provided the training, equipment, and possibly the leads of potential clients, and the contracted itinerant, who was often a woman, was responsible for filming the town and collecting the revenue necessary to pay for it. More entrepreneurial itinerants, such as H. Lee Waters, who is discussed at length in the next chapter, created their own business enterprises, devising promotional materials and business models that allowed them to maximize profits. Some directors like Waters had experience as photographers, while others were new to moviemaking entirely.

If many producers of local views were camera operators first, and only later learned the ways of the road, others were experienced itinerants who added a movie camera to their repertoire of attractions. For example, the Universal Producing Company, a commercial home talent producer based in Fairfield, Iowa, was known throughout the country for its coarse comedies and fundraising success, producing more than three thousand shows in 1934 alone.[29] Female directors traveled throughout the United States producing plays like *Aunt Lucia,* whose highlight was a "flapper chorus" that consisted of community businessmen in drag.[30] Enlisting as many as two hundred people in the cast, directors would sell advertising to local businesses, work with newspapers to ensure a steady stream of publicity, and put on several performances, all in the course of a week.

One of the advance men for Universal, Lauren Kenyon Woods, who had been responsible for persuading civic organizations to sponsor the company's plays, broke off from the group in the early 1930s and started the Amateur Theatre Guild in Boston.[31] In 1935, the new company began producing its own home talent shows, including *The Circus*, a stage show, and *Movie Queen* in small towns throughout New England. A broad farce of the movie industry, *Movie Queen* was different from the Hollywood films discussed in the previous chapter because no one associated with the production seemed to take it seriously. Of course, it seems unlikely that anyone in the towns visited by Don Newland or Melton Barker ever believed that an out-of-work Hollywood filmmaker was there to find the next Mary Pickford or *Our Gang* child star. But the directors themselves never fully let on that their intentions to make a professional picture were anything less than sincere.

In contrast, *Movie Queen* embodied what Lea Jacobs has identified as the "decline of sentiment" in movie culture that began in the 1920s.[32] Rather than traffic in the dopey melodrama of Paragon's booster films, the slapstick of Tinsley's *Tramps* series, or the small town romance of Newland's comedies, *Movie Queen* pushed a cynical, up-to-date take on Hollywood, one in which only suckers would think they had a shot at being in the movies. As a newspaper in Ludington, Michigan, noted in 1937, "People have known about movies a long time. That is they have seen them on the screen since the days when the May Irwin kiss startled the nation and the 'Great Train Robbery' was regarded as a most elaborate feature—one that people could go home and talk about. Now they can know the 'truth' about Hollywood by seeing the Lions Club presentation of the 'Movie Queen.'"[33]

Of course, the "truth" that the play reveals is so jaded that the entire production works as a burlesque of the local film, particularly those made with Hollywood aspirations. But even if audiences were encouraged to mock Hollywood, even when their own friends and family were on screen or stage, the women behind the show took the matter seriously. It was, after all, their responsibility to make it a success.

Pilgrims of the Impossible:
The "Truth" about Hollywood

If the *Movie Queen* itself was a calculated ploy to turn the public's distrust of the movie industry into fodder for a fundraiser, the female directors who realized these productions were led into the itinerant field with hopes for steady employment. Like similar companies, the Amateur Theatre Guild sought out young women, many of them with professional ambitions of working in the theater or movies, and thus would accept long hours, grueling travel, and low pay for the opportunity of putting on their own productions. While the guild spent its early years producing work in New England, by 1936 it had set its sights nationally, first testing the waters in Pennsylvania, West Virginia, Ohio, Virginia, and North Carolina, before venturing to Michigan, Wisconsin, Minnesota, and South Carolina in 1937. Tina Appleton Bishop, a New York native and one of many directors of the guild's other show, *The Circus*, recalled decades later that by 1938, the guild had thirty-five directors under contract and ten show-bookers who were busy drumming up business around the country.[34] Bishop, like many others, learned of the opportunity by answering a classified ad that ran under the "Help Wanted—Female" heading in the back pages of the *New York Times*.[35] The *Times* ad was placed in the commercial-miscellaneous category next to pitches for modeling classes and dental schools, calling for "Three Intelligent Girls": "Boston organization needs amateur play directors; permanent; traveling; Southern territory this Winter; all expenses paid with excellent remuneration after training; we train you in beautiful Maine resort starting Aug. 23; applicant must pay fare to Boston, pay own living expenses for two weeks training; $10 surety bond. Write for details immediately, Amateur Theatre Guild, Skowhegan, Me."[36] Starting in August 1937, this ad, or one similar to it, ran in the *Times* for several years, looking for women to direct amateur plays.[37] Later ads specified that the group was looking for "college girls" between the ages of eighteen and thirty-five, and the training locations shifted from Skowhegan, a town in central Maine known for its summer theater, to Boston, to New York, to Ashton, Rhode Island, before finally ending in Providence, where the last training program advertised in the *Times* started on March 11, 1940.[38]

While the ads do not state the name of the play to be produced, many of these women were likely recruited to direct *Movie Queen*.[39] Copyrighted on August 13, 1934, by an eighteen-year-old Adella Cramer, one of the group's members, the play was produced in scores of towns across the United States from 1933 to 1941, from Florida to Minnesota, Texas to Maine, and most of the states in between.[40] In May 1938, an ad for the organization ran in the Rotary International's magazine, *The Rotarian*, noting, "We have produced amateur plays and movies on a 50–50 basis for Service Clubs throughout the United States. We direct, furnish equipment, and promote productions."[41] Although this ad specified service clubs, the guild would partner with any organization that was willing to share the costs of production and assist with fundraising. In addition to Rotary chapters, Kiwanis and Lions clubs, Moose and Elk lodges, Boy and Girl Scout troops, and local churches all partnered with the guild in hopes of raising money for charity or themselves.

Lauren Woods, like the owners of other home talent producing companies, saw to it that his contract employees, who he euphemistically referred to as "directors," were well trained and, more importantly, closely managed. Surviving accounts of the training process suggest an intense two- to six-weeks of learning the procedure of putting on a show, including a day-by-day checklist of activities to be conducted and emphatic lessons in the hard sale tactics necessary to "pull off" a successful show.[42] Bishop, one of many women who underwent the training in the guild's Boston offices, recalled years later Woods telling the assembled directors:

> Forget any dramatic ability, girls. I've worked out a foolproof way to work with the costs. What you'll need is salesmanship. You'll have just ten days to enter a strange town and talk a lot of people into getting up on a stage and making fools of themselves. You see, it's all a matter of arithmetic. For every person involved there will be three persons in the audience. When you count the cast as well as the stage-hands, ticket sellers, ushers, and so on, it could add up to a hundred people. At seventy-five cents a ticket, plus the money made on the ad sales, this can mount up. The Guild gets half the gate; the sponsoring organization gets the rest.[43]

While Bishop traveled from New York to audition for a director position with the guild, many of their directors were natives of New England. Marion Angeline Howlett became an associate with the company after a long career as a traveling etiquette instructor, lecturer, and freelance writer.[44] Madeline Anne Chaffee wrote plays and poems before becoming a *Movie Queen* director in 1938, and after spending several years on the road moved back to Rhode Island, where she became the editor of the *Cranston Herald* and, later, the first woman president of the Rhode Island State Council of Churches.[45] Margaret Cram, who produced many *Movie Queen* films in Maine, dropped out of a women's college in Ohio in order to become a director for the Boston Amateur Theatre Guild.[46] Intriguingly, there was a smattering of men who also directed *Movie Queen*, though evidence suggests that they were in the distinct minority. Once the directors were fully trained, they hit the road, traveling, often by train, for days on end to small towns where they would frequently meet people who were no longer sure they wanted to commit the time and resources a show like *Movie Queen* required. Through the submission of daily reports, *Movie*

Figure 5.1. Still frame from *Movie Queen*, Lubec, Maine (1936). *Courtesy of Northeast Historic Film, Bucksport, Maine*

Queen directors kept Woods apprised of their work, and he orchestrated their travel schedules from afar, all in the interest of keeping the company's finances in shape. According to Howlett's notes, directors were expected to clear one hundred dollars profit in each town, and if they failed to hit their mark, they risked being pulled off the road.[47]

The fear of losing money, or worse the cancellation of a show altogether, loomed large for the guild's directors, many of whom found themselves having to sell the show all over again when they arrived in town. As Howlett noted in one director's report: "The townspeople talking about the show after the booker leaves bring up objections that the organization cannot answer, and that throws cold water on the show and consequently, when the director arrives they are ready to cancel—through their fear of losing money, fear of a flop show, fear of work, fear because another show flopped, etc."[48]

While all itinerant directors had to calculate and manage the risks that went into their productions, the business model of the commercial home talent company allowed less room for error, in part because so many entities—the company, its hired director, the sponsoring organization—were trying to extract profit from the enterprise. A theater owner, business organization, or newspaper could plausibly write off the costs of a local film to its desire to foster "goodwill" among its readers, patrons, or customers. The directors of *Movie Queen*, on the other hand, were taking advantage of this goodwill to produce their show at the expense of the time, talents, and patience of the communities they visited. But even the most road-weary director would have found it hard to be more cynical about their precarious occupation than the characters in the show they staged in town after town.

A Brief History of *Movie Queen*

When Adella Cramer copyrighted *Movie Queen* in 1934, the term "movie queen" had long been used to describe female movie actors who achieved success through a mixture of talent and cunning. Twenty-one years earlier, in August 1913, the silent film star Martha Russell was described as a "movie queen" in an article about the production of a local film. In the article, Russell was quoted as telling aspiring actresses, "it looks like fun, and sometimes it really is, but it is hard work to act before the camera."[49] In 1914, Warner's Features produced a film titled *The Movie Queen*, one of several pictures with that title produced in the silent era. The following year, the Hazard Motion Picture Company in Kentucky filmed a series of *Movie Queen* home talent films, with the queen elected in a contest.[50] In Zelda Fitzgerald's short story "Our Own Movie Queen," published in 1925, a young woman wins a local screen talent competition only to find that the final cut of the film minimized her role so the daughter of the owner of a local department store could be featured. The woman takes her revenge on the filmmaker, an out-of-work Hollywood director, by conspiring with the film's assistant director to produce her own cut of the film. After the new film is exhibited, with the expected scandal that results, the woman marries the film's assistant director and appoints herself an expert on the movies even though she has never left her hometown.

Although the "movie queen" almost always referred to a female actor, rather than a screenwriter or director, the term connoted not just stardom but also knowledge about the film industry. As early as 1915, film production companies cooperated with newspapers to put on elaborate and lengthy screen acting competitions, with the winner receiving an opportunity to act on film. Later, movie theaters staged similar contests, with local exhibitors, regional advertising or exploitation, and staff and studios cooperating to promote a specific film or studio by holding a "screen test" competition. As beauty pageants became more popular in the 1920s, many theaters and civic groups adjoined the lure of the movies with the pageants, sponsoring "Movie Balls" in which a movie queen contest was the key attraction.[51] By the early 1930s, the term "movie queen" operated as a way to describe a form of domesticated stardom, its royal connotations suggesting that the holder of the title was removed from the everyday labor of the movie world.⁵²

Cramer's play opens with a prologue that takes place at the Podunk railroad station. At the station, the character's speeches are written in a rural, perhaps southern, colloquial dialect, with the station agent, surprised that the "Hollywood 'special'" is stopping in town, noting the reason for the play by saying, "If it hadn't been for Mary Brown's a-writin' that swell essay on home gar'enin' and a-winnin' a free trip to Hollywood, I guess the spacial wouldn't even know Podunk was on the map!"⁵³ Mary Brown, described as "no public speaker," stammers her way through a speech before boarding the train. Before it pulls off, Roy, a local pastor, steps up and says, again in scrambled English, "going off to a far-away town of reputed wickedness as does this gentile girl of our flock, we come and gather to bid her godspeed and goodwill." He then presents her with a flowerpot full of geraniums, which Mary brings with her on board. The train then makes a number of stops in its trip across the country, with each stop being used as a set-up for a joke. The stage goes dark, and when the lights rise again, the Podunk train station has been transformed into one in Hollywood. But instead of waiting for Mary Brown to arrive, the agent James Cain is eager to receive Marlena Slarbo, a Russian actress whose name, Cain says, "will be on every one's lips—it will be a by-word, a password, a magic word!" When Brown arrives, carrying the potted plant, she is mistaken for Slarbo by Cain, who immediately begins touting her arrival as the "colossal, gigantic, stupendous" new star. Startled by the attention, Brown tells Cain that he has mistaken her for someone else and promptly faints.

The first act opens at the Ritz Hotel, where Brown is still being mistaken for Slarbo. Cain and Brown are about to call off their short-lived partnership when Slarbo calls Cain to inform him that she is no longer coming to Hollywood to make her film debut. When the studio executive Abe Goldstein, of Goldstein, Goldstein & Goldstein, accompanied by several "yes men," walks into Brown's hotel room ready to sign who he believes is Slarbo, she decides to keep up appearances. After fierce negotiations, she signs a thirty-thousand-dollar contract. Slarbo, apparently having decided to come to Hollywood after all, overhears how lucrative the contract will be and intends to take it. Meanwhile, Goldstein's wife, Molly, is touching up her screenplay to be used for Brown's screen debut. Cain successfully blocks Slarbo from meeting Goldstein and unmasking his ruse, and Slarbo, frustrated, decides to give up the check and return to New Jersey.

In the second act, the action has moved to a set at a studio, where two prop men are criticizing Brown's debut film for having "about as much emotion in the whole thing as there was in a dead jelly-fish." Part of the problem, one man said, was that the scenario writer, Molly Goldstein, had based the film on a short story from forty years earlier. The director enters the set, complaining about the difficulty of finishing the picture. The production is floundering. The actors are having trouble remembering their lines and places. When Goldstein arrives, flustered, he speaks with a dialect easily read as ethnic and Jewish. Cornball ethnic and regional humor runs throughout the play, as seen when Goldstein tells Molly he's getting a "noivous breakdown," and she responds by telling him, "Abie, you know right well we don't want no more of them foreign cars."

It soon becomes clear that this act is dominated by slapstick comedy, with the film's director abruptly quitting, a horse called "Smoky the Cow" appearing, and Mary, acting as a typical Podunk native, carrying a kitten on set and discussing her plans to marry "Bill Slocum of the Hicksville Slocums." Goldstein, frustrated with Brown's acting, discovers that because she signed the contract as Slarbo, she cannot collect her pay. Brown realizes that her dreams of being a Hollywood actress will not work out, and she apologizes to Cain for causing him trouble. Brown, having had a change of heart, tells Cain she wants to be with him, and Cain tells her, "Mary, darling, you may not mean a thing to moviedom, but you're everything in the world to me." Cain and Brown leave the set as creditors, assuming they would be paid by Goldstein, chase after them.

The third and final act of the stage play opens back at the Ritz. Brown and Cain are packing, making plans to leave Hollywood when they realize that they are not ready for the sleepy life of Podunk Center. By this point, Brown is very down on her performance as an actor, and she and Cain decide to go to New York instead. Before they leave, Cain receives a call and learns that the picture is a success. Startled, he immediately goes to see Goldstein to learn more:

> GOLD: Went over? Why there's been nothing like it in Hollywood for years. Critics are proclaiming Slarbo an actress of a new type. What was it you said, Miss Bowland?
>
> MISS B: Why the restrained type. No emotion. The public is fed up with gushy engenues and hard-boiled bleached blonde gangster molls. This new type of acting Miss Slarbo has will revolutionize acting. Every star in Hollywood will imitate her. (To Mary) You were simply grand this evening, Miss Slarbo. You have all Hollywood at your feet tonight and tomorrow when this film opens in other cities, you will be an idol of the silver screen. The world will acclaim you.

Figures 5.2 and 5.3. Still frames from *Movie Queen*, Lubec, Maine (1936). *Courtesy of Northeast Historic Film, Bucksport, Maine*

Having realized that her acting contract is good again, Brown decides to re-sign it, although she still needs to pretend to be Marlena Slarbo. Goldstein ups her contract to $200,000 a picture, and Cain faints at the good news. Although no stage instructions are given, one assumes that the curtain closes on Cain's swoon, and, after a brief pause, the play's filmed fourth act appears on the makeshift screen.

The "Plot Shots" of the Fourth Act

As Charles Tepperman notes, the very omission of amateur motion pictures from traditional scholarly and popular inquests is due in part to an unsettled debate about what significance, if any, they held as cinema. Tepperman suggests that the work of advanced amateurs at least occupied a "middle ground" between commercial production and the avant-garde. While the former was governed by the needs of the motion picture industry, and the latter indebted to theories of sound and image, Tepperman argues that for amateurs, cinema was "a powerful new tool for both recording and reflecting on everyday life," and thus responsible for developing what he terms a "pragmatic imagination."[54] The producers of local films were not caught up in such debates, but nonetheless were drawn to the mode, in terms of both practice and aesthetic, that dominated the theaters where they showed their movies. Even so, the filmed fourth act of *Movie Queen*, which was shown in the movie theater or community hall after the play's performance, simultaneously embraced and pushed away from Hollywood as its model for how movies should be made. In fact, it seems as if the directors themselves were like the character Mary Brown, making a movie that breaks the rules of the industry but is all the more intriguing as a result.

In the film, we see Mary Brown arrive back in her hometown, which is no longer the fictional Podunk Center but instead the very town where the film is being screened.[55] Each picture, which ranged from twenty to forty-five minutes in length, follows roughly the same trajectory.[56] The movie queen returns home to the train station or, in some cases, boat dock or airport, and immediately takes part in a parade the town stages in her honor. The parade is followed by voluminous footage of the movie queen stopping by the local businesses that sponsored its production. At the end, however, the film returns to the narrative with Slarbo, presumably angry that her role has been taken by Brown, convincing several local men to kidnap the movie queen. Brown is kidnapped, but she is quickly found and freed by James Cain, thus reuniting the couple. The films abruptly end at this point, leaving it uncertain whether Brown and Cain return to Hollywood or decide to stay in her hometown.

Unlike other itinerant filmmakers, who tended to shoot films in a day or two, *Movie Queen* directors shot intermittently throughout the seventeen-day (not counting Sundays) production, with the closing reel taken the final weekend before the play's premiere. Like other itinerants, the guild's directors sold movie "advertising," which was usually just a few dozen feet taken of factory plants, shops on Main Street, and automobile dealerships. The directors were expected to make selling the film a priority and to schedule meetings with local businesses as soon as they arrived in town. Also on the first day, directors were asked to go to the post office to check film and mail processing time for Agfa Ansco, which provided service out of New York; Chicago; Jacksonville, Florida; and Kansas City, Missouri. Filming began on the sixth day, usually a Saturday, with Brown's arrival on a train. The parade was filmed immediately after, and directors were encouraged to make plans to film churches on Sunday, starting with the largest congregations. Sunday was the first big shooting day, with country clubs, bakeries, soda bottling facilities, and nightclubs all potential subjects for the movies. Directors were also expected to splice film titles and send exposed film to Agfa for processing.

In his instructions for the "plot shots," Woods suggested that directors aim for scenes with slapstick and action, taken in the shortest period of time, in the smallest amount of space, with the interest of keeping crowds engaged and in the picture. Monday and Tuesday, the seventh and eighth days of a director's visit, were significant days for picture taking, as she was encouraged to film additional industries as well as school children and service clubs. Woods suggested that directors be aware of the tight shooting schedule necessary to film every business, particularly because many merchants were waiting for the camera operator to arrive before unloading a truck of goods or otherwise performing for the camera. Directors were expected to continue to shoot advertising pictures for the rest of the week and finish no later than the twelfth day, a Saturday, in time for the "gangster pictures," a fictional sequence featuring townspeople as criminals, that would serve as the closing scenes for the entire production. *Movie Queen* opened on the seventeenth day, a Thursday, which suggests that the film was able to be processed and returned to town within just a few days after the closing scenes were shot.

The *Movie Queens* that are extant all appear to be products of the method outlined in Woods's day-by-day instructions. While premade intertitles were ready for use, the extant prints suggests that they were not deployed systematically, perhaps because they added little value to the audience, who would recognize the churches, businesses, schools, and civic organizations that appeared in the film. Instead, these films function as semifictional depictions of a town as if the location were being visited by a Hollywood star, with the camera operator often flitting back and forth between subjective and objective viewpoints. For example, the Van Buren, Maine, show opens with what appear to be point-of-view shots taken from the perspective of the Mary Brown character as she arrives back home. A high-angle shot depicts crowds of people waving, suggesting just how overwhelming the fictional experience must have been for Brown. Soon, however, the camerawork becomes more ordinary, filming parade scenes and, later, the Brown character herself shaking hands with town leaders. The character playing Monsieur Flowers, a costume designer, is particularly prominent in these scenes, hamming up his performance as an effeminate man. The continual presence of the movie queen reminds the viewer that this is a fictional narrative, yet everything else that appears is observational, as if it were ordinary life in the small town.

But *Movie Queen* breaks from showing views of everyday life in its final sequence, featuring the so-called gangster pictures, which attempted to replicate Hollywood storytelling techniques. While Woods gave fairly general guidance for the shooting of most scenes, he offered exacting instructions for what he called the "plot shots," thirty-seven shots that were intended to incorporate some of the "business shots," such as a scene at the local drug store, with the narrative that was set out in the three-act play that preceded the film. In the training materials he prepared for *Movie Queen* directors, Woods noted that these scenes were essential to the production's success: "Your plot shots are most important in making your film interesting. They are to be made as humorous as possible and are to be cut up in scenes and spliced in between and throughout the commercial paid shots. There is a stock title for each scene, to be run previous to the respective shot.... Another important reason for plot shots is the added publicity obtained by taking them. It has been definitely proven in town after town that the plot shot day is as important a factor of 'Movie Queen' procedure as the 'Movie Queen' parade."[57]

Even though the director's manual described each shot in detail, discussing such matters as stage directions and distance of the camera from the scene of action, such instructions appear to have been mostly ignored, and some *Movie Queens* appear to eschew the gangster pictures entirely. However, several extant *Movie Queens* do depict those scenes, which feature the kidnapping and rescue of Mary Brown, the star of the hour. While one could argue that home talent plays like those produced by the Amateur Theatre Guild were overly scripted and, in the end, stale attempts to provide local entertainment on the cheap, the *Movie Queen* films counter such assumptions by revealing how different directors, and townspeople, interpret even the most detailed instructions. (See Moving Image 5.1.)

For example, the Lincoln, Maine, production of *Movie Queen* appears to invert the order of several key shots even as many of them depict more or less what is suggested by Woods. After a shot of several kidnappers entering a building and capturing what appear to be two businessmen, the first shot in Woods's list, of a "Ford coupe" coming down the road, is quickly followed by his second shot, in which Slarbo; Public Enemy no. 999, the gang leader; and nine kidnappers—not eleven, as Woods suggested—exit the vehicle. This visual gag, common to slapstick comedy, does not require particular technical proficiency, yet Woods warned the director to forbid the kidnappers from smiling for the camera. The third shot, which was intended to provide continuity between exiting the car and going to the gangsters' hideout, is not included in the film and instead replaced by the second half of what was intended to be the fourth shot, in which Slarbo describes Mary Brown using hand gestures to indicate her hourglass figure.

The next four shots, which were to depict the gangsters visiting a confectionary store for a treat and traveling to the scene of their first kidnapping, are omitted entirely, and the gangster pictures resume with shot nine, a medium shot with two kidnappers, one carrying rope and the other a rifle, preparing to capture their first victim. The next shot features a young woman, clearly not Mary Brown, standing in front of a restaurant's glass window. The kidnappers are reflected in the window before they enter the frame and quickly cover the woman's face with a handkerchief before other kidnappers come into view. Two of them carry the woman off, and the camera pans right to follow her. Shots eleven through nineteen, which were to depict the transport of the kidnapped woman to the gang's hideout and a police chase, are omitted. Instead, we see another kidnapping shot, this time of an elderly woman, and then the story jumps to shot twenty, where Slarbo is waiting to see whether the kidnappers have successfully found Mary Brown. Two brief shots show Slarbo revealing that the kidnappers have failed to find Brown, and Slarbo gestures as if to lead the gangsters herself. The next shot depicts several of the gangsters with lassos, standing on a busy street. The camera pans right again, and we cut to a shot of several kidnappers attempting to lasso a passerby. She is quickly caught and thrown into Slarbo's automobile.

These scenes diverge sharply from the plot shots—which make no mention of lassos, and instead imagine Slarbo spotting Brown and then enlisting the gangsters to chase her down. Instead, the story advances to shot twenty-six, with the kidnapper's car racing through the town's main street. The next shot depicts a man one assumes to be James Cain, who, from the plot shots, is there to save Brown. Cain jumps into another vehicle, but before he can turn the ignition, the film cuts once again to shot thirty-five, with Brown tied up and the gangsters all guarding her. Cain enters from the left-hand side of the frame, knocking down the gangsters as if they were bowling pins and hugging Brown, who remains tied up. Although this final scene is described as a series of three shots—a close-up of the gangster's hideout, a medium shot with the gangsters on the ground, and a close-up of Cain and Mary embracing—in the Lincoln film these three actions are presented as a single take. While the plot shots serve as a rough guide to the only fully narrative section of the *Movie Queen* films, the director ignored so many sections that we can safely assume she was willfully disregarding Woods's orders.

Other *Movie Queens* strayed even further from the plot shots, allowing directors, with the input of the actors, to explore darker aspects of the show. The Lubec, Maine, film, for example, featured four violent kidnappings, each of which features the gangsters putting a full-body white sack over unsuspecting women and carrying them kicking and screaming into the gangsters' car. While James Cain's use of a bicycle to chase the car may be read as comic, the drawn out fight sequence that follows is also unsettling, with the scene resembling a battlefield rather than a hideout. In the Belfast, Maine, film, all of the gangsters wave pistols before they go out to search for Brown. The kidnapping shots show the woman in the foreground, and a crowd of gangsters run forward to capture her, inverting the logic of the typical crowd shot in which people walk toward, and past, the camera with little consequence. In Belfast, Brown is tied to a tree, and Cain's successful take down of the gangsters is followed by close-ups of each gangster lying on the floor. Even if the directors were following a script, their embrace of these violent and sexually transgressive scenes suggests that *Movie Queen* was more than just an innocent romp through Hollywood's hoariest genres.

The Cultural Anxiety of the Movies

While producers of other local Hollywood movies sought to assuage concerns about the moral turpitude of Tinseltown, the guild's staging and filming of *Movie Queen* mercilessly mocked the film industry and its small-town fans. Brown and other residents of Podunk Center are presented as naive, uneducated, and, at least in the version submitted for copyright, southern. Hollywood, on the other hand, is presented as a place dominated by ethnic Jews, foreigners, and, in one of the play's minor characters, the costume designer Flowers, gay men. In Middlebury, Vermont, where *Movie Queen* was staged in the late 1930s, the director's name was changed from Mr. Williamson to Von Vonheim, an obvious play on Erich von Stroheim.[58] In effect, the *Movie Queen* demonstrates the flip side of the "decline of sentiment" identified by Lea Jacobs. Once one disregarded the sincerity of motion picture actors and the stories in which they appeared, it became easier to apply nativist suspicions of urban America to the movie industry full cloth.[59] And, once one is comfortable with mocking the very movie fans who, through their loyalty to particular genres and stars, ensured the industry's economic stability, it becomes easier to suggest that the movie star and the star-struck fan are equally to blame for degrading American culture.

Thus, the efficiency of the *Movie Queen*'s production was undermined by the play's suspicions that such industriousness was a sign of a worthwhile enterprise. The sharp satire of the play cast doubt on the sincerity of many of the newspaper articles that advertised its production. For example, like other itinerants, the guild's directors used the casting process, particularly the selection of the movie queen, to build interest in the production. In 1938, the Butte, Montana, newspaper noted that "Mary Brown, stage name of the lead in 'Movie Queen,' is a Butte girl, selected from a group of hundreds of aspirants for this important role, whose identity will not be made known until she steps from the plane at the Butte airport."[60] In Menasha, Wisconsin, the local paper noted that "the production is expected to be something entirely different than ever stages in Menasha before. Stage show, style show, comedy, dancing choruses and local movies are all combined in the play." When the movie queen arrives to town, "ostensibly from Hollywood," she was to be feted with a "royal welcome and will be given the key to the city by the mayor. A parade will be staged in her honor and movies will be taken of both the parade and spectators along the way."[61] Unlike the "movie-struck girls," to use Shelley Stamp's phrase, who pined so much to be in the movies that they represented a danger to the industry, the local people involved in the production of *Movie Queen* were able to reproduce the excitement of the movies without making plans to run off to Hollywood.[62]

As *Movie Queen* demonstrates, a take on Hollywood could envelop many competing ideas and stereotypes about rural and urban life, native and immigrant populations, and other minority groups. By reproducing the industry's most hackneyed plots and stereotypical characters, these films suggest that Hollywood lacked original ideas and was out of touch with the desires of rural audiences. By "kidnapping" the movie queen from Hollywood, the directors of the Boston Amateur Theatre Guild encouraged local people to mock the nation's leading culture industry at the height of its power. While the producers of other Hollywood local films may have taken themselves seriously, the experience of *Movie Queen* suggests that rural audiences saw the chance to "see yourself in the movies" for what it was, a clever scheme to get them to participate in that eternal fantasy of Hollywood: anyone can be a star.

Amateur Equipment with Professional Results

The directors of *Movie Queen* were not the only itinerant entertainers to take up 16mm cameras in the 1930s, even among home talent producers. Late in that decade, a competing company, John B. Rogers, began making its own copycat production, the more plainly titled *We're in the Movies*. In Rogers's version, a Hollywood director comes to town and conducts a movie queen competition. The winner of the competition was actually set in advance, as the sponsor held its own competition before the filmmakers arrived to stage one.[63] Unlike the Amateur Theatre Guild, the Rogers Company concentrated its efforts in the upper Midwest and employed male directors, but they too appeared to cut short their work before the United States' entry into World War II. Other fictional local films were made by amateurs, including members of cinema clubs like those discussed earlier in this chapter, who nonetheless managed to show their movies in movie theaters and municipal auditoriums.

Exhibitors, desperate to find new ways to attract audiences, also expressed renewed interest in acquiring movie cameras, but instead of producing home talent films, they wanted to make their own local newsreels. In October 1937, the *Motion Picture Herald* suggested that theater managers, "looking about for some device to take the place of chance games, pot-and-pan giveaways and other gift forms as the seemingly necessary added attraction," should begin using local newsreels, which featured local events, to win over audiences.[64] There was even an attempt to create a national network of local newsreels. In November 1937, the *Motion Picture Herald* reported a plan by the Herman A. DeVry Company, a manufacturer of 16mm projectors, to lease film-making equipment to cinemas so that they could make their own local newsreels.[65] The company would then use the footage to produce a national newsreel, which would be screened, in 16mm, alongside the local newsreels in each community. The article reported local newsreel activity in Colorado, Oklahoma, Wisconsin, Iowa,

Illinois, Indiana, Minnesota, and North Carolina, suggesting that its use by theater managers was widespread by the end of 1937.⁶⁶ Although many of these local newsreels do not survive, collections in Britton, South Dakota, and Warsaw, Indiana, suggest the vibrancy of the practice in the late 1930s.⁶⁷

But the itinerant filmmakers who produced impressionistic non-narrative and nonfiction works were particularly successful in the 1930s. In 1941, a representative of Amateur Service Productions of Lancaster, Pennsylvania, claimed that the company had produced 1,500 movies in 27 states, a boast that is supported by the many surviving examples of their work.⁶⁸ An independent producer, Arthur J. Higgins, made movies in at least 114 towns throughout the United States between 1936 and 1942, shooting in places like Agua Dulce, Texas, which reported just two hundred residents in the 1940 census.⁶⁹ But despite the frenetic activity of these itinerants, they left few traces of their practice, other than the occasional reel with an edge code that reveals its age and the premade title cards that mark its provenance. Produced just a few years before home movies became the dominant mode of amateur filmmaking, these town portraits offer another way of thinking about the local film, as a motion picture of life "caught unawares" in a particular time and space, unencumbered by larger ideas of what those moments might signify.

It is telling, then, that the best-known producer of these town portraits, H. Lee Waters, who ran a portrait studio in Lexington, North Carolina, referred to his practice as "Movies of Local People." Made between 1936 and 1942, Waters focused on a specific region of the country, the mid-Atlantic, mostly towns within a few hundred miles of his home, and kept both his films and production records, providing a surfeit of detail for what is otherwise a largely undocumented phenomenon. But Waters's attention to recordkeeping was outmatched by his film style, which, in its use of camera tricks, staged events, and endless personal encounters between the cameraman and his chosen subjects, created work that captured and reproduced the communities he depicted. By operating in a smaller gauge, Waters realized the ambitions many itinerants had for their work—to show a community to itself.

Notes

1. For more on Gleason, see Swanson, "Inventing Amateur Film."
2. *An Amateur Photoplay in the Making: The Story of "Fly Low Jack and Game" Produced by the Rochester Community Players*, c. 1927, Eastman Kodak, 3. http://digital.hagley.org/cdm/ref/collection/p268001co1112/id/8018.
3. Swanson, "Inventing Amateur Film," 130.

4. "Home Movie Pioneers Recall Films of Early 20s," *Evening News* (Newburgh, N.Y.), December 7, 1968, 6.

5. My claim rests on examination of trade and popular publications produced by Kodak in the 1920s, including the *Eastman Kodak Company Trade Circular, Kodakery*, and materials kept in company scrapbooks. None of them suggested that 16mm equipment ought to have been used to make local movies, and few discuss how it might have been used outside the home. Haidee Wasson notes that Kodak did introduce a projector for traveling salesmen in the late 1920s but also suggests that projectors with bulbs bright enough for theatrical exhibition were not widely available until around 1934. See Wasson, "Suitcase Cinema." For more on domesticity and home movies of the 1920s, see Wasson, "Electric Homes! Automatic Movies!"

6. As Charles Tepperman suggests, determining the exact relationship between the prices of camera equipment and the demographic makeup of amateur movie enthusiasts in the 1930s is a difficult task, particularly because new technologies, such as 8mm, introduced in 1932, and fluctuating prices made moviemaking more accessible over the course of the decade. Nevertheless, the Great Depression helped ensure that amateur moviemaking would not be a mass phenomenon until after World War II. See Tepperman, *Amateur Cinema*, 80–81.

7. Even though 8mm was introduced as a cheaper alternative to 16mm in 1932, I have not come across any examples of itinerants working in 8mm, most likely because obtaining a bright and large enough projected image would have been impossible in the 1930s. There was an 8mm itinerant film series made in Canada in the postwar period called *Stars of the Town*.

8. "Amateur Theatre Guild: Director of "The Circus" on the Road, 1937–8," MAH (5).

9. In both the United States and Europe, small-gauge cameras and projectors were primarily the toys of the elite until the 1930s, and it was not until after the Second World War that they were inexpensive enough to be purchased by middle-class consumers. See Nicholson, *Amateur Cinema*, 3–5.

10. Luckett, *Cinema and Community*, 115.

11. Advertisement, *Kodakery*, March 1924, 30–31. In her history of Kodak's marketing for the camera, Nancy Martha West argues that this slogan refers to the company's wish to position photography as a playful activity. See West, *Kodak and the Lens of Nostalgia*, 12–13.

12. According to Charles Tepperman, Kodak released its professional grade Cine-Kodak Special in 1933, and it was not until 1936 that "advances in 16mm projector illumination and optical sound track reproduction" made it possible to show amateur-made films in movie auditoriums. See Tepperman, *Amateur Cinema*, 121.

13. Ibid., 218–219. As Tepperman notes, the ACL turned against "practical films" after World War II, in part because of the awareness that there was a large 16mm nontheatrical film industry that met the needs previously filled by amateurs. The magazine *Home Movies*, which was published out of Los Angeles starting in the mid-1930s, also covered practical—and profitable—uses for motion pictures.

14. J. H. McNabb, "The Amateur Turns a Penny," *AMM*, December 1926, 19, 30–31.

15. "Through the Telephone," *AMM*, March 1927, 2.

16. "Finance!" *AMM*, November 1927, 50.

17. "Amateur—Typical?" *AMM*, May 1928, 295.

18. Epes W. Sargent, "For Charity's Sweet Sake," *MM*, November 1928, 712.

19. Ibid., 735.

20. Zimmermann, *Reel Families*, 83–89.

21. See Horak, "The First American Film Avant-Garde," and James, *The Most Typical Avant-Garde*, 137–154. David James explores the connection between the avant-garde and

amateur filmmaking in the chapter "The Idea of the Amateur," which argues that in the post–World War II period, the lines between the two were diminished in favor of a more broadly defined experimental cinema.

22. Jerome Beatty, "The Great Yonkers Jewel Robbery: An Amateur Scenario," *MM*, February 1927, 12. Bernard Kemper produced this script in 1926 and 1927, making a film he titled *The Great Perham Jewel Robbery*. The 16mm print is held by the Minnesota Historical Society.

23. "The Free Screen," *MM*, February 1935, 61.

24. Theodore Huff, "The Mirror of Burlesque," *MM*, October 1932, 428. Charles Tepperman argues that Huff's films were in "an awkward position between amateur and avant-garde filmmaking of the 1930s." See Tepperman, *Amateur Cinema*, 264.

25. Tepperman, *Amateur Cinema*, 448.

26. "Closeups—What Filmers Are Doing," *MM*, November 1935, 498.

27. While synchronous sound was not used, itinerants often played music to accompany their films and spoke over a loudspeaker to identify people and places.

28. "Cinematic Progress in 1933: A Technical Review," *American Cinematographer*, April 1934, 495. The article notes that the first projectors, introduced eleven years earlier, featured 250-watt bulbs, while recently introduced projectors used 750-watt bulbs, permitting projection on screens that were between 15 and 18 feet wide. The projector used by the *Movie Queen* directors required a 750-watt bulb. See "Amateur Theater Guild, 1937–1938," MAH.

29. Kett, *The Pursuit of Knowledge under Difficulties*, 388.

30. See Senelick, *The Changing Room*, 328.

31. For example, Woods visited Portsmouth, New Hampshire, in 1931. See *Portsmouth Herald*, January 14, 1931, 4.

32. Jacobs, *The Decline of Sentiment*.

33. "The Truth about Hollywood Life," *Ludington* (Mich.) *Daily News*, July 9, 1937, 8.

34. Tina Appleton Bishop, "A Southern Odyssey (How to Succeed in Show Business)," http://web.archive.org/web/20131210185044/http://tinabishopauthor.com/short-story-a-southern-odyssey/.

35. The *Boston Globe* also ran such ads.

36. Classified advertisement, *New York Times*, August 1, 1937, 173.

37. Ads in the *Boston Globe* appeared as early as 1934, though some of these ads were for the company's other plays.

38. Classified advertisement, *New York Times*. January 26, 1940, 17.

39. The guild's other productions included *The Circus* and *Boomerang*.

40. *Catalog of Copyright Entries. Part 1. [C] Group 3. Dramatic Compositions and Motion Pictures*, vol. 7, Nos. 1–123 (Washington, DC: Government Printing Office, 1934), 4814.

41. *The Rotarian*, May 1938, 64. While the ad notes other productions, including *Boomerang* and *Dress Rehearsal*, to my knowledge *Movie Queen* was the only production that had a film component.

42. One of the directors of *Movie Queen*, Marion Angeline Howlett, kept the memoranda and instructions produced by the Amateur Theatre Guild, as well as her own records of her experience as a director, and donated her collection to Harvard in the early 1970s.

43. Bishop, "A Southern Odyssey."

44. One brochure lists Howlett's accomplishments as follows: "Lectured at University of Phillipines, in Manila; Was received by the Sultan of Zulu; Was fifteen days alone in the jungle of Cambodia; Was received by Crown Prince of Siam; Was entertained by Arabian Sheiks; Was at the mercy of Chinese coolies in North China; Learned * Pung Chow (Mah

Jongg) in an exciting adventure in plenty of Chinese atmosphere, and is now an expert player of this most fascinating game." Brochure, MAH, series 3, folder 3.

45. "Madeline Chafee [sic] Clark," in Sharon Coleman, *A Salute to Rhode Island Independent Women* (Providence: Rhode Island Commission on Women, 1976), 11.

46. Jill Tatem, Western Reserve University, personal correspondence with the author, February 15, 2010. Cram was enrolled in the university from 1932 to 1934 but did not graduate.

47. Directors received fifty dollars' salary for each production. The advance booker was paid twenty dollars. Profits were split with the sponsoring organization after local costs, such as renting the theater or hall. Directors were expected to generate $150 profit for each venture, which meant that the home office would receive $8 after the director's salary and the booker's salary were paid. See L. K. Woods to Howlett, November 11, 1927, MAH (2).

48. "Amateur Theatre Guild: Director of 'The Circus' on the Road, 1937–8," MAH (8).

49. "Essanay Artist—A Movie Queen—Says Local Girls Fine Actresses," *News-Palladium* (Benton Harbor, Mich.), August 8, 1913, 7.

50. "Louisville Notes," *MPW*, August 14, 1915, 1187.

51. For two examples of this use of the "movie queen" contest, see "Grand Movie Parade One of Many Features for Movie Ball," *Delphi* (Ind.) *Journal*, January 8, 1931, 1, and "Local Beauties to Compete in Shore Contest," *Denton* (Md.) *Journal*, July 8, 1933, 1. Some of these movie balls were run in connection with the production of civic films, which are discussed in chapter 6.

52. For more on women and labor in early Hollywood, see Hallett, *Go West Young Women!*

53. Adella Cramer, "The Movie Queen," August 13, 1934, Manuscript Division, Library of Congress, Washington, DC. All quotes from the play refer to this unnumbered edition. Another copy is found in MAH, series 3, folder 9.

54. Tepperman, *Amateur Cinema*, 191.

55. It is not clear whether the Amateur Theatre Guild substituted the name of its host town in the play, or if "Podunk Center" was used to stand in for all small towns. Although the classified ads printed in the *New York Times*, as well as the dialect of the Podunk natives, indicate that it was intended to be produced only in the South, the play was in fact performed in many regions of the United States.

56. While many of these films no longer survive, more than a dozen films made in New England are available due to collection and preservation efforts by Northeast Historic Film. In addition, copies of films made in Bogota, New Jersey, and East Palestine, Ohio, circulate online.

57. "Plot Shots ('Gangster Pictures')," MAH (12).

58. "Middlebury Movie Queen Welcomed by Big Parade," *Middlebury* (Vt.) *Register*, 1939, Sheldon Museum Collection, Northeast Historic Film.

59. As Francis G. Couvares has noted, such tensions between small-town audiences and the motion picture industry developed in the 1910s, and were encouraged by exhibitors in small towns, who sought to use concerns about the morality of the movies in order to secure economic advantages, such as making the "block booking" of pictures illegal. See Couvares, "Hollywood, Main Street, and the Church."

60. "'Movie Queen' Arrival Is Set," *Montana Standard* (Butte), August 7, 1938, 35.

61. "Proceed with Plans for Lions' Stage Production," *Appleton* (Wis.) *Post-Crescent*, May 30, 1938, 13.

62. Stamp, *Movie-Struck Girls*, 37–40.

63. See "'Hollywood Premier' for 'Glamour Girl' of Indiana," *Indiana (Penn.) Gazette*, November 27, 1940, 3.

64. "Theaters Turn to Local Newsreel as Substitute for Chance Game," *Motion Picture Herald*, October 16, 1937, 16. Chance games were used by theater mangers in the 1930s to win audiences. But theater managers ran into trouble in the late 1930s when states started to investigate their use as a form of illegal gambling. One cash giveaway chance game, known as "Bank Night," was particularly popular during this period, and many state and local governments tried to shut it down using antigambling laws. For an account of this phenomenon, see Gomery, *Shared Pleasures*, 32.

65. "Sixth National Newsreel on 16 mm., Starts Jan. 1," *Motion Picture Herald*, November 20, 1937, 13.

66. See Johnson, "'An Added Bonus.'"

67. The Britton, South Dakota, films are on the internet, while the Warsaw, Indiana, films are held by the Kosciusko County Historical Society.

68. "Altoona Motion Picture Is Planned," *Altoona* (Penn.) *Tribune*, February 6, 1941, 10. See the filmography.

69. Steg, "The Itinerant Films of Arthur J. Higgins."

6

THE CAMERAMAN HAS VISITED YOUR TOWN
The Local Film and the Politics of Recognition

IN FEBRUARY 2005, LOCAL FILMS shot by H. Lee Waters, a North Carolina–based itinerant filmmaker who was active between 1936 and 1942, were screened once again in Kannapolis, North Carolina, a former mill town located just north of Charlotte. This showing was particularly significant because Waters's films of Kannapolis had just been named to the National Film Registry, an honor reserved for motion pictures of historical or aesthetic significance. For almost three hours, 16mm preservation prints of reels originally shot in 1936, 1938, and 1941 were projected before a mixed-age crowd at the 960-seat Gem Theater. Many of those in the audience were Kannapolis natives, a city that had experienced a number of recent hardships, most notably the 2003 closing of the clothing manufacturer Cannon Mills, which had built the town nearly a century earlier and once employed most of its inhabitants.[1]

For much of the screening there was a familiar murmur in the crowd, with a rotating set of narrators identifying who was on the screen as others in the audience carried on their own conversations about the memories spurred by pictures of their hometown in more prosperous years. But when Corine Cannon, the first African American woman to work a production job at Cannon Mills in 1962, was handed the microphone to narrate the section of the film taken in the African American community, a silence fell over the mostly white crowd. As Cannon described the footage, recalling names and places that were unknown to those at the Gem, it became clear that segregation, both then and now, marked how Waters's films were received by audiences. Waters advertised his own itinerant film practice, which he called *Movies of Local People,* in democratic language, asking audiences to "See Yourselves as Others See You," a turn of phrase that assumes a reflexive, and equal, public. But in practice, this act of recognition, whether of oneself or others, schools or factories, neighborhoods or business districts, was shaped by a social geography of difference that existed

163

in Kannapolis and many other towns visited by itinerant filmmakers in the first half of the twentieth century, and continues to resonate today. Even if some itinerants attempted to impose their idealized, and commercially suitable, view of a community on itself, or encouraged the film's sponsors to do the same, most local films represented social, racial, and economic differences, providing views that often served at odds with the stated intentions of the filmmaker.

In this chapter, I consider the role recognition played in the production and reception of local films. Rather than speculate more broadly about the encounter between the filmed subject and the movie camera, I am interested here in how assumptions about the form and function of the local film are built into the mode's aesthetic and social operations. Nowhere is this more apparent than in the oeuvre of H. Lee Waters, whose work is uniquely situated for this kind of analysis.[2] First, the vast majority of Waters's films are extant, making it possible to consider his representational strategies across different geographic locations and time periods. Second, Waters shot in a non-narrative, nonfiction style that allowed him to develop his own approach to filming local communities. Third, Waters made repeat visits to most of the communities he filmed, which meant that over time, he became familiar with the nuances of particular places. He filmed 118 communities in North Carolina, South Carolina, Virginia, and Tennessee, almost all of which were small towns. Many of these towns were, or were bordered by, mill villages, so-called because their economic, social, and political life revolved around a mill or factory. In most cases, the factory owners, in some cases a single individual, financed the construction of the villages as well, and workers lived in company-owned housing, shopped in company stores, and relied on their employer for municipal services. While, of course, no town is alike, the geographic limitations Waters placed on his work makes it possible to consider the relationship between his ordinary, and iterative, strategies of representation and his efforts to convince audiences that they were seeing something different from what they saw in Hollywood films, namely themselves.

In contrast to representation, recognition has been an undertheorized phenomenon in film studies, perhaps because the experience of seeing oneself in the movies was assumed to be more unusual than was actually the case. Even though Walter Benjamin notes that "any man today can lay claim to being filmed" in his classic essay on art in the age of mechanical reproducibility, his brief analysis on the subject considers being in the movies as a form of aspirational labor, rather than a social experience. For Benjamin, seeing oneself on screen is an experience that produces a false sense of accomplishment, like a writer who considers herself an author after the publication of a letter to the editor.³ Psychoanalytic theory assumes that recognition is an act of misrecognition, in which the subject identifies with the characters on screen, thus suturing the gap between the individual viewer and the universal subject position. These approaches to the question of recognition assume *a priori* that recognition of the self does not take place in the cinema, making these theories of limited value when applied to the local film. Instead, I turn to the work by social and political theorists, including Charles Taylor, Nancy Fraser, Axel Honneth, and particularly Paul Ricouer, on the philosophical and political valences associated with the act of recognition. Although the contemporary version of these debates was inaugurated in the early 1990s, with Taylor's 1994 essay on "The Politics of Recognition" focusing on the tensions between multiculturalism and late capitalism, the term "recognition" has since been adapted by a number of disciplines, including film studies, to describe the struggle for minority groups to gain political, civil, and social rights through visual media.⁴ As Paula Rabinowitz has argued about documentary film, its purpose is "to remand, if not actively remake, the subject into a historical agent," and thus is a form of politics "overlaid with a gloss of objectivity."⁵ Although local films were rarely so pointed in their critique, I argue that Waters's *Movies of Local People* actively challenged stable notions of self and other by depicting all people as equals before the camera. In this way, *Movies of Local People* can be seen as an effort to produce a community capable of recognizing itself not as it sees itself but as others, including minority groups, see it. After all, what is most interesting about the 2005 screening of the Kannapolis films is not that members of the audience could recognize their community but that they could also fail to recognize many of its members.

TO SEE YOURSELF AS OTHERS SEE YOU:
RECOGNITION AND THE MEDIATED SUBJECT

Although I have argued in previous chapters for the specificity of local film practices in particular historical moments and contexts, the assumed pleasure of recognizing oneself on the screen appears to transcend geographic boundaries and historical time periods. For example, a sign produced by the British itinerants Sagar Mitchell and James Kenyon in 1907 advised audiences to "See Yourself as Other People See You," a phrase used by many itinerants over the next half century, including Waters.⁶ The call was likely a reworking of a line from the well-known Robert Burns 1785 poem "To a Louse, On Seeing One on a Lady's Bonnet at Church," deployed for an

Figure 6.1. H. Lee Waters with camera. *Courtesy of Davidson County Historical Museum, Lexington, N.C.*

age in which self-awareness comes at the hands of a camera rather than an insect.[7] While Mitchell and Kenyon's advertisement can be read as a plain statement for a show in which what is on the screen is nothing more than local views, it is the very call to an individual viewer—"see yourself"—that underscores the local film's peculiar alchemy of display and perception.

But the local film is not a mirror, a point that is emphasized by the second half of the phrase, "as other people see you." Instead of the chain of looks that aligns the classical cinema spectator with the ideologies of movie characters, local films assume a socialized and embodied viewer, one who is already familiar with the other people on screen, who may in fact be in the very same audience with those people, who are also viewing themselves. When Stephen Bottomore defines the local film as a motion picture in which there is a "significant overlap" between the members of the audience in the theater and those individuals pictured on screen, he is calling attention to the fact that the mode relies on a particular form of recognition in which seeing oneself, seeing others, and seeing oneself as if one was seen by others are bound together in a mediated form.[8]

This question of recognition has been addressed most substantially by scholars who have researched local films made during the first two decades of cinema. As Mary Ann Doane observes of early cinema more generally, such films are suffused with what she calls the contingent, "that which is beyond or resistant to meaning." She observes that cinema has the capacity to "perfectly *represent*" the contingent, but this attribute has long been suppressed by classical cinema, which places the mechanical recording of reality in service of fictionalized narratives.[9] Recognition, in this context, might be seen as the act of recovering elements of what was thought to be contingent within the film frame, identifying and signifying people, places, and objects that go undescribed by the title cards that take the place of narrative cues in early cinema.

In fact, local views, even more so than companion genres, such as nonlocal "actualities," assume that their purpose is to produce moments of recognition that are illegible to a film's producer and exhibitor. When we look back at these films, we correctly place the emphasis on their localness, but in so doing miss the very specific appeals these films had for audiences. As Doane notes of the early moving images made by Auguste and Louis Lumière, the wealth of information offered within these films includes "the different types of clothing of various workers, the use of bicycles, the direction of gazes," but this material is ignored because of these films' status as the first projected moving images.[10] Local films offer similar information, but their depiction of what might be thought of as pure contingency effaces their value as texts. The Lumière films, Doane suggests, function as both a "record and performance" of what they depict, implying the presence of both archival and spectacular impulses.[11] Even after these archival and spectacular impulses began to separate from the conventions of mainstream classical cinema, local films retained this dual functionality. They were events when they were first exhibited and historical artifacts the day after.

Local films foreground the problem of the contingent precisely because their definition rests on a temporally and spatially situated encounter between an audience and a film that in most cases is preceded by an equally complex encounter between an individual and a motion picture camera.[12] For the local film, the threat of contingency is quelled by the act of recognition, but as soon as the last reel runs through the projector, the contingent looms again, as the audience that gives the film meaning quickly dissipates. The German film scholar Uli Jung makes a similar observation when he describes two films made in Cologne, Germany, the first produced by Lumière in 1896 for sale to audiences worldwide, and the second shot by Peter Marzen, a theater operator in Trier, Germany, in 1904. Jung argues that the two films are "generic" and "typical" of the period as they both "depict large masses of individuals moving about, . . . use major Catholic churches as backdrops, and . . . utilize the end of high mass to make sure a large number of people will fill the space in front of the camera." Jung argues that the popularity of scenics in the early cinema period (1895–1907) makes it difficult to tell local films apart from motion pictures made for global audiences without additional contextual evidence, creating what he calls a "blind spot in film historiography," referring, evidently, to a historiography that is built on analysis of extant prints.[13] To press Jung's point from another direction, one could argue that almost any motion picture is a local film at some moment—from Lumière's workers viewing their own exit from the company factory to an actor watching the daily rushes of a Hollywood feature. The presence of the contingent alone, and its temporary disappearance, which occurs when a viewer recognizes all that is contained within the frame, is not sufficient to mark a film as local.

Jung argues that it is within histories of exhibition that local films become more discernable, if not always discrete, objects. While I agree with this turn to exhibition, I also find within the films themselves looks of recognition, the very quality many itinerants, particularly Mitchell and Kenyon, emphasized. In Vanessa Toulmin's extensive research on this collection, which consists of several hundred reels produced between 1899 and 1913, she has uncovered an astonishing amount of contextual information about the celebrations, sporting events, modes of transportation, and spaces of work and leisure that are visible in these films.[14] And yet, Toulmin notes that Mitchell and Kenyon themselves saw their local movies as "a simple marketing venture to film as many faces as possible, thus providing a ready made paying audience, desiring to see themselves reproduced on screen."[15] In a coauthored essay, Toulmin and Martin Loiperdinger argue that the twin pleasures of self-recognition—seeing oneself and seeing oneself with the awareness that others are watching—were present in theatrical settings before cinema, with the reflective "Looking Glass Curtain" debuting at the Royal Coburg Theatre in London in 1821, and quickly crossed over to both photography and cinema. As Toulmin and Loiperdinger note, "Audiences attending the projection of local films were clearly aware that they were both the subject and object of the show."[16] As they observe, the local film is a "simple" motion picture genre, one whose appeal is, to borrow a phrase from David Bordwell, "excessively obvious."[17]

Although Toulmin and Loiperdinger, writing in 2005, were aware of just a handful of itinerant producers of local films, they correctly assumed that itinerant filmmakers, unfamiliar with the intricate cultures of the communities they visited, resorted to using a shooting script of sorts—factory gates, downtown business districts, schools, churches—in order to find the crowds of people they needed to fill their theaters. But the central appeal built into local films—self-recognition—also initiates a complex mode of moving image production, one negotiated by the filmmaker, the sponsor, the filmed subject, and the social group in which the subject is located. When seen in this light, true contingency is not the things that can be seen but remain unidentified in the frame, but rather the complex social formations that are reduced to a series of personal and group shots of people made by an outsider with remuneration in mind. It is the recognition of the self as seen by others that gives local films their currency as a distinct mode of moving image production and exhibition.

The Look Away: Toward a Theory of Mediated Mutual Recognition

In his inquiry into what he calls the "course of recognition," Paul Ricouer considers how recognition has been an essential, yet neglected, component of the Western philosophical tradition. Bringing together phenomenological and ethical approaches to the subject, Ricouer is primarily interested in the "transfer from the positive act of recognition to the demand to be recognized" that marks much of the contemporary discussion about the subject.[18] Just as Burns's poem noted that by recognizing another's foibles—seeing a louse on an upper-class woman's bonnet—one also has the opportunity to reflect on their own, the act of recognition generates awareness of social difference and, with it, empathy. Although local films were not intended to generate such thoughts, I argue that Waters's films of *mutual recognition* privileged such experiences.

As Ricouer reminds us, recognition has a long history in Western philosophy. For example, Immanuel Kant emphasized the role judgment plays in our ability to synthesize objects and their appearances with our prior knowledge about them. Building on Kant's theory of judgment and perception, Ricouer argues that change, particularly changes in time, "give rise to operations of recognition," which then push up against their limits, misrecognition and nonrecognition.[19] When we see an object, we register certain perceptions of it so that when we see it again, we are able to recognize it as the same object. But if we do not recognize an object, our failings are of little consequence, as a Kantian perspective assumes that time itself is objective, giving the object *a priori* definition.

But mis- and nonrecognition of people and certain familiar objects have very different implications, Ricouer suggests, as they bring about a recognition that what we perceive is governed by changes within ourselves, rather than the exterior world. In other words, when we fail to recognize someone or something that we have encountered before, we look within ourselves to discover the cause of this misrecognition. As Ricouer observes, this process of self-recognition draws on a dialectical relationship between "sameness and ipseity," the former being an "immutable identity" that does not change with time, the latter referring to the self, which develops ethically over time. The tensions in this dialectic are heightened in two acts, Ricouer argues, memory and promises. While both cases are "moments of actualization" in which the self becomes recognizable, the latter relies on an assertion of sameness—I remember myself in the past—while the other asserts ipseity—in the future, I will commit to this action.[20] Although these two capacities push against different aspects of the self, when paired together they make visible the stakes for self-recognition. If one fails to recognize the past, one has forgotten an essential aspect of oneself, and if one does not make good on a promise, one is committing a betrayal of the self. Self-recognition, then, is the act of identifying oneself as an ethical being who has constancy in a changing world.

This act of self-recognition takes on new dimensions, Ricouer claims, when one considers the relationship between "individual forms of human capacities and their social forms," the latter of which initiate what he calls "mutual recognition," quite simply, the awareness the self-recognition is dependent on the awareness, and presence, of others. Drawing on the work of Bernard Lepetit, who was associated with the Annales school of

French historiography, Ricouer suggests that collective representations shape social practice by acting as "symbolic mediations contributing to the instituting of the social bond," which in turn makes mutual recognition possible.[21] As William H. Sewell, Jr., notes, this cultural turn in French historiography inverts the economic and sociological determinism of earlier Annales scholarship and instead asserts the historical importance of the "formation, mutation, and disappearance" of the social order that is produced by individuals within a society and often reflected culturally.[22] In other words, societies create the conditions for mutual recognition to occur through the production of social and cultural formations, from the newspapers and broadsides that, according to Jürgen Habermas, constitute the "public sphere" of the eighteenth century to the rise of the novel in the nineteenth.[23] By emphasizing the sociality of recognition, Ricouer links these earlier discussions of the subject with more recent debates on the privileges associated with, and demanded for, particular identities, including those of racial, ethnic, and sexual minorities.

While aesthetic and analytic philosophers have associated recognition with problems of identification and perception, Paul Ricouer notes that political and economic philosophers have instead focused on the struggle for participation in the civic sphere. In this context, the threat of misrecognition is outweighed by what he calls a "refusal of recognition" by others who do not see themselves as belonging to the same social and political order. Drawing on Axel Honneth's work, Ricouer observes that "recognition intends two things: the other person and the norm," which offers an approach to this problem that is at once specific—one either recognizes another person or does not—and extensive, as a "norm" can be delimited in any number of ways. As a result, Ricouer argues that struggles for recognition have largely taken place on two planes: one that proposes "an enumeration of personal rights defined by their content" and one that allows for the "attribution of these rights to new categories of individuals or groups."[24] While the first category of rights belong to a familiar framework—borrowing from T. H. Marshall's division of rights into civil, legal, and social classes—the second category challenges longstanding divisions between and within societies.[25] As Ricouer comments, the politics of recognition has largely played out as a conflict between those who advocate for rights specified in the first plane, such as the redistribution of wealth, and those who advocate for rights specified in the second plane, such as legal protections for minority groups.

Without choosing a side in this longstanding argument, Ricouer expresses concern that the debate might be interminable and proposes that we instead look toward "peaceful experiences of mutual recognition, based on symbolic mediations as exempt from the juridical as from the commercial order of exchange." Recalling the anthropologist Marcel Mauss's work on the gift, Ricouer argues for the value of gratitude, as it "lightens the weight of obligation to give in return."[26] By seeing recognition as a kind of social esteem, one in which mutuality, not struggle, is central, Ricouer allows for a definition of social recognition that is dependent on mediation.[27] This argument echoes that of the political theorist Chantal Mouffe, who imagines the common good as a "'vanishing point,' something to which we must constantly refer when we are acting as citizens, but that can never be reached," or, crucially, defined.[28] But, unlike Mouffe, Ricouer emphasizes the role self-recognition plays in the mutual recognition he calls for. As he closes his book, he argues that "reception" is the "pivotal term between giving and giving in return."[29] In other words, it is the act of seeing oneself as others might see you that gives recognition its political, social, and ethical potency.

From Seeing Yourself as Others See You to Seeing Yourself in the Movies

In previous chapters I have suggested that the local view was augmented, and quickly replaced, by local films that sought to do more than just allow people to see themselves in the movies. Here, I suggest that what I call "films of mutual recognition" deployed the techniques of perception and display used in local views for an era in which the cinema was associated with sociality and commercialism, which in the United States was often subsumed under the Hollywood sign. Film historians have long argued that the medium has a unique capacity to reflect society, including individuals and groups at the margins who are not represented in other spheres of public life, particularly politics and business.[30] Although local views possessed this reflective quality in early cinema, the possibilities for mutual recognition were limited, as neither the local film nor the cinema was durable enough to sustain social critique. City booster films purposefully excluded many people from appearing in the pictures, and home talent and Hollywood local movies also sought to control how townspeople were depicted. But the 16mm itinerant filmmakers of the 1930s embraced an expansive and inclusive recognition as a core principle and developed business models that relied on the appeal self-recognition had for many in the communities they visited. Broader trends in visual culture, such as the increased use of documentary photography in popular magazines, gave credence to candid, unadorned images that were intended to tell a larger story. As a result, the local films of the 1930s came to serve as a social imaginary, a site where individuals could reflect on how they presented themselves to their communities and how others might perceive them.

This transition from the local view to the film of mutual recognition can be observed by considering the intersection between two phrases, both of which were used by Waters and others to promote their practice. The first was the aforementioned "See Yourself as Others See You"; the second was "See Yourself in the Movies." I have already discussed some of the implications of the first phrase for how these films constructed the experience of recognition. In what follows, I extend this analysis, and compare it with the sets of promises made by its companion phrase, "See Yourself in the Movies." When paired together, these phrases imply a theory of mutual recognition that underlines how local films both reflected and recreated communities.

As I have already suggested, the first phase, "See Yourself as Others See You," likely originated in a Burns poem from the late eighteenth century, a historical moment now associated with the French and American Revolutions, both of which sought to place individual rights—as opposed to the state—at the center of political and social systems. One can read the phrase, particularly in the context of the Burns poem, as implying a certain kind of shame that comes from an awareness of the political, social, and economic systems in which we participate. In this way, the phrase can be thought as a form of calling, asking the subject to participate as a member in a community that is already defined by others. This is a peculiar form of recognition, as one is asked to see oneself as a certain kind of actor—a citizen, perhaps, or maybe just someone who functions primarily in a certain social or economic role, such as a schoolchild, a mill worker, or a housewife.

This phrase is further complicated when the person who is seen is ordinarily invisible, often not by choice. As Ricouer notes, much of the "politics" in the politics of recognition comes out of a desire by members of excluded minority groups to seek rights granted to those who are in the majority group. In other words, seeking recognition is also a search for the rights and privileges granted to those who are recognized. At the same time, because one's quest for recognition may be denied or even punished, such a push for visibility carries with it considerable risk. For example, members of a minority group who are seeking rights granted to the majority might find, as a result of their push for recognition, that they are instead made targets for retaliation. As the Martinique writer Édouard Glissant has argued, the right *not* to be seen, which he calls "opacity," might be just as critical as recognition itself.[31] By remaining in the shadows, one can retain a certain degree of independence from a society that refuses to recognize its members in the manner they prefer. From this perspective, the call to see yourself is a threat, rather than an opportunity.

But this view of recognition is tempered by Waters's other clarion call—"see yourself in the movies"—which locates his practice in a particular medium, the cinema, and an historical moment, the mid-1930s, in which the "movies" is understood to be indistinguishable from Hollywood. The "see yourself" here is a less complicated one, more akin to earlier ideas of recognition as simply a form of identification. The viewer that is implied here is expected to see him- or herself, and those people, places, and objects that are an extension of one's identity—"that's me," "that's my school," "that's my workplace," "that's my town." Also implicit in this statement is the assumption that the movies will contain things that are not oneself, and in fact might belong to others.

The "movies," on the other hand, imply a narrowly defined cinema, that of Hollywood in the middle of the studio era. This moment was significant because of the studio system's dominance and the weakness of the nontheatrical sector, as 16mm film exhibition did not pick up until World War II. The "movies" also imply what we could call the fiction of fictional cinema, the idea that cinema is predominantly a medium for telling stories, usually couched within a particular genre, and delivering stars. Waters played up both notions—first, suggesting that the camera has the capacity to identify a movie star merely by filming them, and second, by suggesting that his films represented a kind of genre picture, the *Movies of Local People* that has its own logics of display, continuity, and narrative. And, of course, the "movies" suggest a larger representational system, one that is not limited to a particular community but instead carries with it much larger assumptions about the cinema's role in society, and its preeminent status as a medium that captures and documents everyday life, most often in newsreels.

Creating *Movies of Local People*

In Waters's oeuvre one finds a particularly sharp expression of the local film as a privileged form of mutual recognition. While many local films possess this quality, Waters was uniquely positioned to produce movies of mutual recognition. Like many of his film subjects, he grew up in a mill village and worked in the small town of Lexington, North Carolina. Waters also trained as a portrait photographer and possessed the entrepreneurial zest and bonhomie such a position required. He had a strong sense for how to elicit a response out of the subjects he approached in just a few feet of film, which meant that his films were well composed and intricately structured. Even if recognition in his early films rested on claims of identification, he very quickly moved to claiming the possibilities for mutual recognition and, soon, recognition of oneself and others as they were, rather than as they are. In this way, Waters self-consciously created a film style that revealed a community to itself.

Born in Caroleen, North Carolina, in 1902, Waters moved often as a child, as his parents chased factory work in mill towns in the Carolinas before settling in Lexington, North Carolina, a town of five thousand in the middle of the state. At the Erlanger Cotton Mills, located on the outskirts of town, Waters worked alongside his parents and lived with them in Erlanger Mills Village, a new community that was built and owned by his employer. By 1925, Waters had decided against a life as a millworker and began pursuing other opportunities. He was a musician and projectionist for Young's Theater, one of the two movie theaters in Lexington; a reporter for *The Dispatch*, the town's twice-weekly newspaper; and an apprentice at J. J. Hitchcock's Studio, a photography studio.[32] In May 1926, he graduated from Lexington High School. His father, Thomas Butler Waters, died the next month at the age of fifty-five from complications after major dental work. Waters and his mother were forced to move out of family housing and into a "hotel" the company kept for single workers. Shortly after his father died, Waters, with the help of his mother, purchased the photography studio and renamed it the H. Lee Waters Studio, beginning what would be a seventy-year career as a commercial studio photographer.

Perhaps because of his familiarity with small-town life, Waters made modest—yet more radical—claims for his movies. Unlike his predecessors, he did not promise townspeople that he would represent their community as a site of investment, an untapped reserve of acting talent, or even a place that has its own stories to tell. Instead, he took on the hometown as its own distinct topoi, something he could easily do because so many of the towns he visited were places just like Lexington, small towns experiencing an influx of population as the Carolinas became home to the nation's textile industry. Of the locations Waters visited, most owed their recent population growth, or even existence, to the mill villages that sprouted up in the North Carolina Piedmont and upstate South Carolina at the turn of the century. In just a few decades, local entrepreneurs created these sizeable industrial communities with the singular aim of producing textiles for the world market. Entire factories employing hundreds of people were constructed to make towels or hosiery or yarn, and their employees were housed by the company nearby so as to make it possible for one's entire life to be bound up in the mill. Waters likely sought out these communities because he knew that he could accomplish his goal of filming as many people as possible due to the systemic and totalizing ordering of space in the mill village.³³

In addition to his experience as a millworker, Waters's training as a commercial photographer made him well suited for itinerant filmmaking. Soon after starting his studio, Waters attended a summer course at the Winona Lake School of Photography in Indiana, which focused on technical training, and continued to keep up with the field by subscribing to trade publications. Like many photographers in the period, Waters supplemented his portraiture work with commercial projects, shooting for businesses and, on occasion, the local newspaper.³⁴ In the early 1930s, Waters purchased a home movie camera, which allowed him to learn the craft of filmmaking before he set out on the road.³⁵ His training and experience as a studio photographer provided him with the business and personal skills he needed for success on the road.

By most accounts, Waters became an itinerant filmmaker for pecuniary reasons. His studio business in Lexington was slow, as portrait photography was considered a luxury that few families, even in the relatively prosperous mill villages, could afford in the 1930s. In one of many newspaper interviews he gave later in life, he recalled that the idea for *Movies of Local People* came out of conversations he had with other studio photographers.³⁶ Although he had considered projecting still photographs of local people with lantern slides, another localizing tactic used by theater managers at the time, he decided to make movies instead because he thought it would be more profitable.³⁷ Waters worked on spec, shooting 16mm film of people and places as soon as he reached an agreement with the manager of the local movie theater to give him a cut of the box-office proceeds after his films were shown.

Like many itinerants, Waters ran his business largely by himself, creating the demand for the product he offered in every town he visited. Although his early films were black and white, he soon turned to color, shooting a few hundred feet in each community. In order to live up to his own advertising, Waters filmed as many people as possible when he visited a town and selected his shooting locations accordingly. He visited schools, where he filmed every grade and often the teachers as well. If the town had mills, he went to the gates when the shift changed in order to film people who were surprised to see a camera after a hard day's work. He went downtown, where young mothers and businessmen congregated in largely

Figure 6.2. The car used by H. Lee Waters when he made his *Movies of Local People*. Courtesy of Davidson County Historical Museum, Lexington, N.C.

empty streets. While there, he also shot footage of local businesses who had paid for the privilege of parading their products and employees before his camera. He went into neighborhoods where he found children playing and elderly people sitting on their front porch. After finishing his rounds, which rarely lasted more than a day, he returned to Lexington and sent his film to Kodak for processing. He assembled the developed footage into several reels and went back to the town to show his movies for a several-day engagement.

Waters, more than most itinerants, created the demand for his films by using every trick out of the showman's book—banners, flyers, posters, and other forms of ballyhoo, much of which he documented in photographs. For example, one photograph depicts the car he drove through town, a late-model, four-door Pontiac—a long, Dachshund-like car with gentle curves over the wheel wells, protruding headlights, and a toothy grill for a face, with two large, bell-shaped loudspeakers attached to the front and rear of the car, connected to the inside by long, thick speaker wire. A large banner, emblazoned with the name of his enterprise, "Movies of

Local People," hangs over the side of the car, covering up the two rear side windows and extending past the back of the car. Waters also printed round, mirror-backed buttons—underscoring the reflective nature of his film practice—to hand out so that people could pin an advertisement for his practice on their shirts. The buttons read, simply, "I'm in the Movies."

Since Waters kept detailed financial records, it is easy to determine his business model. From the beginning, his two streams of revenue were a percentage of ticket sales, in most cases ranging from a 30- to 50-percent take of the box-office gross, and advertising that was sold to local businesses on a per-foot basis. In fact, advertising often made up the majority of his revenue and, because it was collected in advance, allowed Waters to pay for fixed costs, including film stock, before he sold the first ticket. While the advertisements may have been sold to businesses as purely promotional segments, an opportunity for a store to display its wares and employees, Waters rarely held to the format, filming whatever appeared of interest at the time, from small children wandering through a shop to someone who decided to mug for the camera.[38]

The connection between *Movies of Local People* and Hollywood came up frequently in the newspaper advertising and articles printed in advance of Waters's visit, particularly in the initial two years of his operation when he was most likely to be visiting a town for the first time. For a visit to Siler City, North Carolina, one newspaper observed that its residents "will have the opportunity to determine whether or not our little metropolis is withholding from the screen world a Gable, Harlow, or a Zasu [sic] Pitts, by going to the Gem Theatre Monday and Tuesday and seeing moving pictures of many local citizens."[39] A newspaper account of a film made a month earlier, in Albemarle, North Carolina, revealed some of the same tensions and emphasized the novelty of Waters's equipment. In August 1936, the *Stanly News and Press* noted that while still images of the town's people had been projected by the manager a few months earlier, Waters's films will be "the first time that moving pictures of local citizens have been shown, and the unique feature is expected to draw large crowds to the theatre. The pictures were made several days ago, the regular paraphernalia of the picture studios being used."[40]

Other newspaper accounts of Waters's filmmaking emphasized their ordinariness, not their connection to Hollywood, particularly those that were published after his second, third, or fourth visit to town. While few itinerants sought to discredit associations others made between the movie industry and their own artisanal practices, Waters was particularly successful in producing movies that audiences read as being both engaging and distinct from what the movie industry had to offer. In Concord, North Carolina, the local paper noted that Waters had been making "motion pictures of Concordians as they went about their work, hobby or recreation as the case might be."[41] Instead of screen tests, Waters appeared to be making moving image equivalents of the kind of candid photography that one saw in magazines such as *Life* and *Time*. The people who appeared in the movies were not caught up in the camera; rather, it was the camera that had caught them. For Waters's return trip to Siler City, the paper observed that Waters's familiar presence was part of his style, as "he will catch folks just as they appear in everyday life."[42] As the *Henderson Daily Dispatch* reported, Waters's filmmaking presence was so ordinary that "you may see yourself on the screen as many people were photographed unaware."[43]

The possibility of being filmed without one's knowledge appeared to be new for Waters's audiences. Local filmmakers working in 35mm carefully staged their shots, so it was highly unlikely that a camera would appear as a surprise. Even so, Waters's visits to town were announced in advance, and relatively few people in the films appear to be surprised by his camera. Perhaps his discussion of people being caught unawares meant merely that they were filmed without being warned beforehand that a cameraman was on his way. One review of Waters's films noted that the "cameraman 'caught' many of our citizens on the streets—some comical, others dignified and self-conscious."[44] After what might have been a somewhat hostile reception in Forest City, North Carolina, the local theater placed a newspaper advertisement to reassure would-be film subjects that "Cameraman Waters has not been sent to Forest City by the US Department of Justice to obtain evidence against any citizens suspected of crime: he has not been sent to photograph the lay of the land for any government for use in war time."[45] There were a few occasions when Waters's filmmaking activities were announced in the paper, such as a call placed in the *Roxboro Courier* for "mothers with children under school age" to appear at the Dolly Madison Theater so that Waters can make a group picture of them, though his tight shooting schedules seemed to limit such notices.[46] It is also clear from viewing the films that many of the pictures, especially ones taken at schools, were clearly choreographed, if not posed, and thus distinct from Waters's street scenes. This distinction between "aware" and "unaware" shots might also be similar to that made between studio and candid photography which preoccupied still photographers in magazines like *Popular Photography*.[47] The lines between the two were not as clear as they first seemed, and in effect worked to enlist local people in the production of images that appeared to be spontaneously filmed.

Even if Waters was able to film people unawares on his first visit to a town, he was unlikely to find the same success on return visits. He visited many towns several times, either to make more movies or to show old ones to meet demand. Although Waters had limited competition, mostly from locals who tried their hand at filmmaking, his use of semi-professional filmmaking equipment and his skill as a cinematographer meant that he could return to a town again and again and know that he would draw a crowd of paying customers. As a result, he was able to create films of mutual recognition that explored the social dimensions of local places.

The Mediated Recognition of *Movies of Local People*

So far, I have established that Waters carried out his film practice in a systematic manner and worked in places that were similar to one another in terms of their demographics, economies, and social organizations. Not surprisingly, these towns also had very similar media infrastructures. Almost all of the towns Waters visited had a movie theater, and most also had a local newspaper that reported community and national news and would have been able to receive local and regional radio signals. Of these three media, however, newspapers were the most local, in part because they could rely on economies of scale—such as printing at another facility—to reduce costs and sustain a lower rate of publication, once or twice weekly in many cases, in order to serve its community. As Benedict Anderson has famously argued, newspapers helped to produce an "imagined community" by sustaining a belief that a publication both represented and reproduced the world of its readers.[48] Local newspapers in small communities had a particularly intimate relationship with the people they covered in the 1930s and 1940s. Many printed not just the news of the town's officials but also the events of everyday life, with something as slight as a vacation or a visit from an old friend being reported in full. In many cases, the proof of one's membership in a community could be delivered by a person's appearance in the local newspaper.[49]

Newspapers were particularly important for movie theaters and, by extension, Waters's film practice, as they dedicated considerable advertising and editorial space to the coverage of all things related to the cinema. While this outsized presence of Hollywood news items, movie star photographs, and gossip columns in local papers could be written off as just further evidence of the industry's successful publicity efforts, to do so ignores the impact of seeing such material in a paper that identifies itself with a local community. Many small theaters were independently owned and managed, and thus had a greater stake in how Hollywood was covered locally, as untimely or negative coverage could hurt interest in the theater's own programs. In many cases, theater managers were personally credited with bringing particular film programs to town, even if they had relatively little sway over what they screened on a given week.

By covering movie stars as well as their own community, local newspapers helped collapse the distance between their small town and Hollywood. A cinematic language even permeated the language of the newspaper. One column that appeared under a number of names in assorted newspapers sought to write about the events of the town as if it were a moving portrait of the people in town. For example, the *Davie Record*, in Mocksville, North Carolina, ran a column called "Seen along Main Street," written pseudonymously by "The Street Rambler," who once caught Waters's own activities in the midst of a busy day:

> Old maid and old bachelor talking things over—Miss Ruby Angell drinking coffee and eating doughnuts—Miss Mary Foster shopping in Mocksville Cash Store—Phillip Johnson raising a dust on Main street—J. T. Angell cleaning sidewalk after heavy wind storm—Albert Boger telling about how hard the wind blew—Mrs. Ralph Morris and little daughter on their way to school—Three C boys going to the movies—School children watching snowflakes—Policeman and wife walking up street—Jim Burgess having his picture made for the movies—Sheriff Bowden on his way to ball game—Dr. Garland Greene leaving court house—C.F. Merouev, Jr, walking around bareheaded on cold morning—Miss Helen Page getting mail—Drug clerks busy delivering cold drinks to Johnstone building—Two girls falling out about boy friend—Fellow drinking bottle of beer, bottle of wine and glass of water—Mrs Frank Fowler selling theatre tickets—Miss Mary Alice Binkley on way to telephone office—Bill Merrell going south with bunch of rugs.[50]

The brevity and vividness of these descriptions, and the action implied, makes them read not only as images but as moving images, with the em-dash serving to splice each scene so that they may be read not as one continuous action but rather dozens of individual actions, some related—a dust is raised, cleaned up, then discussed—and others not at all. In contrast to the local news gathering of an earlier generation, in which a dutiful reporter went from house to house collecting news—a mode of reporting deftly captured in Sherwood Anderson's 1919 short story collection *Winesburg, Ohio*—this new form of news writing could have been prepared by a reporter looking out his or her window, or perhaps walking up and down Main Street. This dominance of the visual collection of information, and of cinematic language as a way of ordering this information, emerged in these "snap shots" columns, and within new expectations for how one

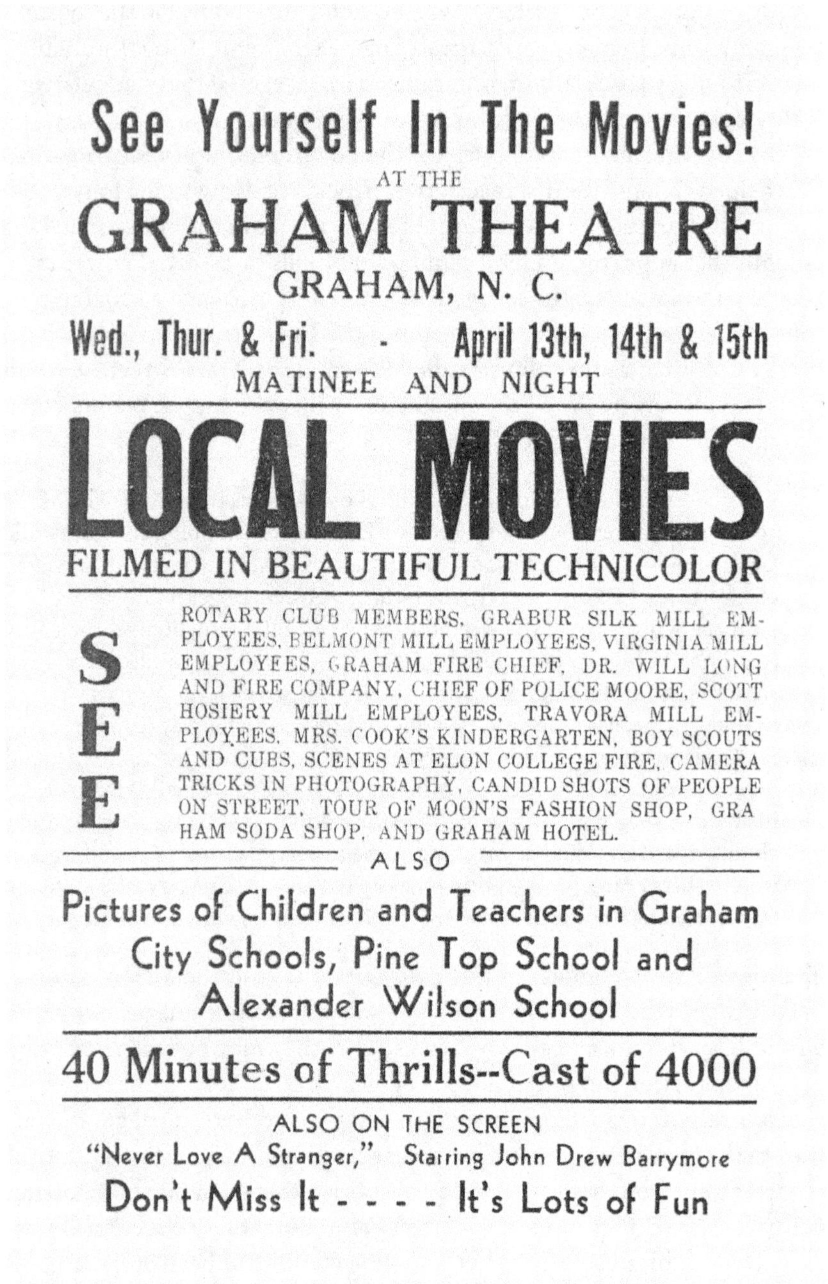

See Yourself In The Movies!
AT THE
GRAHAM THEATRE
GRAHAM, N. C.

Wed., Thur. & Fri. - April 13th, 14th & 15th
MATINEE AND NIGHT

LOCAL MOVIES
FILMED IN BEAUTIFUL TECHNICOLOR

S E E ROTARY CLUB MEMBERS, GRABUR SILK MILL EMPLOYEES, BELMONT MILL EMPLOYEES, VIRGINIA MILL EMPLOYEES, GRAHAM FIRE CHIEF, DR. WILL LONG AND FIRE COMPANY, CHIEF OF POLICE MOORE, SCOTT HOSIERY MILL EMPLOYEES, TRAVORA MILL EMPLOYEES, MRS. COOK'S KINDERGARTEN, BOY SCOUTS AND CUBS, SCENES AT ELON COLLEGE FIRE, CAMERA TRICKS IN PHOTOGRAPHY, CANDID SHOTS OF PEOPLE ON STREET, TOUR OF MOON'S FASHION SHOP, GRAHAM SODA SHOP, AND GRAHAM HOTEL.

ALSO

Pictures of Children and Teachers in Graham City Schools, Pine Top School and Alexander Wilson School

40 Minutes of Thrills--Cast of 4000

ALSO ON THE SCREEN
"Never Love A Stranger," Starring John Drew Barrymore

Don't Miss It - - - - It's Lots of Fun

Figure 6.3. Flyer for H. Lee Waters's *Movies of Local People,* Graham, North Carolina. H. Lee Waters Collection, David M. Rubenstein Rare Books and Manuscript Library, Duke University, Durham, N.C.

participated in mediated culture. Because no one would report their news, they had to make themselves be seen as to be included in the newspaper.

It is not surprising, then, that Waters's films were often advertised in the form of lists of scenes closely resembling these snapshot columns, which might have encouraged audiences to read the films as a series of short scenes. Before Waters had even shot the film of Siler City, the paper, or perhaps Waters himself, felt confident enough in his intentions to film "local people, industry, athletic teams and other organizations" to include them in print.[51] After the film had already been made, the descriptions became more exact, particularly in Waters's own flyers, which he handed out to help bring people to the movie theater. For a 1942 showing in Graham, North Carolina, Waters's flyers let his audience know that they could see: "Rotary Club members, Grabar Silk Mill Employees, Belmont Mill Employees, Virginia Mill Employees, Graham Fire Chief, Dr. Will Long and fire company, Chief of Police Moore, Scott Hosiery Mill Employees, Travora Mill Employees, Mrs. Cook's Kindergarten, Boy Scouts and Cubs, Scenes at Elon College Fire, Camera Tricks in Photography, Candid Shots of People on Street, Tour of Moon's Fashion Shop, Graham Soda Shop and Graham Hotel."[52]

All of this and "pictures of children and teachers in Graham City Schools, Pine Top School and Alexander Wilson School" were promised by Waters in this list of scenes. It also included the various government, civic, and education groups that made up most of the news in a local newspaper. A community that could be captured in snapshots in print could also be captured in "cinema shots," as the *Valdese News* described them, making a film practice like *Movies of Local People* possible.[53] The presence of these cinematic newspaper columns in the papers of the towns Waters visited suggests that seeing oneself as if one were in the movies was something that could easily be imagined by the people in the communities he visited, even if those movies had not been made before Waters came to their town.

Like these anonymous newspaper columnists, Waters used a systematic approach to filmmaking that allowed him to meet his objective of capturing as many faces as possible without foreclosing the opportunity to shoot whatever captivated him. As the sociologist and film theorist Daniel O'Connor observes of cinema more generally, Waters used his camera as a "social apparatus," which, as O'Connor notes, "evokes a power relation between an anonymous viewership and those made into its image." Like other scholars, O'Connor invokes the work of Michel Foucault to cast the cinema as "an extension of disciplinary vigilance," but instead of focusing on the disciplining of bodies in the theater, O'Connor instead argues that "disciplinary cinema structures the visual field so as to produce and reproduce the opposition of viewer and image."[54] For him, the disciplinary cinema, which we could also term a cinema of surveillance, both monitors social relations and transforms them through the use of montage, putting disparate images of society in relationship to one another, producing what he calls a "mobile social interface." Filmmakers like Waters embraced the disciplinary potential of the cinema to produce an image of the local that is imbricated in what O'Conner terms a "relatively closed, fixed, and territorially bounded space for idiosyncratic events and activities that are particular to its inhabitants."[55] Even though O'Connor suggests that disciplinary cinema makes local culture "largely obsolete," filmmakers like Waters simultaneously embraced a sociological definition of the local and the broader moving image culture that made his work legible to movie audiences.

Seen in this light, Waters's films can be read as a disciplinary cinema that aims to produce mutual recognition through montage. In a 1990 NBC television news segment, Waters demonstrated his filmmaking style for television audiences.[56] In the three-minute piece, he can be seen calling out to his film subjects, asking them to engage with him and his camera. Unlike classical cinema, in which looking at the camera is a threat to the "fourth wall" that separates spectators from the world on screen, almost all of the people seen in Waters's films are looking directly at the camera. In many cases, Waters filmed subjects standing still, as if posing for the camera, before he was able to persuade them to respond to the camera in some way. In other cases, Waters filmed people walking by the camera, giving them either an opportunity to stop and pose or cover their face so they can avoid being seen or, in some cases, avert their eyes while straining to appear as if they do not notice the camera at all. Camera avoidance, part of what Sarah Keller has termed "cinephobia," appears to be gendered in Waters's films—with women hiding from the camera perhaps ten times as frequently as men.[57] While one might imagine that such responses to the camera are situational—with factory exit scenes, taken after a long day's work, being one site where men and women would prefer not to be filmed—such looks—and looks away—can be seen in almost every environment.

The production of these scenes occur as if they were scripted in advance. For school shots, which made up the largest part of almost any film Waters made, he would often film entire classes that were lined up for his film as if he was going to take a still photograph of them. Holding the camera, he would pan over the faces of the students, often moving the camera across the crowd several times to make sure he included everyone. He would also film school activities, most often children's games or sporting events, and again would hold the camera so as to give himself the most flexibility. While he would occasionally film close-up shots of particular students, he used the medium-length shot most often so that several students were in the frame at the same time.

For shots of the mill, almost always taken at shift change, Waters used a different approach. He placed his camera on a tripod, which meant that people would approach the camera and then walk off screen. As older people were more reluctant to be filmed by Waters than schoolchildren were, the use of a tripod gave his film subjects the option of not appearing on film because they knew they could easily escape the camera's view. In these shots it was common for people, especially women, to cover their faces while exiting the mill, suggesting that they were not interested in being filmed, which, as I explore below, has interesting implications for how we read recognition in these films. Waters also used a tripod for scenes taken downtown, and he would often speed up the film, accomplished by winding the hand-cranked camera more slowly than usual, to produce the effect of a busy street.

For other street scenes and for advertisements, Waters used a mixture of approaches. He occasionally used a tripod but would also hold the camera to give himself more leeway in his filming. While the length of his shots taken at the school tended to be brief, as the motion of the children there tended to be frantic, he could use longer shots downtown, taking the time to capture a toddler walking down the street or a business owner demonstrating a product. The shot lengths were also longer in African American neighborhoods, which Waters filmed often, most likely because he could not film African Americans in other places. In both his black-and-white and color films Waters was able to consistently produce sharp, high-contrast work, particularly remarkable because he made manual adjustments to his camera on the fly. Waters used one-hundred-foot rolls, roughly four minutes in length, and edited his films in camera, which meant that whatever he filmed next would appear next when he showed his film a few weeks later. Although there was not necessarily any relation between one shot and the next, Waters's films almost always started with a reel shot at the school, followed by several reels of advertisements and other downtown shots, before he returned to the second reel shot at the school. Even though it would have been possible to make his films into narratives by using title cards to separate certain scenes from others, or by structuring the film so it progressed from one part of town to the next, Waters did not do so. Instead, his films have an organic logic in which the town is made out of disparate scenes held together by their location in a shared social space.

By making *Movies of Local People,* Waters not only inverted Hollywood's construction of the movie theater as a nonlocal, nondifferentiated space where one sees but is not seen but also challenged a community's conception of itself, where its primary gathering spaces—the school, places of work, the home—are segregated along age, gender, economic, and racial lines. As folklorists Beverly J. Stoeltje and Richard Bauman note in an article on a community festival in Luling, Texas, the presentation of place through a demarcated event allows for what they call a "centralization in reverse" that presents the community to itself for contemplation by itself. As Stoeltje and Bauman observe, the presentation of community in a festival "set[s] things off in special contexts, marking them with special intensity as being on view, available for examination, contemplation, reflection, whether the object is woman, flag, agricultural product, or association."[58] The function of the festival, then, is to make the town visible to itself, so it may be subject to analysis, which allows for, in the words of Stoeltje, a "regeneration through the rearrangement of structures, thus creating new frames and processes."[59] Waters's films had the potential to challenge and regenerate how a community saw itself because he could, unlike almost anyone else in town, visit the factory, the schoolyard, downtown, African American neighborhoods, and even fly in an airplane to take aerial views in the course of a day's visit. The underpinning promise of his film enterprise—seeing yourself as others see you—is one that implies a community of "others" and the inability for any one person in that community to see how he or she is perceived by these "others." Just as festivals can challenge the social order while remaining pleasurable events, Waters's films contain latent critiques of the communities he depicted even when they were entertaining. One witnesses scenes of poverty, humiliation, and prejudice in these films, and yet, they still appear celebratory, as if all aspects of the community are worth seeing on the big screen.

Waters's films, like festivals, work in part by inverting the normal order, making the familiar exotic and the exotic familiar. The community that is being filmed is allowed to see itself in the movies, as if their town was a subject worthy of a Hollywood film. Likewise, by filming the community, Waters made the once very unusual experience of being in

Figure 6.4. *Movies of Local People* showing at an unidentified theater. *Courtesy of Davidson County Historical Museum, Lexington, N.C.*

a film an ordinary one for his audience. As the *Journal-Patriot* in North Wilkesboro, North Carolina, noted of a repeat visit by Waters to their town in 1941, "Mr. Waters, who travels throughout this and surrounding states, with a carload of expensive movie equipment, has helped many in making their first appearance on the silver screen. He has appeared in this city before and movie fans know the type of entertainment he offers."[60] While Waters began by offering something that was very unusual for his audiences, his enterprise became something familiar for the people in the towns he visited.

The Mutual Recognition of Difference and the Color Line

Even if Waters made the local film a routine experience in the towns he visited, the mutual recognition that his films advanced was far more challenging than appears to be the case from a cursory reading of the films. As Ricouer reminds us, mutual recognition asks us to be cognizant of both the other, the person who is asking to be recognized, and the norm, the figure against which we measure our capacity to recognize someone. Working in a medium that was by the 1930s strongly encoded with normative ideas of social difference, Waters asked the people who saw his films to simultaneously compare people to these norms and to recognize those depicted as themselves and their neighbors.

Nowhere was this difficulty more apparent than in Waters's films of African American residents. Although African Americans were excluded from many of the sites Waters filmed, particularly mill villages, they were nonetheless part of the larger community, and white audiences would have recognized many of their African American neighbors, even if they were in places that whites rarely visited. African American residents would have likely recognized many whites but would have also been particularly aware of the dangers posed by the movie camera. As Shawn Michelle Smith notes, W. E. B. Du Bois defined "double consciousness" as the "sense of always looking at one's self through the eyes of others," thus arguing for the importance of visual culture in understanding the history of blackness in the United States.[61] Applying Henry Louis Gates's concept of "signifying," in which African Americans manipulate signs to convey a doubled meaning, to visual culture, Smith suggests that African American photography has the capacity to "denaturaliz[e] both images and viewing positions" by repeating the tropes of white photography. For example, she suggests that Du Bois's contribution to the Paris Exhibition of 1900, a photographic series titled "Types of American Negroes," played with the "color" lines that separated the "criminal mugshot" from the "middle-class portrait." She argues that the photographs selected by Du Bois, some of which appeared to be signifying both criminality and middle-classness simultaneously, worked to "disrupt the authority of white observers by collapsing the distance between viewers and objects under view that is held traditionally to empower observers."[62] Because of photography's association with objectivity and neutrality, that is, both depicting reality without manipulation and operating in much the same way regardless of who is front of or behind the camera, Smith suggests African Americans are heavily invested in the medium as a mode of representation.

For obvious reasons, the cinema does not offer the same opportunity for this kind of manipulation, which makes Waters's films a particularly important site where African Americans encountered the movies. Unlike classical Hollywood cinema, which so distorted views of African American life that it gave rise to an alternative cinema practice that operated at a near complete remove from the industry in Los Angeles, Waters depicted

African Americans in a largely neutral and objective fashion.[63] As a result, Waters was often *more* apt to capture looks of racial difference and racial recognition than other filmmakers, as he was seeking to film a community as it was rather than produce a carefully constructed image of it.

Even after the first wave of the Great Migration, North Carolina still had a significant African American population, with the 1940 census reporting that 27.5 percent of its residents were African American, the sixth highest percentage in the country. Segregation ensured that whites and African Americans participated in markedly distinct economic, social, and political spheres, which had the effect of creating two parallel worlds within many of the towns in the state. For example, while textile mills employed 19 percent of the white labor force in the state, they only employed 1.5 percent of the African American labor force. In contrast, just 1 percent of whites worked in "domestic service" while 17 percent of African Americans did.[64] With the 1898 Wilmington insurrection, in which white supremacists forcibly overturned a democratically elected local government, still within living memory, many African Americans operated with the awareness that racial violence was a very real threat.[65]

Not surprisingly, African Americans were also less likely than whites to be able to attend the movies at all. In 1937, one exhibitor publication counted just 14 African American theaters in North Carolina, with a total of 5,600 seats, or one seat for approximately every 175 African American residents of the state.[66] This compared unfavorably with the nation on the whole, with the *Motion Picture Herald*, who ran the article, noting that there was one seat for every eighty-nine African Americans in African American theaters, compared to one seat for every twelve whites. While many theaters were spatially or temporally segregated—balcony seating in larger towns and Sunday night shows in smaller ones—and thus were more open to African Americans than these numbers suggest, segregation limited African American participation in film culture. Other exhibition sites, such as churches, may have made cinema available to African American audiences in nontheatrical settings, but this did not change the fact that many African Americans in the state had limited access to the most recent films screened in movie theaters.

Given these financial and logistical challenges, it is somewhat surprising that Waters filmed African American communities at all. And yet, of the 118 communities he visited, Waters screened films to African American audiences in 32 of them, or just over one-quarter of the total. While a few of these screenings were either in nontheatrical settings, such as an African

American school in Hillsborough, North Carolina, or African American theaters, such at the Hollywood Theater in Chapel Hill and the Palace Theater in Kannapolis, most were in theaters with a balcony. As a result, most scenes of African Americans in Waters films were made with the expectation that they would have been shown to either white audiences alone, or white and African American audiences in a segregated theater. In what follows, I consider films from three North Carolina communities—Henderson, Chapel Hill, and Kannapolis.

Waters first visited Henderson, a township of 16,137, in December 1936, not long after he began making *Movies of Local People*, and returned to the town twice, first in September 1938 and then again in October 1939.[67] Even though the Stevenson Theater, which opened in 1927 and sat eight hundred, had a balcony, Waters's first screening at the theater appeared to take place without the presence of a African American audience.[68] For the two later screenings, African Americans were in the audience, although Waters recorded receiving just a handful of dollars from African American audiences, $20.05 from the 1938 visit and just $4.65 from the 1939 visit. While Waters did not provide attendance records as he did for white audiences in Henderson, the balcony revenue made up just 3.5 percent of the $716.35 box office received during these two visits. This poor showing came despite the fact that two-fifths of Henderson's population in 1940 was African American, meaning that a substantial portion of the town was missing from the theater the nights Waters's films were screened. S. S. Stevenson, who ran a small theater chain from his home in Henderson, including his eponymous theater, appears to have not been interested in the African American movie audience, as the closest African American theater was in Raleigh, forty miles to the south. When Waters came to Henderson, it seemed clear that he was to make a film for its white residents only.

The 1939 film of Henderson opens with a typical scene of students exiting a school building. In fact, the entire film is fairly ordinary, with Waters filming schools, downtown businesses, and sites of employment, in this case scenes at a tobacco packhouse. Rather than focus on these rather ordinary scenes, I want to call attention to the moments where African Americans, who, again, were not considered to be the audience for this film, appear. In fact, the opening two shots of the film, in which schoolchildren parade in front of the camera, depict a middle-aged African American man sitting in the background, suggesting he occupies some unidentified role with the school. Children play baseball and other school-yard games, all without the presence of African Americans, underscoring how segregated social life was during this period. Even when Waters showed large crowd scenes, such as those taken at the high school, only white faces appear, producing the illusion that Henderson was a white community.

When African Americans do appear, such as a young man depicted in one of Waters's portrait shots, the look returned to Waters is skeptical; in one case, an African American man runs away from the camera. While the footage of workplaces includes African American employees, they are often in the background and do not smile like their white coworkers. In this film, Waters presents African Americans as laborers attending to the upkeep of white life. In one of the film's more poignant scenes, we see African American men and women assisting white children at the playground, helping them go down slides and pushing them on swings.

Waters also filmed African Americans in downtown Henderson, though here again it is clear that visibility was a threat for many African Americans. For example, in one shot a young heavyset boy is walking confidently in the center of a downtown sidewalk when he passes by an older African American woman, who stops and turns to watch him. In the next shot, we see the boy continue to walk while the woman stands off to one side, witnessing the film's production as if she is concerned that some harm would come to him as a result of being on camera.

The Henderson film ends with a series of trick shots for which Waters was well known. In one, he slow cranks the camera to produce the illusion of an extremely busy downtown, and then fast cranks the camera and holds it upside down to produce the illusion of reverse motion. In both cases, the town becomes automated, as if it is running of its own accord rather than as the product of individuals walking the streets, driving cars, and otherwise acting on the physical landscape. Waters follows this special effect shot with a long panning shot of downtown, as if to remind audiences of the surveillance qualities of his practice. The next shot returns to the sidewalk, only this time Waters has split the screen horizontally, with the intended effect of matching the torsos of passersby to the legs of others. But one African American, standing still on the right side of the frame, looks away from the camera, as if to observe people's reaction to Waters as he films. When he turns toward the camera, the shot ends, and soon after, so does Waters's movie of Henderson. (See Moving Image 6.1.)

If Waters's films of Henderson largely ignored African American life, the single picture he made in Chapel Hill, home to the University of North Carolina, instead imagined a community where African Americans were the most important members of society. While the university did not admit its first African American student until 1951, African Americans had long played an important part in the community, living near campus and performing many service-related roles, such as building maintenance and preparing food in the cafeterias. If Waters had instead made a film at the university, it might have looked much like the Henderson film, depicting an entirely white campus in which African Americans appear only at the margins of the frame.

Instead, Waters produced a picture of the African American community from within, depicting inhabitants as individuals who lived in the segregated neighborhoods that bordered the university. With a township population of 8,903, Chapel Hill's economy centered around the university. Like Henderson, a significant portion of Chapel Hill's population, 32.8 percent, was African American, and the town's African American community was prosperous enough to support its own movie theater, which opened in 1939. Waters visited the theater twice, first in October 1939 and then again in April 1941, though he only recorded the revenue from the first visit, $64.94 in three screenings, which was significantly lower than Waters would receive on a typical visit to a white theater.

Almost all of the footage in the two films is taken outside people's homes, with the characters in the center of the frame, suggesting that Waters asked permission to film people and had them pose for the camera. The people smile before the camera, and there are few instances of either men or women hiding from the camera. If African Americans were portrayed as caretakers in Waters's film of Henderson, in Chapel Hill whites are not visible at all. While we see scenes of African American businesses and institutions, such as schools and churches, the white world is rendered invisible in these films. Instead of displaying the availability of consumer goods in stores, here African American businesses demonstrate their services, such as taxi cabs and automotive repair shops.

In Kannapolis, Waters made the rare decision for his 1941 visit to film white and African American communities and screen his films in both white-only and black-only theaters, the Dixie and the Palace, respectively. Not surprisingly, this segregation was reproduced in the film itself, with the "white" reels featuring the city's white residents and the single "black" reel featuring its African American inhabitants, who made up 15 percent of the township's population.[69] Waters's footage of the African American community is very similar to that taken in Chapel Hill, filming schoolchildren and some businesses but mostly the everyday lives of African Americans. Because the film was presented alongside films of Kannapolis's white communities, however, economic disparities became visible to all of the town's population, an important development even if, unlike documentaries of the period, there was no associated call to action.

But Kannapolis is significant for another reason. Like many mill towns, Kannapolis was a new community, one whose residents were from elsewhere and had none of the deep ties that bound natives to their hometowns. Furthermore, what identity Kannapolis did have was often tied up with that of the person who owned the mills, making these towns more extensions of a single person's vision than a collective project. When Waters visited a town, he did not just lay bare the divisions that existed in the town. He also gave townspeople an opportunity to see the various schools, factories, stores, churches, and buildings as belonging to a community they could identify as their own. It was the mutual recognition of place that made the local film such an enduring artifact of the period for many communities.

While Waters did not make his films with the intention of making social inequities visible, seen today it is clear that the problems of difference—from the inequalities in housing and work opportunities to the gender- and race-coded responses to the camera—are continuously addressed in his films. Although the opportunities for recognition that are presented by Waters's films are not matched with a redistribution of economic, psychic, or legal resources, these movies do allow us to imagine the possibilities for mutual recognition in the local film.

From Mutual Recognition to Place Recognition

If the emphasis on mutual recognition in Waters's films destabilized social identities, his films also produced place-based identities. By filming everyone he anticipated might come to the theater, Waters created a moving image record that served as a cognitive map of the community he filmed. Even though his films named particular places, incorporated towns, as their site of production and exhibition, his flyers revealed that such place-names were capacious, containing schools, mills, and small villages far outside of city limits. In this way, place recognition is a constitutive act, one that employs identification in order to inform a mutual recognition of one's common membership in a community with others. And for Kannapolis and many similar towns, such acts of place recognition resulted in more durable associations of people and the built environments they inhabited with place-names.

This process of place recognition was particularly important for the many Waters films that included mill towns. Because these towns were often plotted on land purchased by their owners, who then proceeded to design and manage their operations, they functioned as distinct "topias," purpose-built modern economic projects that were uneasily expected to fulfill social and cultural demands by its residents. Like most company towns, Kannapolis had a life, a history, a presence outside the confines of the imagination of its creator and owner. As Edward L. Rankin Jr. notes in the company history, produced for the hundredth anniversary of Cannon in 1987, "Whether it was or is a company town, Kannapolis people love their community and are proud of its history and heritage, its growth and development and its quality of life."[70] The rhetorical moves in this statement—putting into question whether it is a company town, asserting that it has history and heritage and that those are linked to growth, development, and quality of life—lay out the terrain for the kinds of questions that are asked about place when it is determinedly modern. Both "history" and "heritage" signal, but do not replicate, a past, one that, in Kannapolis's case, is particularly fraught, in part because the city was unincorporated for most of its existence, which meant that its residents had little say in what went on in their community. Likewise, "growth" and "development" are bound up in discussions of urban life, and their apparently benign presence runs rampant through many tropes of modernity.

As the geographer J. Nicholas Entrikin notes of place-names, "the meanings given to place range from the personal, relatively subjective understanding of place associated with personal experience to the relatively objective sense of place as location." He locates between these two endpoints, one bound by its subjectivity and the other by its lack of subjectivity, the "cultural symbols of a place associated with a particular cultural community." Thus, as Entrikin argues, place-names are "intertexts," shared cultural symbols that pass among films, novels, and the physical world, allowing for meaning outside of any one context. The intertextual nature of place-names puts them at the center of larger arguments about modernity and meaning.[71]

For Kannapolis residents, including those who were present in the Gem Theater on a February afternoon in 2005, H. Lee Waters's films of the city are now one of the key intertexts that allows for reflection on a place that they called home. Even though these films, shot in 1939, 1941, and 1942, captured just a few hours of life in the community, its cultural status permits, as Michel de Certeau suggests is possible of New York sidewalks, a reading of "footsteps" on the film text, each frame mapping the place.[72] The emphasis on recognition in the local film calls attention to the gap between collective and individual naming, which is also the difference between the name of a place and a place-name. If a place-name is deeply personal, one that is determined more by the imagination than the name, producing a truly arbitrary system in which a place-name is unrelated to place, it is difficult to imagine the recovery of any place whose name has been lost. But, if one can, as Entrikin suggests, find a place-name that serves as an "intertext" between individuals, one close to de Certeau's sidewalk of a thousand stories yet also networked or woven, allowing for a collective that can name, it is possible to imagine place-names that are not the product of an author but of a community.

At the same time, this emphasis on place recognition in the local film, which only accelerated after World War II, works against mutual recognition as it demarcates who is worthy of recognition by emphasizing their relationship to the named community. Waters's films are compelling examples of the possibility of mutual recognition precisely because he depicted people who were excluded from political life and yet intricately connected to the town's economy and, revealingly, many aspects of its social life. At the same time, the democratic quality that distinguished films of mutual recognition from other local movies was under constant threat of being undermined by sponsors who desired to associate the movies with the places of their choosing. Waters's autonomy gave him the ability to film where and when he pleased, but many other itinerants worked as clients for civic and business clubs who had a heavy hand in determining the places that would and would not be filmed.

The Hometown Movie Idea

Itinerants like Waters were everywhere in the 1930s and early 1940s, shooting so frequently that local films like his became what a Valdese, North Carolina, newspaper called the "Home Town Movie Idea," a mode of moviemaking that "comes right down to everyday life."[73] While these small-gauge pictures were largely free of the genre and narrative impositions placed on local movies in the 1910s and 1920s, they were not without structure, and, in fact, their assumption of mutual recognition meant that they had potentially greater power to challenge how a community thought of itself than their predecessors.

In contrast to these earlier modes of local filmmaking, the decline of these movies of mutual recognition occurred somewhat swiftly, due to a series of large events. First, and most obviously, the US entry into World War II had several direct consequences for itinerant filmmakers. Gas was rationed, making any itinerant practice difficult to sustain. The US military purchased 16mm moving image equipment from amateur moviemakers for wartime use, which encouraged itinerants like Waters to give up on filmmaking altogether. The draft and war-related employment discouraged men and women from continuing their itinerant work, as they could find, or were forced to find, other opportunities.

After the war ended, local film production resumed but not with the same variety as before. Home movie cameras were more widely available in the postwar period, making moving images more commonplace than had been the case just a few year earlier. And the film industry itself was struggling to retain its audience in the face of competition from television. Small-town theaters, who had long fought to stay in business, started to close. Their audiences went either to theaters in larger communities or to drive-in theaters, which drew moviegoers from a wider geographical range.

In the face of these changes, some itinerants found a different way to promote their films. Rather than selling the potential of mutual recognition or of Hollywood stardom, these itinerants instead appealed to the increasingly national sensibilities of small-town residents. Local films could be used to celebrate the civic qualities of postwar life, a universe in which many imagined themselves to be residents of small towns, and those who actually did live in these towns saw an advantage in documenting and commemorating their contributions to civic life. Local films, then, became tools to celebrate the familiar, and it was the nationalization—and the banalization—of everyday life that became their *metteur en scène*, not movies where seeing yourself was the greatest thrill of them all.

Notes

1. Rankin, "A Century of Progress," 6. Built by James Cannon in 1908—its name, from the Greek, means "City of Looms"—the Cannon Mills of Kannapolis became, by 1914, the "largest manufacturer of huck towels in the United States." An unincorporated town until 1984, meaning that its residents had no local representation, Kannapolis, like so many mill towns, was dominated by its largest employer, who owned 8.8 percent of the land within town boundaries, including 1,600 houses. The company fought, and defeated, multiple efforts by its employees to unionize. After a series of corporate takeovers and mergers, the mill finally closed its doors in July 2003, which was widely covered at the time as a death-knell for mill towns in North Carolina. For one account of Cannon's anti-labor history, see James Surowiecki, "Strikes, Lies, and Videotape," *Slate*, August 29, 1997, http://www.slate.com/articles/arts/the_motley_fool/1997/08/strikes_lies_and_videotape.html.

2. Robert C. Allen first pointed out to me the centrality of recognition, as opposed to identification, in the work of Waters. In *Nickelodeon City*, Michael Aronson argues that an exhibitor-filmmaker active in the 1910s, Charlie Silveus, created a "cinema of recognition" in which "the gaze is not projected outward toward a disembodied spectator, but inward to a known and very corporeal audience" (229).

3. Benjamin, "The Work of Art in the Age of Mechanical Reproduction," 234.

4. Taylor, "The Politics of Recognition." Mette Hjort is one of the few film studies scholars to discuss recognition in what she has termed the "cinema of small nations." See Hjort, "Danish Cinema and the Politics of Recognition."

5. Rabinowitz, *They Must Be Represented*, 8.
6. Widdowson, "Mitchell and Kenyon," 141.
7. The Burns poem reads, in translation, "O would some Power the gift to give us / To see ourselves as others see us!"
8. Bottomore, "From the Factory Gate to the 'Home Talent' Drama."
9. Doane, *The Emergence of Cinematic Time*, 10, 22.
10. Ibid., 23. This is a problem for early cinema in general, and could be one for Waters's films as well. If a genre of film, whether it be local film or early cinema, is seen as important largely because it is representative of that genre, a reading of what is present in the film is often made difficult or deemed unnecessary because the existence of the film, as either the first, only, or rare record of whatever subject, is seen as an end in itself.
11. Ibid., 24.
12. One obvious exception would be motion pictures that were made with a hidden camera.
13. Jung, "Local Views," 253–255.
14. Some of these discoveries are her own, while others were made by contributors to a volume she coedited. See Toulmin et al., eds., *The Lost World of Mitchell and Kenyon*, as well as Toulmin's monograph *Electric Edwardians*.
15. Toulmin, "'Local Films for Local People,'"118.
16. Toulmin and Loiperdinger, "'Is It You?'" 9, 16.
17. Bordwell refers to classical Hollywood cinema as having an "excessively obvious" aesthetic, by which he means that all information is communicated to the spectator in a very clear and straightforward manner. See Bordwell, *The Classical Hollywood Cinema*, 3. Likewise, local films have at base a very understandable and accessible appeal.
18. Ricouer, *The Course of Recognition*, 19.
19. Ibid., 62.
20. Ibid., 101, 102, 110.
21. Ibid., 134, 137.
22. Sewell, *Logics of History*, 73.
23. See Habermas, *Structural Transformation of the Public Sphere*. For example, while some have argued that Edgar Allan Poe's 1840 short story "Man of the Crowd" is a very early example of the effacement of the individual in mass culture, one could instead suggest that it reflects the narrator's failed attempt to engage the "man of the crowd" in mutual recognition.
24. Ricouer, *The Course of Recognition*, 161, 199.
25. Marshall, *Citizenship and Social Class and Other Essays*. Ricouer attributes Marshall's concept to Robert Alexy, Talcott Parsons, and Honneth.
26. Ricouer, *The Course of Recognition*, 219, 243.
27. Nancy Fraser, among others, critiques those, like Honneth, who privilege calls for recognition over redistribution, when she suggests that both should be addressed in tandem, as many groups "suffer both maldistribution and misrecognition *in forms where neither of these injustices is an indirect effect of the other, but where both are primary and co-original.*" Pursuing this debate further would lead us far outside the context of recognition in the local film, which is why I have not addressed it further. However, following Rabinowitz's work on documentary, I would argue that recognition leads to calls for redistribution. See Fraser, "Social Justice in the Age of Identity Politics," 19.
28. Mouffe, *The Return of the Political*, 85.
29. Ricouer, *The Course of Recognition*, 263.
30. Robert Sklar makes the claim forcefully in his cultural history of the movies. See Sklar, *Movie-Made America*.
31. Édouard Glissant, "For Opacity," in Glissant, *Poetics of Relation*, 189–194.
32. *Miller's Lexington, N.C. City Directory*.

33. See Hall et al., *Like a Family*, particularly chapter 3, for more on mill life in North Carolina.

34. Surprisingly, there are few scholarly studies of photographers like Waters, as their work tends to attract only local interest, or, in the well-known case of Michael Disfarmer, attention from those who value their photographs as a form of outsider art, rather than as a common cultural practice. In his collection of essays *Each Wild Idea: Writing, Photography, History,* Geoffrey Batchen argues that research on what he terms vernacular photography has been suppressed by historians of photography because "to deal with it directly would be to reveal the shallow artifice of their historical judgment, and of the notion of artwork on which it is based" (58). One rare exception, as Batchen notes, comes from Canada, *Mining Photographs and Other Pictures, 1948–1968*. In a long essay that appears at the end of the volume, Allan Sekula suggests that small-town commercial photographer Leslie Shedden aspired to be the "model of a photographic craftsman and small entrepreneur," thus making work that aestheticized, and also reproduced, the social and economic landscape of the community (255).

35. Kodak saw camera stores and photography studios as potential distributors for their amateur movie cameras and likely provided Waters with, at the very least, brochures for their products.

36. Ray Rollins, "Old Movies Appeal to Nostalgia," *Winston-Salem* (N.C.) *Journal*, January 12, 1976, 17.

37. Ven Carver, "Playing on People's Vanity Pays off Big," *High Point* (N.C.) *Enterprise*. April 22, 1973, D1–2. The projection of "lantern slides" produced by the local photography studio might have been common in movie theaters in this time period. Charles Abel's 1931 book *Money Making Ideas for Portrait Studios*, which was owned by Waters, suggests that "photographers who are located near neighborhood motion picture houses can get, for comparatively low prices, the privilege of running lantern-slides during the time when reels are being changed, or the audience is moving in or out" (72).

38. Because Waters did not document the costs he incurred in making his films, it is difficult to establish what his profits were, but his business model is relatively clear. For example, Waters recorded a gross of $153.54 in four screenings in early October 1941 at the Center Theater in Mount Airy, North Carolina, taking 30 percent of the box-office gross, $355.40, and recording an additional $50 in advertising revenue. Alan Kattelle, a collector who specializes in amateur technology, estimates that in 1935, Kodachrome film ran $9 for a 100-foot roll. In Waters's business records he notes that he shot 800 feet of Kodachrome film in Mount Airy, which meant that he would have spent $72 for a twenty-eight-minute film. If this number is correct, roughly 20 percent of his gross from that screening went to film costs alone.

39. "Moving Pictures of Local People to Be Shown at Theatre," *Chatham* (N.C.) *News*, September 11, 1936, 1.

40. "Local Pictures to Be Shown on the Screen at Stanly," *Stanly* (N.C.) *News and Press*, August 18 1936, 5.

41. "Local Movies at Pasttime Today," *Concord* (N.C.) *Daily Tribune*, August 13, 1936, 2.

42. "Movies of Local Residents to Be Taken on Streets," *Chatham* (N.C.) *News*, February 28, 1941, 4.

43. "Local People in Film at Stevenson," *Henderson* (N.C.) *Daily Dispatch*, September 14, 1938, 3.

44. "Local Movies," *Rockingham* (N.C.) *Post-Dispatch*, June 15, 1939, 6.

45. Advertisement, *Forest City* (N.C.) *Courier*, June 17, 1937, 11. Of course, this statement could have been printed as a joke to encourage talk about Waters's visit. But it does seem clear that Waters was not as well-received in Forest City as he was in other towns.

46. "Mothers Invited to Have Pictures Made on Tuesday," *Roxboro* (N.C.) *Courier*, February 22, 1937, 1.

47. In response to a letter inquiring about the use of the word "candid," the editors of *Popular Photography* defined it in the August 1941 issue as being "either a picture which is snapped without the subject's knowledge or one which is carefully planned to make it appear spontaneous and unposed. Some of the best candid pictures that are taken are really rehearsed over and over again before the shutter is clicked" (18). This slippery definition—candid photographs are either unposed or appear unposed—allowed Waters to claim that his movies were "candid" even when they did not appear to be so.

48. Anderson, *Imagined Communities*.

49. The exception to this would be a town's African American residents, whose exclusion from public life was often mirrored by an exclusion from the newspaper.

50. "Seen along Main Street," *Davie* (N.C.) *Record*, February 26, 1941, 1.

51. "Movies of Local Residents to Be Taken on Streets."

52. Flyer, H. Lee Waters Collection, David M. Rubenstein Rare Books and Manuscript Library, Duke University, Durham, N.C.

53. "To Take Pictures of Local People," *Valdese* (N.C.) *News*, December 11, 1941, 1.

54. O'Connor, *Mediated Associations*, 7, 8. Lee Grieveson, for example, is more concerned about the cinema as a physical site where bodies are disciplined, and draws connections between the regulation of theater space and the regulation of the movies themselves. See Grieveson, *Policing Cinema*.

55. O'Connor, *Mediated Associations*, 19. In some of Waters's films, this connection between discipline and cinema is made explicit. For example, in the 1941 Granite Falls, South Carolina, color footage, Waters films a police officer pretending to arrest passersby, thereby making literal his oft-used phrase, "many were caught by the movie camera."

56. "The Movie Man: H. Lee Waters," *Assignment America*, NBC Nightly News, January 19, 1990.

57. Keller, "Cinephobia."

58. Stoeltje and Bauman, "Community Festival and the Enactment of Modernity," 170.

59. Stoeltje, "Festival," 270–271.

60. "Local People on Screen at Allen," *Journal-Patriot* (North Wilkesboro, N.C.), February 27, 1941, 5.

61. Smith, "'Looking at One's Self through the Eyes of Others,'" 581. These ideas are developed further in her book *Photography on the Color Line*.

62. Smith, "'Looking at One's Self through the Eyes of Others,'" 586, 587.

63. While Waters did depict Native Americans, Asians, Latinos, and other racial and ethnic minority groups, individuals from these groups were a distinct minority in his films and in North Carolina, where he shot most of his films. According to the 1940 US Census, North Carolina, with a population of 3.5 million, had just 22,545 residents who were Native Americans (here classified as "Indian") and a scant 104 residents who were Chinese or Japanese, plus another 40 identified as "other." Only 9,046 residents were foreign-born. In all, 71.9 percent of the state's population was classified as "white" while 27.5 percent was classified as "Negro," leaving just 0.6 percent of the population as "other." People of Hispanic descent were classified as white, though the census reported very low rates of immigration from Central and South America.

64. US Census. The calculations are my own.

65. See Cecelski and Tyson, eds., *Democracy Betrayed*.

66. "232 Negro Theatres 1 ½ % of All Houses," *Motion Picture Herald*, April 24, 1937, 78. This number is approximate because I am using the theater data from 1937, while the population data is from 1940. A number of African American theaters opened in the late 1930s, including the Hollywood Theater in Carrboro (1939) and the Palace Theater in Kannapolis (1938).

67. The US Census recorded the populations of townships, sub-county districts that included towns and outlying rural areas. Since North Carolina, even in 1940, was a

markedly rural state, I have chosen to use townships to record town populations, as they more accurately reflect the number of people who would have thought of a community, and its theater, as being part of their economic, social, and political life.

68. "New Theaters," *Film Daily*, March 14, 1927, 4.

69. Because Kannapolis was an unincorporated place, the US Census classified the township as "Cooks Cross Roads." Part of the town was in neighboring Rowan County, whose China Grove township boasted another 15,668 people, 860 of whom were African American.

70. Rankin, "A Century of Progress," 11.

71. Entrikin, *The Betweenness of Place*, 55, 56, 57.

72. de Certeau *The Practice of Everyday Life*, 97.

73. "To Take Pictures of Local People: Cameraman to Visit Community and Take Informal Movies of Local People," *Valdese* (N.C.) *News*, December 11, 1941, 1.

7

EVERY TOWN HAS ITS MAIN STREET
The Banal Localism of the Civic Film

IN THE 1920S, THERE WAS a moment when the small town was seen as the last holdout against commercial culture. In his analysis of this brief period, the literary scholar John Beck notes that the famed educator John Dewey, critiquing those who thought the United States should have a singular cultural form, believed that the "richness of local life in all its idiosyncrasies [was] the bedrock of what it means to be American."[1] Writing in a time when a robust and increasingly restrictive Americanism was promoted by business forces and nativists alike, Dewey, along with other small-town defenders, including the poet William Carlos Williams, promoted the provincial as the bulwark against mass conformity. In their view, the small town, with its distinctive culture, social groups, and even local dialect, was both a suitable site for resistance to nationalism and for establishing connections across cultures. As Dewey wrote in 1920, "the locality is the only universal," an inversion that survives today in discussions of the local and the global.[2]

In this chapter, I consider the local film as a site where questions of national identity, particularly in its political and economic valences, rose to the forefront. My focus here is on a mode of local film practice that I identify as the *civic film*. I use the word "civic" here to signal a particular form of publicity that was invested in a citizenship informed by national practice but carried out in local space. Although the civic was experienced and reproduced in everyday life, in this period it was often tied to national service and business organizations, such as the Rotary Club or the chamber of commerce, whose local chapters played a significant part in the standardization of social and political life. Civic films, whether they were commissioned at the behest of one of these organizations or made by an itinerant filmmaker who persuaded these organizations to sponsor the film, reproduced their political and social imaginary. Unlike the films of mutual recognition described in the previous chapter, these movies spotlighted individual community leaders and organizations, often putting them at the center of a narrative that focused on progress in the community. In many cases, these films were produced as moving image time capsules of town life as it was imagined to exist, with the reels often given to a local institution for safekeeping.

In civic films there was little mention of a world outside the locale in which it was filmed, although the movies themselves suggested, in vague and abstract language, that the community was part of a larger civic and social economy that included other towns like it. In this way, the relationship emphasized was not between local and national culture, as was the case for Hollywood local films, but instead a regional sphere where towns competed for markets and industry. The civic culture produced by service and business organizations, coupled with references to mass culture, enabled the use of local film practices to reproduce and historicize small-town life as imagined by the theater manager in cooperation with the sponsoring organization and filmmaker. By putting forward a civic imaginary, filmmakers were able to ignore both the particularity of local people and places as well as Hollywood.

The Banality of the Local

Even though "local" is, in its most common uses, a scalar term, it is usually set in a binary relationship with something that defines it in the negative. The local is that which is not national nor global nor general nor, countering Dewey, universal. Conversely, the local is assumed to have a positivist bent, associated with the particular, individual, specific, topical. As a result, the definition of the local is assumed to be obvious to distant and nearby observers alike even though the term is defined precisely by listing the things that it is not. In fact, the "local" in local film is often made to take on various generic, aesthetic, and sociological burdens that are often in direct conflict with its capacity to represent particular people and places. As a result, the local envelops both what makes it particular to a specific time and space and the ideas that make it legible to a broader population. To use a contemporary example, local food is both recognizable in a generic sense, as food, and in a specific sense, as food that comes from a particular place and may have culinary and ethnic associations with the people who live in that place. In this way, the "local" connotes specificity without directly betraying any hint of what the term implies.

What I described earlier as the nationalization of everyday life, or the transformation of ordinary social activities into ones that were coordinated, to some degree, at a national scale, was extended and amplified after the Second World War. As Robert Wiebe has argued, as early as the 1920s, regional- and class-based politics was giving way to a division between a "national class," which loosened its hold on local politics in order to secure "central, strategic positions in American society," and a "local middle class" that retained its interests in local and regional economies. As Wiebe observes, these classes also sorted themselves out socially and culturally, with those in the national class joining professional interest groups, such as the American Bar Association, and the local middle classes instead fueling the growth of service clubs, like Rotary and Kiwanis.[3] While these latter organizations positioned themselves in opposition to the urban metropolises of the early twentieth century, by midcentury they instead found that the processes of standardization and homogenization that they had once embraced were now being used by boosters in these metropolises to smooth over, or even erase, the difference between the storied small town and the newly constructed suburban community.

In this chapter, I argue that many of the local films made after the Second World War evacuated any claims for local distinctiveness in favor of what I call "banal localism." I adapt this term from Michael Billig, whose 1995 book *Banal Nationalism* reconsiders the meaning and practices of nationalism for a postmodern, and global, era. Countering key theorists of nationalism, such as Benedict Anderson, Billig suggests that the "imagi-nation" required for being a member of a nation is more ordinary than romantic, and relies on a persistent, if often unacknowledged, "flagging" of national identity in everyday routines. Like a language, Billig argues that a nation must be "put to daily use" through "banal practices, rather than conscious choice or collective acts of imagination." In essence, Billig suggests, the nation is a way of life in which "'we' are constantly invited to relax, at home, within the homeland's borders." But instead of nationality serving as a prime mover in society, one that provides the motivation for wars and other acts of fealty to the state, Billig emphasizes its "low key, understated tone," something that appears so ordinary that it is almost imperceptible to the average observer.[4]

While a number of scholars have used the term "banal localism" as a parallel to Billig's term, such uses tend to describe phenomena that are more consistent with what Roland Robertson has called "glocalization," the idea that in a globalized society the local becomes imbricated in the global and vice versa.[5] Billig himself is critical of such theories, as he suggests that even local cultures are embedded within the nation. In fact, he argues globalization itself is a kind of fiction that denies the power nation-states, particularly the United States, play in securing economic and cultural exchange between nations.⁶ However, I argue that banal localism is a form of "flagging" communities, which often identify themselves as small towns, in order to reinforce the social, political, economic, and cultural processes that are necessary for their survival as distinct places. While these identities are linked to the nation, they are not enveloped by it, and the flaggings that occur for specific communities—road signs, references to an assumed "we" in local newspapers, even actual town flags and other symbols—reinforce town identities much in the same way that national symbols and utterances do. At the same time, the town, unlike the nation, is under greater threat of being forgotten, passed by, or simply ignored, as there are other forms of official and semi-official governmental structures—counties, cities, neighborhoods—that could erode and replace its political and economic power. Banal localism, then, allows the town to assert itself without calling attention to the fact that it needs sustained citizen support in order to survive. Because "hot" localism is not an option—few towns are ready for sustained warfare with neighboring communities or with the nation-state—localism in the modern era must be banal.⁷

In the postwar period, film culture became more accessible to ordinary people, which muted the original appeal of the local film. With newly inexpensive amateur film equipment, people could make their own home movies for an audience that was often no larger than the residents of a single household. The decline of single-screen movie theater exhibition was accompanied by the rise in two forms of mobile exhibition—the drive-in theater and the classroom. In the former, one's own automobile was made an extension of the theatrical experience, thus privatizing it, while in the latter, the projector itself moved, turning a multitude of spaces into places where films might be seen.⁸ Although earlier modes of local film production did not cease completely, the declining importance of movie theaters made the "local film" itself a less compelling proposition for sponsors, theater owners, and audiences. The growth of local broadcast media—radio and particularly television—also made mass mediated experiences of one's own community somewhat more common than they had been before, which only further dampened the enthusiasm for local movies.⁹

And yet, the *civic film* thrived in the postwar period, in part because such movies embraced the banal localism that in the early twentieth century would have been anathema to movie sponsors. Instead of promising audiences that they were uniquely suited for motion pictures, itinerants implied that the towns they filmed were just like any other, and that quality was what made them worthwhile. In order to emphasize this point, these films used narration, which was prerecorded and used again and again, to stress the ordinariness of the community in a voice that audience members might recognize from national radio programs and Hollywood newsreels. If local films were once prized for their ability to capture the quotidian, civic films instead embraced the commonplace.

Revitalizing the "Small Town" in the 1930s

The archetypal American small town, with its Main Street shops, friendly neighbors, and tightly knit community, is a modern invention.[10] Many historians have traced its origins to the 1930s, with the creation of popular, and enduring, fictional communities such as Grover's Corners, from *Our Town* (1940); Carvel, from the *Andy Hardy* series (1937–1958); and, slightly later, Bedford Falls, from *It's a Wonderful Life* (1946).[11] Even though all three of these fictional communities had literary origins, their cinematic portrayals endured, both as an ideal for local communities and as American political and social life writ small. A generation removed from the close-minded and backward-looking small towns depicted by writers such as Sherwood Anderson, Willa Cather, and Sinclair Lewis, these new small towns were instead treated as modern-day temples, inhabited by oracles such as *Our Town*'s "Stage Manager," Judge Hardy, and the guardian angel Clarence Odbody in *It's a Wonderful Life*.

Like ancient temples, these towns were often revisited by spiritual seekers for decades to come, finding solace both in their seeming timelessness—even Carvel, the least remembered of the three, was a going concern until the late 1950s—and their ability to reduce the complexities of modern life into pabulum. The wistfulness for a simpler age that runs through the small-town films of the 1930s and 1940s became a stronger current of nostalgia in the postwar period, making the small-town film not as much a relic of the past as it was an alternate vision of the present.[12] As Daniel Immerwahr argues in his study of the community development movement in this period, the experience of the horrors of an alienated modernity—world war, economic calamity, and social unrest—led to a "newfound appreciation for small-scale social solidarities, from the small group to the faraway village."[13] Many of the social movements that emerged in this period, from the organizing strategies of civil rights activists to the neighborhood associations that formed to fight urban renewal projects in cities, can be seen as part of an effort to address major challenges in society by turning them into a series of small, and winnable, fights against the powerful. The small town, in this instance, became both a model of an ideal society and a representative of the favored side in the battle against forces allied with the metropolis.

The utopian tendencies of the small-town films had its apotheosis in *The Truman Show* (1998), a movie about an ersatz small town created for a reality television show in which only one person, Truman Burbank, was "real." The picture was filmed on location in the New Urbanist community of Seaside, Florida, which was itself built in the 1980s and modeled after an idealized image of midcentury America. In the second half of the twentieth century, and now in the twenty-first, the small town, as image and as built environment, is continually coopted and appropriated, capable of absorbing capitalist and communitarian dreams alike. As Ryan Poll observes, "the dominant small town has become an aesthetic form that erases the violences that constitute global capitalism," which makes it an appealing face for corporations who wish to mask the environmental and economic damages caused by their activities.[14] The civic films I discuss in this chapter can be thought of as early iterations of imagining the small town as a particular, yet reproducible, space, one where the comfort found in sameness and individuality is indistinguishable. As Robert Wuthnow argues in a recent sociology of small towns in the United States, while the places themselves are diverse in terms of local landscapes, ethnicity, and racial makeup, residents "tacitly share an outlook that involves a similar lifestyle."[15]

The Banality of Civic Films

While there is no direct evidence that the turn to banalism in local films came in response to the newfound popularity of small towns in the American cinema, such films did seem to whet the appetite for celebrations of ordinary life. By the 1930s, many itinerant filmmakers no longer saw the fact that the communities they visited identified as "small towns" as a liability that needed to be overcome by booster campaigns or blithe comparisons to Hollywood. Instead, these new civic films celebrated the small town as something that was intrinsic to its identity. Scenes of work and home life, schools, civic and fraternal organizations, and government were valuable precisely because they represented the institutions every prosperous and well-functioning town should have and value. Producers of civic films also assumed that the cinema itself was a stable institution, capable of making representations of the local that would be seen from the outset as both broadly accessible and historical.

Rather than focusing on a single filmmaker whose work epitomizes the civic mode, in this chapter I consider several filmmakers—Franklin

Tisdale, H. C. Kunkleman, Shad Graham, Sol Landsman, Arthur Loevin, and Don Parisher—whose practices share stylistic and thematic elements. In some cases, these filmmakers were also linked to one another, either using the same production crew or, in the case of Shad Graham and Arthur Loevin, teaming up together after a period of working independently. Civic film producers used a mixture of old and new tactics to persuade sponsors to invest in their own local movies. Some appealed to the medium's capacity to historicize the present, claiming that the film would be a "permanent historical record" of the community. Others instead suggested that the film would serve a promotional role, enticing visitors to come to the community to see its landmarks and join its many thriving institutions. Television, in particular, was set out as a potential outlet for these films, which may have encouraged sponsors to invest in a new medium the hopes they had once placed in the cinema itself.

Whether they were interested in making movies for memorial or advertising purposes, sponsors appear to have been persuaded of the value of an anodyne aesthetic. In contrast to the local film modes discussed so far in this book, civic films were not intended for the amusement of contemporary audiences. Their productions received comparatively little fanfare in local newspapers, and even directors who claimed experience in Hollywood, such as Graham, did not suggest that they would be giving the town an opportunity to see how things were done on the coast. Initially civic producers wanted to give their work the imprimatur of official movie making and were thus shot in 35mm, but by the 1950s they regularly provided 16mm copies to their sponsors for local use.[16] Some producers, including Robert M. Carson, began shooting in 16mm, making longer and even duller films. While considerable time and expense went into the production of these motion pictures, the results were uneven, showing a marked indifference to film form and narrative structure. The soundtracks used in these films combine prerecorded and often canned narration with musical standards that had little to do with the scenes they accompanied. If local films often crossed the line between footage of local people and places and mere advertisements, movies made in the civic mode eschewed that distinction altogether. In fact, many civic films are better understood as a long series of advertisements for sponsoring businesses, coupled with perfunctory footage of local institutions and landscapes to create the illusion that the motion picture can serve other functions.

In previous chapters, I suggested that the other modes of local film production are best understood as being embedded within cinema history. In this chapter, I expand this view and instead argue for the civic mode's emergence in the context of the transformed identity of the American small town. First, I look at early civic films made by Franklin Tisdale, a Chicago-based filmmaker who began producing motion pictures in the 1910s, and H. C. Kunkleman, an Ohio-based filmmaker who was associated with the Pacific Film Production Company in the 1930s. While several of the filmmakers discussed in this chapter also began producing civic films in the early 1930s, of those with narration only Kunkleman's films are known to survive, and they thus make a useful case study for how the mode emerged. Next, I turn to the *Home Town* series, which reflected a confidence that the banal localism of midcentury America could sustain a filmmaking practice for several decades. By midcentury the fate of the local film was tied to that of small towns, so much so that towns' decline as economic, social, and cultural centers also meant that itinerants no longer had access to the capital, or audiences, required for their work to continue. Although the movies I discuss in this chapter kept up appearances, presenting each town as enduring scenes of human endeavors, at times they betrayed an obvious truth—the banality of the local in midcentury meant that there were few reasons to record its appearance on celluloid.

The Local Film as Commercial Reel

In 1940, the seasoned camera operator Charles W. Herbert published an article in *American Cinematographer* recounting the history of what he called "commercial reels." But rather than providing a sketch of the many efforts by companies to push their products in the movies, Herbert focused on a period in the early 1920s when what he called "goldbricking promoters" dispersed across the country, pushing their "promotional commercials" on naive small-town residents: "High pressure men with convincing letterheads and calling cards would find the town. They quietly hobnobbed with bankers, mayors, leading citizens, expressing wonderment at the fact that the motion picture industry had not discovered this great storehouse of talent and ideal locations."[17] Herbert went on to recount the major modes of local filmmaking, from home talent productions to Hollywood screen tests, though he cast such pictures as scams, what the Riverside, California, Chamber of Commerce called in 1933 "money-getting schemes" that needed to be fully investigated before local businesses handed over their hard-earned dollars to out-of-towners.[18] By describing the local film as a commercial venture, Herbert placed it within a history of industrial and advertising films, emphasizing its profitability for filmmakers, especially fake ones, and diminishing its other values. While Herbert was a bit too quick to cast aspersions on the entire field of itinerant filmmaking, his description of these practices is a window into how those in the industry thought of local films—a huckster's game, conducted by those who were unable to secure steady work in New York or Los Angeles.

Local films were always commercial ventures, despite the occasional protestations to the contrary by their producers, but civic pictures were almost exclusively commercials, produced by professionals who had experience in, or at least ties to, the movie industry. Here, I wish to outline how the very processes of making local films—securing sponsors to pay for production, persuading local theater owners to agree to add them to their programs, requesting community participation—privilege certain social configurations, which over time calcify into pictures that take on generic aspects. Put another way, I seek to answer why the civic film emerged as the dominant mode of local motion picture production after the Second World War.

Perhaps the most important shift that occurred is that film itself came to be thought of in pragmatic terms. Thomas Elsaesser emphasizes the usefulness, or utility, of moving image production as a quality that separated the wheat of the industrial film from the chaff of moving images more generally.[19] Considered in this framework, many of the local films produced in the first several decades of the twentieth century should not be thought of as industrial films at all, as their utility was limited to making money and fulfilling the fantasies of its sponsors and audiences. The primary informative value of local films was their ability to show people and places how they looked on camera. And even this quality was often overcome by other desires, such as an interest in reproducing the form and content of Hollywood films or emphasizing the mutuality inherent in the looks at the camera.

But, starting in the early 1920s, another purpose for local films emerged—to document local institutions as products of civil society. Franklin M. Tisdale's eponymous film company, which began as early as 1911, typifies the migration of local films from amusements to civic fare. When Tisdale came to Pittston, Pennsylvania, in 1916, he brought along one of his "Tisdale Players," an aspiring actress from California, and invited locals to audition before his camera for a movie popularity contest, giving participants both the opportunity to see themselves on screen and to learn whether their neighbors judged them suitable for the movies.[20] But by 1921, when Tisdale visited Decatur, Illinois, the local newspaper plainly stated that "there will be no plot or characters in the picture, the intent being to produce a purely civic and industrial feature."[21] Even though the company had the resources to produce local Hollywood movies, their turn to making civic pictures suggests that such films were treated more seriously by business sponsors. That same year, the Waterloo, Iowa, newspaper emphasized that the company's film in that city would depict "the daily routine of business, also the various steps in the manufacture of Waterloo products," and show them to locals and nonlocals alike who were interested in what went on in the city.²² A few years later, Tisdale started another venture, the Imperial Film Corporation, and inaugurated a new series titled, "Things You Ought to Know About," in which the town name itself was included at the end of the title. In contrast to the 1910s, when including a town's name in a title was thought to limit its distribution possibilities, civic filmmakers invariably invoked the town's name in their productions. Such movies could be thought of as process films in which everyone depicted, from cooks to factory workers to firefighters, were all part of a larger organism, contributing to the town's everyday functioning and necessary elements for its continued growth.

In the 1920s, other independent cameramen, most notably Harry Kunkleman, entered the civic film game, shooting under the auspices of several companies, including the Metropolitan Industrial Film Company, the Civic Arts Film Production Company, and by the early 1930s, the Pacific Film Production Company. Like Tisdale, representatives of Pacific tried a number of business strategies to make their films pay off. Some continued to shoot "screen tests" at a Movie Ball hosted by the film's sponsors. William Ramsell in Iowa found success partnering with local dairies to hold a baby contest, with all children under the age of six invited to participate in a film that was screened alongside more pedestrian views of people and businesses. In 1937, one of the company's enterprising cameramen made a movie at an Ohio roller-skating rink, asking townspeople to "skate yourself into Hollywood" for a Sunday evening shoot.²³

Despite the occasional reference to Klieg lights and Hollywood, civic film producers were not keen to link their work with that of the stars. Instead, their focus was on documenting the town itself, with an eye to the "historical record" their picture would surely become. By the time Kunkleman, a cameraman from Ohio who had started his own company in 1920, was working for Pacific in the 1930s, the company had converted to sound in a way, by adding a soundtrack to each film after shooting had finished. But instead of recording a unique narration for each film, Kunkleman recycled the same commentary, a fact that went unnoted in local newspapers or in the commentary leading up to the film's production. Instead, the extant films from this period signal how producers and sponsors alike

Figure 7.1. H. C. Kunkleman. *Courtesy of David Kuntz*

embraced a routinized view of their town's economic, social, and civic culture. Like other modes of local film production, civic films were a marked success. One prominent producer, Blache Screen Service of San Francisco, reported making 863 "Short Length Ad Films," most of which were likely part of their *Buy at Home* series, in 1939 alone.[24]

In the mid-1930s, Kunkleman traveled to the South to make a series of films in small towns throughout the region.[25] His 1936 picture *Your Town on Parade in 1936*, made in Cordele, Georgia, typifies how civic films began to redefine the form and function of local movies.[26] The picture opens with a series of pans across a group of businessmen, all presumably members of the chamber of commerce, the film's sponsor. The narrator, who Kunkleman had also used for a film made in Anderson, South Carolina, a year earlier, informs the viewer that "this picture is not designed for advertising purposes only, but also to show you the things you should know about the town in which you live," which implies that there were many everyday activities, even in a small community, that were unknown to most of its inhabitants.[27] And, if that alone were not enough reason to continue watching the picture, the narrator presents another case to the viewer—"Perhaps you would have liked to have seen pictures of your city in the past good old grandfather days, when movies were just in its infancy. This picture of your city as it is today will be worth seeing in the years to come." In a few lines, the narrator summarizes the purpose of the civic film: to show people their own town and to record it for future generations. Excised from this account of the local film is any reference to Hollywood and, in many cases, any audience apart from those who reside in the town where it was filmed.

Pacific's films often ran long—six reels, or just about an hour, in Waterloo, Iowa—but the Cordele film is a relatively compact twenty-four minutes.[28] Although the film has a soundtrack, with recorded music and narration, intertitles are also used, most of which appear to be handwritten advertising cards that specify the names of local businesses and were likely filmed onsite. A few title cards, particularly those for the Rotary Club and the Lions Club, are standardized and appear to have been inserted into the film in post-production. Kunkleman's stylistic range was limited. Slow pans from left to right and back again were his trademark, with the occasional medium shot of an individual looking directly at the camera. There is very little left to chance in these pictures, and while the participants seem comfortable participating in their production, there is little joy expressed, as if Kunkleman intended to capture an official, yet ordinary, day in the life of the town, rather than give people an opportunity to express surprise or delight at the camera's presence.

Although Kunkleman's films were exhibited in local theaters, they appear to be directed to an audience who was geographically, or temporally, distant from the place of production. And while one can detect this distance in the image itself, it is the soundtrack, particularly the voiceover narration, that sets apart civic films from their silent nonfiction counterparts. As Charles Wolfe has observed of voiceover narration in documentary films in this period, early reviewers of sound travelogues and newsreels often assumed that the narration was not that of a "voice of God" but rather the voice of a lecturer, who was assumed to be just off screen.[29] The transition from the nearby lecturer to the distant narrator was an important development in early sound documentaries, as it confirmed the film's status as an objective and truthful art form. In his analysis of voiceover in government-sponsored films made in the 1930s, Jonathan Kahana suggests that it often served as "political ventriloquism" or, more pointedly, a "volatile agent of hegemony." As he argues, "The state that speaks in these films was one that gained its authority by an uncanny ability to produce and fill empty spaces: in the land, but also in the American character. This voice projected itself into both places in an uncanny ventriloquizing of the American people, in whose name the state claimed its new powers."[30] Kahana goes on to argue that such use of voiceover, in a period when the documentary form itself was gaining visibility, is allegorical, instrumentalizing particular images in service of a national narrative about state power.

Although civic films operated at a different scale, and their lack of coordination reduced their efficacy, the presence of canned narration allowed for a similar conversion of the local film from something particular to something that was generically particular. After all, it was not just the presence of an off-screen narrator that distinguished these civic films from their predecessors but the presumed place of that narrator, whose very voice—intonation, accent, and elocution—marked him as not being local but rather detached from the place depicted by the camera.[31] As Wolfe notes, the voiceover narration of early documentaries drew on the aural qualities of the radio announcer's voice, which by the mid-1930s was firmly established as a distinct mode of address, typified by the *March of Time's* Westbrook Van Voorhis, whose "odd inflections, teletype cadence and often ironic tone" made him famous in his own right.[32] Although the narrator of Kunkleman's film is unidentified, the postwar civic filmmakers boasted of the celebrity of the radio announcers who narrated their films.

If the civic films of the 1920s and 1930s pointed toward a shift in how local films depict small-town life, the movies made after the Second World War underscored just how dramatic, and seemingly incontrovertible, this shift was. Instead of local films responding to an inchoate set of desires around the cinema, they were now put in service of a civic agenda in which the local was figured as a distillation of national political, economic, and cultural concerns of a prosperous, if anxious, middle class. For these audiences and sponsors, local films were not associated with the pleasure of seeing themselves but rather the security of knowing that their images had been committed to celluloid for posterity.

A New York Story: Casting *Our Home Town*

Like many itinerant filmmakers, Shad E. Graham, as he called himself when he was making his *Our Home Town* film series, constructed an autobiography that placed him, during varying points in his career, at both the center and periphery of cinema history.³³ Born on April 24, 1896, the day after Edison's Vitascope debuted in New York, Graham spent his life staking a claim on all corners of the cinema, from unverified early brushes with film pioneers—a bit part in *The Great Train Robbery* (1903) and work as a "prop boy" for *The Birth of a Nation* (1915)—to associations with Hollywood studios, including William Randolph Hearst's Cosmopolitan Studios, Universal, and MGM.³⁴ During the Second World War, Graham worked for the Office of Strategic Services, the precursor to the Central Intelligence Agency, and in his postwar career became an independent producer of educational, industrial, and newsreel pictures.³⁵ But despite this range of activity in and around the movie industry, Graham's most significant work was on the *Our Home Town* series, which he suggested was "a classic portrayal of small town life" that "made the citizens proud of their town," as it revealed "hidden truths and beauty they had over-looked."³⁶ After his death in 1969, Graham's widow donated several dozen films from the series to the University of Texas at Austin, in what was likely the first attempt to place local films within an academic and archival context.³⁷

For an itinerant filmmaker, Graham was unusually attentive to the historical importance of his own work, but the *Home Town* series, alternately titled *Our Home Town* and *My Home Town*, was not his alone. In fact, a number of other filmmakers, including Sol Landsman, Arthur Loevin, George S. Gullette, Sam Marino, and Don Parisher, all produced versions of the *Home Town* series in the 1940s, operating under a variety of company names. Most of these individuals were based in New York, or at least saw the city as their putative home and source of talent.

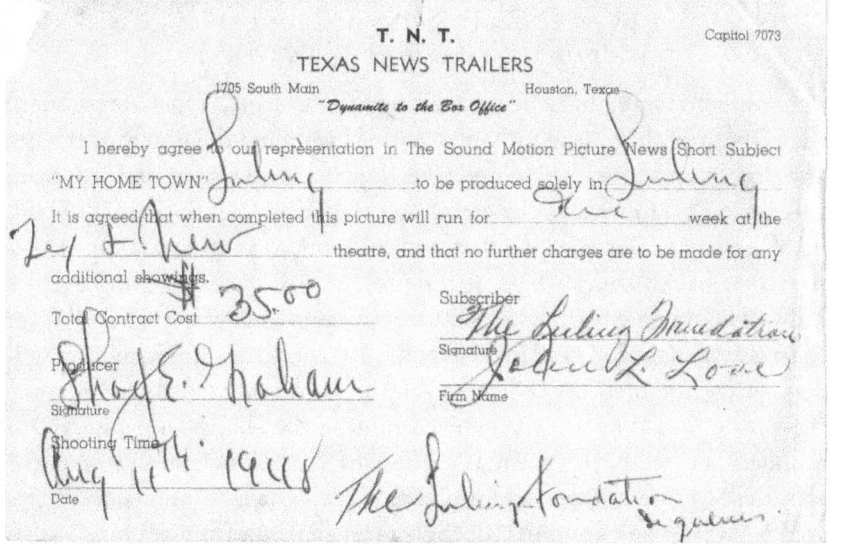

Figure 7.2. Receipt from *My Home Town*, Luling, Texas (1948). *Shad Graham Papers, di_10748, Dolph Briscoe Center for American History, University of Texas at Austin*

Several prominent newsreel and radio announcers provided narration for the films, including Vincent Connolly, whose voice could be heard on the popular Mary Margaret McBride radio show and Paramount's newsreels; John Reed King, who worked in both radio and television; and CBS's Norman Brokenshire, one of radio's best-known announcers. In his memoirs, Brokenshire recalled working in early 1947 with Parisher, who would send him the film and "covering script" so he could record it in New York.[38] But it was Connolly's narration that appeared most frequently in these films, and he occasionally received top billing in their promotion.[39]

While Graham was not the first civic film producer, his championing of the importance of the series underscored its ties to the banal localism that thrived after World War II. Graham and other producers of the *Home Town* films added to the familiar mix of local business boosterism and small-town civic pride a healthy dose of postwar patriotism in which the American small town was not only a respite from international troubles but a model of how conflicts might be resolved. While the canned narration is critical to distinguishing the civic film from its predecessors, for the *Home Town* series it is the text of the narration itself that associates routinized images of service clubs, fire departments, and schoolchildren with a postwar vision of American democracy.

Even When It Rains on Mondays: Codifying the *Home Town* Genre

According to Graham, he began making his *Our Home Town* film series in the early 1930s, but these early productions were not documented by him and do not appear in the voluminous digitized newspaper archives from this period.⁴⁰ However, a through-line can be found in the career of Graham's associate George S. Gullette, whose work as an itinerant filmmaker stretched back to 1912 when, as a representative of the Moving Picture Publicity Company, he made a picture in Allentown, Pennsylvania.⁴¹ Over the next two decades, Gullette was behind at least two significant itinerant film series. The first, which he and John E. Campbell registered for copyright in 1921 as *Who's Who*, involved filming the "backs of persons with numbers for exhibiting them as a guessing contest concluding with the subtitle 'See Them Turn Around Next Week,' at which points audiences could confirm their abilities to recognize local people from behind."⁴² This two-part film, which combined the staged appeal of the star contest with the desire to represent an aspect of life that was "hidden" to its residents, proved to be very successful, with productions in Oregon, Ohio, New Jersey, Massachusetts, North Carolina, Pennsylvania, Wisconsin, and likely many other states. Gullette's other major film series reworked another trope in local filmmaking, the "tourist girl" film, in which the winner of a beauty contest visits local businesses. Gullette began this series in the late 1920s, shortly after he discontinued his *Who's Who* films, and within a few years he was casting the same actor, Kay Gordon, who had fleeting appearances in Hollywood productions, as a representative of the movie industry. This series, titled *Our American Girl*, was also made again and again throughout the United States, demonstrating Gullette's acumen for identifying a profitable formula for local filmmaking.⁴³

In his notes for a planned autobiography, Graham commented that he began the *Home Town* series in the 1930s with Gullette but later decided to cede half of the country to him so he could make films in Texas, where he moved after the Second World War. In interviews, Graham claimed he was "proud of his original idea in motion picture presentation," and in later biographies suggested that, of all his experiences in the movie industry, it was the hometown films he held dearest.⁴⁴ During the war, other filmmakers, including Sol Landsman, Arthur Loevin, Shad Graham, and Don Parisher, began making their own versions of *Home Town* films. By the late 1940s, there were at least a half-dozen itinerants making versions, each pairing anodyne images of small towns with a soundtrack that, to varying degrees, called attention to the ordinary distinctiveness of the community in question.

In previous chapters, I have argued that local film practices are best thought of as a mode, not a genre, as each individual movie was an assemblage of the desires of sponsors, exhibitors, filmmakers, and the people and places that appeared in the finished product. But the *Home Town* film operated within a narrower band of variables, set in large part by the soundtrack and the narrator's script, which prescribed not what could be seen—canned band music serves to fill in the gaps—but what was significant enough to merit description. Furthermore, as suggested earlier, the *Home Town* film operated within a set of genre expectations around how small towns were depicted in the cinema, with the local iteration merely a representation and performance of a national ideal. In matching distinct images with the same, or similar, sounds, the producers of these small town movies accelerated the rise of a banal localism. The movie camera became merely another instrument in the solidification of a dominant, if ordinary, social and economic strata and *topos*, that of the middle-class, white, small-town resident.

Because the *Home Town* series was not associated with a single individual or company, it is difficult to determine the number of productions made or the contours of the practice. Shad Graham claimed to have made between two hundred and five hundred movies over a forty-year period. When they were affiliated with Park Motion Picture Productions, Don Parisher and George Gullette said that they were producing films throughout North Carolina, South Carolina, and Virginia. Sol Landsman and Arthur Loevin made films in Connecticut and Massachusetts during the war, and in Georgia, Florida, New Jersey, and Pennsylvania afterward.[45] In several cases, filmmakers partnered with theater circuits to produce these films, suggesting that the introduction of a prerecorded soundtrack and use of 35mm film made it an easier fit for theater programs. Other producers, including Charles Wecker and A. Lincoln Eskin, made films with similar titles and themes.[46] My focus here, however, is on fourteen extant *Home Town* films made between 1944 and 1954 in a half-dozen states that appear to draw their script from a single, unidentified source.[47] As Jonathan Kahana suggests of voiceover narration more generally, these scripts do more than augment moving images with a comforting narrative of progress and bombastic orchestral music. Instead, the narration structures how these films can be received by audiences, as they make explicit the tacit understanding that the local film is, more often than not, a mass commodity individuated, just barely, for hometown audiences.

The earliest extant *Home Town* film, titled *My Home Town Goes to War*, was filmed in Hickory, North Carolina, in 1944 and produced by Graham, Parisher, and Gullette. Landsman made films with similar titles in New England, including *Greenfield for Victory* (Massachusetts, 1942) and *Hartford for Victory* (1943), though it is not clear whether these films used the same script.[48] (See Moving Image 7.1.) The Hickory film's narrator, who is unidentified, opens with the following lines that announces the film's purpose:

> Yes, this is it. My Home Town. The place we as neighbors in this community call home. Sure we leave from time to time for elsewhere, but it's home sweet home to us all.
>
> They say every town has its Main Street. Well, this is ours. We built it with civic pride, and remain proud of its dignity, and friendly characters.

With minor changes, adding "tolerable" to describe the town's characters, and replacing the "Sure" with an "and" in the first line, these lines are repeated in almost every *Home Town* film, with the narrator, most often Vincent Connolly, speaking in a tone that suggests both resignation and self-confidence. The repetitive nature of the narration, which rarely makes up more than a quarter of the running time of the film, with the remaining soundtrack filled with orchestral music, adds an element of dreariness, making even those rare images in which people engage with the camera operator appear perfunctory. Later in the film, the narrator even admits defeat, noting, "It's not the greatest town in the world—our home town—but can you imagine all these nice, peaceful towns like ours, here in our beloved America, with all its folks like us pulling together?"[49] While the producers of this series, unlike their predecessors, never oversell the import of their movie, the narrator appears to undercut the town at every turn.

These *Home Town* films celebrate what I have identified as banal localism in part because they see it as essential to the narrator's vision of postwar democracy. Although Shad Graham claimed to be nonpartisan, in 1960 he made an anticommunist film titled *To Sow This Seed*, starring Martin Dies Jr., best known as the first chairman of the House Un-American Activities Committee. The film was intended to be a follow-up to the committee's own *Operation Abolition*, released the same year. Although the narrations analyzed here do not betray such explicit political leanings, they do suggest that the small town is a key player in the maintenance of the postwar order, an order that is best kept by cooperation with, and appreciation for, authority figures.[50] We see this milieu of banal localism emphasized in another line that is often repeated in these films, that "our fathers and mothers in our home town are just plain nice living folks, the kind you read about in storybooks, you know, Main Street folks who say hello, nice morning, even when it rains on Mondays. You see we really are the folks folks in other nations would like to change places with. These civic-minded familiar faces we all know in my home town think our town is something to shout about. Don't you?" Even at its most anodyne, the narration reproduces a feeling that everyday life is not just ordinary but largely indistinguishable from "storybooks," those fictional accounts of small towns that were familiar to audiences and part of the mental furniture that constituted cultural and social life in this period. Unlike the booster films of the 1910s, which sought out local landmarks that distinguished a town from its neighbors, the producers of the *Home Town* pictures liked familiar views—fire departments, milk bottling facilities, pharmacies, and churches—all of which were captured with medium shots that kept buildings of architectural distinction, or the surrounding built environment, out of view.

After a few more opening remarks, the narrator gets down to business, that is, the local merchants who sponsored the film's production. As Alison Isenberg notes in her study of central business districts, colloquially known then and now as "Main Streets," local merchants felt threatened on all fronts during the 1930s and 1940s. In addition to facing the same economic uncertainties as everyone else, small-town merchants were beset by two additional crises—the rise of the chain store and the decline of the downtown. Shoppers with limited means were increasingly drawn to chain stores, while well-heeled residents went to cities to make major purchases, leaving behind the small businesses who could not compete on price or selection. While wartime restrictions on gasoline and the entry of women, who were already responsible for the vast majority of retail spending, into the workforce temporarily revived downtowns everywhere, these gains were tempered by the rationing of many consumer goods. When the war ended, rationing subsided, but now businessmen feared that the postwar drop in government spending would bring on another recession.[51]

Although one might expect businesses to put their best face forward in spite of these difficulties, the narrator instead gives voice to these anxieties, introducing the long sequence of shots of local businesses with the following:

> Let's call on some of our business firms and see what they are doing to help make our life more pleasant. Let's see how they work to give us the best the markets have to offer. Their purpose is to please you, to fulfill your desires

and needs, to keep you well dressed and to keep your homes well-furnished, so you may maintain your place in society.

They are always there to greet with you a friendly smile, and to give you the best possible service. You have assurance of their dependability because they are one of us in the permanence of our community.[52]

In the films produced by Arthur Loevin, who worked with both Landsman and Graham, this celebration of local businesses takes on a barbed tone in an added section of the narration, in which a nonprofessional narrator, likely Loevin himself, implores the audience to adopt a "fair response to local buying" and be patient in waiting for consumer goods to arrive to town.[53] In Graham's film of San Marcos, Texas, he makes the point even more explicit, with the narrator commenting, "This is precisely why this movie reminder has been assembled for you—to inform you of the many contributions made by our home town, local merchants and businessmen, for the betterment of our town."[54] While the *Home Town* series was not the only itinerant series to push such a message—Maurice Blaché's *Buy at Home* films were produced with similar aims—the addition of a narration implied that the images themselves were secondary to the importance of supporting local businesses.[55]

Rather than underscoring the collective sentiments that run throughout the narration, this second narrative suggests that the "hometown" is in a defensive posture, under threat from distant forces who seek to undo the economic, and thus social and political, dominance of local merchants. Later in the film, the original narrator returns to note that the service clubs—Lions and Rotary are invariably pictured—are the "backbone" of the town, "for it is through them that our business and social activities are welded together."[56] In effect, the narrator seeks to persuade the audience that the social and cultural goods they associate with their community are actually economic ones, and that their consumer choices may undermine the institutions—tellingly, schools and churches are discussed toward the end of the film—on which they depend.

The narration of the *Home Town* films ends on a brighter note, discussing, as so many films did in this period, the "world of tomorrow" that awaited Americans returning from war. Like corporate-sponsored educational films from the same period, the narrator emphasized the importance of repurposing wartime technologies for the production of domestic goods, thus ensuring the "progress and happiness of America and the world."[57] Later versions of the film omitted this part of the narration but left a final section in which the exhibitor, operating under the guise of "your theater," thanks theater patrons and promises "excellent entertainment for the future."⁵⁸ In the final analysis, it seems, it is the movie theater itself that had the most to gain, or lose, from the exhibition of local moving pictures. The anxieties voiced in these films proved to be well-founded, as both small towns and, even more so, small-town theaters struggled to adapt to other postwar technologies and landscapes—highways, suburban housing developments, and television—making these films a record of a way of life that was fast disappearing.

Recorded on the Celluloid Ribbon—The *Longue Durée* of the Local Film

Even though the banal localism of the *Home Town* series appears, from a certain vantage point, to be an end point for the mode, from another it is the beginning of a genre—the sponsored town portrait film—that persists in a familiar form to this day in television and new media. Although I have suggested earlier that Shad Graham was just one of many producers of *Home Town* films in the 1940s, by the 1950s he was one of the most prolific filmmakers of such pictures, producing dozens of films every year until at least 1959, when he made a picture in El Dorado, Arkansas. In a form letter, Graham noted that his company was in town to make "one of their State wide pictorial reviews, a special motion picture production of what makes El Dorado 'tick'—strictly a Booster subject for our Home Town."⁵⁹ Although theatrical exhibition was still seen as the preferred outlet for the films, when the El Dorado Chamber of Commerce wrote back about their 16mm copy of the film, they noted that they were "notifying the companies who sponsored this film that we have their TV film for them," which they called "much more useful" than the 35mm version.⁶⁰ Even though Graham never wavered in his commitment to theatrical exhibition, business sponsors were less convinced by its value.

In fact, in the 1950s, a number of local films were shown on television stations, whose need for local content might have contributed to a boomlet in the production of local films.⁶¹ For example, in 1953, a new company called Americana Productions first screened its film of Brazil, Indiana, on WTTV in nearby Bloomington.⁶² Those who did not have their own television sets were encouraged to go to the First Presbyterian Church, which invited the community to see the Sunday noon broadcast on their "large screen set."⁶³ Other filmmakers, such as Robert M. Carson, began producing long promotional documentaries, taking advantage of the low costs of 16mm stock to make two-hour movies that would test the patience of all but the most committed local boosters. In the 1950s, Don Parisher relocated his business to Florida and began a second career as a director of promotional films for the towns and cities in the state.

Itinerants who first entered the field in their youth, including H. C. Kunkleman and Melton Barker, remained active filmmakers well into their seventies. In 1969, a seventy-one-year-old Kunkleman, who was making films at the Lorain County Fair in Ohio, put down his camera to tell the newspaper of the historical importance of his own work and to mourn the loss of many early films: "It is a shame that youngsters of today can not sit down and see a good Mary Pickford movie. These have all disintegrated now. Nitrates used in early films were their downfall."[64] Many other itinerants realized that the days of small-town single-screen theaters where they exhibited their films were numbered, and that they had little hope of getting their pictures to play at the suburban multiplexes that had replaced them. Although the heyday of itinerant film production had long passed, the shuttering of small-town theaters proved to be the event that effectively ended the production of the kinds of local films discussed in this book.[65]

However, local films continued to be made, even if they were shot on video and, later, digital media. By the 1980s, the same booster organizations that once backed local films were now investing in the production of videos that promoted a region's business climate and appeal to tourists. With consumer-grade video camcorders, it became possible to record "home talent" performances of all sorts, and many communities regularly documented local functions with video equipment.[66] In 2004, an enterprising Iowan, Scott Thompson, started My Town Pictures, a regional film production company that has made more than fifty feature-length motion pictures in the Midwest, almost all of them written and directed by Thompson himself.[67] In 2013, Thompson asked the residents of Zumbrota, Minnesota, population 3,252, to raise $95,000 for the production of a feature film made in town with a mixture of professional and local actors.[68] While some in town were skeptical of the proposition, the former owner of the town's single-screen theater, which had recently closed and was now in the hands of an arts organization, told a regional newspaper that he would contribute several thousand dollars to see the film produced in Zumbrota. After all, he told the newspaper, "I've thrown money down worse ratholes than this."[69] Even after the local theater closed, and verifying the credentials of an out-of-town filmmaker is an easy web search, there were still people who put their hopes in a motion picture. Thompson's local feature film, *His Neighbor Phil*, had its premiere at the State Theatre in Zumbrota in the fall of 2014.[70]

Notes

1. Beck, *Writing the Radical Center*, 82.
2. John Dewey, "Americanism and Localism," *The Dial*, June 1920, 685.
3. Wiebe, *Self-Rule*, 141–142, 147.
4. Billig, *Banal Nationalism*, 95, 127.
5. Robertson, "Glocalization."
6. See Billig, *Banal Nationalism*, 145.
7. It seems telling that such rivalries between localities are often expressed by loyalties to sports teams, which are, after all, a playful means of battle.
8. I have not found any evidence that local films were made to be shown exclusively in drive-in theaters, though local movies were shown in drive-ins.
9. Of course, local broadcasting has its own vital history. See Kirkpatrick, "Localism in American Media."
10. While there are many books on the cultural history of the small town, Miles Orvell's *The Death and Life of Main Street* is an effective introduction to the subject.
11. Nonfiction examples prevailed also, particularly the Lynds' *Middletown*, which was an increasingly thinly disguised Muncie, Indiana, and has long been a site for documentarians. Local films were also made in Muncie, including *The Manhaters* (1915), discussed in chapter 2, and *Your Own Home Town—Muncie, Indiana* (1936), which is similar to the films of mutual recognition discussed in chapter 6.
12. As Ryan Poll notes in *Main Street and Empire*, Frederic Jameson suggests that postmodernism emerged precisely at the moment when "real, material small towns become obsolete." Poll goes on to argue that what he calls the "ideological small town" in postmodern culture becomes "reified fictions that ideologically block subjects from recognizing the complex, historically mediated social relations that constitute global capitalism" (126).
13. Immerwahr, *Thinking Small*, 8.
14. Poll, *Main Street and Empire*, 158.
15. Wuthnow, *Small-Town America*, 351.
16. Shad Graham supplied 16mm reductions of his films to several cities in the 1950s, including El Dorado, Arkansas. See Ann H. Cordell, El Dorado Chamber of Commerce, to Shad E. Graham, July 6, 1959, 3U307, SG.
17. Charles W. Herbert, "Commercials as They Were—and as They Are Today," *American Cinematographer*, May 1940, 208–209, 247.
18. "Money-Getting Schemes Bared by Chamber of Commerce Committee," *Riverside* (Calif.) *Daily Press*, February 28, 1933, 2. This notice appears to have been distributed widely, though I do not have evidence of its being reprinted in other newspapers.
19. Elsaesser, "Archives and Archaeologies."
20. "Movie Star Will Sign Contract Here," *Pittston* (Penn.) *Gazette*, March 28, 1916, 6. In some cities, theaters displayed photographs of movie aspirants. See "Photos of Leaders Are to Be Shown," *Scranton* (Penn.) *Republican*, April 1, 1916, 3.
21. "To Make Motion Picture of City: No Plot or Characters to Be Used," *Decatur* (Ill.) *Review*, January 18, 1921, 12.
22. "Civic Film Is Near Completion," *Waterloo* (Iowa) *Times-Tribune*, May 20, 1921, 9.
23. Advertisement, *East Liverpool* (Ohio) *Review*, November 13, 1937, 6.
24. Alicoate, ed., *Film Daily Year Book*, 595. Other producers discussed in this chapter did not report their activity to *Film Daily*, making it impossible to know how many films they were producing in a typical year.
25. According to his granddaughter Kathryn Gangel, Kunkleman would travel with his family and set up business in one town, then travel to cities in the region for six months or more. Personal correspondence with the author, September 6, 2015.

26. According to University of Georgia film archivist Margie Compton, only the company, Pacific Film Productions, is credited in the local newspaper articles about the film's production, but Kunkleman, who made several films in the region between 1934 and 1936, was most likely its director. Personal correspondence with the author, November 25, 2015.

27. For more on the Anderson film, see Streible, "Itinerant Filmmakers and Amateur Casts."

28. According to Margie Compton, the film's shorter running length may be due to a lost reel. Personal correspondence with the author, November 25, 2015.

29. Wolfe, "Historicising the 'Voice of God,'" 152.

30. Kahana, *Intelligence Work*, 93, 94.

31. I have not encountered any examples of civic films narrated by women, though the points made here would hold.

32. Wolfe, "Historicising the 'Voice of God,'" 153.

33. Graham's birth name was Edmond S. Walstrum. When he entered the motion picture business in the 1910s, he went by S. Edwin Graham, which may have been a sly reference to Edwin S. Porter. He appears to have adopted Shad as a first name only after the end of the Second World War.

34. Graham's papers at the University of Texas contain several versions of this biography, but the most complete, and seemingly accurate, version appears in the posthumously published *The National Cyclopaedia of American Biography* (Clinton, N.J.: James T. White, 1973), 54:396–397.

35. In a job application to the Office of Strategic Services, where he worked as a ten-dollar-a-day contractor for just under a year, Graham gave a more complete resume, listing stints such as directing a picture of Ridgefield Park, New Jersey, and, with George Gullette, making a newsreel series titled "The Guest Newsreel Reporter." See Personnel File, Edmond Shadrack Walstrum, Record Group 226, Records of the Office of Strategic Services, 1919–2002, National Archives and Records Administration, Washington, DC.

36. Ibid.; "Biographical Sketch," SG, box 3U308. Graham was also proud of his role in filming the Texas City Disaster, a ship explosion that killed more than five hundred people, in 1947 for Fox Movietone. Graham testified before Congress on his role in filming the disaster and in the class action lawsuit that followed.

37. Although the University of Texas still has Graham's films, they are not currently available to be viewed. Graham himself tried, and mostly failed, to sell his films to the towns he visited in the late 1960s, although it appears that he was more successful selling 16mm and 8mm reductions of his films after they were made.

38. Brokenshire, *This Is Noman Brokenshire*, 291.

39. For example, see advertisement, *Middletown* (N.Y.) *Times-Herald*, October 12, 1946, 2.

40. In notes for a planned autobiography, Graham claimed to have made films in Connecticut, Ohio, Illinois, Wisconsin, Missouri, Colorado, Nevada, California, Louisiana, North Carolina, South Carolina, Virginia, and Georgia between 1929, when he left Hollywood, and 1935, when he returned to make the Mexican–US coproduction *The Great Manta*, under the name S. Edwin Graham. Of course, Graham could have been working under yet another name and calling his series something other than *Our Home Town*, but exhaustive searches of newspaper databases have not revealed any films that appear to be related to this series. Other filmmakers, such as Edwin Cooper, made similar films in the 1930s. There is a record of two Graham productions in 1945, *Bangor at War* and *Mount Carmel at War*, both made in Pennsylvania.

41. "Allentown and Allentonians in Moving Pictures," *Allentown* (Penn.) *Democrat*, July 13, 1912, 5.

42. Copyright deposit, April 11, 1921, Moving Image Research Center, Library of Congress, Washington, DC. Gullette began his *Who's Who* series as early as 1918, when he made one in Mansfield, Ohio. See "Who's Who in Mansfield? Th' Movies 'll Show You," *Mansfield News*, August 15, 1918, 3. A film with the title *Who's Who in Corpus Christi* is among the films in the Graham archives at the University of Texas.

43. Several films from this series survive, including ones made in Oshkosh, Wisconsin, and Tulsa, Oklahoma. A similar film, *See America First*, also starring Kay Gordon, was made in Oakland, California, and is also extant. See "To 'Star' in Local Film," *Oakland Tribune*, November 21, 1930, 55. Gullette made an earlier film series, *The Princess Visits*, which follows the same structure as the *American Girl* series. See "To Make Movies of Mansfield," *Mansfield* (Ohio) *News*, May 6, 1915, 5.

44. "Work on Movie of Freeport and Velasco Is Started This Week," *Freeport* (Texas) *Facts*, August 1, 1946, 1.

45. In the early 1950s, Loevin broke off from Landsman and made films in Texas, including one in Bryan, where he may have first met Graham, with whom he later worked. Gullette does not appear to have made any *Home Town* movies after the war and described himself as "retired" in an application to the Motion Picture Pioneers in 1952. See "12 More Apply to Join Pioneers," *Motion Picture Daily*, November 6, 1952, 6.

46. Charles Wecker made films in several towns, all titled *My Home Town*, in Pennsylvania and in Richmond, Virginia, in 1948, with narration by Bill Stern. None of the films are known to survive. A. Lincoln Eskin, under the auspices of the Progressive Pictures Company, made *My Home Town* in Newark, Ohio, using a soundtrack similar to the other films described in this chapter.

47. These films were made in North Carolina, Georgia, New Jersey, Ohio, Pennsylvania, and Texas.

48. "To Make Movie of Local Groups in War Effort," *Greenfield* (Mass.) *Recorder-Gazette*, November 10, 1943, 10; "Local War Effort to Be Subject of Newsreel Picture," *Hartford Courant*, March 15, 1943, 8.

49. *My Home Town*, Hickory, N.C.

50. Starting in 1946, the *Home Town* films added a nod to local police, observing, "for through this force our town is kept in order and we are protected from unlawful influences." *Our Home Town*, Mooresville, N.C. Later films revised the last line to "unlawful and disrupting influences."

51. Isenberg, *Downtown America*, 97–98, 161–162.

52. *My Home Town*, Thomaston, Ga.

53. Ibid.

54. *Our Home Town*, San Marcos, Texas.

55. An earlier film, *Man Power* (1930), made in Council Bluffs, Iowa, tried a different tact, blaming the town's lazy populace for its failure to live up to its potential.

56. *My Home Town*, Monroe, N.C.

57. *My Home Town*, Mooresville, N.C.

58. *Our Home Town*, Denville, N.J.

59. From James W. McWilliams, May 1, 1959, SG, 3U308.

60. Ann H. Cordell to Shad E. Graham, July 6, 1959, SG, 3U307.

61. For accounts of the many efforts to provide local programming on television in the 1950s, see Michael D. Murray and Donald G. Godfrey's edited volume *Television in America*. In the early 1950s, television stations often used the terms "local film" to distinguish prerecorded moving images they held from those that were supplied by a national network. Many radio and television historians have pointed out what David Goodman calls the "paradox" of broadcasting, that these national media were regulated with the assumption that "local service to a place-based community" was paramount. See

Goodman, *Radio's Civic Ambition*, 105. In her analysis of television's depiction of, and relationship to, the Midwest, Victoria Johnson instead focuses on regionalism as the site where "institutional and cultural struggles over networking" congealed. See Johnson, *Heartland TV*, 34.

62. "Brazil Story in Television Show Well Received," *Brazil* (Ind.) *Daily Times*, October 5, 1953, 1.

63. "Brazil Story on TV Tomorrow Is a Local 'Must,'" *Brazil* (Ind.) *Daily Times*, October 3, 1953, 1.

64. "Akron Man Filming County Fair for Benefit of Future Generations," *Chronicle-Telegram* (Elyria, Ohio), August 23, 1969, 7.

65. For more on the decline of the small-town theater, see Robert Sklar's introduction to Michael Putnam's photobook *Silent Screens*. Theaters like the "last picture shows" Putnam photographed hosted local film screenings until the very end.

66. Judi Hedrick has identified these videos as "community vernacular video," which she defines as nonprofessionally produced videos that "document the activities of various communities outside the family." Hedrick, "Amateur Video Must Not Be Overlooked," 79. While this study has excluded local video production, clearly such practices are similar in some ways to local films.

67. "Meet the Creative Director and Screenwriter," http://www.mytownpictures.com/writer.html. Of course, regional and local film production also continued apace in this period, but the directors of such films expected them to play at festivals and, hopefully, be picked up for distribution.

68. Thompson charges towns $4,500 for the production of what he calls "community movies," which are not expected to receive wide release. Personal conversation with the author, December 14, 2015.

69. Rich Larson, "Gone Hollywood? Zumbrota Ponders a Feature Film in Their Back Yard," *Southern Minn Scene Magazine*, September 12, 2013, http://www.southernminn.com/scene/movies/article_e65af6d0-1c28-11e3-af0d-0019bb30f31a.html.

70. Sandy Hadler, "Zumbrota Prepares for Sneak Peak of Film," *Red Wing* (Minn.) *Republican Eagle*, October 17, 2014, http://www.republican-eagle.com/content/zumbrota-prepares-sneak-peak-film.

8

RECLAIMING THE LOCAL FILM
Artifacts, Archives, and Audiences

IN HER STUDY OF FILM preservation in the digital era, Giovanna Fossati refers to the "archival life" of a film, which "indicates the life of film once it has entered the archive, from selection to preservation, from restoration to exhibition and digitization."[1] This reframing of film as an object in flux—a catalogue entry one day, something in need of repair the next, an ephemeral experience on the screen for many evenings, and, finally, a computer file among many others—is generative even if it discounts the materiality of celluloid. In this chapter, I expand on Fossati's notion of the "archival life" of film to include what I call its "second lives" outside the archive, which begin when moving images, particularly those that were orphaned, are rediscovered by community groups, scholars, and artists.

As I discuss later, it was not until the early 1980s that a few archivists had an inkling of the existence, let alone the value, of local films. Another decade passed before film historians and archivists realized that these films, and similar moving images produced outside mainstream commercial and independent spheres, constitute what Paula Amad has called a "counter-archive" in which moving images challenge the traditional archive's "sacred myths of order, exhaustiveness, and objective neutrality" due to their fragmented and fragile status.[2] Given the neglect of local films for the entirety of the period in which they were produced in large numbers, it is surprising that any survived at all.

But even when these films began to circulate in the communities where they were made, their status was far from secured. Reels were found and then lost again. Community copies were created on video cassettes, with new soundtracks and texts identifying people and places on screen, but these videos were not preserved alongside the films they reproduced. In other cases, artists removed local movies from community and archival contexts and instead used them as found footage pieces that commented on their serial nature. In fact, the second lives of local films are just as fragmented, capricious, and multifaceted as the circumstances that allowed them to be produced in the first place.

Although I am primarily interested in how local movies have survived the vicissitudes of time in order to become treasured historical artifacts in the communities where they were made, such travails are also indicative of how the twinned fields of film preservation and film history have shifted to accommodate local motion pictures. The itinerants who kept the movies they made, including Shad Graham and H. Lee Waters, sold or donated some of their work to universities and film archives in the early 1970s but were met with middling interest, and the collections were subsequently neglected.³ It was not until the late 1990s that local films were considered "orphans," unprotected by copyright and thus a priority for preservation efforts. Early academic studies of the cinema centered on the medium's status as an art form, not historical record or cultural artifact. Only after a series of "turns" in the field of cinema studies—the theoretical turn, the historical turn, the cultural turn, and, finally, the archival turn—did local movies even show up on the research agendas of film specialists. To paraphrase Norma Desmond, local films were big; it was the field that was small.

Years Rolled Back: Finding and Losing Local Films

Although some local films were never really lost, narratives of loss and recovery are critical to how scholars and communities alike understand these movies, and, one could argue, much of cinema history. In her history of motion picture archives, Janna Jones suggests that in the early 1990s, archivists began rejecting earlier commitments that privileged feature-length commercial cinema in order to focus on "constructing the history of the twentieth century by way of their attention to maintenance, preservation, and restoration of archival film materials."⁴ This shift in archival practices and priorities at a national level created both the infrastructure necessary for local films to be recovered in the first place and fostered a community of archivists and scholars who were invested in bringing such moving images into popular and critical discourses.⁵ In other words, local films were no longer seen as curios, the equivalent of a mass-produced manufactured good made by a factory that closed long ago, but instead as windows into the history of a community and, by extension, the United States.

By the late 1990s, archivists, funding sources, and scholars were in a position to identify and, more importantly, prioritize the preservation of local films. The National Film Preservation Foundation (NFPF), a federally chartered corporation that selected and administered film preservation grants, began making awards in 1998. In its very first year it gave more than seven thousand dollars to the Nebraska State Historical Society for the preservation of *Kearney and Its People in Motion Pictures* (c. 1926).[6] In the historical society's application to the foundation, curator Paul J. Eisloeffel noted that the film was conceived as an "actuality piece," not as one of the "local talent" motion pictures that were popular at the time. Eisloeffel further argued that the films were made in collaboration with Universal, and thus were "a rare collaboration between a major studio and a local community." Because they had been left in the towns where they were filmed, they were orphaned by the film studio. Eisloeffel observed that such films were a "unique testament to the power of the moving image as a documentary medium," and, moreover, valuable to the study of state and local history.[7]

Since 1998, the NFPF has proved to be a reliable funding source for the small archives, from public libraries to historical societies, that hold local films. For example, it has funded the preservation of thirty-five reels of H. Lee Waters's *Movies of Local People* (1936–1942); Paragon Feature Film Company's production of *The Lumberjack* (1914); a home movie depicting the making of Don Newland's *Americus's Hero* (1928); Park Motion Picture Production's *My Home Town* in Mooresville, North Carolina (1946); and many other local films. While the presence of the NFPF alone has not caused the revival of interest in local films, its support for such pictures has smoothed the journey from discovery to preservation. Other funding sources, from privately raised money from the communities where the picture was made to a mixture of federal, state, and regional grants has given the holders of such movies a range of options when seeking funds for preservation, video and digital transfers, and, in some cases, reproduction for sale. In order to get a better sense of how such films are found, understood, and preserved as "local films," the following case studies of three of the filmmakers or film companies discussed in this book—O. W. Lamb of the Paragon Feature Film Company, the female directors of the Amateur Theatre Guild, and H. Lee Waters—illustrate how historians and archivists alike have interpreted these films.

Paragon Feature Film Company

Although just three of the dozens of pictures made by the Paragon Feature Film Company are extant, the fact that the company was active in the 1910s, the decade in which the movie industry itself was organized, makes its work of considerable value, particularly because relatively few films from this period survive. Not surprisingly, these films were of interest to archives even before the turn to an interest in orphans, and, in fact, one of Paragon's movies, *Blissveldt Romance*, was featured in a 1993 congressional report that led to the establishment of the NFPF. At the same time, these reels were, in two of three cases, held by archives that had neither significant film collections nor staff who specialized in audio-visual preservation. While these three pictures survived exceptional odds in order to make it to their hundred-year anniversaries, each of them demonstrates the difficulties of preserving local films after they are discovered.

BLISSVELDT ROMANCE

When the Paragon Feature Film Company shot the *Blissveldt Romance* in August 1915, the company was near its peak, making movies that challenged narrative and aesthetic conventions of the booster film. After the film was made, it was presumably given to the Grand Rapids Association of Commerce, which sponsored the film, though in this case it may have been left directly in the hands of Benjamin Hanchett, president of the local streetcar company and owner of two properties that were featured prominently in the picture—the Blissveldt farm and the Lakewood mansion. In any case, the film was found in the attic of Hanchett's Lake Michigan cottage in the 1980s, when it was sold to another prominent Grand Rapids family. After a few years, the family donated the nitrate reels to the Grand Rapids Public Library, which decided to apply for an American Film Institute–National Endowment for the Arts (AFI-NEA) grant to pay for its preservation. In a written statement submitted for a congressionally mandated 1993 report on the state of film preservation in the United States, Grand Rapids city historian Gordon L. Olson noted that the $1,100 received from the federal government allowed them to attract matching local funds and produce a new 35mm negative and print, a 16mm reduction negative and print, and two video masters. In his statement, Olson argued that "it is important that films such as these are preserved, not only for the local images they contain, but also to document their role in the development of the movie industry," tying them into a national narrative of the rise of Hollywood.[8] At the same time, the publicity the *Blissveldt* project received resulted in the preservation of other films made in Grand Rapids, thus ensuring greater awareness of the community's own moving image history.

Film historians Annette Melville and Scott Simmon, the authors of the 1993 report that was commissioned by the Library of Congress, came to a somewhat different conclusion than Olson. After noting that motion pictures of "historic or cultural interest" were being held by "government offices, historical societies, museums, universities, libraries, and nonprofit associations" that were ill-equipped to handle film, Melville and Simmon observed that the Grand Rapids Public Library successfully took advantage of an AFI-NEA grant to preserve and transfer the film to video so it could be shown in the community. But, as they go on to note, "the point here is that most small public organizations with historically valuable films are not equipped to preserve them without expert technical advice and support."[9] Although these comments appear to be unnecessarily critical, they proved prescient, as the 35mm elements of *Blissveldt Romance* were left at John E. Allen, Inc., the laboratory that preserved the film and produced the transfers, and the 16mm elements went missing sometime before they were requested for a screening at the 2012 Orphans Film Symposium.[10] Even though the film continues to be screened in Grand Rapids, local audiences now see a DVD copy of a video transfer, which is far from the quality of the original print.

PRESENT AND PAST IN THE CRADLE OF DIXIE

While *Blissveldt Romance*'s preservation was made possible thanks to a federal grant, another Paragon production, *Present and Past in the Cradle of Dixie* (1914), was preserved because it had been given in 1921 to the Alabama Department of Archives and History by the manager of the Empire Theater, part of a local theater chain.[11] But rather than keeping the nitrate film in their own collections, the archives department gave it to the state treasurer so it could be stored in that department's safe, and by 1940 had forgotten about it when the archives moved to another building. The film was discovered in 1986 when the treasury department temporarily vacated their offices for a renovation to the state capitol building.[12]

Although *Present and Past* was lost for half a century, once it was rediscovered state archivists located a considerable amount of material about its production, including a copy of the script, a program, and even a list of proposed titles (including "The Court of Love Unites the Blue and the Grey"). As the archivist Tanya L. Zanish notes in a 1993 article, the film "is a romanticized view of both the early twentieth-century South and Montgomery's role in the formation of the Confederacy," which made its preservation problematic, particularly given the city's uneasy relationship to both the Confederacy and the long civil rights struggle of African Americans following the end of the Civil War.[13] Nevertheless, the film was screened again publicly, and a local television produced a sympathetic documentary about its discovery, which included interviews with the children of some of the film's stars.[14]

THE LUMBERJACK

Of the three extant Paragon productions, *The Lumberjack*, shot in Wausau, Wisconsin, is unique in that the film was never lost. Even so, it took almost a century for the film to enter an archive. According to a 1983 documentary on the film's production, the 35mm print, made for the film's star, Hans Hagge, was kept in the vault at the Wausau Theatre until the theater's manager died in 1945, when it was moved to the Employers Mutual Liability Insurance Company of Wisconsin, based in Wausau.[15] Later, the film was moved again, this time to city hall, where it was kept in a basement vault, and screened on occasion. In his 1983 documentary, *When You Wore a Tulip and I Wore a Bright Red Rose*, Stephen Schaller accounts for the film's production history and the memories of those who remember seeing the film when it was exhibited. He even interviews one person who appeared in the film, who refers to herself as the "last leaf on the tree," the one surviving cast member.

While Schaller's film is remarkably aware of *The Lumberjack*'s historical significance as an example of a broader phenomenon, there are no direct references to other extant works from this period, in part because neither *Blissveldt Romance* nor *Present and Past* had yet been found. In this way, *When You Wore a Tulip* offers a window into an alternate history in which these films were found and identified when archivists and historians were first looking more closely at cinema history, which could have placed such pictures at the center of these inquiries, rather than the margins. In other words, rather than describing such movies as *orphan* films, we might have instead referred to them as *hometown* movies and seen them as the leading edges of an account of the cinema in which there were many sites of production—from family homes to industrial production companies to Hollywood—all worthy of study and preservation. Instead, both *The Lumberjack* and *When You Wore a Tulip* languished for a time after the latter was produced, and it was not until 2011 that the Wisconsin Historical Society received a NFPF grant to preserve the Paragon film.

Movie Queen

In her study of film preservation, Caroline Frick emphasizes the role regional film archives play in the United Kingdom in finding and caring for materials that would be passed over by national film archives. In the United States, state archives sometimes have taken on this function, but collecting policies and budgets mean that they could be unprepared for the task of collecting their state's moving image history. Since 2000, several independent state and regional film archives have been created, including the Texas Archive of the Moving Image, which Frick started in 2002; Chicago Film Archives (2003); and the Tennessee Archive of Moving Image and Sound (2005).[16] Although these archives differ in important ways, they all took their cue from an independent regional film archive, Northeast Historic Film (NHF), which was founded in Maine in 1986 by Karan Sheldon and David Weiss, and now holds 10 million feet of film and more than 8,000 hours of video.[17]

In just the third year of the organization's history, NHF received a donation of the 16mm film print *Movie Queen, Lubec* (1936), which spurred an ongoing research project on the films that, as Sheldon notes, layers "firsthand production and reception testimonies, documentary research, physical preservation, public presentations, and discussions of accreted meanings" in order to turn them into "significant cultural records."[18] The archive has now collected ten *Movie Queen* prints, all made in New England, although the company produced films throughout the United States.[19] Like many itinerants active in the 1930s, the directors of the *Movie Queen* films tended to leave the 16mm reels with the production's sponsor, which increased the likelihood of their survival. At the same time, relatively few *Movie Queen* productions used intertitles or other identifying markers, which meant that many titles were unidentified until an archivist from NHF inspected them.[20]

Due to NHF's regional focus, and the large numbers of *Movie Queens* made in New England, the archive has been able to approach the films collectively as a long-term research and preservation project. Starting with an early preservation project, funded by an AFI-NEA grant, to preserve two *Movie Queen* films in 1989, the archive has made the film series a priority. Over time, archivists have located new films, identified the people and places depicted in them, and researched the elusive directors and their employer, the Amateur Theatre Guild, who made them.[21] While the three extant films made by Paragon were each discovered and preserved as independent works, the *Movie Queen* films were from the beginning seen as the products of an itinerant practice.

One of the more unusual outcomes of this research was the 2000 production of a new *Movie Queen* in Bucksport, Maine, the home of NHF. Written and directed by archivists Andrea McCarty and Don Radovich, the opening credits note that it was inspired by the *Movie Queen* films made by Margaret Cram, who for a time was thought to be the sole producer of these movies. The black-and-white 16mm production includes images of the community that take after the tropes of the 1930s films, including shots of road signs welcoming the queen, intertitles, and her arrival by boat. At the same time, McCarty and Radovich play with the conventions of silent-era melodrama, with a flashback scene introduced by the title "Insert flashback here." In this way, the Bucksport *Movie Queen* belongs to the neo-silent cinema of directors such as Guy Maddin, Veit Helmer, and Charles Lane. Although the film follows the loose narrative structure of the earlier *Movie Queens*, no one appears in period dress, and an additional love story is added to the plot. In this way, the Bucksport *Movie Queen* suggests a desire for movies with a stronger narrative structure, one closer to Hollywood than the decisively amateur aesthetics of the guild's versions. At the same time, the townspeople in the Bucksport film appear to have enjoyed the experience of making the movie just as much as those who were in the original movies, even if the Bucksport film winks at its source material, having fun with a film that never took itself seriously. Although NHF has also engaged in more conventional preservation work, the creation of the "new" version of *Movie Queen* suggests that they are invested in creating a vibrant culture around these films. Even though the original films were left with individual communities, NHF has gathered them together again, making what might have appeared to be a one-off local effort into a regional film practice shared by many New England communities.

H. Lee Waters

In other cases, local films survived because the filmmaker kept them and continued to exhibit them locally. Although an untold number of movie theater owners and hobbyists kept their movies close, H. Lee Waters's care of his films suggests how local pictures fell from popular awareness even as they circulated within the communities where they were made.

H. Lee Waters's brief career as an itinerant filmmaker ended in 1942, when wartime restrictions on gasoline, the birth of a third child, and a revived portrait studio business brought him back to stay in Lexington. But Waters retained an interest in itinerant exhibition. He continued to revisit the communities where he made *Movies of Local People* to show them his films from the 1930s and 1940s. He undertook a twenty-year anniversary tour during which he visited a number of towns, including Fort Mill, South Carolina, where he called his movies *Way Back in 1940*. In a flyer, Waters promised that the audience will "enjoy seeing the year's [sic] rolled back for you" and assured them that the movies will "bring back fond memories of people and places that are gone . . . But Not Forgotten!" Elsewhere in the same flyer, however, Waters suggested that the films revealed a certain

Figure 8.1. H. Lee Waters later in life. *Courtesy of Davidson County Historical Museum, Lexington, N.C.*

continuity in the community, asking audiences to "see yourselves and your friends as you looked 20 years ago" and suggesting that "you won't believe what you see . . . but the camera doesn't lie!"²² While Waters's films may have not initially been received as historical works, with the twenty-year tour such an association was his primary calling card.

In making these return visits, Waters also prompted exhibitors to recall the decline of moviegoing, which had dropped considerably in the postwar period. In a 1960 letter, O. T. Kirby, manager of the Dolly Madison Theater in Roxboro, thanked Waters for bringing his former patrons back to the theater:

> We played your MOVIES OF LOCAL PEOPLE, taken in Roxboro during the years of 1938 and 1939 over May 12–13–14, 1960 to very good results at the box office. It would be quite a job to dig back into our records this far to determine how this recent engagement stood up against the original ones, but off hand, I would say there was an increase in business this time. In fact, I think there was considerably more enthusiasm among our townspeople who remember these twenty-year-old films.

Figure 8.2. Flyer for H. Lee Waters's *Movies of Local People in 1940*, Fort Mill, South Carolina. *H. Lee Waters Collection, David M. Rubenstein Rare Books and Manuscript Library, Duke University, Durham, N.C.*

It is our intention to return another series of these old pictures some time in the very near future. Needless for me to say, this attraction brought in so very many of our friends whom I have not seen since the advent of television.²³

While Waters's original *Movies of Local People* was one of many things used by theater managers to get people to come to the movies, his twenty-year anniversary tour took place after the cinema had already lost a substantial part of its audience, thus making his films one of the few things that could get people to turn off their television sets and go to their local theater. Kirby, like many movie theater owners in small towns, got out of the business in the 1970s, and the movie theaters in Roxboro have since been converted to other uses.²⁴

In 1976, the *Winston-Salem Journal* ran an article about Waters with the headline, "Old Movies Appeal to Nostalgia." Identifying Waters as a "vintage Lexington photographer," the article notes that he was back on the road selling his films, but this time he was "phasing himself out as he goes—first showing and then selling the old movies to any willing buyer in the various towns and villages." Making the point that he was showing his films at civic club gatherings, not movie theaters, the article stated that it was "nostalgia," not seeing oneself on the screen, that drove the interest in these films.²⁵ Along with Milo Holt, a film distributor from Siler City, North Carolina, Waters sold as many of the films as he could during the 1970s. Waters's decision to sell his movies meant the end of his film practice, transferring the responsibility of storing and screening of the films to those institutions—in most cases, libraries, schools, or civic organizations—that purchased them.²⁶

In 1985, Tom Whiteside, a filmmaker who was teaching at Isothermal Community College in Spindale, North Carolina, came across Waters's films of Cliffside, which had been purchased by Philip White, a local historian and principal of the Cliffside School.²⁷ Soon after, Whiteside went to Lexington to meet Waters and began a long relationship that resulted in the establishment, in 1988, of the H. Lee Waters Collection at Duke University. The collection received an early dose of publicity in 1989, including an NBC News segment on Waters and articles in several major newspapers in the region. With Waters's financial records as a guide, Whiteside began contacting libraries and other community groups who might have purchased the films to convince them to donate the originals to Duke with the understanding that they would receive several viewing copies of the film in return so they could continue to show their movies as they wished. Duke University received a number of NFPF grants, beginning in 2002, to preserve these films. In 2004, Waters's films of Kannapolis, North Carolina, were nominated to the National Film Registry, the first local movies to be so honored, which made the collection an even greater priority for Duke Special Collections and the NFPF. In 2015, ninety-five films from the collection, along with Waters's financial records, were placed online.²⁸

Although these three narratives of discovery appear to be unlikely and singular events, the history of film preservation is full of such stories, such as the 1978 excavation of more than five hundred silent films found in the permafrost in Dawson City, Canada.²⁹ While some films were genuinely discovered, in many cases this narrative of finding a "lost treasure" was foisted on these pictures; in fact many such films were well known in the communities where they were made. For example, residents of Huntingdon, Pennsylvania, had long been aware that Don Newland had shot a movie in their community in the 1930s as it was screened in the local theater in 1966 during the town's bicentennial festivities, but the film appeared to have disappeared shortly after. The film resurfaced in 2001, when the theater's longtime manager finally revealed that he had kept it.³⁰ Many other local movies remain lost, but memories of their production have been sustained by local history columns in town newspapers, photographs, oral histories, and, in the case of the Bucksport *Movie Queen*, recreations.

So far, I have focused on discovery narratives in which an archive swoops in to collect, preserve, and, most importantly, identify the importance of local motion pictures to the history of the cinema. But many local films are not in archives or, at the very least, are not part of an archive's priorities in terms of preservation and access. Instead, they are held by residents of the community where they were produced, who have sought to make them legible to contemporary audiences by adding music, commentary, and other media, such as photographs. By reclaiming local films for their own purposes, communities have remade them for the video and digital eras.

No Longer in Use: Reclaiming the Local Film

In her 1986 defense of the work and craft of local historians, Carol Kammen argues that, counter to the assumptions of academic historians, local history is a "broad field of inquiry" that encompasses a range of approaches, from cultural history to environmental history, and methods, including oral history, statistical analysis, and literary studies.³¹ As she observes, many of the research methodologies that were commonplace in local history are now being adopted by academic historians, a migration that has only accelerated in recent years, and film history is no exception.

Most often, the discovery of local films prompt community groups to identify the people and places in the film and then inscribe their work into the film text, usually through the addition of an audio track, with narration and musical sequences, to what was a silent film. More recently, these movies have been radically transformed by being placed online, with some communities taking frame grabs of the film and presenting them as a series of digitized stills, while others simply upload their movies, with or without annotation, to commercial video sharing sites.

In *The Archive Effect: Found Footage and the Audiovisual Experience of History*, Jaimie Baron defines what she calls the "appropriation film," which contains moving images the film viewer experiences as "'archival'—that is, as coming from another time or from another context of use or intended use." Challenging longstanding distinctions between archival footage, which carries with it the authority of its holding facility, and found footage, which is assumed to lack this authority because of its uncertain provenance, Baron suggests that "foundness" is a quality of all historical moving images, which become "archival" as they are integrated into documentaries, experimental film, and other appropriation films. She suggests that the "archive effect" occurs in appropriation films when the gap between the present of the film and the past of the image is acknowledged within the film itself. As she argues, the archive effect "is a function of the relationship between *different elements* of the *same text*."[32] Even minor alterations to the image, such as layering on a textual description or adding a narration, is enough to produce this effect, thus transforming how the text can be read and, presumably, experienced by the viewer.

In *reclaimed* local films, found moving images are incorporated into new works that subtly but pointedly change how they are understood by residents of the community that was filmed. The term "reclaim" has historically been used to indicate the recovery of something that was lost, often with moralistic undertones. In recent decades, however, the idea of reclamation has been deployed in environmental contexts, in which something that is defiled or wasted—soil, water, and wood are just a few examples—is saved, recovered, and put to use. My use of the term indicates both the assumed status of local films when they are found and the hopes historical societies, public libraries, and community groups have for these images once their reclamation work is complete. In contrast to restoration, which in a film context means to bring the work back to a form that is as close as possible to its original state, reclamation acknowledges the desire to bring something back while also holding to its status as something that was once lost or devalued. Many reclaimed local films are videos, a medium that, as

Michael Z. Newman has argued, has a long history of fostering utopian thinking.³³

In this context, these movies are not valued for their "historical, cultural, or aesthetic significance," the qualities that would make them candidates for inclusion on the National Film Registry, or for their evidentiary status as historical artifacts. Rather, they are of interest because they facilitate the matching of previously unknown moving images of the past with other media, from audio commentaries by local historians and long-time residents of the community that was filmed to textual descriptions of the people and places who are identified. While archives often privilege preservation over access, and seek out grants in order to ensure the original artifact will survive in perpetuity, community groups prioritize access and are less likely to consider the film itself as something worth preserving. For this reason, it is as access copies, and copies of access copies, that these movies thrive.

THE ARTIFACT AND THE ACCESS COPY: RECLAIMING THE MOVIES OF AMATEUR SERVICE PRODUCTIONS

The films of the often anonymous directors of Amateur Service Productions (ASP) are, in many ways, the most ordinary of local pictures. In almost all cases, they were made at the behest of a civic or service organization with relatively little fuss. While the films were screened at movie theaters, there is no evidence of the pomp other itinerants called up, such as parades, fictional scenarios, or trick camerawork. Rather, these movies were merely records of everyday life, filmed following what seemed like a shooting list—a shot of the entrance to town; its main street; and, dutifully, key businesses, schools, and social organizations. Even their titles were ordinary: *See Yourself and Your Town in Movies* was commonly used.

Although the company was active for just a few years, from 1935 to 1941, company representatives claimed that they produced as many as four thousand films during this period. The movies they left behind have become footage for local historical videos, which transforms these works into ruminations on a period that has long been associated with economic hardship and social solidarity. From the outset, it is clear that these videos are not invested in the films themselves as artifacts. For example, in a 1991 video of ASP's 1938 film in Reedsburg, Wisconsin, the scrolling introductory text informs the viewer that "music, sound effects and subtitles have been added to enhance your viewing pleasure and to help identify some scenes," and "various sequences in this film have been rearranged to provide better continuity."³⁴ The Reedsburg video uses band music and advertising jingles in the soundtrack, and sound effects—children playing, cars driving, creaky doors opening—are deployed in a manner similar to that used in the "sound" versions of silent films that were made in the 1930s. Instead of a narrator identifying scenes, white text, which the introduction identifies as "subtitles," notes the names of local businesses and places, leaving people unidentified. The closing credits note that the original film was donated to the Wisconsin Historical Society, further severing the connection between the artifact and the access copy.[35]

If the Reedsburg video adds relatively little detail to the film, other local historical videos attempt to place the movies within the context of the time in which it was made. For example, when community historians in Aliquippa, Pennsylvania, acquired the 1937 film *See Yourself and Your Town in the Movies* in the 1990s, they created a videotape copy, which they retitled *Aliquippa in 1937* (1997), adding both music and commentary.[36] The video was sponsored by a local historical society, the Center for Industrial Heritage of Beaver County, and was narrated by five people with different relationships to and interests in the people and places presented in the film. For example, the video opens with scrolling text that discusses a 1937 Supreme Court decision that is relevant only because it happened to involve a labor dispute between Aliquippa workers and Jones and Laughlin Steel, the town's major employer. The scrolling text continues by introducing the production of the film as the other significant event that year. This tension between the national and the local runs through the piece, and many like it, in part because such movies only become legible when read either as very specific images of people and places or as a general window to life as it was once experienced by people living in a particular place.

We see this tension express itself in the soundtrack, which alternates unidentified big band music presumably from the period in which the film was made and the voices of the narrators, whose identifications resonate with familiarity and often intimacy. Because the Aliquippa film, like most others, features hundreds of people, identifying individuals is a time-consuming task, particularly considering that the video was made sixty years after the original film. And yet, what stands about the video is not the surfeit of information about the people and places depicted but rather the narrator's musings on the past's relationship to the present. For example, when one of the town's future celebrities, the composer Henry Mancini, who was fourteen at the time, appears in the marching band sequence, the narrator briefly identifies him and then moves on to the next name. But when shots of the dedication of a pavilion in St. Joseph Park in the neighboring town of Center Township appear, the narrator muses on the gap between the present of when the narration is recorded and the past of the images. (See Moving Image 8.1.)

In this footage, the narrator goes beyond merely identifying the scenes in order to call attention to both the historical circumstances that led to the pavilion's dedication and, implicitly, the recognition that this "happy gathering" is firmly in the past. At one point, the narrator notes that the park is near a cemetery, which is not seen in the footage, only to further comment that it is no longer in use, underscoring the decline of the community. In fact, as *Aliquippa in 1937* continues, it becomes clear that the narrators are interested in the film in part because it documents a moment when the town was near its peak in terms of population, political power, and social solidarity, and thus underscores the tragedy of its subsequent decline.[37]

This process of reclaiming privileges what Allison Landsberg has called the "affective mode of historical engagement." Local historical productions are more than just videos; instead, as Landsberg suggests of historical film more broadly, they produce "visceral experiences—the oscillation between proximity and distance, alienation and intimacy," that she suggests allow viewers to think historically.[38] Although she focuses on historical fiction films, her emphasis on affect, rather than representation, seems particularly important for local historical videos. The affect local films were intended to produce—the bodily experience of seeing yourself on screen—is replaced by something different, seeing one's own community as a mediated and historicized moving image.

The presence of the narrator, whose intimate relationship to the people and places pictured gives him or her authority over these images, encourages viewers to see these films as storehouses of memories, narratives, and experiences, not just representations of the past. For example, in another local history video, made using Amateur Service Productions' footage of Sauk City, Wisconsin, the narrator, W. J. "Shimmel" Coenen, notes the following over an image of a two men in front of what appears to be a house: "Now this is August Marquardt on the left and Oswald Homberger on the right. They started a real estate business after the banks went broke in nineteen hundred and whatever and it's interesting to note that August Marquardt is blind but he's a real estate dealer. I think that's interesting." In contrast to the Aliquippa film, dates are fairly unimportant to the narrator, who instead uses the images on screen to discuss what is imperceptible in the film itself—such as the fact that the man wearing dark glasses is blind—and thus binds these stories to the film. In *The Ethics of Memory*, the philosopher Avishai Margalit delineates *common* memory, an aggregate of "the memories of all those people who remember a certain episode which each of them experienced individually," from *shared* memory, which "integrates and calibrates the different perspectives of those who remember the episode." Unlike common memory, which is only held by those who experienced a particular event, Margalit argues that shared memory cuts across time, binding members of a "community of memory" to one another. Shared memory depends on these communities of memory, as Margalit defines it, "a network of people and organizations to carry out the division of mnemonic labor," as well as the association of the remembered items, in order for it to function.[39] In effect, local historical videos serve to make the common memories of those who assembled the video a shared memory for the community.[40]

Although I have focused here on videos that were produced using films shot by Amateur Service Productions, similar videos have incorporated a wide range of historical moving images, including other local films, home movies, and newsreels, as well as photographs, maps, newspapers, and other ephemera. These reclaimed copies are less likely to be in archives than local films, and, given the comparatively short shelf-life of video, are now more vulnerable to being lost than the films that they were intended to save. Meanwhile, many communities have turned to another new medium, the internet, in an effort to share their movies with a much larger audience, one very different from the geographically and spatially circumscribed communities they knew best.

Remember Cliffside: Local Films on the Web

When H. Lee Waters sold his films in the 1970s, he found eager buyers among those who grew up in mill towns. Like the Aliquippa film, Waters's movies depicted mill towns at their peak of productivity and population, and many former residents looked back at mill life with fondness, particularly those who were children in the 1930s. But if the Aliquippa film was seen in the context of the community's decline, many mill town movies were among the only moving image records of these communities, which no longer existed as such. Beginning in the 1960s, mills shuttered operations, and in many cases companies dismantled worker housing, shops, and other buildings once they were no longer needed.

Cliffside, in the North Carolina Piedmont, was one of those communities. In 1901, Raleigh Rutherford Haynes, who had already developed several textile mill communities, chartered Cliffside Mills, which went into operation the following year. By 1922, the community had grown large enough to support its own public school building, and by the 1940s, its population reached 2,500, larger than many municipalities in the state, even though it remained a company-owned village. The homes were reserved for employees of the mill, which, over time, fell into disrepair. By the 1960s, all company housing was removed from Cliffside, against the wishes of some residents who would have preferred to purchase their homes from the new owner, Cone Mills. Soon after, the once-thriving village became a ghost town, even though the factory itself was active for another three decades.

In 2002, former Cliffside resident Reno Bailey, a software developer who had recently retired, created *Remember Cliffside*, a website that exhaustively documents the town. The hand-coded site contains primary and secondary source materials, including oral histories, photographs, images of a scale model an artist made of the town, and, in one section, more than three hundred stills that were taken from H. Lee Waters's film of the community.[41] Each still is labeled, and most of the individuals who appear in them are identified. While Lois Womack and Sue Crowe, the "twin reporters" for the *Cliffside News*, suspected in 1937 that Waters's visit meant that "Hollywood doesn't seem so far off now as it used to," and that "movie contracts" would be on their way for Cliffside's residents, these images had lost any association with the movie industry.[42] Rather, it is their specificity to the community that gives them meaning. Visitors to the site can now see the film either as a series of stills or as moving images. Waters's films, then, are not only a media artifact, left unconnected to the rest of the material, but rather incorporated into the community's history.[43]

In fact, it is their placement on a local history website that reveals how local films on the web are different from the community history videos discussed earlier. While the need to match sound with image forces narrators and editors to make decisions about what to emphasize in their reclaiming of local films, when these films are placed on the web, there are no similar restrictions on how they are used. For example, on the Cliffside site it is possible to document those left out of the films, most notably the community's African American residents, by including photographs, maps, and other documents pertaining to the African American community in Cliffside. Instead of representing a film as the account of a place and a time, *Remember Cliffside* permits a more expansive notion of what it means to document and revisit the past, with Waters's films serving to reveal just how many stories might be told about the community.

Unlike many local history websites, *Remember Cliffside* is a remarkably robust and well-tended site, one that is itself in need of preservation, as the design and infrastructure has not changed since it was first created.[44]

But, many local films are not handled with such care, even though digital tools now make it easy to work with moving images. Instead, they are commonly found on video sites, including YouTube and the Internet Archive, where they are left open for interpretation and reuse by those who come across them.

The Indeterminacy of Now

In his 2004 book *The Remembered Film*, Victor Burgin observes that one of the consequences of the ubiquity of digital media in our contemporary moment is its capability to change our expectations for how the past is represented in visual media.[45] In a world that sees itself, and often its past, as a motion picture, local films compensate for the absence of moving images from many histories. And on video sharing sites, movies themselves become the medium of history writing, as people create video essays out of photographs, texts, maps, and other media. While certain visual and aural artifacts, including VHS hiss, projector noise, and audio buzz, hint at how the films were transferred and remediated for online streaming, this work is rarely commented on in the descriptions. In fact, local films are uploaded online with just the barest of details, leaving commenters to speculate on the date of the footage, its initial purpose, and the people and places pictured. On occasion, even the identity of the person or organization who has uploaded the video is obscured, making it difficult to discern the origins of these films.

At the same time, their obscurity generates a broader range of responses online. Video sharing sites encourage their users to engage with moving images by commenting on them, and in many cases individuals take on the task of supplementing these videos with their own reactions. These comments range from the identification of individuals and places to digressions about someone's experience living in the place pictured. In some cases, such comments go in surprising directions, such as those for the 1940 production of *Movie Queen* in Bogota, New Jersey, in which one surprised commenter asks "son bogotanos gringos?"[46] Another goes on to note that Bogota was named after the Bogert family, who helped settle the area, and has no connection to the Colombian capital.

More often, however, users comment about where relatives appear, identifying specific sections of interest, or time stamps, in order to direct subsequent viewers to scenes of interest. In a comment on *It Happened in Norristown*, a user writes "Puts family life in late 30's Norristown into perspective. I think I see my grandfather, Frank Wildman. Now I understand how people got into Philadelphia with relative ease."[47] In other instances, users observe moments that are incongruous with contemporary decorum. In a comment on *This Is Progressive Wilkes County* (1948), one asks, "29:50 Did he say what I think he said?" leading the curious viewer to go to the section of the film and hear the narrator note, "One of the principal reasons for the county's industrial stability is the capable industrious source of *white* American labor."[48] While none of these responses are particularly surprising as YouTube comments, they do suggest the ways in which responses to local films online are different from those that occur in other contexts. While the comingling of the archival with the contemporary, and the local with the global, has its own pleasures, it often comes at the expense of identifying the local film as a cultural artifact, belonging to a particular place and time.

But the most surprising reuse of local films once they leave their community context occurs not online but in the black box theaters and white cube galleries where art is both produced and received. Filmmakers, musicians, and installation artists have reworked, repurposed, and interpreted local films. While this work is distinct from the kinds of local historical research discussed above, artists explore how these moving images may be reinterpreted for future audiences who will think about moving images in contexts far removed from the movie theater where the films were once screened.

Artist Reuses of Local Films

Unlike community groups, artists rarely have strong investments in identifying the people and places in specific motion pictures, and instead emphasize the films' aesthetic qualities. At the same time, these images are received as something more than footage, as their production history is often either incorporated into the work itself or takes on an important role in how these new pieces are received by critics and audiences. While both community and artistic reuse of local film transforms the original, artists also radically shift how these films are valued and interpreted. As a result, the three examples discussed here—Vanessa Renwick's 2003 film *Britton, South Dakota*; Jenny Scheinman and Finn Taylor's 2015 multimedia work *Kannapolis, A Moving Portrait*; and Gareth Long's 2014 installation *Kidnappers Foil*—suggest some of the ways these films might be read when their ties to specific people and places are no longer what is most interesting about them. In other words, these artists are exploring the attractions these films have for people who do not see themselves, or their collective histories, on screen.

Even though they were produced by itinerants, most local films were not intended to travel. Their primary audience, and in many cases their only audience, consisted of people who recognized the scenes before them. This intimacy between the films and their subjects began to separate soon after their first screenings; almost all of the local films that are extant were shown to many local people who were not present for the movie's premiere over a period of decades. And yet, it was not until these films entered archives that they attracted an audience that consisted mostly of people who were not from the community depicted.

One of the primary places where such screenings occurred was the Orphan Film Symposium, which, from its very first meeting in 1999, sought to connect the "film scholars, archivists and preservation experts" who found these motion pictures in archives throughout the world with the "filmmakers and historians" who might use them.[49] Filmmakers such as Alan Berliner, Péter Forgács, and Bill Morrison were invited to share their work with archivists and scholars, who in turn took interest in how filmmakers were using materials that archivists and scholars had studied and preserved. By bringing together professional communities with interests in orphan films, Dan Streible, who founded and continues to run the symposium, raised awareness of local films produced in the United States.

This model of archivist-artist partnership is seen in Vanessa Renwick's 2003 film *Britton, South Dakota*, which reuses local newsreels shot by Ivan Besse in 1938 and 1939. In 1991, the archivist Rick Prelinger acquired two and a half hours of Besse's films from a collector in Texas. Soon after, he brought the films back to Britton, where Besse again narrated them in front of an audience of people who recognized themselves and their neighbors in footage shot a half-century earlier. In early 2003, Renwick contacted Prelinger in search of footage she could use for a screening and performance event in Portland, Oregon.[50] He sent her a large sampling of films from his archives, including a video copy of Besse's films. Renwick was immediately struck by the faces of the children in the films and selected two sequences to be scored by Johnne Eschleman, a multimedia artist who performed music under the name the Distance Formula. Shortly after the live performance and screening, Renwick invited Eschleman to record his score in a studio and matched it to the footage.

The nine-minute video opens with a black screen or, more precisely, a blank screen, as if to suggest the presence of a projector. On the soundtrack, one hears the hiss of a sound recording, as well as a selection of eerie sounds that may be coming from birds and amphibians or possibly electronic instruments. When the images appear an organ is heard on the soundtrack, creating an atmosphere of melancholia. The film transfer is exceptionally sharp, and Besse's aesthetic, which, like many films of the period, borrows conventions from portrait photography, gives the impression that the children on screen were filmed out of a documentary impulse. In a brief comment, the filmmaker James Benning observes the "structural" quality of *Britton, South Dakota*, suggesting that the iterative practices used by many itinerants to maximize profits, particularly capturing every person who might be persuaded to see themselves on screen, could also be read as an experiment with film form.[51]

If Renwick reinterprets the *Britton* films as structuralist Americana, the musician and composer Jenny Scheinman, along with the filmmaker Finn Taylor, turned H. Lee Waters's *Movies of Local People* into a series of small town portraits for *Kannapolis: A Moving Portrait*.[52] The project was prompted by a new initiative, titled *From the Archives*, in which Duke Performances, the university's performing arts organization, asked artists to create work inspired by, and in dialogue with, materials held by Duke's Special Collections. In 2010, Aaron Greenwald, director of Duke Performances, approached Scheinman about writing songs based on Waters's movies. Although Scheinman conducted extensive research about Waters and the culture of the mid-Atlantic South, in a radio interview she emphasized that she not did see her project as a documentary.[53] Rather, she sought to inhabit the lives of the people pictured, creating pieces that captured their perspectives while simultaneously considering how contemporary viewers, immersed in social media, might see the people and places depicted in Waters's films.

In the performance, which premiered at Duke University's Reynolds Industries Theater in March 2015, Scheinman accommodates this dual perspective by constructing narratives out of Waters's footage. Although the work takes its name from one of the many cities Waters visited, Taylor uses footage from several dozen films, which he treats as material to be reedited, slowed down, color-corrected, and otherwise manipulated to fit Scheinman's songs. Other sounds, such as the steady hum of textile machinery and the noises of children playing, are added to the soundtrack, breathing an aural life into the silent images. One of the hokiest moments in Waters's films, when two embarrassed school-aged children, always a boy and girl, hold a large cardboard heart inscribed with the words "Be My Valentine," is here presented as the early signs of a courtship. Character-centered songs, along with the repetition of certain images, allows for a reading of Waters's films as little narratives, much in the way stories were constructed out of the best known images of the 1930s, photographs taken on behalf of the Farm Security Administration.⁵⁴ In this way, what appears to be intimacy in the work—particularly those songs that explore the inner lives of these characters—is instead an artifact of Scheinman's and Taylor's distance from the footage, which allows them to create their stories without concern for the identities of the people in the films. The processes of identification and recognition that were an essential part of the local film's appeal are traded for more generalized pleasures of immersion in a distant and unfamiliar past.

Although Scheinman's songs, such as one plainly titled "Good Old Days," question the temptation to look back at these films with fondness, subtle manipulations of the original footage emphasize nostalgic, rather than critical, readings of the films. For example, Taylor makes considerable use of one of Waters's trademark camera tricks—the reversal of time, most often used to show young boys leaping up from the ground and back onto the top of a cliff. Waters achieved this effect in camera, which means that in the films themselves we only see the action once. But Taylor is able to deliver us this movement over and over, in effect creating a hierarchy of images in which we are encouraged to fix our eyes on certain figures and movements. The work's title, *Kannapolis: A Moving Portrait*, signals what distinguishes Scheinman's and Taylor's approach from other interpretations of Waters's films: we are expected to see them as portraits, pictures planned and produced with the expectation that they would be studied with care, rather than the fleeting glances of someone we might recognize. In this way, Scheinman and Taylor suggest one possible future for local films—repositories of stories that we must imagine, rather than research, and wells of visual records that we can draw on continuously.

While Jenny Scheinman reimagines local films as containers of short narratives created out of arresting images, the installation and conceptual artist Gareth Long sees the narrative, fiction films of the itinerant filmmaker Melton Barker as being "littered with questions of amateurism [and] amateur participation," which have long been preoccupations of his artistic practice.⁵⁵ Long came across Barker's films shortly after they were listed in the Library of Congress's National Film Registry in 2012. Although the registry is typically thought of as a place to honor specific films, Barker's entire oeuvre was added, even presumably those films that are not known to have survive or that still lie in dusty corners of small towns, waiting to be found. In an interview, Long emphasized his interest in exploring the "copying and iteration and seriality" that goes on in Barker's work, seeing it not only as a prototype of later cultural forms, such as reality television, but also as a late version of early cinema, in which copying was a "distribution method," a way to get around copyright by creating a work again rather than merely duplicating another's chase sequence or waves crashing against the shore.[56]

For the piece, which was exhibited at the Kunsthalle Wien, a contemporary art museum in Vienna, Austria, Long arranged eleven large screens in a dark cube, some translucent and hanging from the ceiling, others set against the wall. Barker's films are shown simultaneously, even retaining the crinkle of the soundtrack, creating a cacophony of mismatched sounds when the films are playing. Although the films start at the same time, very quickly minor differences emerge. In an essay that accompanied the exhibit, Erika Balsom observes that the films's seriality "might be understood as [a] violent imposition of sameness that liquidates historicity and authenticity."[57] Instead of the locality of these works emerging as their core quality, we instead see their sameness, with difference read as imperfection rather than something that makes each version unique. Although Balsom nods to the film's documentary value at the end of her essay, such characteristics are not relevant to Long's presentation of the films, and there is no attempt to locate them within a particular geography, a social context, or even a cultural milieu.

Artistic renditions and reuse of local films are, unsurprisingly, provocative, and in fact might be seen as affronts to the kind of careful, local historical work community groups have done with these motion pictures. And yet, these examples demonstrate the very alien qualities of local films, the fact that they represent not only people and places that are distant from the contemporary moment but also a past that is not well-known and does not circulate in other contexts. At the same time, these creative works do not attempt to recast local films as something they were not—home movies, raw footage, or ethnographic work—and thus wrestle with notions of representation, community, and seriality, all of which are at the core of itinerant practices. In fact, by reusing the local film for other purposes, these works underscore what, exactly, makes it such a distinct mode of motion picture production in the first place.

Local Films, the Archive, and the Academy

For film historians and archivists, there is the temptation to return to the original, to make the moving image legible in its moment of origin, and to recreate the conditions under which it was initially seen. But for those who work with local films, realizing this goal is impossible, as such movies assumed a temporal and spatial wholeness that was inherently unstable. In addition, the quest to preserve films has the unintended consequence of making the access copies that were produced in local communities secondary to the prints that are preserved in archives. In effect, the best practices for researching and preserving many kinds of films, particularly those feature-length commercial productions that, over time, have come to be received as movies of artistic and historical interest, are insufficient, and potentially harmful, to local films.

Instead, the experiences of discovery, reclaiming, and reuse outlined here suggest another approach to preservation, which would add contextual information to make cinema legible to a wider range of audiences. If the chasm between contemporary viewers and film artifacts is ever widening, the processes of recovery, reclamation, and reuse serve as a drawbridge between the two, allowing the viewer to connect with local movies without threatening the integrity of the original artifact. Although residents of a depopulated factory town; museum visitors in Vienna, Austria; and a thirty-year-old looking for movies of their hometown online all view these works in different ways, the fact that they are able to see these movies at all suggests the impact of the considerable effort that has been put into disseminating these films to a larger public.

If local films were intended to be an evening's entertainment, shown one evening and then forgotten, their survival alone has confounded expectations. In the last few decades, though, their recovery by archives, reclamation by community groups, and reuse by artists has offered something even more challenging—a picture of what the world might look like if every movie was thought to be a local film, one of unknown thousands, copies of copies, forever moving in and out of focus.

Notes

1. Fossati, *From Grain to Pixel*, 23
2. Amad, *Counter-Archive*, 4.
3. After his death in 1969, Graham's widow, Ruth Esther Graham, established the Shad E. Graham Memorial Film Library, a collection of his *Our Home Town* films and other productions, at the University of Texas at Austin. The reels were held by the College of Communication until 1983, when they were transferred to the Dolph Briscoe Center for American History, also at the University of Texas. As for the Waters films, William H. Brown, archives registrar for the Division of Archives and Records, part of the State Archives of North Carolina, noted that a number of public libraries and historical societies donated Waters's films to the state archives between 1974 and 1977 but these films were not available to the public for many years. Viewing copies of the films are now available, and some of the films have been digitized and put online.

4. Jones, *The Past Is a Moving Picture*, 17.

5. Thanks to Karan Sheldon for suggesting I should emphasize the role archivists at small institutions played in changing national preservation priorities.

6. Among the other state archives and historical societies that recognized the importance of their moving image collections were the Rhode Island Historical Society, Oregon Historical Society, Minnesota Historical Society, and Chicago History Museum.

7. NFPF Grant Application, courtesy of Paul Eisloeffel, Nebraska State Historical Society.

8. Gordon L. Olson, "Statement Regarding Library of Congress National Film Preservation Board Reauthorization," in *Film Preservation 1993: A Study of the Current State of American Film Preservation* (Washington, DC: National Film Preservation Board of the Library of Congress, 1993), 4:159–160.

9. Annette Melville and Scott Simmon, *Film Preservation 1993*, vol. 1 (Washington, DC: National Film Preservation Board of the Library of Congress, 1993), https://www.loc.gov/programs/national-film-preservation-board/preservation-research/film-preservation-study/current-state-of-american-film-preservation-study/

10. It is still unclear where the elements for the *Blissveldt Romance* preservation are located, though correspondence with Jim Winslow, a local historian in Grand Rapids, suggests that all elements remain at the Allen labs.

11. Zanish, "Present and Past in the Cradle of Dixie," 28. The film premiered at the Grand Theater, which was part of the same theater chain.

12. Ibid., 25.

13. Ibid., 28. For more on Alabama's approach to its multiple, and conflicting, heritage sites, see Eskew, "From Civil War to Civil Rights."

14. The film was produced by Bill Schaum and written and narrated by Bob Ingram, a longtime reporter for the *Montgomery Advertiser*. It aired on WSFA, a Montgomery television station, in 1987.

15. *When You Wore a Tulip and I Wore a Bright Red Rose*, directed by Stephen Schaller, 1983.

16. University and state archives have also taken an interest in collecting regional film. For an extensive list of such archives, see Karan Sheldon and Karen Glynn, "Regional Moving Image Archives, United States" (2006), http://www.oldfilm.org/files/file/RegionalArchives.pdf.

17. "About Us," Northeast Historic Film, 2010, http://oldfilm.org/content/about-us.

18. Sheldon, "Meeting the Movie Queen," 80.

19. Two other *Movie Queen* films, from Bogata, New Jersey, and East Palestine, Ohio, circulate online.

20. For example, members of the Van Buren Rotary Club held on to their *Movie Queen* production but over time forgot what was on the 16mm reel. See "Collections: Movie Queen Mania," *Moving Image Review*, Winter 2003, 7. Likewise, the Ellsworth, Maine, *Movie Queen* was discovered in 2015 in a collection that had been held by NHF since 1999.

21. Many of these archivists, including Andrea McCarty, Don Radovich, and Dwight Swanson, were trained at the L. Jeffrey Selznick School for Film Preservation in Rochester, New York, which started in 1996.

22. Flyer, H. Lee Waters Collection, David M. Rubenstein Rare Books and Manuscript Library, Duke University, Durham, N.C.

23. Letter, personal collection of the author.

24. According to Kirby's grandson Bob Morgan, now a pharmacist in Roxboro, Kirby left the business because he found it increasingly difficult to compete with multiplex theaters in Durham, North Carolina, thirty miles to the south, and was dissatisfied with the quality of films, whose content meant that the theater could not keep to its mission of showing "family entertainment."

25. "Old Movies Appeal to Nostalgia," *Winston-Salem* (N.C.) *Journal*, January 12, 1976, 17.

26. As noted above, many of these films were soon after transferred to the State Archives of North Carolina.

27. Tom Whiteside, "Up for Adoption? The Adaptability of H. Lee Waters' Movies of Local People," http://www.sc.edu/orphanfilm/orphanage/symposia/orphans1/whiteside.html.

28. Duke University Libraries, H. Lee Waters Film Collection, http://library.duke.edu/digitalcollections/hleewaters/.

29. Kula, "Up from the Permafrost."

30. Wagoner, "The *Huntingdon's Hero* Story."

31. Kammen, *On Doing Local History*, 5.

32. Baron, *The Archive Effect*, 9, 22.

33. Michael Z. Newman, *Video Revolutions: On the History of a Medium* (New York: Columbia University Press, 2014), 105.

34. Reedsburg 1938 film, YouTube, https://www.youtube.com/watch?v=NmvNNgeF618.

35. In fact, when I viewed the copy at the Wisconsin Historical Society, I was unaware of the reclamation of the film, which was later uploaded to YouTube.

36. Counter to what the narrator of the film implies, the movie had been found several decades earlier by Robert Casoli, a visual education instructor at Hopewell High School in Aliquippa, who screened it from time to time at community events. See "In One Ear," (Aliquippa, Penn.) *Beaver Valley Times*, November 26, 1959, 1. Don Inman acquired the film in 1990, when it was sent to the Boston-based Blackside, Inc., for use as footage for a WGBH documentary series about the Great Depression. Although the footage was not included in the documentary, the video transfer enabled the production of *Aliquippa in 1937*.

37. This rather unhappy story is emphasized in other local histories. For example, Rade Vukmir's 1999 history of the Jones and Laughlin steel mill in Aliquippa notes in the introduction that "the greed of the 1980's driven by Wall Street and the desire for shareholder and corporate profits had shut the mill down and ended a way of life forever," and goes on to document, with photographs, oral histories, and production data, exactly what was lost. See Vukmir, *The Mill*, 15.

38. Landsberg, *Engaging the Past*, 29.

39. Margalit, *The Ethics of Memory*, 51, 58–59, 79.

40. Maurice Halbwachs's work on collective memory is also useful here because he identifies the tension between efforts to establish and cultivate a national memory and the very localized, and often familial, nature of our own memories. See Halbwachs, *On Collective Memory*.

41. "Remember Cliffside," remembercliffside.com.

42. "Cliffside News," *Forest City* (N.C.) *Courier*, August 9, 1937, 9.

43. More recently, Duke University has created a companion website for the Waters collection, effectively a moving image equivalent of Roy Stryker's Farm Security Administration photography unit in which the films themselves become secondary to a visualization of small-town culture in the Depression-era South.

44. In fact, in 2015, a fundraising campaign was launched to pay for the site's preservation. See "Preserve 13 Years of Historical Research," https://www.indiegogo.com/projects/preserve-13-years-of-historical-research#/.

45. Burgin, *The Remembered Film*.

46. Tommy Carlock, "Movie Queen - 1940's Bogota NJ Part 1," YouTube, https://www.youtube.com/watch?v=4nC-msW5gm8&list=PLChMSN94D1H1_2jbiM1eCm5O13LYNqcn0&index=3.

47. Carl Christensen, "Norristown Pennsylvania - 1937 promotional film by the Chamber of Commerce," YouTube, https://www.youtube.com/watch?v=sELHCpBkLs0&index=77&list=PLChMSN94D1H1_2jbiM1eCm5O13LYNqcn0.

48. https://www.youtube.com/watch?v=SfUz13Lg22o&index=42&list=PLChMSN94D1H1_2jbiM1eCm5O13LYNqcn0.

49. "Call for Participants: Preservation of Film Conference," Columbia, S.C. (September 23–25, 1999)," http://h-net.msu.edu/cgi-bin/logbrowse.pl?trx=vx&list=h-announce&month=9906&week=d&msg=Z0KRZsEI49dkeSOc5u4xGQ&user=&pw=.

50. Vanessa Renwick, personal conversation with the author, November 7, 2015.

51. "Britton, South Dakota," http://www.odoka.org/the_work/britton_south_dakota/.

52. Film editor Rick Lecompte and sound designer Trevor Jolly also contributed to the piece's production. See "World Premiere Presentation: Duke Performances Commissions Acclaimed Musician Jenny Scheinman to Create New Work Inspired by North Carolina Films of H. Lee Waters," December 9, 2014, https://dukeperformances.duke.edu/sites/default/files/u75/Press%20Release%20Duke%20Performances%20Jenny%20Scheinman%20%2B%20H.%20Lee%20Waters%20'Kannapolis'%2012-09-14.pdf.

53. Jenny Scheinman, interview, WUNC, March 20, 2015, http://wunc.org/post/kannapolis-moving-portrait.

54. For more on the Farm Security Administration, see Smith, *Making the Modern*, chapter 8.

55. Gareth Long, interview with the author, November 9, 2015.

56. Ibid.

57. Balsom, "Repeat Performance."

CONCLUSION
See Your Town Disappear—
The Historicity of the Local Film

FOR THE FIRST THREE QUARTERS of the twentieth century, local films were everywhere. They were made by theater managers, hobbyists, and traveling filmmakers with varying amounts of experience and expertise. They were shot in big cities, suburban neighborhoods, small towns, and even in villages and hamlets that struggled to support regular film exhibition. Camera operators created moving image records of big events and notable townspeople, and turned the crank as amateur actors staged home talent performances. Others caught people unaware as they walked through town on what was, in every other way, an ordinary day, commemorated merely because a camera was there.

Local films were the products of a huckster's hustle, the realizations of a narcissist's wish, the results of a starry-eyed business club's fanciful publicity campaign. If one were to unspool all of the local films ever made, with each frame covering a map of the places and people pictured, we would likely have a more comprehensive view of life in the United States in the twentieth century than if the same were done for any other mode of professional or amateur film production. For all their worldly ambitions, Hollywood producers were provincials when it came to selecting shooting locations, with most movies made in New York or Los Angeles studios. Industrial and educational picture companies occasionally ventured out of their smaller, geographically dispersed offices, but only to capture the people and places selected by their clients. Newsreel camera operators trained their eyes on events, not everyday life. Home movie makers, who were more numerous than itinerant producers of local films, were not active in large numbers until the 1940s, providing comparatively few views of the United States before then. Itinerant filmmakers, in contrast, traveled everywhere, from the beginnings of cinema, and continued making local movies in large numbers into the 1970s.

At the same time, local films were from the moment after the final reel wound its way through the projector especially vulnerable to loss. The business and civic associations who sponsored these films were, in many cases, given them for safekeeping, but those groups were usually unprepared to keep archives at all, let alone something as fragile as film. While some theaters retained local films, the projection booth was not seen as an obvious home for motion pictures. Local movies shot on 16mm were more likely to be saved, often by people who had access to a projector, but film damage and the loss of playback equipment made them functionally obsolete. A few filmmakers decided to retain their movies, knowing that the pictures shot today had historical value that could be commercialized in three, ten, or twenty years hence. But in most cases, local films were an ill fit for even informal systems of distribution, circulation, and preservation, making their survival all the more unlikely. Those that did survive constitute, collectively, a vast and unwieldy moving image archive of twentieth-century America.

In many ways, this book has been interested in making sense of this archive. Distributed in a variety of small institutions rather than centralized in a national one, the local film archive is both rare and nearby. Modest in its aims, this archive invites uses, and users, of all sorts. Most studies of local film and adjacent genres—travelogues, amateur film, home movies—have focused on their capacity to capture and reproduce scenes from everyday life. As I have shown, the itinerant producers of local films from the early teens forward had other ambitions. By integrating fictional plots, narrative storytelling techniques, and special effects into their local films, these producers adapted to fast-changing industry norms. Rather than mapping the small worlds created by these movies, this book has sought to describe the social, political, and cultural climates in which local films were produced. In my conclusion, I want to suggest, first, how this other archive of cinema might challenge how we conceptualize the work of film history, particularly our own "local views" of the discipline, and, second, how local films themselves might open up new horizons of inquiry in fields that continue to treat cinema in nationalist and generalist terms.

Where Is the *Local* in Film History?

In Siegfried Kracauer's posthumously published book on historiography, he argued that historians should seek to find middle ground, or a "medium shot," between histories that are too distant from or too close to the ground of historical experience.[1] Written in the 1960s, Kracauer's work anticipated arguments about the research and writing of history, from microhistories that celebrate minutiae to work in the digital humanities that uses algorithms to mechanically read large volumes of historical data. Although Kracauer's use of film concepts to describe his thoughts on historiography is not surprising given his interest in cinema, film history in particular is well-suited for "medium shot" analysis, in part because films themselves travel from the granular to the global. In fact, the local theater itself could be thought of as a middle ground between close analysis of individual films and investigations into the operations of the motion picture industry. Furthermore, I want to suggest that local films especially represent this "medium shot" of film history, as they capture the specificity of particular places using modes of production devised for almost any place whatsoever.

In this book, I have discussed the local film as a historical film practice that was recognized as such in its own time—contemporary newspapers often referred to the production of these movies as "local films"—and as a way to conceptualize an entire archive of moving images that confound the divisions film historians have long used to demarcate certain types of cinema. Local films were professional and amateur, fiction and documentary, narrative and non-narrative, commercial and noncommercial. In fact, as I have shown, such labels meant less than those that were commonplace at the time—home talent, booster, hometown—but have fallen into disuse.

By calling these movies "local films," I bring attention to the similarities they share and the possibilities for analyses that cut across historical periods, genres, and functions. At the same time, I have tried to avoid reading them through a single interpretive framework, namely, films that gave people the pleasure of seeing themselves in the movies. Jane Gaines has suggested that film historians need to guard against over-determining their readings of the past. As an example, she observes that the transformative, if now universally accepted, notion of a "cinema of attractions" that predated narrative film can be used to produce a particular reading of early cinema texts, thus cutting against its very potential to provoke new understandings of moving image culture at the turn of the twentieth century. As she notes, a history of the cinema that is invested in fictional narrative will locate the origins of such works. Likewise, histories of the documentary will seek out early *actualités*. With digital archives, such readings are remarkably easy to reproduce, as long as one ignores the search results that confound one's expectations.

Rather than tossing out old paradigms for new ones, Gaines proposes borrowing from the work of the anthropologist Michel-Rolf Trouillot, in which we look for an overlap, rather than a gap, in the "historicity of that which is said to have happened" and the "historicity of what happened."[2]

Instead of locating historical facts in the past, using evidence—newspapers, films, ephemera—that is, by necessity, widely accepted as valid and using them to fill in the gaps of history, Gaines suggests that we also account for the ways in which the interpretations of these facts are shaped by another, and more recent, set of historical facts about how the cinema came to be and is understood.

Expanding the Frame: The Scale of Local Film

Rather than seeing the "local film" as yet another phenomenon of early cinema that persisted, in a subterranean way, until the 1970s, I want to suggest that we can see interest in the local film as something that is related to our investment in the "local" as a way to conceptualize an alternative to global culture. This way of looking at the local film opens up new approaches to adjacent fields, particularly those that ascribe social, economic, and geopolitical importance to the American small town and its surplus of representations. Because local films were not mere pictures of everyday life but rather structured, layered, and organized representations of certain people and places, looking at them through contemporary eyes provides insight into both the small-town imagination and those who, willingly or not, were cast as bit players in its realization. Instead of seeing such films as historical evidence, I suggest that we look at these movies as "special effects" that collapsed hierarchical and proportional scales of cultural production. Because cinema was from its inception understood to be a global medium, which was experienced in local and communal settings, local motion pictures glide effortlessly from the particular to the general. This is why these films can simultaneously be seen as detailed, even microscopic studies of place and as an epiphenomenon of the development of the movies as mass culture.

By claiming that local films were not really, or at least not only, "local," I want to underscore other ways in which they may be analyzed and understood. Anna McCarthy has argued that the "politics of scale" was essential to the development of cultural studies as an academic discipline, with scholars studying the marginal, the ordinary, and the everyday in order to challenge "conventional assumptions about scale and value, generality and importance."[3] As Alan Liu has noted, many localized studies, whether of particular works of literature or specific communities, present themselves as a challenge to global and hegemonic studies. At the same time, by embracing "detailism" as a way of researching and writing history, such scholars produce what he terms "bubble universes" that are even more closed off and atomized than the larger views they are intended to supplement or replace. Furthermore, such universes are often depicted as if they were mediated using contemporary technologies, which, not surprisingly, are often seen as scalar instruments. As he argues, such histories are dispensed "through the 'orifices' of lenses, microphones, screens, and sundry other instructions of mediation that, via the act of mediation itself, register the paradox of immersive freedom from history constitutive of contingency." Rather than accepting mediation on its own terms, Liu, echoing Kracauer, suggests scholars embrace "actual media innovation" that allows one to "see history as a compound relation of proximity and distance between past and present."[4] Here, I wish to propose that we look at local films as texts with "compound relations," offering specificity while implicitly acknowledging their universality. By reading such films as being as much about a particular place as they are about ideas of how such places should be depicted in the cinema, it is possible to retain this "medium shot," seeing the local as a middle ground between the particular and the abstract.

Even so, there remains the question of just what kind of "local" is present in the local film. I propose that we should see the local as a special effect. Although not all local films were narrative fictions, almost all itinerants shot scenes that can be read as special effects. Whether they were camera tricks, such as under-cranking or over-cranking the camera in order to produce the illusion of fast or slow motion, or staged effects that relied on stop-motion cinematography and the manipulation of the mise-en-scène, such as fake fires and automobile accidents, special effects were ubiquitous in local films. Furthermore, the production of the local was itself a kind of special effect, as it emerged from an ideology of place that was reinforced by sponsors and exhibitors who saw much to be gained in controlling who was granted a few minutes on screen. The presence of special effects in local films challenge our understanding of these moving images as representations of the everyday, the ordinary, or the real, and suggests that their capacity to transform the appearance of the local was as important as its mere depiction.

In other word, the towns that appeared in local films have disappeared, but not because of a special effect produced by a particularly clever director. Rather, these towns disappeared because they have been replaced, in our historical imagination, by the moving images, photographs, and other textual materials that survive, which are now the basis for both specific and general histories. And although local films in particular appear to bring them back to life with a vividness not found in other media, the presence of special effects, even ones that only become visible on close reading, remind us of our need to find an overlap between film as historical evidence and film as a means of manipulating reality.

We see this concern about the historicity of the local film in a somewhat unusual place, the editorial pages of the *Moberly Weekly Monitor*, a Missouri newspaper that had a striking reaction to a motion picture of a coon hunt that was produced by the Paragon Feature Film Company in the autumn of 1913. Like many early assessors of the cinema, the unidentified editorial writer from Moberly realized characteristics of the medium that would only become clear to film theorists decades later. In a section that reminds us of the cinema both as a special effect and, contradictorily, as a machine that produces historical evidence, the editorialist observed, "We will sit in the picture show hereafter and see ourselves living in the past, the resurrection of the past, and live again this day. And soon there will be some on the picture screen whom we once knew but know no more. The panorama of the world is passing. All creation is a moving picture."[5]

Local films used special effects both as a way to exploit the capacities of cinema and as a way to remind us of the medium's fallibility as historical evidence. As archivists, scholars, and community groups continue to discover, identify, and reclaim these moving images for our own time, it is critical that we are reminded of what they represent: images of particular people and their interest in appearing in a medium whose reach and influence seemed to be limitless.

Notes

1. Kracauer, *History*. The suggestion that Kracauer's preferred mode of historical analysis should be referred to as a "medium shot" comes from Gerd Gemünden and Johannes von Moltke's introduction to *Culture in the Anteroom*, 4–5.
2. Gaines, "What Happened to the Philosophy of Film History," 71.
3. McCarthy, "From the Ordinary to the Concrete," 34.
4. Liu, *Local Transcendence*, 25.
5. "The Pictures of Today," *Moberly* (Mo.) *Weekly Monitor*, November 7, 1913, 2.

FILMOGRAPHY

Thousands of local films were produced in the United States in the twentieth century. I have included complete filmographies for the companies and titles discussed in detail in this book, with two exceptions—Arthur J. Higgins and Melton Barker, as substantial filmographies for both can be found elsewhere.[1] In cases where many films had the same title, or the title is unknown, I include it at the beginning of the filmography and list productions by city, separated by a semicolon, with the production year in parentheses. All films that are underlined are extant.

Advance Motion Picture Company (Chicago), 1911–1919
Producers: George L. Cox, Alvin B. Giles; *Cinematographers*: Eugene Newman, Columbus D. Behan, Clarence W. Hutton
The Battle of Cameron Dam, Cameron Dam, Wis. (1913)
Famous Illinois Canyons and Starved Rock, Starved Rock State Park, Ill. (1913)
The Girl of Wonder Cave, Monteagle, Tenn. (1913)
Made-in-La-Crosse, La Crosse, Wis. (1913)
Untitled Films: **Georgia**: Atlanta (1914); **Illinois**: Springfield (1913); **Iowa**: Cedar Rapids (1913); **Kansas**: Kansas City (1913); **Texas**: San Antonio (1913); **Wisconsin**: Green Bay (1914)

Amateur Service Productions (Cleveland; Akron, Ohio; Waco, Tex.; Jefferson City, Mo.; Lancaster, Penn.; Kansas City, Mo.), 1935–1941
Manager: Augusta Kells; *Advance Agent*: R. E. Prillaman; *Camera Operators*: J. C. Brannon, Robert Doer, W. G. Elliott, William A. Kimber, Victor Marvel, Kenneth R. Roberson, R. A. White; *Directors*: Miss Beckter, Lois D. Benton, Carol Dittmar, Kathryn Ekler, Wilson Elliott, I. R. Hall, Elizabeth Heiland, Martha Linder, Evelyn Lindstrom, Jean Long, Katherine Mulcahy, Rita O'Bryant, Vera Piersol, R.E. Prillaman, Ruth A. Ritchie, Blanche Stouffer, Ruth Strickland, Rose Tikton, Dallas I. Weiser, Eva Wilson, Margaret Yost
Know York Better, York, Penn. (1941)
Our Town, New Cumberland, Penn. (1941)
See Yourself and Your Town in the Movies: **Illinois**: Albany, Andrews, Rossville (1937); Highland (1938); **Indiana**: Batesville (1937); Columbus, North Manchester (1938); **Maryland**: Frostburg (1938); Hagerstown, Keyser (1941); **Missouri**: Chillicothe, Kirksville, Maryville, Moberly, Washington (1939); **New Jersey**: Hackettstown (1940); Chatham (1941); **New York**: Jamestown, Pulaski (1938); Mechanicville, Olean (1940); **Ohio**: Independence, St. Clairsville (1935);

Coventry (1936); Orrville, Zanesville (1937); Portage Lakes (unknown); **Pennsylvania**: Aliquippa, Beaver Falls, Etna, Lewisburg, Mifflinburg, Point Marion, Reading, Rochester, York (1937); California, Littlestown (1938); Hamburg, Hatboro, Hazleton, Lansford, New Holland (1939); Bradford, Danville, Greenville, Pittston, Tyrone, Wellsboro (1940); Altoona, Bellefonte, Bellwood/Antis, Lititz, New Cumberland, Shippensburg (1941); **Texas**: Brownsville, Bryan, Kerrville, Mexia, Mission, Olney, San Benito, Stamford, Weslaco (1939); **West Virginia**: Elkins (1937); Charles Town (1941); **Wisconsin**: Neenah, Reedsburg, Rhinelander, Sauk City, Prairie du Sac (1938)
Your Home Town in the Movies, Franklin, Penn. (1940)

Amateur Theatre Guild (Boston), 1934–1941
Head: Lauren Kenyon Woods; *Writer*: Adella Cramer; *Associates*: Violet McClure Woods; *Directors*: W. Robert Anderson, Edwin W. Arnold, Emilene Bouge, Esther Griffin Card, Jeanne Carney, Madeline A. Chaffee, Paddy Chessman, Ross R. Cote, Margaret Cram, Barbara Demack, Virginia Gibeau, Catherine Gough, Ralph Gram, Doris Hamel, Marion Angeline Howlett, William S. Jeffs, Mary Kinhan, Anne L. Lambert, Mildred Lamson, Marilyn B. Lundy, Alice O'Leary, Margaret Showalter, Nancy Spencer, Dorothy Stone, Marjorie Turner, Agnes Winslow
Movie Queen: **Connecticut**: Willimantic (1940); **Florida**: Bradenton, Sarasota (1938); **Illinois**: Dixon (1938); **Indiana**: Frankfort, Logansport (1938); **Maine**: Auburn, Bath, Belfast, Caribou, Ellsworth, Houlton, Lincoln, Millinocket (1935); Bar Harbor, Eastport, Lubec, Newport, Old Town (1936); Rockland (1938); Sanford (1939); Bucksport, Camden, Rumford/Mexico, Van Buren, Waterville (unknown); **Massachusetts**: Conway (1934); Concord, Greenfield, Leominster, Norwood (1935); Abington, Orange (1936); Groton (1939); Cohasset (1940); Framingham (1941); Reading (unknown); **Michigan**: Escanaba, Ironwood, Ludington, Niles (1937); **Minnesota**: Brainerd (1937); **Missouri**: Carthage (1938); **Montana**: Anaconda, Butte, Havre, Helena (1938); **New Hampshire**: Nashua (1938); Exeter (1940); **New Jersey**: Rahway (1939); Bogota, South Amboy (1940); **New York**: Ballston Spa, Dunkirk, Malone, Oswego (1935); Tupper Lake (1936); Mineola (1939); **North Carolina**: Burlington (1936); Hickory, Lumberton (1937); Wilmington (1938); **North Dakota**: Valley City (1938); **Ohio**: Barnesville, East Sandusky, Mingo Junction, Norwalk (1936); East Palestine (1937); Findlay (1941); **Pennsylvania**: Towanda (1935); Elwood City (1936); Hazleton (1937); Connellsville, Kingston (1940); Belle Vernon (1941); **South Carolina**: Marion (1937); Florence (1938); **South Dakota**: Huron, Yankton (1938); **Tennessee**: Kingsport (1938); **Texas**: Abilene, Big Spring (1938); **Vermont**: Middlebury (1939); **Virginia**: Harrisonburg, Martinsville, Pulaski (1936); **West Virginia**: Bluefield (1936); **Wisconsin**: Wisconsin Rapids (1937); Menasha (1938)
Note: Other plays produced by the Amateur Theatre Guild did not feature a film production and thus are unlisted.

Blache Screen Service (San Francisco), 1922–1941
Director: Maurice Blache; *Sales Director*: William F. Thomas; *Camera Department Head*: Verne Rucker; *Field Manager*: E. C. MacGlashan; *Camera Operator*: Amos Stillman

Buy at Home Campaign: **California**: Etna/Fort Jones/Callahan, Fortuna (1937); Dunsmuir (unknown); **Colorado**: Longmont (1940); **Idaho**: Idaho Falls (1939); Weiser (unknown); **Montana**: Deer Lodge (1939); **Nebraska**: Lincoln (1940); **Oregon**: Forest Grove (1934); Enterprise (1935); Prineville (1937); Coquille, McMinnville, St. Helens (unknown); **Washington**: Tekoa (1938); Wilbur (1939)
... On Parade: **Montana**: Phillipsburg (1939); **New York**: Ellenville (1941)

Robert M. Carson Productions (Mason City, Iowa; Winter Park, Fla.), 1953–c. 1970
Producer: Robert M. Carson; *Directors*: Hal Black, Don Nestingen, Jim Richards; *Camera Operators*: R. A. Hereford; *Script*: Wanda Borr; *Editorial Supervision*: Robert Braverman; *Narration*: S. Norton Berry
Keeping Pace with Tomorrow, Winter Park, Fla. (1962)
This Is Our Town: **Illinois**: Monmouth (1954); Cicero, Crystal Lake, Elgin, St. Charles, Urbana (unknown); **Iowa**: Spencer (1954); **Kansas**: Garden City (1953); Manhattan (1955); **Minnesota**: Red Wing (1953); Fairmont, Winona (1954); Lake City (unknown); **Missouri**: St. James, St. Joseph (1954); St. Charles (unknown); **Nebraska**: Beatrice, Syracuse (1953); **Texas**: Waco (1955); Amarillo, Lubbock (unknown); **Wisconsin**: Eau Claire (1953); Chippewa Falls, Stevens Point (1954)

Chouinard Filming Company (Pittsburgh), c. 1929
C. J. Chouinard
Our American Girl's Visit to Altoona, Altoona, Penn. (1929)

Civic Art Film Production (Warren, Ohio), c.1930
President: E. J. Baumer; *Cameraman*: H. C. Kunkleman; *Representative*: Charles B. Copperman
Things You Ought to Know About: **Pennsylvania**: Charleroi, Franklin, Monongahela, New Castle, Oil City (1930)

Community Film Company; Community Photoplay Company (Los Angeles), 1920–1921
Director: Charles Le Witt; *Camera Operators*: Paul L. Hoefler, J. L. Roop, G. V. Smith; *Associates*: H. L. Hartman, K. Hoddy Milligan
Betty from ... : **Kansas**: Hutchison, Salina (1921); **Missouri**: Springfield, St. Joseph (1921); **Nebraska**: Lincoln (1921)
The Girl from ... : **Colorado**: Denver, Fort Collins, Greeley (1920); **Kansas**: Burrion, Emporia, Moberly, Pittsburg, Topeka (1921); **Texas**: Corsicana (1920); **Wyoming**: Cheyenne, Laramie (1920)
Home Town Romance, Bakersfield, Calif. (1920)
The Parisian Romance, Paris, Texas (1920)

Cosmopolitan Industrial Film Corp. (Springfield, Ill.), 1923; **Metropolitan Industrial Film Company** (Youngstown, Ohio), 1923–1925
Directors: Ted Kennedy, H. C. Kunkleman; *Cameraman*: Don Malkames; *Advertising Manager*: J. Arnett Fisk; *Associates*: F. W. Kunkleman, B. F. Taylor
Unknown Titles: **Indiana**: Bloomington, Princeton (1923); **Pennsylvania**: Clearfield, Franklin, Greenville, Huntingdon, Tryone (1923); Carlisle (1924); Titusville (1925)

Dixie Film Productions (Clarksburg, W.Va.), c. 1926
Associates: H.C. Kunkleman, Adam Montgomery, W.E. Brooks, P.W. Bailey
Unknown Titles: **North Carolina**: Greensboro (1926); **Virginia**: Danville (1926)

Dixie Film Productions (Florence, Ala.), 1951–1966
Associates: Amos Bond, W. K. Flint, Jim H. Killen
The Hopkinsville Story, Hopkinsville, Ky. (1966)
This Is Your Town: **Alabama**: Tuscumbia (1952); Decatur, Gadsden, Hartselle (unknown); **Arkansas**: Blytheville (1954); Mountain Home (1955); **Kentucky**: Hopkinsville (1952); Hopkinsville (1957); **Missouri**: Sikeston (1954); **Tennessee**: Columbia, Cookeville, Humboldt (1952); Kingsport (1953); Cleveland (1956); Dickson, Fayetteville, Lawrenceburg, Lewisburg, Manchester, McMinnville, Shelbyville, Tullahoma, Winchester (unknown)

Empire Film Company; New York Publicity Company; Gullette & Harris Empire Amusement Company (New York), 1915–1917
Directors: George S. Gullette, Nelson A. Harris; *Actor:* Agnes Laing
Aunt Sally Visits Knoxville, Knoxville, Tenn. (1915)
Down in Old Carolina, Charlotte, N.C. (1917)
The Princess Visits: **Indiana**: Logansport (1915); **North Carolina**: Durham, Gastonia, Hickory, High Point, Salisbury, Statesville (1917); **Ohio**: Ashtabula, Mansfield, Massillon (1915); **West Virginia**: Bluefield (1915)
Winston-Salem, the City of Industry, Winston-Salem, N.C. (1917)
Unknown Titles: **Alabama**: Birmingham; **Georgia**: Rome; **Ohio**: Youngstown; **Pennsylvania**: Erie (all dates unknown)

Florida Productions, Inc. (Tampa), 1926
Director: George S. Gullette
Horns and Hearts, Tampa, Florida (1926)
Unknown Titles: **Florida**: Arcadia, Brooksville, Lakeland, Orlando, Sanford, Tarpon Springs (1926)

Globe Films (New York), 1924–1926
Directors: Jack Allen, J. B. Launt; *Cameraman:* Philip J. Armand; *Casting Directors:* Charles E. Fulner, Roy B. Jones
I Love You Truly, Providence, R.I. (1926)
New Castle Adopts a Baby, New Castle, Penn. (1925)
The Reporter, Altoona, Penn. (1925)
The Story without an End: **Maryland**: Cumberland, Hagerstown (1925); **New York**: Niagara Falls, Olean (1925); **Pennsylvania**: Kane, Harrisburg, Monessen (1925); Lewiston, Reading (1926)

Shad E. Graham Productions; Texas News Trailers (Missouri City, Texas), 1947–1969
Director: Bobby Bass, Jack Gardner, Arthur Loevin, Shad Graham Associates, Clyde Waddell; *Narration:* Vincent Connolly
…at War: **Pennsylvania**: Bangor, Mahanoy City, Mt. Carmel (1945); Tamaqua (unknown)
Cowboy Sweethearts on Parade, Bay City, Texas (1950)

Our Home Town: **Arizona**: Safford (unknown); **Arkansas**: El Dorado (1959); North Little Rock, Pine Bluff (unknown); **Idaho**: Coeur d'Alene (1956); **Louisiana**: Houma, New Iberia (1954); **Montana**: Bozeman, Butte, Havre, Kalispell (1956); **New Mexico**: Pueblo (1954); Alamogordo, Las Cruces (1958); **North Dakota**: Williston (unknown); **Texas**: Brazosport, Freeport, San Marcos, Wharton (1946); Huntsville, McKinney, Waxahachie (1947); Colorado City, Galen Park, Houston, Luling, West University and the Village (1948); Bryan, College Station, Laporte (1949); Freeport (1950); Eagle Lake, Liberty (1951); Baytown (1953); Odessa (1957); Bay City, Brenham, Coleman, Crockett, Dumas, Durant, El Campo, Hillsboro, Houston-Harrisburg, Humble Road, Killeen, Mineral Wells, Pasadena, Terrell, Texas City, Victoria, Weatherford, Wichita Falls, Yoakum (unknown); **Wyoming**: Casper (1954)

Gullette Film Company; **Gullette-Nedell Company**; **Gullette-Kelley Company** (New York), 1926–1930
Director: George S. Gullette; *Assistants*: F. G. Gullette, Andrew Kelley, X. F. Sutton
Our American Girl: **California**: Oakland (1930); **Indiana**: Indianapolis (1928); **Iowa**: Mason City (1930); **Missouri**: Springfield (1930); **New York**: Syracuse (1926); Cornell (1930); **Oklahoma**: Tulsa (unknown); **Texas**: Amarillo, El Paso (1927); **Wisconsin**: Manitowoc (1928); Oshkosh (unknown)
Who's Who: **Iowa**: Davenport (1927); **New Jersey**: Trenton (1925); **Ohio**: Mansfield (1918)
Unknown Titles: **New York**: Jamaica (1927); **Louisiana**: Monroe (1925); **Pennsylvania**: Lebanon (1922)

Holt Film Company (Topeka, Kans.), c. 1914
Dedication of the G.A.R. Memorial Hall, Topeka, Kans. (1914)

Hudris Film Company (New York; Los Angeles), c. 1915–1926
Directors: Sidney Buck, W. Josh Day, George Henry, John Stahl, Walter Steiner, Albert Stoman; *Camera Operators*: Beverly B. Dobbs, George Hardy, William Harris, Jr., Granville L. Howe, Ned K. Miller, Erwin Nadel, Daniel Raphael
The Belle of . . . : **Maine**: Biddeford (1917); **New Hampshire**: Nashua (1917); **Ohio**: Sandusky (1923); **Wisconsin**: Kenosha (1923)
It Happened in Jackson, Jackson, Mich. (1917)
Milwaukee Love, Milwaukee, Wis. (1926)
A Romance of . . . : **California**: San Bernardino (1918); Bakersfield, Oakland, San Diego, Santa Ana (1919); Riverside (1922); **Connecticut**: New London (1915); **District of Columbia**: Washington (1921); **Illinois**: Decatur (1917); Galesburg (1922); Freeport (1925); **Indiana**: Elkhart (1916); Kokomo (1917); **Iowa**: Waterloo (1920); **Kansas**: Wichita (1921); **Maine**: Biddeford and Saco (1916); Bangor (1917); **Maryland**: Frederick (1916); **Massachusetts**: Fitchburg, Quincy, Springfield, Worcester, (1916); Lowell (1918); **Michigan**: Bay City, Kalamazoo (1917); **Montana**: Butte, Helena (1920); **Nebraska**: Omaha (1920); **New York**: Gloversville, Niagara Falls (1916); **North Carolina**: Asheville, Durham (1916); **Pennsylvania**: Pittsburgh (1924); **Utah**: Ogden, Salt Lake City (1920); **Washington**: Bellingham, Seattle, Walla Walla (1919); **Wisconsin**: Appleton, Madison, Manitowoc, Oshkosh (1920); La Crosse (1922)

Industrial Film Syndicate; Commercial Film Syndicate; Independent Film Syndicate (New York), 1911–1912
Director: Edwin S. Carman
Unknown Titles: **Iowa**: Des Moines (1911); **Minnesota**: Brainerd (1911); **New York**: Mount Vernon (1911); Schenectady (1912); **New Jersey**: New Brunswick (1912)

Industrial Moving Picture Company (Chicago), 1910–1916; **Rothacker Film Company** (Chicago; New York), 1916–1930
Producers: Robert Cochrane, Carl Laemmle, Watterson Rounds Rothacker; *Cinematographers*: Oliver Chadwick, H. A. DeVry, Freeman Owens
Confederate Veterans and Sons, Little Rock, Ark. (1911)
Muskegon in Motion, Muskegon, Mich. (1912)
War Bonnet Roundup, Idaho Falls, Idaho (1912)
Unknown Titles: **Illinois**: Chicago (1911); Springfield (1912); Freeport, Joliet, Nokomis and DuQuoin, Rock Island, Springfield, Wilmette (1913); University of Illinois Homecoming, Zion City (1914) **Indiana**: Gary (1911); Elkhart (1912); Michigan, Panama-Pacific Expo, Vincennes (1914) **Kentucky**: Mammoth Cave (1912) **Michigan**: Kalamazoo; **Montana**: Anaconda (1911) **Nebraska**: Omaha (1913) **New Jersey**: Jamesburg (1912) **Ohio**: Grand American handicap trap-shoot, Columbus (1911) Lima (1912) **Oklahoma**: Oklahoma City (1913) **South Dakota**: Aberdeen (1911) **Tennessee**: Chattanooga (1911) **Unknown location**: Elks Convention (1911) **Wisconsin**: Racine (1912) Waukesha (1917) **Wyoming**: Cowboy Convention (1911)

Interstate Film Producers; Consolidated Film Producers (Los Angeles; New York), 1915–1934
Directors: Charles Fetty, Don O. Newland; *Assistant Director*: Jack Vance; *Cinematographers*: Jack Flanagan, Willis Foremans, Russell Parham; *Casting Director*: Albert Kaufman; *Associates*: F. C. Crosby, Charles Norman David, James Morris, R. D. Phillips, Howard M. Prager
Adopts a Baby (1915–1922): **Illinois**: Centralia, La Salle, Mattoon, Taylorville (1915); Anderson, Bluffton, Decatur, DuQuoin, Peru, Wabash, Winchester (1916); Robinson (1917); **Indiana**: Michigan City (1915); Huntington, Mishawaka (1916); Clinton, Sullivan (1917); Huntington (1919); Buchanan, Whiting (1921) Kokomo, Logansport (as *Logansport's Baby*, 1922); Huntington (as *Huntington's Baby*, 1923); **Iowa**: Davenport, Iowa City, Washington (1920); **Kansas**: Parsons (1919); Iola, Ottawa (1922); **Kentucky**: Owensboro (1916); **Michigan**: Marshall (1915); Port Huron, Three Rivers (1916); **Ohio**: Defiance (1916), Elyria, Kent, Massilon (1922); Coshocton (as *Coshocton's Baby*), Steubenville (1923); **Wisconsin**: Wisconsin Rapids (1920), Marinette (unknown)
Alexandria Adopts Twins, Alexandria, Ind. (1916)
A Day in Hollywood (1926–1928): **Illinois**: Carbondale, Murphysboro (1926); **Kansas**: Lawrence (1928); **Louisiana**: Monroe (unknown); **Mississippi**: Hattiesburg (1926)
Hero (1923–1934): **California**: Woodland (1924); **Florida**: Sarasota (1929); **Georgia**: Americus (1928); Fitzgerald, Macon, Thomasville (1928); **Illinois**: Alton, Belvidere, Mattoon, Rockford (1926); **Indiana**: Logansport, Muncie (1924); **Maryland**: Cumberland (1923); Salisbury (1924); Salisbury (1929); Cumberland (as *My Hero*, 1931); **New York**: Rome (1927); Cortland (1928); **North Carolina**:

Durham, Salisbury, Wilmington, Wilson, Winston-Salem (1925); **Ohio**: Hamilton, Sandusky (1923); Toledo (1925); Portsmouth (1926); Lima (1928); Athens, Circleville, Delphos, Pickaway (as *Pickaway Co's Hero*), Wellston (1932); **Pennsylvania**: Shamokin, Wellsboro (1928); Connellsville, Greenville, Scottdale (1930); Huntingdon, Lebanon, Tyrone (1934); **South Carolina**: Gaffney (1930); **Tennessee**: Kingsport (1926); **Virginia**: Danville, Richmond (1925); Harrisonburg, Staunton, Winchester (1929); **West Virginia**: Charleston (1930); Bluefield (1933); **Wisconsin**: Janesville (1927); Staunton (1929)
Mama's Choice, Gloversville, N.Y. (1928)
Queen: **Pennsylvania**: Wellsboro (1933); Towanda (1934)

Hugh V. Jamieson (Dallas, Texas), 1915–1923
Won from the Flames: **Kansas**: Arkansas City, Hutchinson, Iola, Ottawa (1915); **Missouri**: Macon (1915); **Oklahoma**: Cushing, Perry (1915); **Texas**: Cleburne, Denton, Fort Worth, Port Arthur, Victoria, Waco (1916); Corsicana, McKinney (1923)
Note: Melton Barker made the McKinney film. Jamieson operated an industrial film production company in Dallas until the 1970s.

Carl Laemmle (Los Angeles), 1912
Producer: Carl Laemmle; *Cinematographer*: Charles Kaufman; *Associate*: Watterson Rothacker
Oshkosh in Motion, Oshkosh, Wis. (1912)
Note: Laemmle had close ties to Oshkosh, and it is unknown whether he produced films elsewhere on behalf of his company, Universal.

Liberty Film Company (Joplin, Mo.; Kansas City, Mo.), 1911–1912
General Manager: J. W. Cotter; *Director*: Calvin Mayhew
In and Around Rogers, Rogers, Ark. (1912)
Unknown Title, Iola, Kans. (1912)

Arthur Loevin Productions; Landsman Production Company (New York), 1943–1954
Directors: Sol Landsman, Arthur Loevin, Jessie Marcus; *Associate*: Bill Burkett; *Narration*: Vincent Connolly
Augusta Marches On, Augusta, Ga. (1946)
... for Victory: **Connecticut**: Hartford (1943); **Massachusetts**: Greenfield (1944)
Our City, Hartford, Conn. (1948)
Our Home Town: **Florida**: Fort Pierce (1948); **Georgia**: Augusta (as *Augusta Marches On*), Douglas, Fitzgerald, Tifton (1946); Americus, Dublin, Savannah, Waycross (1946); Swainsboro, Thomaston (1947); **Louisiana**: Lake Charles (1954); **Pennsylvania**: Doylestown, Levittown (1954); **Tennessee**: Kingsville (1953); **Texas**: Baytown, Bryan (1953); Austin, Beaumont, Harlingen, McAllen, Victoria (unknown); **Virginia**: Pulaski (1953); Petersburg (1954)

Majestic Amusement Company; New York Publicity Company (New York), 1912–1914
George S. Gullette
Unknown Titles: **Pennsylvania**: Allentown (1912); **Tennessee**: Nashville (1914)

McHenry Film Company (Akron, Ohio), 1915–1916
Producer: Basil McHenry; *Director*: Carl Shaner
The Man Haters: **Indiana**: Logansport, <u>Muncie</u> (1915); <u>Anderson</u>, New Albany (1916); **Kentucky**: Lexington, Louisville (1916); **New York**: Dunkirk, Utica (1916); **Ohio**: Lima (1915); Hamilton, Piquo (1916); **Virginia**: Lynchburg (1916); **West Virginia**: Bluefield, Charleston (1916)
T'was School Days, Newark, Ohio (1916)

Metropolitan Film Productions; National Film Productions; Associated Film Productions; H. C. Kunkleman & Associates (Akron, Ohio), 1927–1969
General Managers: T. J. Carroll, E. J. Baumer; *Cameraman*: H. C. Kunkleman; *Promotional Director*: Robert Beasley
The Coschoton Story, Coschoton, Ohio (1969)
The Parade of Progress of Columbiana for 1950, Columbiana, Ohio (1950)
Salem at Mid-Century, Salem, Ohio (1950)
Things You Should Know about . . . : **Ohio**: Piqua (1939)
This Is Our Town: **Ohio**: Delphos (1952)
Unknown Titles: **Indiana**: Elwood (1960); **Maryland**: Hagerstown (1927); **New York**: Oneonta (1939); **Ohio**: Mansfield (1938); Norwalk (1949); New Philadelphia (1950); Columbiana (1951); Wellington (1969); **Canada**: Niagara Falls (1931)

Richard E. Norman (Des Moines; Chicago), 1915–1917
The Wrecker: **Alabama**: Mobile, Montgomery (unknown); **Arkansas**: Little Rock (unknown); **Florida**: Gainesville (unknown); **Georgia**: Columbus (1917); Brunswick (unknown); **Illinois**: Decatur (1917); Aurora, Belleville, Blue Island, Carbondale, La Salle, Murphysboro, Peoria, Quincy, Streator (unknown); **Michigan**: Mainstee, St. Joseph and Benton Harbor, Traverse City (unknown); **New Jersey**: Trenton (unknown); **Ohio**: Columbus, Lorian (unknown); **Oklahoma**: Tulsa, West Tulsa (unknown) **South Carolina**: Columbia (unknown); **Wisconsin**: Marinette and Menominee (unknown); **Canada**: Ottawa (unknown)
Unknown Titles: **Illinois**: Alton (1915); Carbondale (1916)
Note: Norman stopped working as an itinerant filmmaker in the late 1910s and moved to Jacksonville, Florida, where he established a studio to shoot race films.

Pacific Film Production Company (Erie, Penn.; Springfield, Ill.; Washington, N.C.; Kingsport, Tenn.), 1931–
Directors: E. J. Baumer, C. E. McMullen; *Cinematographer*: H. C. Kunkleman; *Location Manager*: William Ramsell
Anderson on Parade, Anderson, S.C. (1935)
Things You Ought to Know about . . . : **Illinois**: Belvidere (1933)
Things You Should Know about . . . : **Georgia**: <u>Cordele</u> (1936); **Illinois**: Clinton, Jacksonville, Mattoon (1932); Herrin (1936); **Iowa**: Burlington, Muscatine, Waterloo (1933); Algona, Emmetsburg, Humboldt, Mason City (1934); **Kentucky**: Middlesboro (1935); **New Jersey**: Bridgeton (1937); **New York**: Olean (1931); **North Carolina**: Rockingham (1934); Reidsville (1935); **Ohio**: Xenia (1937); **Pennsylvania**: Bradford (1931); **South Carolina**: <u>Florence</u>, Gaffney, Greenwood, <u>Orangeburg</u> (1935); **Tennessee**: Kingsport (1935); **West Virginia**: Beckley (1935)

Paragon Feature Film Company; Special Scenic Film Company (Denver, Col.; Omaha, Neb.; New York; Des Moines), 1912–c. 1917

Director: O. W. Lamb; *Cinematographer*: William Preston Mayfield; *Scenario Writer*: William Lou Gullet; *Other Personnel*: John S. Conger, Gilbert P. Hamilton, Jr., Edward Rosenthal

Pilgrim Scenario (1912–1913): Five young women are selected to act as tourists visiting the city. They take in the various sights of the town.

Wedding Scenario (1913–1916): A young man and woman, usually from notable families, are cast to play the leads in an industrial romance.

An American Citizen, San Antonio, Texas (1914)
The Awakening of Muskogee, Muskogee, Okla. (1913)
Blissveldt Romance, Grand Rapids, Mich. (1915)
The Call of the Hills, Dubuque, Iowa (1916)
The Cedar Valley Romance, Waterloo, Iowa (1916)
The College Hero, Omaha, Neb. (1914)
A Council Bluffs Courtship, Muscatine, Iowa (1914)
Fifty-Thousand Feet of Kansas, Kansas (1914)
A Fortunate Accident, Birmingham, Ala. (1914)
From Wedding Bells to Cotton Bolls, Memphis, Tenn. (1915)
Greater Tulsa in the Movies, Tulsa, Okla. (1913)
Into the Future, New Orleans, La. (1914)
The Lumberjack, Wausau, Wis. (1914)
The Maid of the Miami, Dayton, Ohio (1915)
The Maid of the Mississippi, Rock Island, Ill. (1916)
The Mine Owner's Daughter, Springfield, Ill. (1915)
One Wonderful Day, Fond du Lac, Wis. (1914)
A Political Touchdown, Austin, Texas (1915)
Present and Past in Cradle of Dixie, Montgomery, Ala. (1914)
Pretty Pilgrims at the Peerless Princess of the Plains, Wichita, Kans. (1913)
A Race for a Bride, Jackson, Mich. (1914)
Romance of a Southern Fort, Fort Smith, Ark. (1914)
Romance of Lovers Lane, St. Joseph, Mo. (1914)
Seeing McAlester, McAlester, Okla. (1912)
Seeing Oklahoma City in the Days of '89, Oklahoma City (1913)
The Spirit of Columbus,1865–1915, Columbus, Ga. (1915)
Sunny Hours in St. Joe Valley, South Bend, Ind. (1914)
Texas as It Is Today, Austin, Texas (1916)
Unknown Titles: **Arkansas**: Little Rock (1913); **Colorado**: Denver (1913); **Illinois**: Quincy (1914); Alton (1916); **Kansas**: Kansas City (1913); **Michigan**: Lansing (1914); **Missouri**: Independence, Moberly, Sedalia (1913); **Montana**: Billings (1913); **Nebraska**: Omaha (1913); **Texas**: Denison, Sherman (1912); Dallas, Fort Worth, Galveston (1913); Houston, Port Arthur (1914); El Paso (1915); **Wisconsin**: Eau Claire, Sheboygan (1914); **Wyoming**: Cheyenne (1913)

Don Parisher Productions (New York; Miami), 1947–1965

Director: Don G. Parisher; *Camera Operators*: Lloyd McComber, Ken Stambaugh; *Script*: Mabel Lawrence; *Music*: Emil Velazco; *Sound Recording and Special Effects*: Holly Smith; *Other Crew*: Ted Ramo; *Narrators*: Norman Brokenshire, Joe Given, Harry Hennessey, John Reed King, Clyde McLean

Charlotte, Queen City of the South, Charlotte, N.C. (1948)
Chattanooga, Scenic Center of the South, Chattanooga, Tenn. (1952)
Deland, City of Gracious Living, Deland, Fla. (1955)
Delightful Deland, Deland, Fla. (1965)
Fort Lauderdale Story, Fort Lauderdale, Fla. (1950)
Fun in the Sunshine, Miami Beach, Fla. (c. 1967)
Happy Beach Adventure, Jacksonville, Fla. (unknown)
Hollywood-by-the-Sea, Hollywood, Fla. (1961)
King of Casselberry, Casselberry, Fla. (1953, 1964)
Miami Beach, U.S.A., Miami (1960)
Missing Person, Pompano Beach, Fla. (1967)
Negro Durham Marches On, Durham, N.C. (1947)
A New Adventure in Living, Pompano Beach, Fla. (c. 1964)
North Miami Beach: Gateway to Interama, North Miami Beach, Fla. (c. 1967)
The Pompano Beach Story, Pompano Beach, Fla. (1961)
Spartanburg, My Home Town, Spartanburg, S.C. (1947)
This Is Bluefield, Bluefield, W.Va. (1947)
This Is Chapel Hill, Chapel Hill, N.C. (1948)
This Is Greensboro, Greensboro, N.C. (1947)
This Is Progressive Rutherford County, Rutherfordton, N.C. (1948)
This Is Progressive Wilkes County, Wilkesboro, N.C. (1948)
This Is Statesville, Statesville, N.C. (1948)
Thomasville: City of Roses, Thomasville, Ga. (1951)
The Torch of Friendship, Miami (1962)
Valdosta, The Azalea City, Valdosta, Ga. (1953)
Where Florida Prepares for the Future, Gainesville, Fla. (1951)
World's Most Beautiful Beaches, Pompano Beach, Fla. (1952)
The World's Most Famous Beach, Daytona Beach, Fla. (1950)
World's Winter Strawberry Capital, Plant City, Fla. (unknown)
Unknown Title, Columbus, Ga. (1952)

Park Motion Picture Productions (New York), 1944–1947
Directors: Shad Graham, George S. Gullette, Don G. Parisher; *Camera Operator:* Sam Marino; *Narrators:* Norman Brokenshire, Vincent Connolly
My Home Town: **New Jersey**: Freehold, Lakewood (1947); **North Carolina**: Burlington, Charlotte, Fayetteville, Hickory, Rockingham (1944); Lumberton, Mooresville (1946); Monroe, Wilmington (1947); **South Carolina**: Bennettsville, Clover (1946)

Raymond Film Company (New York; Philadelphia), 1919–1927
Producer: George R. Raymond; *Associate:* George S. Gullette
Making Motion Pictures, Decatur, Ill. (1927)
Who's Who in . . . ? **Kansas**: Hutchinson (1924); **Missouri**: Springfield (unknown); **Nevada**: Reno (1921); **New Jersey**: Trenton (1919); **North Carolina**: Charlotte, Concord, Greensboro, High Point, Winston-Salem (1920); Winston-Salem (1922)

John B. Rogers (Fostoria, Ohio), 1939–1940
Camera Operators: J. Barton Elliott, B. J. Gudenkuf, Jerry Moore, Max Willetts; *Directors:* Robert H. Dore, Harry Dorrington, W. Frederic Reider, Florence Strauch, Don Vest, R. D. Wile

We're in the Movies: **Illinois**: Arlington Heights, Harvey, Maywood (1940); **Indiana**: Ellwood (1940); **Michigan**: Ann Arbor (1939); Birmingham, Marshall, Sault Ste. Marie, Traverse City (1940); Albion (unknown); **Missouri**: Cape Girardeau (1940); **New York**: Salamanca, Silver Creek (1940); **Pennsylvania**: Curwensville (1940)

Note: John B. Rogers, who produced home talent plays, was active from 1903 until 1977 but only made films for this production.

Russell Motion Picture Company (Unknown), c. 1928
Who's Who in . . . : **Indiana**: Valparaiso (1927); **Ohio**: Hamilton (1928)

Scenic Film Company (Atlanta), c. 1914–c. 1916
President: Carl Rountree; *Director*: J. Garnett Starr; *Cinematographer*: V. L Walker
Buy-A-Bale, Atlanta (1914)
Big Movie Ball, Atlanta (1916)
Georgia, the Empire State of the South, Atlanta (1915)

Mack Sennett Comedies Corporation (Los Angeles), 1917–1923
The Crossroads of . . **Indiana**: Fort Wayne (1922); **Iowa**: Dubuque (1923); **Kentucky**: Lexington, Louisville (1922); **New York**: Syracuse, Watertown (1922); **Ohio**: Cincinnati (1922)

Sowers Motion Picture Company (Denver), c. 1913
Proprietor: Arvine W. Sowers; *Cinematography*: Max Schneider
Unknown Titles: **Colorado**: Colorado Springs (1913); **Utah**: Salt Lake City (1913)

Special Event Film Manufacturing Company (New York), c. 1913
Director: Fred Beck
Unknown Titles: **New York**: Elmira; Utica (1913)
Note: Contemporary newspaper accounts note that Beck was traveling widely for his series of local views, though such activities might have been taken to promote the exhibitor camera his company was offering.

St. Louis Moving Picture Company (St. Louis), 1911–c. 1914
Arthur L. Kimball
The Pageant and Masque of St. Louis, St. Louis (1914)

Superior Film Company (Des Moines), c. 1913–c. 1916
Richard E. Norman, C. D. Tinsley, Don A. Davis, Morgan Howells, Charles A Vogman, Karl Vinigraff, Robert Blaylock
Laura the Lobbyist, Des Moines, Iowa (1915)
The Making of Chicago, Chicago (1916)
Unto The Least Of These, Des Moines, Iowa (1916)
Unknown Titles: **Iowa**: Maquoketa, Oelwein (1913); Des Moines, Muscatine (1914); **Missouri**: Trenton (1914)

Tinsley Film Company (Corning, Iowa), 1914–1941
Director: Charlie David Tinsley; *Assistant*: H. E. Christie
Adams County Gold, Corning, Iowa (1922)
Ak-Sar-Ben Parade, Corning, Iowa (1914)

Between Two Fires, Corning, Iowa (1914)
Chariton's Heroes, Chariton, Iowa (1914)
The Church in the Wildwood, Unknown location (1928)
Ezra and June Take in the White City Corning, Iowa (1914)
The Fisherman's Reward, Crystal Lake, Iowa (1914)
Hiram and Mandy see the Races, Creston, Iowa (1914)
An Innocent Prisoner, Afton and Creston, Iowa (1919)
Iowa Beautiful, Unknown location (1931)
Kohly's Flying Circus, Corning, Iowa (1922)
Last Drill of the Boys of '61, Corning, Iowa (1914)
Lazy Bones, Moville, Iowa (1935)
The Man at the Throttle: **Iowa**: Oelwein, Muscatine, Iowa City (1915)
Married on the Run, Oskaloosa, Iowa (1915)
The Mexican Raid, Corning, Iowa (1916)
Miss Lee's Flirtation, and Hiram's Mistake, Creston, Iowa (1914)
Not by a Dam Site, Corning, Iowa (1917)
On the Mexican Border, Corning, Iowa (1917)
Our Boys at Camp Cody, Corning, Iowa (1918)
Our Rainbow Boys, Corning, Iowa (1919)
Over There, Corning, Iowa (1918)
Red Oak Coursing Meet, Corning, Iowa (1914)
Rosebud Indian Reservation, Rosebud Indian Reservation, S.Dak. (1919)
Safety First, Corning, Iowa (1923)
Saved by the Stars and Stripes, Corning, Iowa (1914)
Turkey Day, Unknown location (1927)
Two Troublesome Tramps: **Arkansas**: Harrison (1931); **Illinois**: Carlinville (1926); **Iowa**: Afton, Malvern (1915); Anita, Carroll, Griswold (1917); Bedford (1919); Hamburg, Hawarden (1921); Glenwood (1922); Atlantic (1923); Lenox (1928); Lemars, Mason City (1930); Humboldt (1932); **Kansas**: Iola (1927); **Missouri**: Chillicothe, Maryville (1933); **Minnesota**: Wadena (1932); **Nebraska**: Plattsmouth (1919); Beatrice (1929); **North Dakota**: Grand Forks (1920); **South Dakota**: Aberdeen (1920); Deadwood (1927)
Watch Your Speed, Unknown location (1941)
The Wolf Hunt, Corning, Iowa (1915)

Tisdale Industrial Film Corp. (Chicago), 1914–1923
Director: R. J. Fahrer, Franklin M. Tisdale; *Cinematographer*: E. H. Davey; *Assistants*: A. J. Cooper, J. P. Knight, F. R. Martin
Unknown Titles: **Kentucky**: Fulton, Mayfield (1914); **Illinois**: Freeport (1920); Bloomington, Decatur, Evanston, Kankakee, Monmouth, Pekin, Peoria, Springfield (1921); **Iowa**: Burlington, Davenport, Ottuma, Waterloo (1921); **Massachusetts**: Fitchburg (1923); **Michigan**: Adrian (1920); **New York**: Binghamton (1916); Syracuse (1918); **Ohio**: Springfield (1920); **Pennsylvania**: Pittston (1915); **Wisconsin**: Eau Claire, La Crosse, Racine (1921)

Tourist Girl Film Company, 1915
Director: J. L. Siple
Tourist Girl: **Alabama**: Birmingham, Mobile, Montgomery (1915); **Kentucky**: Mammoth Cave (1915)

Towns and Cities Film Company, c. 1912
Producer: W. H. Frank
Unknown Titles: **New York**: Buffalo (1912); **Pennsylvania**: Scranton, Wilkes-Barre (1912); Carbondale (1913)

United Film Associates; Salvatore Pace Bondanza Cudia (New York), 1920–1934
For the Love of Dell, Philipsburg, Penn. (1928)
For the Love of Marcia, Huntingdon, Penn. (1928)
Mt. Holly in the Movies, Mt. Holly, N.J. (1924)
Three Wives, Baltimore (1934)
Unknown Titles: **Indiana**: Elwood (1932); **New Jersey**: Washington (1925); **Pennsylvania**: Lock Haven (1928)

Victor Film Advertising Company (Topeka, Kans.), 1912
O. W. Lamb, C. H. Strawn, R. C. Strawn, H. F. Charles
Seeing Topeka First, Topeka, Kans. (1912)

H. Lee Waters (Lexington, N.C.), 1936–1942
Movies of Local People: **North Carolina**: Albemarle, Belmont, Boone, Concord, Cooleemee, Henderson, Kannapolis, Kernersville, Liberty, Mount Holly, Roxboro, Sanford, Siler City, Thomasville, Troy (1936); Angier, Benson, China Grove, Clayton, Cliffside, Concord, Draper, Durham, Erwin, Forest City, Fuquay Springs, Gastonia, Granite Falls, Hillsboro, Kernersville, Kings Mountain, Leaksville Boulevard, Lenoir, Louisburg, Mooresville, North Wilkesboro, Roxboro, Rutherfordton, Selma, Shelby, Siler City, Smithfield, Spindale, Spray, Thomasville (1937); Asheboro, Charlotte, Cherryville, China Grove, Cramerton, Elkin, Gastonia, Granite Falls, Henderson, Kannapolis, Lexington, Mocksville, Mooresville, Mt. Gilead, Newton, North Wilkesboro, Norwood, Oxford, Raeford, Red Springs, Rockingham, Roxboro, Shelby, Spencer, Spindale, Swannanoa, Troy, Wadesboro, Winston-Salem (1938); Angier, Asheboro, Burlington, Chapel Hill, Concord, Cooleemee, Cramerton, Denton, Erwin, Gastonia, Gibsonville, Greensboro, Henderson, Hillsboro, Jackson, Kernersville, Liberty, Lillington, Madison, Mebane, Mooresville, Nashville, Newton, North Wilkesboro, Oxford, Pilot Mountain, Pineville, Pittsboro, Rockingham, Roxboro, Scotland Neck, Siler City, Spencer, Taylorsville, Thomasville, Troy, Wake Forest, Warrenton (1939); Asheboro, Burlington, Cliffside, Cooleemee, Durham, Elkin, Gastonia, Kernersville, Kings Mountain, Lexington, Mocksville, Roxboro, Salisbury, Statesville, Thomasville, Troy (1940); Apex, Asheboro, Burlington, Concord, Conover, Denton, Elkin, Gastonia, Granite Falls, Hickory, Kannapolis, Kings Mountain, Lumberton, Madison, Mayodan, Mocksville, Monroe, Mt. Airy, North Wilkesboro, Oxford, Pittsboro, Rockingham, Rockwell, Roxboro, Siler City, Spencer, Valdese, Warrenton (1941); Bessemer City, Burlington, Concord, Conover, Fort Mill, Gastonia, Graham, Granite Falls, Haw River, Pittsboro, Rockwell, Siler City, Spencer, Valdese (1942); **South Carolina**: Winnsboro (1936); Blacksburg, Chester, Fort Mill, Gaffney, Great Falls, Lancaster, Lockhart, Rock Hill, York (1937); Bishopville, Camden, Cheraw, Chesterfield, Gaffney, Great Falls, Hartsville, Rock Hill, Timmonsville (1938); Fort Mill, Fountain Inn, Rock Hill, Whitmire, Woodruff (1939); **Tennessee**:

Mountain City (1940); **Virginia**: Bassett, Fieldale, Martinsville (1937); Bassett (1938); Danville, Martinsville, Wytheville (1939); Damascus, Dante, Lebanon, Saltville (1940); Bassett, Fieldale (1941)

Western Producing Association (Seattle), 1919–1920
Director: Gladys Parker; *Assistants*: Gladys West, Bernice Agatz; *Cinematography*: Frank Jacobs
Helen's Dollars: **Washington**: Aberdeen, Olympia (1920)

Zenith Motion Picture Company (Chicago; New York), 1914–1921
Associates: W. E. Aten, Otto A. Brinner, M. W. McGee, H. S. Moss; *Camera operator*: Morris E. Hair, G. L Howe
The Girl and the Tramp, Lima, Ohio (1915)
Making Good, Clinton, Iowa (1914)
The Man Who Made Good, Racine, Wis. (1914)
Rochelle under the Commission Form of Government, Rochelle, Ill. (1915)
Secret Orders, Racine, Wis. (1916)
Unknown Titles: **Illinois**: Morris (1915); **Indiana**: Kokomo (1914); **Iowa**: Dubuque (1916); **Missouri**: Joplin (1916); **Wisconsin**: Janesville, Oshkosh (1914)

Notes

1. The filmography for Melton Barker can be found on the website http://www.meltonbarker.org/film-search/, which is maintained by Caroline Frick. Frick's 2010 filmography for itinerant filmmakers includes the films of Arthur J. Higgins: http://www.meltonbarker.org/wp-content/uploads/2012/10/Filmography.pdf.

BIBLIOGRAPHY

Archive Collections

Graham, Shad. Papers, 1949–1970, Dolph Briscoe Center for American History, University of Texas at Austin

Howlett, Marion Angeline. Papers, 1909–1973, Harvard Theatre Collection, Cambridge, Mass.

Howlett, Marion Angeline. Papers, 1880–1983. Arthur and Elizabeth Schlesinger Library on the History of Women in America, Radcliffe Institute for Advanced Study, Harvard University, Cambridge, Mass.

Norman, Richard. Collection, Black Film Center/Archive, Indiana University

Panama Pacific International Exposition. Records, BANC MSS C-A 190, Bancroft Library, University of California, Berkeley

Sennett, Mack. Collection, Margaret Herrick Library, Academy of Motion Picture Arts and Sciences, Beverly Hills, Calif.

Waters, H. Lee. Collection, 1936–2005, Duke University Special Collections, Durham, N.C.

Selected Periodicals

Adams County (Corning, Iowa) *Free Press*
Adams County (Corning, Iowa) *Union Republican*
Amateur Movie Makers (New York)
Daily Oklahoman (Tulsa)
Emporia (Kans.) *Gazette*
Hutchinson (Kans.) *News*
Montgomery (Ala.) *Advertiser*
Movie Makers (New York)
McAlester (Okla.) *News-Capital*
Moving Picture World (New York)
New Brunswick (N.J.) *Times*
Springfield (Ill.) *News Record*
Waterloo (Iowa) *Evening Courier*
Waterloo (Iowa) *Evening Courier and Reporter*

Books and Articles

Abel, Charles. *Money Making Ideas for Portrait Studios*. Cleveland: Charles Abel, 1931.
Abel, Richard. *Americanizing the Movies and "Movie Mad" Audiences, 1910–1914*. Berkeley: University of California Press, 2006.

———. "Charge and Countercharge: 'Documentary' War Pictures in the USA, 1914–1916." *Film History* 22, no. 4 (December 2010): 366–388.

———, ed. *Encyclopedia of Early Cinema*. New York: Routledge, 2010.

———. "Film Discourse in the Heartlands: The Early 1910's." *Film History* 18, no. 2 (2006): 140–153.

———. *Menus for Movieland: Newspapers and the Emergence of American Film Culture*. Berkeley: University of California Press, 2015.

Abel, Richard, Giorgio Bertellini, and Rob King. *Early Cinema and the "National."* New Barnet, Herts, U.K.: John Libbey, 2008.

Alicoate, Jack, ed. *Film Daily Year Book*. New York: The Film Daily, 1940.

Allen, Robert C. "Manhattan Myopia; or, Oh! Iowa!" *Cinema Journal* 35, no. 3 (Spring 1996): 75–103.

———. *Vaudeville and Film, 1895–1915: A Study in Media Interaction*. New York: Arno Press, 1980.

Allen, Robert C., and Douglas Gomery. *Film History: Theory and Practice*. New York: Knopf, 1985.

Amad, Paula. *Counter-Archive: Film, the Everyday, and Albert Kahn's Archives de la Planète*. New York: Columbia University Press, 2010.

American Film Institute Catalog: Feature Films, 1921–1930. Berkeley: University of California Press, 1971.

Anderson, Benedict. *Imagined Communities: Reflections on the Origin and Spread of Nationalism*. Revised and extended edition. New York: Verso, 1991.

Anderson, Mark Lynn. *Twilight of the Idols: Hollywood and the Human Sciences in 1920s America*. Berkeley: University of California Press, 2011.

Aronson, Michael. *Nickelodeon City: Pittsburgh at the Movies, 1905–1929*. Pittsburgh: University of Pittsburgh Press, 2008.

Arvold, Alfred. "The Little Country Theatre." *The Drama: A Quarterly Review*, no. 21 (February 1916): 87–98.

Atherton, Lewis. *Main Street on the Middle Border*. Chicago: Quadrangle Books, 1966.

Bailey, Liberty Hyde. *The Country-Life Movement in the United States*. New York: Macmillan, 1911.

Balio, Tino, ed. *The American Film Industry*. Revised edition. Madison: University of Wisconsin Press, 1985.

Balsom, Erika. "Repeat Performance: *Kidnappers Foil* (1936–1952/2014)." Exhibition Guide for *Kidnappers Foil*. Kunsthalle Wien, Vienna, Austria, November 13, 2014.

Baron, Jaimie. *The Archive Effect: Found Footage and the Audiovisual Experience of History*. New York: Routledge, 2014.

Barron, Hal S. *Mixed Harvest: The Second Great Transformation in the Rural North, 1870–1930*. Chapel Hill: University of North Carolina Press, 1997

Batchen, Geoffrey. *Each Wild Idea: Writing, Photography, History*. Cambridge, Mass.: MIT Press, 2001.

Bean, Jennifer M., "The Imagination of Early Hollywood: Movie-Land and the Magic Cities, 1914–1916." In *Early Cinema and the "National,"* edited by Richard Abel, Giorgio Bertellini, and Rob King, 332–341. New Barnet, Herts, U.K.: John Libbey, 2008.

Bean, Shawn C. *The First Hollywood: Florida and the Golden Age of Silent Filmmaking* Gainesville: University Press of Florida, 2008.

Beck, John, *Writing the Radical Center: William Carlos Williams, John Dewey, and American Cultural Politics*. Albany: State University Press of New York, 2001.

Benjamin, Walter. "The Work of Art in the Age of Mechanical Reproduction." In *Illuminations*, edited by Hannah Arendt, translated by Harry Zohn, 217–251. New York: Schocken Books, 1969.
Bernstein, Matthew, and Dana F. White. "'Scratching Around' in a 'Fit of Insanity': The Norman Film Manufacturing Company and the Race Film Business in the 1920s." *Griffithiana* 62–63 (May 1998): 81–127.
Billig. Michael. *Banal Nationalism*. Thousand Oaks, Calif.: Sage, 1995.
Bledstein, Burton J. *The Culture of Professionalism: The Middle Class and the Development of Higher Education in America*. New York: Norton, 1978.
Boorstin, Daniel J. *The Americans: The National Experience*. New York: Vintage Books, 1965.
Bordwell, David, Janet Staiger, and Kristin Thompson, eds. *The Classical Hollywood Cinema: Film Style and Mode of Production to 1960*. New York: Columbia University Press, 1985.
Bottomore, Stephen. "From the Factory Gate to the 'Home Talent' Drama: An International Overview of Local Films in the Silent Era." In *The Lost World of Mitchell and Kenyon: Edwardian Britain on Film*, edited by Vanessa Toulmin, Simon Popple, and Patrick Russell, 33–48. London: British Film Institute, 2004.
Bowers, William L. *The Country Life Movement in America, 1900–1920*. Port Washington, N.Y.: Kennikat Press, 1974.
Braudel, Fernand. *On History*. Chicago: University of Chicago Press, 1980.
Braudy, Leo. *The Hollywood Sign: Fantasy and Reality of an American Icon*. New Haven, Conn.: Yale University Press, 2011.
Brokenshire, Norman. *This Is Noman Brokenshire: An Unvarnished Self-Portrait*. New York: Van Rees Press, 1954.
Buchloh, Benjamin H. D., and Robert Wilkie, eds. *Mining Photographs and Other Pictures, 1948–1968: A Selection from the Negative Archives of Shedden Studio, Glace Bay, Cape Breton*. Halifax: Press of the Nova Scotia College of Art and Design, 1983.
Burgin, Victor. *The Remembered Film*. London: Reaktion Books, 2004.
Cameron, James R. *The Taking and Showing of Motion Pictures for the Amateur*. New York: Cameron, 1927.
Cecelski, David S., and Timothy B. Tyson, eds. *Democracy Betrayed: The Wilmington Race Riot of 1898 and Its Legacy*. Chapel Hill: University of North Carolina Press, 1998.
Chansky, Dorothy. *Composing Ourselves: The Little Theatre Movement and the American Audience*. Carbondale: Southern Illinois University Press, 2004.
Condee, William Faricy. *Coal and Culture: Opera House in Appalachia*. Athens: Ohio University Press, 2005.
Cousins, Volney D. "Combination for Better Engineering: Outline of a Co-operative Plan and Its Probable Results." *Telephony* 59, no. 27 (1910): 756.
Couvares, Francis G. "Hollywood, Main Street, and the Church: Trying to Censor the Movies before the Production Code." *American Quarterly* 44, no. 4 (December 1992): 584–616.
Crafton, Donald. *The Talkies: American Cinema's Transition to Sound, 1926–1931*. Berkeley: University of California Press, 1997.
Danbom, David B. *Born in the Country: A History of Rural America*. Second edition. Baltimore: Johns Hopkins University Press, 2006.

de Certeau, Michel. *The Practice of Everyday Life*. Translated by Steven Rendall. Berkeley: University of California Press, 1984.

de Cordova, Richard. *Picture Personalities: The Emergence of the Star System in America*. Urbana: University of Illinois Press, 2001.

Delamoir, Jeannette. "Louise Lovely: The Construction of a Star." Ph.D. dissertation, La Trobe University, Bundoora, 2002.

Dench, Ernest A. "Openings for the Free Lance Cinematographer." *Photographic Times*, July 1915, 285–287.

Des Moines City Directory. *Polk's Real Estate Register and Directory of the United States and Canada*. 5th revised edition. Detroit: R. L. Polk, 1913.

Doane, Mary Ann. *The Emergence of Cinematic Time: Modernity, Contingency and the Archive*. Cambridge, Mass.: Harvard University Press, 2002.

Eaton, Walter Prichard. "The Real Revolt in Our Theatre." *Scribner's Magazine*, November 1922, 596–605.

Eckey, Lorelei F., Maxine Allen Schoyer, and William T. Schoyer. *1,001 Broadways: Hometown Talent Stage*. Ames: Iowa State University Press, 1982.

Elsaesser, Thomas. "Archives and Archaeologies: The Place of Non-Fiction Films in Contemporary Media." In *Films That Work: Industrial Film and the Productivity of Media*, edited by Vinzenz Hediger and Patrick Vonderau, 19–34. Amsterdam: Amsterdam University Press, 2009.

Elshtain, Jean Bethke. *Jane Addams and the Dream of American Democracy*. New York: Basic Books, 2002.

Entrikin, J. Nicholas. *The Betweenness of Place: Towards a Geography of Modernity*. Baltimore: Johns Hopkins University Press, 1991.

Eskew, Glenn T. "From Civil War to Civil Rights: Selling Alabama as Heritage Tourism." In *Slavery, Contested Heritage, and Thanatourism*, edited by Graham Dann and A. V. Seaton, 201–214. New York: Haworth Press, 2001.

Fielding, Raymond. *The American Newsreel: 1911–1967*. Norman: University of Oklahoma Press, 1972.

Fitzgerald, Zelda. "Our Own Movie Queen." *Chicago Sunday Tribune*, June 7, 1925. Reprinted in *Red Velvet Seat: Women's Writing on the First Fifty Years of Cinema*, edited by Antonia Lant, 607–622. New York: Verso, 2006.

Fossati, Giovanna. *From Grain to Pixel: The Archival Life of Film in Transition*. Amsterdam: Amsterdam University Press, 2009.

Franklin, Harold B. *Motion Picture Theatre Management*. Garden City, N.Y.: Doubleday, Doran, 1928.

Fraser, Nancy. "Social Justice in the Age of Identity Politics: Redistribution, Recognition, and Participation." In Nancy Fraser and Axel Honneth, *Redistribution or Recognition? A Political-Philosophical Exchange*, translated by Joel Golb, James Ingram, and Christiane Wilke, 7–109. New York: Verso, 2003.

Frick, Caroline, comp. and ed. "Itinerant Filmography, North America." *The Moving Image* 10, no. 1 (2010): 170–181.

———. "Jackrabbit Genius: Melton Barker, Itinerant Films, and Creating Locality." *The Moving Image* 10, no. 1 (Spring 2010): 1–22.

———. *Saving Cinema: The Politics of Preservation*. New York: Oxford University Press, 2010.

Frykholm, Joel. *Framing the Feature Film: Multi-Reel Feature Film and American Film Culture in the 1910s*. Stockholm: US-AB, 2009.

Fuller-Seeley, Kathryn H. *At the Picture Show: Small-Town Audiences and the Creation of Movie Fan Culture*. Charlottesville: University Press of Virginia, 2001.
———, ed. *Hollywood in the Neighborhood: Historical Case Studies of Local Moviegoing*. Berkeley: University of California Press, 2008.
Gaines, Jane. "First Fictions." *Signs* 30, no. 1 (Autumn 2004): 1293–1317.
———. "From Elephants to Lux Soap: The Programming and 'Flow' of Early Motion Picture Exploitation." *Velvet Light Trap* 25 (1990): 29–43.
———. "What Happened to the Philosophy of Film History." *Film History* 25, no. 1 (2013): 70–80.
Gaudreault, André. *Film and Attraction from Kinemtography to Cinema*. Translated by Timothy Barnard. Urbana: University of Illinois Press, 2011.
Gemünden, Gerd, and Johannes von Moltke, eds. *Culture in the Anteroom: The Legacies of Siegfried Kracauer*. Ann Arbor: University of Michigan Press, 2012.
Glassberg, David. *American Historical Pageantry: The Uses of Tradition in the Early Twentieth Century*. Chapel Hill: University of North Carolina Press, 1990.
Glissant, Édouard. *Poetics of Relation*. Translated by Betsy Wing. Ann Arbor: University of Michigan Press, 1997.
Gomery, Douglas. *The Hollywood Studio System*. New York: St. Martin's Press, 1986.
———. "The Picture Palace: Economic Sense or Hollywood Nonsense?" *Quarterly Review of Film Studies* 3, no. 1 (1978): 26.
———. *Shared Pleasures: A History of Movie Audiences in the United States*. London: British Film Institute, 1992.
Gomes, Maryann. "Working People, Topical Films, and Home Movies: The Case of the North West Film Archive." In *Mining the Home Movie: Excavations in Histories and Memories*, edited by Karen L. Ishizuka and Patricia R. Zimmermann, 235–248. Berkeley: University of California Press, 2008.
Goodman, David. *Radio's Civic Ambition: American Broadcasting and Democracy in the 1930s*. New York: Oxford University Press, 2011.
Grau, Robert. *The Theatre of Science*. New York, Benjamin Blom, 1914.
Grieveson, Lee. *Policing Cinema: Movies and Censorship in Early-Twentieth-Century America* Berkeley: University of California Press, 2004.
Gunning, Tom. "Before Documentary: Early Nonfiction Films and the 'View Aesthetic.'" Reprinted in *The Documentary Film Reader: History, Theory, Criticism*, edited by Jonathan Kahana, 52–63. New York: Oxford University Press, 2016.
———. "Crazy Machines in the Garden of Forking Paths: Mischief Gags and the Origins of American Film Comedy." In *Classical Hollywood Comedy*, edited by Kristine Brunovska Karnick and Henry Jenkins, 87–105. New York: Routledge, 1995.
———. "Pictures of Crowd Splendour: The Mitchell and Kenyon Factory Gate Film." In *The Lost World of Mitchell and Kenyon: Edwardian Britain on Film*, edited by Vanessa Toulmin, Simon Popple and Patrick Russell, 49–58. London: British Film Institute, 2004.
Habermas, Jürgen. *Structural Transformation of the Public Sphere: An Inquiry into a Category of Bourgeois Society*. Translated by Thomas Burger. Cambridge, Mass.: MIT Press, 1989.
Halbwachs, Maurice. *On Collective Memory*. Edited, translated, and with an introduction by Lewis A. Coser. Chicago: University of Chicago Press, 1992.
Hall, Jacquelyn Dowd, et al. *Like a Family: The Making of a Southern Cotton Mill World*. Chapel Hill: University of North Carolina Press, 1987.

Hallett, Hilary. *Go West Young Women! The Rise of Early Hollywood*. Berkeley: University of California Press, 2013.

Halsey, Stuart & Company. "The Motion Picture Industry as a Basis for Bond Financing" (1927), reprinted in *The American Film Industry,* ed. Tino Balio, 195–217. Madison: University of Wisconsin Press, 1976.

Halttunen, Karen. *Confidence Men and Painted Women: A Study of Middle-Class Culture in America, 1830–1870.* New Haven, Conn.: Yale University Press, 1982.

Hampton, Benjamin. *History of the American Film Industry.* 1931; New York: Dover Publication, 1970.

Hansen, Miriam. *Babel and Babylon: Spectatorship in American Silent Film.* Cambridge, Mass.: Harvard University Press, 1991.

Harris, Neil. *Humbug: The Art of P. T. Barnum.* Boston: Little, Brown, 1973.

Hedrick, Judi. "Amateur Video Must Not Be Overlooked." *The Moving Image* 6, no. 1 (Spring 2006): 66–81.

Hertogs, Daan, and Nico de Klerk, eds. *Nonfiction from the Teens: The 1994 Amsterdam Workshop.* London: British Film Institute, 1994.

Hill, J. Wilbur. "Will the Moving Picture Camera Pay?" *Camera Craft,* July 1916, 271–274.

Hjort, Mette. "Danish Cinema and the Politics of Recognition." In *Post-Theory: Reconstructing Film Studies,* edited by David Bordwell and Noel Carroll, 520–532. Madison: University of Wisconsin Press, 1996.

"Home Talent." *American Education* 5, no. 2 (October 1901): 94.

Hoorn, Jeanette, and Michelle Smith. "Rudall Hayward's Democratic Cinema and the 'Civilising Mission' in the 'Land of the Wrong White Crowd.'" In *New Zealand Cinema: Interpreting the Past,* edited by Alistair Fox, Barry Keith Grant, and Hilary Radner, 65–82. Chicago: Intellect Press, 2011.

Horak, Jan-Christopher. "The First American Film Avant-Garde: 1919–1945." In *Lovers of Cinema: The First American Film Avant-Garde: 1919–1945,* edited by Jan-Christopher Horak, 14–66. Madison: University of Wisconsin Press, 1995.

Houghton, Norris. *Advance from Broadway: 19,000 Miles of American Theater.* New York: Harcourt, Brace, 1941.

Hulfish, David S. *Motion-Picture Work: A General Treatise on Picture Taking, Picture Making, Photo-Plays and Theater Management and Operation.* Chicago: American School of Correspondence, 1913.

Immerwahr, Daniel. *Thinking Small: The United States and the Lure of Community Development.* Cambridge, Mass.: Harvard University Press, 2015.

Iowa Department of Agriculture. *The Iowa Year Book of Agriculture,* vol. 14. Des Moines: Robert Henderson, 1914.

Isenberg, Alison. *Downtown America: A History of the Place and the People Who Made It.* Chicago: University of Chicago Press, 2004.

Jacobs, Lea. *The Decline of Sentiment.* Berkeley: University of California Press, 2008.

Jacobs, Lea, and Ben Brewster. *Theatre to Cinema: Stage Pictorialism and the Early Feature Film.* New York: Oxford University Press, 1998.

Jacobs, Lewis. *The Rise of the American Film: A Critical History.* New York: Harcourt, Brace, 1939.

James, David. *The Most Typical Avant-Garde: History and Geography of Minor Cinemas in Los Angeles.* Berkeley: University of California Press, 2005.

Jauss, Hans Robert. "Literary History as a Challenge to Literary Theory." *New Literary History* 2, no. 1 (Autumn 1970): 7–37.

Johnson, Martin L. "'An Added Bonus': Local Films, Local Newsreels and the Strand News in Warsaw, Indiana (1938–1955)." *Historical Journal of Film, Radio and Television* 32, no. 3 (2012): 401–417.

Johnson, Victoria. *Heartland TV: Prime Time Television and the Struggle for U.S. Identity.* New York: New York University Press 2008.

Johnson, A. P., comp. and ed. *Library of Advertising: Methods of Advertising.* Chicago: Cree, 1911.

Jones, Janna. *The Past Is a Moving Picture: Preserving the Twentieth Century on Film.* Gainesville: University Press of Florida, 2012.

Jowett, Garth. *Film: The Democratic Art.* Boston: Little, Brown, 1976.

Jung, Uli. "Local Views: A Blind Spot in the Historiography of Early German Cinema." *Historical Journal of Film, Radio and Television* 22, no. 3 (2002): 253–273.

Kahana, Jonathan. *Intelligence Work: The Politics of American Documentary.* New York: Columbia University Press, 2008.

Kammen, Carol. *On Doing Local History: Reflections on What Local Historians Do, Why, and What It Means.* Nashville: American Association for State and Local History, 1986.

Kane, William R. *1,001 Places to Sell Manuscripts.* Ridgewood, N.J.: The Editor Company, 1915.

Karr, Kathleen. "Hooray for Providence, Wilkes-Barre, Saranac Lake—and Hollywood." In *The American Film Heritage: Impressions from the American Film Institute Archives*, 104–109. Washington, DC: Acropolis Books, 1972.

Kasson, Joy S. *Buffalo Bill's Wild West: Celebrity, Memory, and Popular History.* New York: Hill and Wang, 2000.

Kattelle, Alan. *Home Movies: A History of the Amateur Motion Picture Industry in the United States.* Nashua, N.H.: Transition, 2000.

Kaufman, Jason. *For the Common Good? American Civic Life and the Golden Age of Fraternity.* Oxford: Oxford University Press, 2002.

Keil, Charlie. *Early American Cinema in Transition: Story, Style and Filmmaking, 1907–1913.* Madison: University of Wisconsin Press, 2001.

———. "1913: Movies and the Beginning of a New Era." In *American Cinema of the 1910s: Themes and Variations,* edited by Charlie Keil and Ben Singer, 92–114. New Brunswick, N.J.: Rutgers University Press, 2009.

Keller, Sarah. "Cinephobia: To Wonder, to Worry." *LOLA* 5 (2015), http://www.lola-journal.com/5/cinephobia.html.

Kember, Joe. *Marketing Modernity: Victorian Popular Shows and Early Cinema.* Exeter: University of Exeter Press, 2009.

Kessler, Frank, and Eef Masson. "Layers of Cheese: Generic Overlap in Early Non-Fiction Films on Production Processes." In *Films That Work: Industrial Film and the Productivity of Media,* edited by Vinzenz Hediger and Patrick Vonderau, 75–84. Amsterdam: Amsterdam University Press, 2009.

Kessler, Frank, and Nanna Verhoeff. *Networks of Entertainment: Early Film Distribution, 1895–1915.* Eastleigh, U.K.: John Libbey, 2007.

Kett, Joseph F. *The Pursuit of Knowledge under Difficulties: From Self-Improvement to Adult Education in America, 1750–1990.* Stanford, Calif.: Stanford University Press, 1994.

Kirby, Lynne. *Parallel Tracks: The Railroad and Silent Cinema.* Durham, N.C.: Duke University Press, 1997.

Kirkpatrtick, Bill. "Localism in American Media, 1920–1934." Ph.D. dissertation, University of Wisconsin–Madison, 2006.

Klenotic, Jeffrey. "Putting Cinema History on the Map: Using GIS to Explore the Spatiality of Cinema." In *Explorations in New Cinema History*, ed. by Richard Maltby, Daniel Biltereyst and Phillip Meers, 58–84. Malden, Mass.: Wiley-Blackwell, 2011.

Kracauer, Siegfried. *History: The Last Things before the Last*. New York: Oxford University Press, 1969.

Kuehn, Shelly. "Jamieson Leaves the Scene: Early Movies to TV Commercials—Rise and Fall of a Film Company." *Journal of the SMPTE* 83, no. 11 (November 1974): 912–914.

Kuhn, Annette. *Dreaming of Fred and Ginger: Cinema and Cultural Memory*. New York: New York University Press, 2002.

Kula, Sam. "Up from the Permafrost: The Dawson City Collection." In *This Film Is Dangerous: A Celebration of Nitrate Film*, edited by Roger Smith, 213–218. Brussels: FIAF, 2002.

Landsberg, Allison. *Engaging the Past: Mass Culture and the Production of Historical Knowledge*. New York: Columbia University Press, 2015.

Levine, Lawrence. *Highbrow/Lowbrow: The Emergence of Cultural Hierarchy in America*. Cambridge, Mass.: Harvard University Press, 1990.

Lewis, Jon, and Eric Smoodin, eds. *Looking Past the Screen: Case Studies in American Film History and Method*. Durham, N.C.: Duke University Press, 2007.

Lewis, Howard T. *The Motion Picture Industry*. New York: D. Van Nostrand, 1933.

Liepa, Torey. "Entertaining the Public Option: The Popular Film Writing Movement and the Emergence of Writing for the American Silent Cinema." In *Analyzing the Screenplay*, edited by Jill Nelmes, 7–23. New York: Routledge, 2011.

———. "Figures of Silent Speech: Silent Film Dialogue and the American Vernacular, 1909–1916." PhD dissertation, New York University, 2008. UMI 3320809.

Lindsay, Vachel. *The Art of the Moving Picture*. New York: Macmillan, 1915.

Lingeman, Richard. *Small Town America: A Narrative History, 1620–the Present*. Boston: Houghton Mifflin, 1980.

Liu, Alan. *Local Transcendence: Essays on Postmodern Historicism and the Database*. Chicago: University of Chicago Press, 2008.

Luckett, Moya. *Cinema and Community: Progressivism, Exhibition, and Film Culture in Chicago, 1907–1917*. Detroit: Wayne State University Press, 2014.

Lupack, Barbara Tepa. *Richard E. Norman and Race Filmmaking*. Bloomington: Indiana University Press, 2013.

Lybcza, Fabrice. "Fictions incarnées: Pratiques publicitaires du Ballyhoo et regard spectatoriel dans le cinéma muet hollywoodien." *1895: Revue d'Histoire du Cinéma* 82 (2014): 37–63.

Lynd, Robert, and Helen Merrell Lynd. *Middletown: A Study in Contemporary American Culture*. New York: Harcourt Brace, 1929.

———. *Middletown in Transition: A Study in Cultural Conflicts*. New York: Harcourt Brace, 1937.

MacGowan, Kenneth. *Behind the Screen: The History and Techniques of the Motion Picture*. New York: Delacorte Press, 1965.

Macober, Ben. *The Jewel City*. San Francisco: John H. Williams, 1915.

Maltby, Richard, Daniel Biltereyst, and Philippe Meers, eds. *Explorations in New Cinema History: Approaches and Case Studies*. Malden, Mass.: Wiley-Blackwell, 2011.

Maltby, Richard, Melvyn Stokes, and Robert C. Allen. *Going to the Movies: Hollywood and the Social Experience of Cinema*. Exeter: University of Exeter Press, 2007.

Margalit, Avishai. *The Ethics of Memory*. Cambridge, Mass.: Harvard University Press, 2002.

Marshall, T. H. *Citizenship and Social Class and Other Essays*. Cambridge: Cambridge University Press, 1950.

Massey, Doreen B. *For Space*. Thousand Oaks, Calif.: Sage, 2005.

McCarthy, Anna. "From the Ordinary to the Concrete: Cultural Studies and the Politics of Scale." In *Questions of Method in Cultural Studies*, edited by Mimi White and James Schwoch, 21–53. Malden, Mass.: Blackwell, 2006.

McNamara, Brooks. "Popular Entertainment." In *The Cambridge History of American Theatre*, vol. 2, *1870–1945*, edited by Don B. Wilmeth and C. W. E. Bigsby, 378–410. Cambridge: Cambridge University Press, 1998.

Melnick, Ross. *American Showman: Samuel "Roxy" Rothafel and the Birth of the Entertainment Industry, 1908–1935*. New York: Columbia University Press, 2012.

Melnick, Ross, and Andreas Fuchs. *Cinema Treasures: A New Look at Classic Movie Theaters*. St. Paul, Minn.: MBI, 2004.

Miller, Mark Stuart. "Promoting Movies in the Late 1930s: Pressbooks at Warner Bros." Ph.D. dissertation, University of Texas at Austin, 1994.

Miller's Lexington, N.C. City Directory. Asheville, N.C.: Southern Directory, 1925–1926.

Misulia, Charles A. *Columbus, Georgia, 1865: The Last True Battle of the Civil War*. Tuscaloosa: University of Alabama Press, 2010.

Moore, Paul S. *Now Playing: Early Moviegoing and the Regulation of Fun*. Albany: State University of New York Press, 2008.

Moore, William G., comp. *Fun with Fritz: Adventures in Early Redlands, Big Bear, and Hollywood with John H. "Fritz" Fisher*. Redlands, Calif.: Moore Historical Foundation, 1986.

Moran, James M. *There's No Place Like Home Video*. Minneapolis: University of Minnesota Press, 2002.

Morey, Anne. "Early Art Cinema in the U.S.: Symon Gould and the Little Cinema Movement of the 1920s." In *Going to the Movies: Hollywood and the Social Experience of Cinema*, edited by Richard Maltby, Melvyn Stokes, and Robert C. Allen, 235–247. Exeter: University of Exeter Press, 2007.

———. *Hollywood Outsiders: The Adaptation of the Film Industry, 1913–1934*. Minneapolis: University of Minnesota Press, 2003.

Moskowitz, Marina. *Standard of Living: The Measure of the Middle Class in Modern America*. Baltimore: Johns Hopkins University Press, 2004.

Mouffe, Chantal. *The Return of the Political*. New York: Verso, 2005.

Murray, Michael D., and Donald G. Godfrey, eds. *Television in America: Local Station History from across the Nation*. Ames: Iowa State University Press, 1997.

Musser, Charles. *The Emergence of Cinema: The American Screen to 1907*. Berkeley: University of California Press, 1990.

———. *High-Class Moving Pictures: Lyman H. Howe and the Forgotten Era of Traveling Exhibition, 1880–1920*. Princeton, N.J.: Princeton University Press, 1991.

———. "Itinerant Exhibitors." In *Encyclopedia of Early Cinema*, edited by Richard Abel, 340–342. New York: Routledge, 2010.

———. "Towards a History of Theatrical Culture: Imagining an Integrated History of Stage and Screen." In *Screen Culture: History and Textuality*, edited by John Fullerton, 3–19. Eastleigh, U.K.: John Libbey, 2004,

———. "The Travel Genre in 1903–1940: Moving Towards Fictional Narrative." In *Early Cinema: Space, Frame, Narrative*, edited by Thomas Elsaesser with Adam Barker, 123–132. London: British Film Institute, 1990.

Nelson, Richard Alan. *Florida and the American Motion Picture Industry, 1898–1980*. New York: Garland, 1983.

Newman, Michael Z. *Video Revolutions: On the History of a Medium*. New York: Columbia University Press, 2014.

Nicholson, Heather Norris. *Amateur Cinema: Meaning and Practice, 1927–1977*. Manchester: Manchester University Press, 2012.

Novak, William J. *The People's Welfare: Law and Regulation in Nineteenth-Century America*. Chapel Hill: University of North Carolina Press, 1996.

O'Connor, Daniel. *Mediated Associations: Cinematic Dimensions of Social Theory*. Montreal and Kingston: McGill-Queen's University Press, 2002.

Orgeron, Marsha. "'You Are Invited to Participate': Interactive Fandom in the Age of the Movie Magazine." *Journal of Film and Video* 61, no. 3 (Fall 2009): 3–23.

Orvell, Miles. *The Death and Life of Main Street: Small Towns in American Memory, Space, and Community*. Chapel Hill: University of North Carolina Press, 2012.

Pearson, Roberta E. "The Menace of the Movies: Cinema's Challenge to the Theater in the Transitional Period." In *American Cinema's Transitional Era: Audiences, Institutions, Practices*, edited by Charlie Keil and Shelley Stamp, 315–331. Berkeley: University of California Press, 2004.

Peiss, Kathy. *Cheap Amusements: Working Women and Leisure in Turn-of-the-Century New York*. Philadelphia: Temple University Press, 1986.

Peterson, Jennifer Lynn. *Education in the School of Dreams: Travelogues and Early Nonfiction Film*. Durham, N.C.: Duke University Press, 2013.

Poll, Ryan. *Main Street and Empire: The Fictional Small Town in the Age of Globalization*. New Brunswick, N.J.: Rutgers University Press, 2012.

Potamianos, George. "Hollywood in the Hinterlands: Mass Culture in Two California Communities, 1896–1936." Ph.D. dissertation, University of Southern California, 1988.

Putnam, Michael. *Silent Screens: The Decline and Transformation of the American Movie Theater*. Baltimore: Johns Hopkins University Press, 2000.

Rabinowitz, Paula. *They Must Be Represented: The Politics of Documentary*. New York: Verso, 1994.

Ramsaye, Terry. *A Million and One Nights*. London: Frank Cass, 1926.

Rankin, Edward L., Jr. "A Century of Progress: Fieldcrest Cannon, Inc. Salutes Cannon Mills Company and Its Employees, Past and Present." Kannapolis, N.C.: Fieldcrest Cannon, 1987.

Report of the Country Life Commission. Washington, DC: Government Printing Office, 1909.

Reeves, Bradley, and Louisa Trott. "Itinerant Filmmaking in Knoxville in the 1920s: A Story Told through Unseen Movies." *The Moving Image* 10, no. 1 (Spring 2010): 126–143.

Reps, John W. *The Making of Urban America: A History of City Planning in the United States*. Princeton, N.J.: Princeton University Press, 1992.

Ricouer, Paul. *The Course of Recognition*. Translated by David Pellauer. Cambridge, Mass.: Harvard University Press, 2005.

Robertson, Roland. "Glocalization: Time-Space and Homogeneity-Heterogeneity." In *Global Modernities*, edited by Mike Featherstone, Scott Lash, and Roland Robertson, 25–44. London: Sage, 1995.

Rosenzweig, Roy. *Eight Hours for What We Will: Workers and Leisure in an Industrial City, 1870–1920*. Cambridge: Cambridge University Press, 1983.
Salt, Barry. *Film Style and Technology: History and Analysis*. London: Starword, 1983.
Sargent, Epes Winthrop. *Picture Theatre Advertising*. New York: Chalmers, 1915.
Schaefer, Eric. *"Bold! Daring! Shocking! True!" A History of Exploitation Films, 1919–1959*. Durham, N.C.: Duke University Press, 1999.
Schwartz, Vanessa, and Leo Charney, eds. *Cinema and the Invention of Modern Life*. Berkeley: University of California Press, 1995.
Senelick, Laurence. *The Changing Room: Sex, Drag and Theatre*. New York: Routledge, 2000.
Sewell, William H., Jr. *Logics of History: Social Theory and Social Transformation*. Chicago: University of Chicago Press, 2005.
Sheldon, Karan. "Meeting the Movie Queen: An Itinerant Film Anchored in Place." *The Moving Image* 10, no. 1 (Spring 2010): 80–88.
Sherk, Warren M. *The Films of Mack Sennett: Credit Documentation from the Mack Sennett Collection at the Margaret Herrick Library*. Lanham, Md.: Scarecrow Press, 1998.
Singer, Ben. "Feature Films, Variety Programs, and the Crisis of the Small Exhibitor." In *American Cinema's Transitional Era: Audiences, Institutions, Practices*, edited by Charlie Keil and Shelley Stamp, 76–100. Berkeley: University of California Press, 2004.
———. "Home Cinema and the Edison Home Projecting Kinetoscope." *Film History* 2, no. 1 (Winter 1998): 37–69.
Sklar, Robert. *Movie-Made America*. 1975. Reprint, New York: Vintage, 1994.
Slide, Anthony. *Nitrate Won't Wait: A History of Film Preservation in the United States*. Jefferson, N.C.: MacFarland, [1992] 2000.
Smith, Shawn Michelle. "'Looking at One's Self through the Eyes of Others': W. E. B. Du Bois's Photographs for the 1900 Paris Exposition." *African American Review* 34, no. 4 (2000): 581–599.
———. *Photography on the Color Line: W. E. B. Du Bois, Race, and Visual Culture*. Durham, N.C.: Duke University Press, 2004.
Smith, Terry. *Making the Modern: Industry, Art, and Design in America*. Chicago: University of Chicago Press, 1993.
Spears, Timothy. *Chicago Dreaming: Midwesterners and the City, 1871–1919*. Chicago: University of Chicago Press, 2005.
Stamp, Shelley. "'It's a Long Way to Filmland': Starlets, Screen Hopefuls, and Extras in Early Hollywood." In *American Cinema's Transitional Era: Audiences, Institutions, Practices*, edited by Charlie Keil and Shelley Stamp, 332–351. Berkeley: University of California Press, 2004.
———. *Movie-Struck Girls: Women and Motion Picture Culture after the Nickelodeon*. Princeton, N.J.: Princeton University Press, 2000.
Steedman, Carolyn. *Dust: The Archive and Cultural History*. New Brunswick, N.J.: Rutgers University Press, 2002.
Steg, Albert. "The Itinerant Films of Arthur J. Higgins." *The Moving Image* 10, no. 1 (2010): 115–125.
Stewart, Jacqueline. *Migrating to the Movies: Cinema and Black Urban Modernity*. Berkeley: University of California Press, 2005.
Stewart, Stephanie Elaine. "*Movies of Local People* and a Usable Past: Mill Town Treasures and Transcendent Views, 1936–1942." *The Moving Image* 7, no. 1 (2007): 51–77.

Stoddard, Ralph P. *The Photo-Play: A Book of Valuable Information for Those Who Would Enter a Field of Unlimited Endeavor*. [Cleveland?]: Malaney and Stoddard, 1911.

Stoeltje, Beverly J. "Festival." In *Folklore, Cultural Performances and Popular Entertainments*, edited by Richard Bauman, 261–271. New York: Oxford University Press, 1992.

Stoeltje, Beverly J., and Richard Bauman. "Community Festival and the Enactment of Modernity." In *The Old Traditional Way of Life*, edited by Robert E. Walls and George H. Schoemaker with Jennifer Livesay and Laura Dassow Walls, 159–171. Bloomington, Ind.: Trickster Press, 1989.

Stokes, Melvyn, and Richard Maltby, eds. *American Movie Audiences: From the Turn of the Century to the Early Sound Era*. London: British Film Institute, 1999.

Strasser, Susan. *Satisfaction Guaranteed: The Making of the American Mass Market*. Washington, DC: Smithsonian Institution Press, 1989.

Strauven, Wanda, ed. *Cinema of Attractions Reloaded*. Amsterdam: Amsterdam University Press, 2006.

Streible, Dan. "Itinerant Filmmakers and Amateur Casts: A Homemade 'Our Gang,' 1926." *Film History* 15, no. 2 (2003): 177–192.

Susman, Warren. *Culture as History: The Transformation of American Society in the Twentieth Century*. New York: Pantheon, 1984.

Swanson, Dwight. "Inventing Amateur Film: Marion Norris Gleason, Eastman Kodak and the Rochester Scene, 1921–1932." *Film History* 15, no. 2 (2003): 126–136.

Taylor, Charles. "The Politics of Recognition." In *Multiculturalism: Examining the Politics of Recognition*, edited by A. Gutmann, 25–73. Princeton, N.J.: Princeton University Press, 1992.

Teaford, Jon C. *Cities of the Heartland: The Rise and Fall of the Industrial Midwest*. Bloomington: Indiana University Press, 1993.

Tepperman, Charles. *Amateur Cinema: 1923–1960*. Berkeley: University of California Press, 2014.

Toulmin, Vanessa. *Electric Edwardians: The Films of Mitchell and Kenyon*. London: British Film Institute, 2006.

———. "'Local Films for Local People': Travelling Showmen and the Commissioning of Local Films in Great Britain, 1900–1902." *Film History* 13, no. 2 (2001): 118–137.

Toulmin, Vanessa, and Martin Loiperdinger. "'Is It You?' Recognition, Representation and Response in Relation to the Local Film." *Film History* 17, no. 1 (2005): 7–18.

Toulmin, Vanessa, Simon Popple, and Patrick Russell, eds. *The Lost World of Mitchell and Kenyon: Edwardian Britain on Film*. London: British Film Institute, 2004.

Turner, Nancy. *Having Fun with It: The Man Haters Project*. Indianapolis: Indiana Humanities Council Program, 1996.

Uricchio, William. "The Recurrent, the Recombinatory and the Ephemeral." In *Ephemeral Media: Transitory Screen Culture from Television to YouTube*, edited by Paul Grainge, 23–36. London: British Film Institute, 2011.

Usai, Paolo Cherchi. *Vitagraph Co. of America: Il cinema prima di Hollywood*. Pordenone, Italy: Studio Tesi, 1987.

Vaughn-Roberson, Courtney Ann, and Glen Vaughn-Roberson. *City in the Osage Hills: Tulsa, Oklahoma*. Boulder, Col.: Pruett, 1984.

Verhoeven, Deb. "What Is a Cinema? Death, Closure and the Database." In *Watching Films: New Perspectives on Movie-Going, Exhibition and Reception*, edited by Albert Moran and Karina Aveyard, 33–51. Bristol, U.K.: Intellect Books, 2013.

Vukmir, Rade. *The Mill*. Lanham, Md.: University Press of America, 1999.

Wagoner, Nathan. "The *Huntingdon's Hero* Story." *The Moving Image* 10, no. 1 (Spring 2010): 144–149.
Waller, Gregory A. *Main Street Amusements: Movies and Commercial Entertainment in a Southern City, 1896–1930*. Washington, DC: Smithsonian Institution Press, 1995.
———, ed. *Moviegoing in America: A Sourcebook in the History of Film Exhibition*. Malden, Mass.: Blackwell, 2002.
———. "Robert Southard and the History of Traveling Film Exhibition." *Film Quarterly* 57, no. 2 (2003–2004): 8.
Ward, Stephen Victor. *Selling Places: The Marketing and Promotion of Towns and Cities, 1850–2000*. New York, Routledge, 1998.
Warner, Michael. *Publics and Counterpublics*. New York: Zone Books, 2005.
Wasson, Haidee. "Electric Homes! Automatic Movies! Efficient Entertainment! 16mm and Cinema's Domestication in the 1920s." *Cinema Journal* 48, no. 4 (2009): 1–21.
———. *Museum Movies: The Museum of Modern Art and the Birth of Art Cinema*. Berkeley: University of California Press, 2005.
———. "Suitcase Cinema." *Cinema Journal* 51, no. 2 (2012): 148–152.
West, Nancy Martha. *Kodak and the Lens of Nostalgia*. Charlottesville: University Press of Virginia, 2000.
Whalley, Robin, and Peter Worden. "Forgotten Firm: A Short Chronological Account of Mitchell and Kenyon, Cinematographer." *Film History* 10 (Spring 1998): 35–51.
Widdowson, John. "Mitchell and Kenyon: Ceremonial Processions and Folk Traditions." in *The Lost World of Mitchell and Kenyon: Edwardian Britain on Film*, edited by Vanessa Toulmin, Simon Popple, and Patrick Russell, 137–149. London: British Film Institute, 2004.
Wiebe, Robert. *The Search for Order: 1877–1920*. New York: Hill and Wang, 1967.
———. *Self-Rule: A Cultural History of American Democracy*. Chicago: University of Chicago Press, 1995.
Wilinsky, Barbara. "Flirting with Kathlyn: Creating the Mass Audience." In *Hollywood Goes Shopping*, edited by David Desser and Garth S. Jowett, 34–56. Minneapolis: University of Minnesota Press, 2000.
Williams, Linda. *Playing the Race Card: Melodramas of Black and White from Uncle Tom to O. J. Simpson*. Princeton, N.J.: Princeton University Press, 2002.
Witmer, A. S. "Motion Picture and City Publicity." *American Municipalities* 38, no. 2 (November 1919): 198.
Wolfe, Charles. "Historicising the 'Voice of God': The Place of Vocal Narration in Classical Documentary." *Film History* 9, no. 2 (1997): 149–167.
Wrobel, David M. *Promised Lands: Promotion, Memory, and the Creation of the American West*. Lawrence: University Press of Kansas, 2002.
Wuthnow, Robert. *Small-Town America: Finding Community, Shaping the Future*. Princeton, N.J.: Princeton University Press, 2013.
Zanish, Tanya L. "Present and Past in Cradle of Dixie." *Alabama Heritage* 27 (Winter 1993): 25–29.
Zimmermann, Patricia. *Reel Families: A Social History of Amateur Film*. Bloomington: Indiana University Press, 1995.
Zunz, Olivier. *Making America Corporate: 1870–1920*. Chicago: University of Chicago Press, 1990.

INDEX

Page numbers in italics refer to figures.

16mm film, 12, 134n31, 135–142, 157, 159n5, 159n7, 159nn12–13, 160n22, 163, 174, 176, 207, 221, 224n37, 231, 233, 256
35mm film, 12, 90n48, 90n52, 179, 207, 217, 230–232

Abel, Richard, 59, 83
actualities, 1, 4–5, 83, 167
Adopts a Baby series, 117, 119, 123–124, 129, 133n23. *See also* Interstate Film Producers
advertising, film, 27, 53n92, 86, 87; of camera equipment, 64–65; by theaters, 100; in local films, 152, 178, 208–209, 212; municipal, 22–24, 28. *See* industrial films; industrial romances; municipal booster films
"Advertising for Exhibitors," 67, 99–101, 140. *See also* Sargent, Epes Winthrop
Agfa-Ansco, 141, 152. *See also* 16mm film
Allen, Robert C., 4–5, 18–19, 90n40, 91n58, 118, 196n2
amateur. *See* home talent
Amateur Cinema League (ACL), 139, 141, 159n13. See also *Amateur Movie Makers/Movie Makers*
amateur fiction films, 3, 6, 9, 12, 57, 62, 64–66, 86, 88n2, 90n35, 90n48, 90n52, 135–142, 144, 151, 157–158, 159n6, 159n12, 160n21, 195, 198n35, 198n38, 204, 255–257; avant-garde films and, 160n24. *See also* 16mm film
Amateur Movie Makers/Movie Makers, 139–140
Amateur Service Productions, 142, 158, 240–243

Amateur Theater Guild, 9, 12, 89n34, 137, 143–145, 153, 157, 160n42, 161n55, 229, 233
American Film Institute-National Endowment for the Arts (AFI-NEA) grants, 230–231, 233
American Citizen, An, 39–40
archival collections, 8–9, 95
archive, the, 227, 231, 233, 239
Aronson, Michael, 15n21, 91n77, 196n2
Arvold, Alfred, 60–61, 88, 89n23. *See also* Little Country Theater

ballyhoo, 101, 104–105, 111n20, 112n27, 177. *See also* exploitation (publicity stunt)
banal localism, 13, 208, 215, 217–218, 221; relation to banal nationalism, 203–204
Barker, Melton, 6, 94n157, 115, 132, 134n44, 134n46, 143, 222, 249–250
Barnum, P.T., 119. *See also* confidence men
Biograph, 4, 102
Birth of a Nation, The, 40, 214
blackface, 85, 94n147
Blissveldt Romance, The, 40, 46–47, 230–231
booster films. *See* municipal booster films
Bordwell, David, 169, 197n17
Bottomore, Stephen, 15n24, 63, 167
Bunny, John, 11, 73, 122
business culture, 17–18, 38, 111n8

cameras. *See* exhibitor cameras; small-gauge cameras
Carson, Robert M., 207, 221
Cedar Valley Romance, A, 47–48
cinema: historical significance of, 19; institutionalization of, 2, 5, 20, 23. *See*

289

also classical era cinema; transitional era cinema
civic films, 3, 13, 161n51, 201–202, 205–215, 224n31
civic organizations, 58, 62, 111n8, 143, 153, 237. *See also* fraternal service organizations
civil rights, 165, 205, 231
Civil War, 24, 32, 40–41, 43, 72, 74, 231
classical era cinema, 2, 5, 8, 10, 17–18, 34, 111n16, 115, 132, 167, 184, 188, 197n17; look of, 136
Cliffside, North Carolina, 237, 243–244
confidence men, 119, 123
Country Life Commission, 59, 89n22
Cram, Margaret Showalter, 6, 145, 161n46, 233
Cramer, Adella, 144, 147–148. *See also* Amateur Theater Guild
Crossroads series, 11, 103–107, 110, 112nn39–40, 112n50. *See also* First National Exhibitor's Circuit
Cudia, Salvatore, 94n147, 115, 131–132

de Certeau, Michel, 194–195
Dewey, John, 201–202
Doane, Mary Anne, 167

East Is West, 108–109, 113n61
Edison, Thomas, 1, 5–6, 14n12, 64, 86, 94n154, 214
Elks Lodge, 52n58, 65n145
Elsaesser, Thomas, 209
empathy, 20, 170
Entrikin, J. Nicholas, 194–195
Eskin, A. Lincoln, 217, 225n46
exhibitor cameras, 64–65, 66, 91n77
exhibitors, 1–2, 4–5, 8, 11, 14n12, 14n15, 64–68, 76, 95–104, 106–107, 109–110, 111n8, 111n12, 111n16, 112n29, 140, 142, 147, 157, 161n59, 217, 235, 259
exploitation (publicity stunt), 11, 98–105, 107–110, 111nn20–21. *See also* ballyhoo
exploitation managers, 11, 100, 102, 132

Fifty Thousand Feet of Kansas, 21, 48
film: as commodity, 2, 217; narrative fiction, 2, 5, 35, 38, 56–57, 63, 88, 117, 249, 259

film industry, 17, 25–26, 66, 115, 123, 147, 196; consolidation in Hollywood, 57, 102, 114; localization of, 96–97, 101–102, 111n8; *Movie Queen*'s mockery of, 155–156; in New York, 131; nontheatrical, 159n13
film production, 2, 23; amateur, 136, 138, 141, 255; booster, 10; Hollywood, 115; itinerant, 222; local, 3, 7–8, 14n4, 15n21, 21, 95, 110, 115, 136, 196, 204, 207, 212, 226n67
film technology, 12, 64–65, 119, 130, 135–137
Finch, Flora, 11, 122
First National Exhibitor's Circuit, 97, 99–101, 103–106, 108; exploitation staff, 103–104, 109, 112n43, 113n55
folk drama, 57, 61
Fraser, Nancy, 165, 197n27
Frick, Carolyn, 132, 134n44, 232–233
Fuller-Seeley, Kathryn H., 111n12
fraternal service organizations, 58, 62, 111n8, 206. *See also* Elks Lodge, Kiwanis Club, Rotary International Club

Gaines, Jane, 15n26, 98–99, 109, 111n20, 257–258
Gleason, Marion, 135, 158n1
Goldwyn Pictures Corporation, 98, 109, 113n66
Graham, Shad E., 13, 207, 214–218, 220–221, 223n16, 224n33, 224nn35–36, 224n40, 225n45, 228; archives of, 224n37, 225n42, 251n3; papers of, 224n34. *See also Our Home Town* series
Great Depression, 159n6, 253n36, 253n43
Gullett, William Lou, 38, 40, 53n90
Gullette, George S., 214, 216–218, 224n35, 225nn42–43, 225n45
Gunning, Tom, 2, 4, 7, 19, 131, 133n14

Hagge, Hans, 45, 232. *See also Blissveldt Romance, The*
Halttunen, Karen, 119
Hansen, Miriam, 4–5, 18
Harris, Neil, 119. *See also* operational aesthetic
H. B. B. Motion Picture Company, 32, 75

historical reenactments, 10, 38–41, 43, 45–46, 80, 82–83
Hollywood, 10–12, 86, 88, 95, 108, 114–120, 123, 125, 136–138, 140–141, 153, 155, 172, 178, 206–207, 210, 212, 214, 232, 234, 244; culture, 12, 95, 131; directors, 114–115, 121–123, 129; era, 17; fans and, 132n5; films about, 103, 109, 113n69, 121–122, 156; history of, 132n1; movie theaters and, 186; newspapers and, 180–181; as pejorative, 141; producers, 141, 255; rise of, 230; stars/stardom, 109, 153, 196; studio system, 11, 96, 111n14, 174
Hollywood films, 87, 125, 133n14, 135, 143, 164, 168, 186, 205; classical, 18, 188, 197n17; local, 3, 14, 96, 103, 109–110, 115, 119–120, 129, 132, 155, 172, 202, 209; *Movie Queen* and, 147–149, 151, 156–157
home movies, 3, 5, 69, 135–136, 138, 158, 159n5, 204, 243, 250, 256. *See also* 16mm film, amateur fiction films
home talent, 57–62; relation to amateur, 10, 62, 88n2
home talent films, 3, 10–11, 14, 47, 56–65, 67–73, 75–78, 80, 83–88, 88n2, 90n35, 91n76, 92n103, 93n115, 95, 104, 115, 117–121, 124–125, 133n11, 137, 142–143, 145–147, 153, 157, 172, 208, 222, 255, 257
hometown, 89n14, 175, 220; movies, 13, 48, 102, 163, 216–217, 232, 251, 257. *See also* small towns
Honneth, Axel, 165, 171, 197n25, 197n27
Howlett, Marion Angeline, 9, 137, 145–146, 160n42, 160n44. *See also* Amateur Theater Guild
Huff, Theodore, 141, 160n24. *See also* Amateur Cinema League (ACL)

industrial films, 26–27, 31, 38, 86, 88, 94n163, 209. *See also* industrial romances
Industrial Film Syndicate, 28–29, 31, 34, 51n38
Industrial Moving Picture Company, 26–27, 35, 49
industrial romances, 17–18, 38, 45, 53n92, 71, 87
Interstate Film Producers, 115–117, 121–123, 133nn23–24. *See also* Newland, Don O.

intimacy, 20, 241–242, 247, 249
itinerant filmmakers, 8, 11, 39, 49, 56, 73, 88, 94n147, 106, 110, 110n3, 114, 121–122, 129, 132, 138, 141, 152, 158, 163–164, 169, 201, 206, 214, 216, 255; business models of, 35–36, 75, 78, 145–147, 161n47, 198n38, 207, 226n68; fraud and, 95, 119; inclusive participation among, 136; small-gauge, 136–137, 172, 195

Jacobs, Lea, 143, 156
Jamieson, Hugh V., 86, 88, 94n154, 94n157, 134n46
Jowett, Garth, 14n7, 16

Kahana, Jonathan, 213, 217
Kannapolis, North Carolina, 163–165, 190, 192–194, 196n1, 199n66, 200n69; African American residents of, 188–192; Waters's films of, 163, 194, 238
Kannapolis: A Moving Portrait (Taylor), 246, 248–249
Kember, Joe, 19–20
Kirby, Lynne, 76, 78
Kirby, O. T., 235, 237, 252n24
Kiwanis Club, 145, 203
Kodak, 135–138, 141, 159n5, 159nn11–12, 177, 198n35. *See also* 16mm film
Kunkleman, Harry C., 207–208, 210–213, 222, 223n25, 224n26

Lamb, Oliver William, 33, 35–41, 43, 45–50, 54nn119–20, 132n3, 229. *See also* Special Event Film Manufacturing Company
Landsman, Sol, 207, 214, 216–218, 220, 225n45. *See also Our Home Town* series
Lindsay, Vachel, 16–17, 50n2
Lions Club, 143, 145, 212
Little Country Theater, 60–61. *See also* Arvold, Alfred
local, the, 2–4, 10, 201–203, 206, 214, 259; banality of, 208 (*see also* banal localism)
local businesses, 13, 17, 29, 33, 72, 78, 143, 151–152, 177–178, 208, 212, 215–216, 219–220, 241
local culture, 57, 59, 96, 184, 203
local film: bad effects of, 110n3; as commercial ventures, 208–209; Hollywood

and, 95–96, 109 (*see also* Hollywood films: local); as mode, 3, 13, 18, 21–22, 25, 67, 115, 151, 167, 169, 195, 201, 206–209, 217, 250, 255; practices, 7, 9, 136, 165, 202, 217; preservation of, 6, 10, 13, 161, 16, 228–234, 238, 246–247, 252n10, 256; reclamation of, 13, 239, 251, 253n35; recovery of, 13, 228, 239, 251; reuse of, 13, 245–246, 250–251; self-recognition in, 5, 8, 18, 25, 169, 172 (*see also* self-recognition); screen tests and, 103; small towns and, 208, 249, 255; sponsors of, 2–3, 8, 10, 13, 17–21, 24–29, 32, 34, 36, 38–39, 41, 45, 47–49, 51n17, 57, 62, 72–73, 75, 78, 85, 87, 90n35, 114–115, 118, 123–125, 128–129, 143, 145–147, 151, 157, 161n47, 164, 169, 195, 201–202, 204, 207, 209–210, 212–214, 217, 219–221, 230, 233, 241, 256, 259; video and, 222, 226n66, 227, 229–231, 233, 238–245, 247, 253n56. *See also* actualities; amateur fiction films; civic films; film production: local; home talent films; local filmmakers; local views; municipal booster films; mutual recognition: films/movies of

local filmmakers, 2, 67, 179

local newspapers, 8, 27–28, 37, 57, 59, 72–73, 76, 78, 80, 87–88, 104, 117, 122–125, 156, 176, 179–181, 183, 204, 207, 209–210, 224n26

local newsreels, 73, 91n77, 113n66, 135–136, 157–158, 247

local views, 1, 4–5, 10, 12, 14n7, 17–18, 20–21, 25–26, 29–30, 32–33, 48, 54n104, 56–57, 66–67, 71, 88, 103–104, 107, 131, 136, 142, 166–167, 172–173, 256. *See also* actualities

Loevin, Arthur, 207, 214, 216–217, 220, 225n45. *See also Our Home Town* series (Graham)

Long, Gareth, 246, 249–250

Lovely, Louise, 103, 112n35, 115

Lumberjack, The, 40, 45, 229, 232

Lumière, Auguste and Louis, 1, 4, 6, 167

Main Street, 141, 155, 181, 205

Maltby, Richard, 8, 118

Man at the Throttle, The, 71, 76–79, 93n118. *See also* Norman, Richard E.; Superior Film Manufacturing Company; Tinsley, Charles D.

Margalit, Avishai, 242–243

Marshall, T. H., 171, 197n25

mass culture, 3–4, 9, 19, 57, 71, 88, 88n1, 197n23, 202, 258. *See also* local culture

Massey, Doreen, 8

Melnick, Ross, 14n2, 111n12

melodrama, 10, 17–18, 46–47, 87, 103, 108, 143; silent-era, 234

memory, 170; collective, 253n40; common, 242–243; shared, 243

memory pictures, 41

Mexican Raid, The, 79, 80–82. *See also* Tinsley, Charles D.

Mine Owner's Daughter, The, 16–17, 67, 91n66

misrecognition, 165, 170–171, 197n27

Mitchell and Kenyon Company, 5–6, 165–166, 168. *See also* Toulmin, Vanessa

modernity, 19–20, 37, 46, 59, 194, 205

Moore, Paul S., 8, 15n21, 19, 53n100, 118

motion picture industry, 2–4, 8, 11, 111n8, 114–115, 121, 151, 161n59, 208, 257; changes in, 63; home talent and, 68–69; national, 95, 140 (*see also* Hollywood). *See also* film industry

Motion Picture Patents Company, 64, 72

movie fans, 11–12, 59, 69, 71, 96, 100, 109–110, 113n72, 121–122, 132n5, 155–156, 187

Movie Queen series, 6, 12, 137, 141, 143–145, 146, 147, 150, 151–157, 160n28, 160nn41–42, 233–234, 238, 245, 252n19. *See also* Amateur Theater Guild; Cramer, Adella

Movies of Local People (Waters), 163, 165, 174, 176–178, 182, 183, 186, 187, 190, 229, 234–237, 248

movie theater managers, 14n2, 20, 27, 57, 66–67, 93n115, 181; chance games and, 157–158, 162n64; independent, 97, 101; local, 100; local films and, 2, 11, 31, 95, 107, 110, 118, 176, 202, 237, 255; producers and, 69; publicity and, 99, 112n26; small-town, 101–102

movie theaters, 35, 86, 157, 175, 198n37, 237, 204; African Americans and, 189; chains, 11, 66, 97; competitions and, 147; declining importance of, 204;

local, 22; newspapers and, 180; opera houses and, 66, 91n59; purpose-built, 2, 18; small-town, 95–97; sound in, 134n37
Moving Picture World: and amateur film, 140; coverage of local films, 27–28, 31, 33, 75, 87–88; discussion of exhibitor cameras, 64, 66–69; importance of, 8; relationship to small-town exhibitors, 95–98, 100–102; warnings against local films, 49
municipal booster films, 3, 10, 13, 17, 21, 26, 28, 32–33, 38, 45, 48–49, 52n61, 55n129, 56–57, 63, 67, 76, 78, 106, 115, 121, 127, 143, 172, 219, 230; as mode of production, 18, 25. *See also* advertising, film: municipal
Musser, Charles, 4–5, 14n12, 19, 34, 63, 133n14
mutual recognition, 12, 14, 170–175, 195–196, 197n23; films/movies of, 3, 172–174, 180, 184, 187, 193, 195, 201–202, 223n11. *See also* local film: self-recognition in; place recognition; Ricouer, Paul; Waters, H. Lee

National Film Preservation Foundation (NFPF), 228–230, 232, 237–238
Newland, Don O., 9, 11–12, 116–132, 133n8, 133n19, 133n22, 133n24, 134n29, 143, 229, 238. *See also* Interstate Film Producers
newsreels, 3, 32, 37, 43, 52n61, 63–64, 66, 69, 73, 75, 82–83, 174, 213–214, 224n35, 243; announcers, 215; camera operators, 113n55, 255; Hollywood, 205; local, 91n77, 113n66, 135–136, 157–158, 247
Norman, Richard E., 70–71, 75–76, 80, 88, 91n78, 93n114, 93n116, 94n147
Northeast Historic Film (NHF), 233–234, 252n20

operational aesthetic, 119–121, 133n14
Our Gang, 6, 113n70, 132, 143
Our Home Town series (Graham), 13, 214, 216, 224n40, 251n3

Panama-Pacific Exposition (1915), 21, 37, 48
Paragon Feature Film Company, 17, 35–36, 38, 49, 53n80, 229–230, 260; films produced by, 10, 21, 33, 40, 45–49, 87, 91n66, 143, 231–233. *See also American Citizen, An*; *Blissveldt Romance, The*; *Cedar Valley Romance, A*; *Fifty Thousand Feet of Kansas*; Lamb, Oliver William; *Lumberjack, The*; *Mine Owner's Daughter, The*; *Present and Past in the Cradle of Dixie*; Special Event Film Manufacturing Company
Parisher, Don, 207, 214–218, 221. *See also Our Home Town* series (Graham)
Pickford, Mary, 11, 122, 143, 222
place recognition, 8, 193, 195
Poll, Ryan, 206, 223n12
Present and Past in the Cradle of Dixie, 40–41, 44, 231
Progressive movement, 59, 61
public, the, 18, 20–21, 28, 99, 119
publicity campaigns, 9, 99–101, 106, 108–109, 255

Rabinowitz, Paula, 165, 197n27
race films, 63, 70, 76, 94n147, 117
recognition, 5, 7, 10, 12, 14, 20, 163–165, 167–175, 185, 193–195, 196n2, 196n4, 197n27, 249; audience, 12, 80; "gasp of," 131; of one's neighbors, 63; racial, 189. *See also* misrecognition; mutual recognition; place recognition; self-recognition
Redding, Leo L., 25–26
Renwick, Vanessa, 246–248
Ricouer, Paul, 12, 165, 169–173, 187, 197n25
Rotary International Club, 143, 145, 183, 201, 203, 212, 220, 252n20. *See also* fraternal service organizations
Rothacker, Watterson Rounds, 26–28
Rothacker Film Manufacturing Company, 49, 54n126, 55n129. *See also* Industrial Moving Picture Company

Sargent, Epes Winthrop, 27, 67–68, 98–101, 103, 112n26, 112n43, 140. *See also* "Advertising for Exhibitors"
Scheinman, Jenny, 246, 248–249. *See also Kannapolis: A Moving Portrait*
Schneider, Eberhard, 64–65, 90n44. *See also* exhibitor cameras
screen contests, 95, 100, 103, 108, 115, 122. *See also* exploitation (publicity stunt)

segregation, 12, 163, 189, 192
self-promotion, 23, 25, 125
self-recognition, 108, 170, 172
Sennett, Mack, 11, 103–105, 107, 122
sentiment, 53n92; decline of, 143, 156
Sklar, Robert, 14n7, 97, 111n15, 197n30
small-gauge cameras, 137, 159n9, 159n12. See also exhibitor cameras
small-town: audiences, 20, 86, 161n59; culture, 253; films, 60, 205–206, 212; imagination, 258; life, 57–58, 60, 175, 202, 214; movie theaters, 19, 60, 66, 91n59, 95–97, 101, 111n15, 136, 196, 221–222, 226n65, 237; residents/inhabitants, 18, 25, 59, 86, 196, 208, 217
small towns, 13, 32, 58, 63–66, 136, 145, 161n55, 164, 175, 204–206, 223n12; blackface and, 85; Hollywood culture in, 131; home talent films and, 71; in *Home Town* films, 217, 219, 221; itinerant filmmaking and, 12, 35; local films and, 208, 249, 255
Sobler, Al, 104–105. See also First National Exhibitor's Circuit
social imaginary, 21, 173, 201. See also public, the
Souls for Sale, 109, 113n66, 113n69. See also screen contests
sound, 129; synchronous, 130, 136, 160n27
Spears, Timothy, 59, 89n14
special effects, 11, 32, 46, 110, 115, 120–121, 127, 130, 132, 191, 256, 258–260
Special Event Film Manufacturing Company, 31, 33, 65, 91n55
spectatorship, 3, 7–8, 18
Streible, Dan, 6, 113n70, 247
Superior Film Manufacturing Company, 71, 74–76, 78, 80, 117, 142

Taylor, Finn, 246, 248–249. See also *Kannapolis: A Moving Portrait*
Tepperman, Charles, 139, 151, 159n6, 159n13, 160n24
Thompson, Scott, 222, 226n68
Tinsley, Charles D., 11, 56–57, 71–76, 78–88, 92nn83–84, 92n88, 92n103, 92n105; *Tramps* series, 76, 84–85, 143. See also *Mexican Raid, The*; Superior Film Manufacturing Company
Tinsley Film Company, 73, 83

Tisdale, Franklin, 206–210
Toulmin, Vanessa, 6–7, 14n15, 168–9, 197nn14–16
town promotion, 21–24, 47; and planning, 32. See also advertising: municipal
transitional era cinema, 10, 17–18, 20, 50, 56–57, 91nn71–72, 127. See also classical film

Universal Producing Company, 62, 142. See also Woods, Lauren Kenyon

Verhoeven, Deb, 8, 15n28
visual culture, 172, 188
Vitagraph Company, 122–123
voiceover narration, 213, 217
von Stroheim, Eric, 114, 122, 156

Waller, Gregory A., 6, 19, 134n37
Waters, H. Lee, 6, 12, 142, 158, 163–165, 166, 173–195, 196n2, 197n10, 198nn34–35, 198nn37–38, 198n45, 199n47, 199n55, 199n63, 228–229, 234–238, 243–244, 248–249, 251n3. See also *Movies of Local People* (Waters); mutual recognition
Wecker, Charles, 217, 225n46
Whyte-Whitman Company, 65, 90n51. See also exhibitor cameras
Wiebe, Robert, 57, 203
Wilson, Woodrow, 80, 82
women, 108, 219; African American, 191–92; as filmmakers, 12, 136–137, 143–145, 196 (see also Howlett, Marion Angeline); in Hollywood, 161n52; in local films, 34, 37, 41, 43, 124, 139, 155, 184–185; as movie fans, 59; as narrators, 224n31; as theater directors, 90n35, 137, 144
Woods, Lauren Kenyon, 89n34, 143, 145–146, 152–155, 160n31, 161n47. See also Amateur Theater Guild; *Movie Queen* series
World War I, 10, 83–84, 97
World War II, 136, 157, 159n6, 159n9, 159n13, 160n21, 174, 195, 203, 209, 214–216, 224n33

Zimmermann, Patricia, 88n2, 140
Zunz, Olivier, 96, 111n8

MARTIN L. JOHNSON is Assistant Professor of English and
Comparative Literature at the University of North Carolina at Chapel Hill.

www.ingramcontent.com/pod-product-compliance
Lightning Source LLC
Chambersburg PA
CBHW052045220426
43663CB00012B/2455